GRILLPARZER

A CRITICAL INTRODUCTION

COMPANION STUDIES

Grillparzer

A CRITICAL INTRODUCTION

By W. E. YATES

Lecturer in German, University of Durham

CAMBRIDGE

AT THE UNIVERSITY PRESS

1972

Published by the Syndics of the Cambridge University Press
Bentley House, 200 Euston Road, London NW1 2DB
American Branch: 32 East 57th Street, New York, N.Y.10022

© Cambridge University Press 1972

Library of Congress Catalogue Card Number: 77–158550

ISBN: 0 521 08241 2

Printed in Great Britain
at the University Printing House, Cambridge
(Brooke Crutchley, University Printer)

CONTENTS

CONTENTS

ABBREVIATIONS

Wke.: Franz Grillparzer, *Sämtliche Werke,* ed. A. Sauer and R. Backmann (Vienna, 1909–48). All references to Grillparzer's works are to the text of this edition; the orthography has been modernized in passages quoted in the original. References to the plays follow the line numbering in this edition. SD/1529 = stage direction preceding line 1529; 1529/SD = stage direction within, or following, line 1529. Page references for the short stories refer to the text in vol. I/13 [i.e. I. Abteilung, 13. Band].

B: 'Briefe', numbered letters and documents in vols. III/1–5.
G: 'Gedichte', numbered poems in vols. I/10–12.
SB: 'Selbstbiographie', page references to vol. I/16.
T: 'Tagebücher', numbered entries in vols. II/7–12.

No page references are given for quotations from variants to the texts of the plays (from vols. I/17–21), or for Grillparzer's essays (vols. I/13–14), notes on Spanish drama (vol. I/15), and short memoirs (vol. I/16); but the context is specified in each case.

Secondary writings alluded to without detailed page references are all included in the bibliography (pp. 265–70).

Other abbreviations:

Gespr.: numbered entries in *Grillparzers Gespräche und die Charakteristiken seiner Persönlichkeit durch die Zeitgenossen,* ed. A. Sauer (7 vols., Vienna, 1904–41).

Jb.: *Jahrbuch der Grillparzer-Gesellschaft,* vols. 1–34 (1891–1938), Neue Folge (4 vols., 1941–4), 3. Folge (1953ff.).

vii

PREFACE

The main part of this study is critical. The first chapter, which treats Grillparzer's life, is not an interpretative biography, but a purely factual chronological account, of a kind that is not at present available in any language. It places the genesis of Grillparzer's works in the context of his life and charts the progress of their composition, with various works sometimes developing slowly side by side over a decade or more.

I have no new comprehensive formula to offer for the interpretation of Grillparzer's work: indeed, I believe his work has too much diversity for any such simple formula to exist. I have tried in chapters 2–6 to bring out the main thematic links between his major works by grouping them according to their subjects; within these groupings, however, it seemed most useful, especially to readers in schools and universities, to discuss the works separately. My aim has been to stimulate the kind of appreciation and discussion that are based on detailed reading of the texts and close reference to them. Relating my criticism to Grillparzer's own aims of dramatic effectiveness and consistency of characterization, I have tried to suggest where his finest achievements lie: in five plays which show his full mastery – the series of four dramas that he completed between 1823 and 1832, and the posthumous tragedy *Ein Bruderzwist in Habsburg* – and in the short story *Der arme Spielmann*. I have also tried to indicate the virtues that are characteristic of his work in general – particularly to bring out the subtlety of his characterization, his concern with moral values, the consistent ideals underlying his view of history and the human condition, and the essential theatricality of his drama. The kind of appreciation for which he himself would have hoped a hundred years after his death would not be limited to academic study (for he had little faith in academic literary historians) but would rather be based on performances of his plays. Precisely because, to an extent that is unusual in German drama, his work has lively theatrical qualities which do not depend on the words alone, stage production of the best of his plays should not be confined, as it largely tends to be at present, to the German-speaking countries. The centenary of his death may, indeed, be an appropriate occasion to suggest how rich an asset they would be, in new translations, to the repertory of the National Theatre.

It did not seem appropriate to include in an introductory study a comprehensive treatment either of Grillparzer's many occasional poems or of his dramatic plans and fragments, which are mainly of interest to specialists; but I have discussed the most important fragment, *Esther*, and a select number of the lyrical poems and epigrams which help to illuminate his major works. Nor have I attempted to give a full account of his critical and historical essays. These writings do not form a homogeneous whole, and many of them are fragments or mere notes. I have, however, drawn on them extensively (together with the epigrams) in the first section of chapter 6 as evidence of Grillparzer's concern with the cultural trends of his times.

At the request of the Cambridge University Press, I have quoted Grillparzer's prose writings in translation, except where there is a special quality in the German, and have added in footnotes prose translations of all passages of verse and prose quoted in the original German. In these translations I have concentrated on conveying the sense of the original rather than attempting either a poetic style or word-for-word literalism.

I am very conscious of how much I owe to the writings of previous Grillparzer critics, especially to those of Reinhold Backmann and Erich Hock. I should also like to express my thanks to the many friends and colleagues who have helped me in various ways. I owe a special debt of gratitude to Mr M. H. Black, of the Cambridge University Press, and to my former teacher Dr Ronald Gray, for valuable suggestions about the organization of my material; to Dr and Mrs J. W. Smeed, who read a complete draft of the typescript and have given generously of their advice on hundreds of points both of matter and of style; and finally – my deepest debt of all – to my wife, who has assisted me with Grillparzer's Spanish sources, has discussed and checked successive drafts of the book in detail, drafted the index and a large proportion of the translations, and has helped at every stage of preparing the typescript.

W.E.Y.

Durham

1

GRILLPARZER'S LIFE

'And *who is he?*' wrote Byron in his diary on 12 January 1821, after reading Grillparzer's tragedy *Sappho*. 'I know him not; but *ages will*. 'Tis a high intellect.' And again, later the same night: 'Grillparzer is...altogether a great and goodly writer.' Grillparzer died a hundred years ago, and posterity has confirmed Byron's judgment. His works have been translated into more than two dozen languages, from Finnish to Turkish, from Rumanian to Japanese. There is indeed a flourishing branch of the *Grillparzer-Gesellschaft* in Tokyo. In England and America his plays and short stories are studied in schools and universities; and as one English scholar has observed, he is 'for some of us the greatest dramatist of the German tongue'.[1]

In his writing Grillparzer drew so deeply on his experience that even when we are chiefly concerned with the finished works, rather than the man, the story of his long life is still indispensable for the study of the works. Moreover, Grillparzer's life is also intrinsically interesting in several respects. It forms a part of one of the richest periods of the artistic life of Vienna. It was lived against a background of significant political and cultural changes in Europe, which are reflected in some of his works. And in its successive phases it presents a story of achievement and disappointment which is well worth telling for its own sake.

Youth (1791–1816)

Franz Grillparzer was born in a house in the Bauernmarkt, in the centre of Vienna, on 15 January 1791, some eighteen months 1791 after the outbreak of the French Revolution and about a year after the death of the reformist Austrian Emperor Josef II. His father, Wenzel Grillparzer, was a lawyer, reserved and strict in character; his mother, a member of the artistic Sonnleithner

[1] L. A. Willoughby, 'Austrian Nationality and Austrian Literature', *German Life and Letters* I (1936–7), 47.

family, was a passionate musician, and music played a prominent part in Grillparzer's early education. The Vienna into which he was born was still the real cultural capital of the German-speaking world, a unique centre of theatre and of course of music. In the very year of his birth Mozart's last opera, *Die Zauberflöte*, received its première in the Freihaus-Theater (30 September); and Schikaneder's libretto for the opera was one of the books he later remembered having read in early childhood. Though Mozart died on 5 December 1791, Vienna retained its musical eminence. In the

1792 following November Beethoven settled permanently in the city,
1800 and he gave his first public concerts in April 1800. Politically, however, this was a bleak period for Austria: defeated on 4 June 1800 at Marengo, the Austrian army was driven out of Italy by Napoleon, whose forces subsequently advanced eastwards towards
1801 Vienna. The peace of Lunéville (2 February 1801) brought the War of the Second Coalition to an end.

In the autumn of 1800, after preliminary private tuition, Grillparzer had entered the Anna-Gymnasium. His first extant epigram ('Auf zwei Vettern') and lyrical poem ('An die Sonne') were
1804 written in the summer of 1804 (14 May and 16 June respectively); in November 1804 he matriculated for an intermediate course at Vienna University. This was the year in which Franz II gave up the title of Holy Roman Emperor (which he had held since his accession in 1792) and became hereditary Emperor of Austria as Franz I. And in the same year the great court theatre, the Hofburgtheater, came under the direction of Grillparzer's uncle Josef Sonnleithner, who held the post of *Theatersekretär* until 1814. It was in Sonnleithner's house that Grillparzer first met
1805 Beethoven in July 1805. But 1805 was another year dominated by Napoleon, who entered Vienna on 13 November and defeated the Austrians and Russians at Austerlitz on 2 December. Grillparzer's patriotic feelings about the ignominious position of his country found expression in a satirical poem, 'Das Rechte und Schlechte'.

1806 In the spring of 1806 he wrote his first play, *Die unglücklichen Liebhaber*, a one-act comedy in which the characters were modelled on his teachers at the university. The next year, on 24 November
1807 1807, he began his successful studies in the law faculty; in the same month he began a one-act comedy, *Die Schreibfeder*, which he
1808 finished the following January (and revised a year later), and which he judged to be the best piece of work he had done so far (T 21).

2

In the spring of 1808, after reading Schiller's early plays, he began his tragedy *Blanka von Kastilien*, influenced by *Don Carlos*. From May 1808 dates his close friendship with Georg Altmütter (1787–1858), who stimulated his belief in his poetic calling – a belief that was to sustain him throughout his creative life but was also to weigh him down with a sense of the obligations his calling imposed on him. The works he wrote in 1808 include the fragmentary comedy *Das Narrennest*, in which he caricatured himself as 'Seraphin Klodius Storch, a poet'. Storch is a thin, lisping, awkward figure: the self-satire reflects the sense of inadequacy Grillparzer felt from the first in relation to his newly formed poetic ambitions.

A year later he was a member of a *Studentenkorps* during 1809 Napoleon's siege of Vienna. Austria had declared war on France on 9 April 1809, with disastrous results: the French entered the capital once more on 12 May. Just over a week later Napoleon was defeated at Aspern by the Austrians under Archduke Karl; but this victory was reversed in July at Wagram. On 8 October Metternich was appointed Foreign Minister of Austria; later in the same month the Peace of Vienna was signed. In the aftermath of the wars, however, Austria was beset by severe economic difficulties. There had already been rapid inflation in the summer months May to July; and the crisis persisted, culminating two years later (15 March 1811) in the devaluation of paper money to one-fifth of its nominal value. The term for the new currency, 'Wiener Währung', long remained synonymous with the falsity of appearances; in the late 1840s (*Die Anverwandten* iii, 5) and early 1850s (*Mein Freund*, Vorspiel, sc. 3) Nestroy still punned on the associations of its initials, 'Weh, Weh!' From the first it was the middle and professional classes who were particularly badly hit. When Grillparzer's father made his will in October 1809 he began by stating how impossible it was for a lawyer to amass wealth by his earnings alone, and proceeded to his testamentary dispositions with the sceptical opening 'Should, however, anything actually be left...' (B 313). He died, at the age of forty-nine, on 10 November. In the course of that same month, however, Grillparzer completed *Blanka von Kastilien*, which he submitted to the Burgtheater in January 1810. In the spring of 1810 his ad- 1810 miration for Schiller waned, giving way to admiration for Goethe: the works he read included both *Faust* (Part One had appeared in 1808) and *Tasso*, and particularly the latter aroused his enthusiasm: his sense of his poethood allowed him to identify himself with Goethe's hero: 'I felt it was myself speaking, acting and loving in the person of Tasso; Goethe, it seemed to me, had merely given words to *my* feelings; I recognized myself in every emotion, every speech, every word' (T 92). In August *Blanka von Kastilien* was returned, rejected, by the Burgtheater.

1811 In 1811 Grillparzer concluded his full-time law studies. He continued to write; his works of this period include another one-act comedy, *Wer ist schuldig?* (October–November 1811), and a poem, 'Cherubin', addressed to the singer Henriette Theimer 1812 and dated 8 February 1812. In mid-March 1812 he became tutor in law studies to the nephew of Graf von Seilern. The Seilern family library gave him access to Shakespeare in the original, and the stimulus bore immediate fruit in the fragment *Alfred der Große*; but then in October 1812 he fell dangerously ill on the Seilern estate in Moravia. A diary-note written in December 1812, the first of the self-analytical notes that he composed using the fictional name 'Fixlmüllner', mentions his fear that he lacked any original poetic talent (T 168). Nevertheless, in this year or the next he formed a plan to write a second part to *Faust*, as he recalled in his diary ten years later (T 1083).

1813 On 18 March 1813, having fully recovered from his illness and having completed the last of his law examinations, he took up a post at the court library (*Hofbibliothek*) in Vienna as an unpaid assistant, and in this position he began a translation of Calderón's *La vida es sueño*, which he took as far as line 181: still a beginner in his study of Spanish, he had to depend on constant reference to dictionaries. This same year saw the première in Vienna of Adolf Müllner's drama *Die Schuld* (27 April), and in the political field the defeat of Napoleon at the Battle of Leipzig (16–19 October). In November Grillparzer bowed to financial necessity by applying for a post in the civil service, recording his regretful farewell to the court library in an ironic poem, 'Lebet wohl, ihr guten Musen'.

1814 On 27 January 1814 he began his career as a civil servant, entering the *Finanzhofkammer* in the first instance as an unpaid assistant (*Manipulationspraktikant*). In the same year Josef Schreyvogel was appointed artistic director of the Burgtheater from 1 April; under him the Burgtheater was to become the leading classical theatre in the German-speaking countries. On 6 April Napoleon abdicated; in September the Congress of Vienna assembled, and 1815 on 9 June 1815 the Final Act was signed. Though Napoleon had

4

escaped from Elba and landed in France in March 1815, the Battle of Waterloo (18 June) finally brought the Napoleonic age effectively to an end. Meanwhile Grillparzer had received his first salaried appointment in the civil service, in a probationary clerical post (as *Konzeptspraktikant*), and had drafted and begun a fragmentary drama *Friedrich der Streitbare*.

In the spring of 1816 he met a friend of his student days, 1816 Johann Ludwig Deinhardstein, who told him that *La vida es sueño* was going to be performed in Vienna, in a translation by someone called 'Wendt' or some similar name – 'Wendt oder ähnlich' (SB 115). Grillparzer mentioned that he had translated part of it himself; Deinhardstein borrowed his manuscript, showed it to the critic Wilhelm Hebenstreit, and finally persuaded Grillparzer to allow it to be published in the *Modenzeitung* (later renamed the *Wiener Zeitschrift für Kunst, Literatur, Theater und Mode*), which Hebenstreit edited. On 4 June 1816 the production that Deinhardstein had mentioned was given its première in the Theater an der Wien; and the name of the translator, as Grillparzer learnt from the theatre-bills, was not 'Wendt', but 'West'. This was Schreyvogel's *nom de plume*. The very next day two scenes of Grillparzer's translation appeared in the *Modenzeitung*. Grillparzer was able, through an intermediary, to convince Schreyvogel that he had not deliberately taken part in an intrigue with Hebenstreit to expose the inferiority of Schreyvogel's translation; and on 22 June he visited Schreyvogel – a meeting which was to prove a turning-point in his fortunes.

First successes (1816–25)

In character Grillparzer was nervous, self-conscious, and indecisive; he badly lacked self-confidence, and had a tendency to indulge in brooding self-criticism. Schreyvogel drew out of him the admission that he had in mind a plan for a play of his own, *Die Ahnfrau*, and encouraged him to proceed with it. He did not in fact manage to make a start, but he was heartened again by a chance meeting on 12 August when Schreyvogel recalled how he himself had once been encouraged by Goethe: 'And then when I said to him, "I can't get going!" Schreyvogel replied: "I once gave the same answer to Goethe, when he was urging me on to literary activity. But Goethe said, 'You simply have to blow on your fingers, then you'll get going!'"' (SB 119f.). This reminiscence

5

of the master's words stayed in Grillparzer's mind and spurred him on: *Die Ahnfrau* was begun that same evening, and the first version was completed, and the last act read to Schreyvogel, by 15 September. On 22 September Schreyvogel returned Grillparzer's manuscript with his comments, and in the course of October and November the text was revised, and then shortened for performance.

1817 Unforeseen difficulties with the censor arose in January 1817, and the play was briefly banned; but on 31 January the première finally took place in the Theater an der Wien, with Sophie Schröder as Bertha. The work was subsequently banned again after both the second and the third performances. In Grillparzer himself the performance of his play aroused a shameful sense of self-exposure: 'There is something in me which says it is just as indecent to show one's inner self naked as one's outer self' (T 204). But he was now in the centre of public attention. On 22 March Alois Jeitteles' critical essay against fate-tragedies, 'Gegen die romantische Schicksalstragödie', appeared in the *Modenzeitung*; at the end of April *Die Ahnfrau* was published by Wallishausser; and in the course of the spring Grillparzer was introduced into Karoline Pichler's salon.

By this time he had conceived his plan for *Der Traum ein Leben*, and in late June he wrote out a scenario for another work of semi-popular type, *Melusina*, and started work on the first manuscript. Then on 29 June the subject of *Sappho* was suggested to him by a lawyer, Felix Joël. The next day he spent in reading the fragments of Sappho's poetry and translating her most famous extant ode, and the morning after that he began the manuscript of his tragedy. He completed it on 25 July, having incorporated the ode to Aphrodite as lines 428ff. He revised the text in August and showed it to Schreyvogel at the end of the month. On 5 September a parody by Karl Meisl of *Die Ahnfrau* was staged in the principal popular theatre of the city, the Theater in der Leopoldstadt, under the title *Frau Gertrud* (the play was later published as *Die Frau Ahndl*); and though Grillparzer began writing the opening scenes of *Der Traum ein Leben* on 21 September, he broke off work in October after the actor Küstner had raised objections at having to play the part of a black man (Zanga). In this same autumn Grillparzer began to be interested in the theme of *Medea*. On 14 November he suffered a sudden bereavement when the youngest of his three brothers, Adolph, drowned himself at the age of seventeen.

On 15 January 1818 Grillparzer's cousin Ferdinand von Paum- 1818
gartten married Charlotte Jetzer, and soon Grillparzer himself
was involved in an affair with Charlotte. He abandoned *Der Traum
ein Leben* as a fragment (having reached a point equivalent to
line 688 of the finished text) after the dream-play *Die Heilung der
Eroberungssucht* by Carl Franz van der Velde had been produced
at the Theater an der Wien; but this setback was outweighed by
the première of *Sappho* which was given in the Burgtheater on
21 April with Sophie Schröder in the title part. 'The play was
a sensational success' (SB 130). On 1 May Grillparzer was appointed
salaried *Theaterdichter*, with a salary of 2,000 fl. per annum,
through the agency of the Finance Minister, Count Stadion (1763–
1824); he was also received, perhaps on the same day, by Metternich,
who promised his support (SB 132). On 14 June he left for Baden
on restorative leave from his regular civil service post, and while
he was there he made plans for his trilogy *Das Goldene Vlies*. On
20 July he left for Gastein, where he remained until 15 August,
commemorating his departure in the poem 'Abschied von Gastein'
(G 18). On 29 September he began work on his trilogy; in later
life he recalled that he had 'never worked on anything with so
much enjoyment' (SB 136). On 5 October he completed *Der
Gastfreund* and on 20 October began *Die Argonauten*; but about
10 November he broke off work at the love-scene in Act III. All
prospect of further progress receded with the suicide of his mother
on 23 January 1819. Grillparzer was badly affected by this blow; 1819
Schreyvogel wrote to the archaeologist Karl August Böttiger: 'The
dear man is so deeply affected by this misfortune that I am
seriously concerned for his own preservation' (*Gespr.* 161).

In February the poem 'Berthas Lied in der Nacht' (G 3) was
set to music by Schubert, and *Sappho* was published by Wallishausser (with a second printing following within a few weeks). But
Grillparzer was still wholly dispirited by his bereavement, and
also disturbed by his continued involvement with Charlotte. His
feelings of guilt about this were not confined to the fact that he
was betraying his cousin. He also accused himself of cold-heartedly
exploiting Charlotte's affections in order to make psychological
observations on which he could draw in his trilogy. Increasingly,
too, he was concerned to preserve the independence and solitude
which he felt he needed in order to achieve a state of inspiration
and creative concentration. His belief that emotional involvements
endangered this solitude was an inhibiting factor in his conduct

of all his love-affairs, and a major reason – together with his temperamental indecisiveness and lack of confidence – why he never married.

The poem 'Der Bann' (G 19) expresses his determination to break off his relations with Charlotte. On 13 March he applied for three months' leave on the grounds that his health had been undermined by 'sad events of various kinds, foremost among them the recent death of my beloved mother' (B 155). The application was sanctioned on 27 March, and antedated to 24 March (B 159); for on that day Grillparzer had already left for Italy. He remained in Italy until mid-July, spending most of his time first in Rome (where the imperial court had already arrived on 2 April, six days before him, and where he stayed till 26 April), later in Naples and Florence. It was in Rome, on 20 April, that he began the poem 'Campo vaccino' (G 26), a lament for the glories of antiquity which celebrates the greatness of the ancient ruins in contrast to the insipid spirit of the present ('die neue, flache Zeit') in the city of Christianity. On 3 July, in Rome again on his way northwards from Naples to Florence, he kissed the Pope's slipper, and was half amused, half horrified at the ceremony: 'Had I known the fawning manner in which the kissing is performed, I should have stayed away. Since the feeble old man cannot raise his foot, one practically has to lie down on one's belly...' (T 484).

On the day before Grillparzer left for Italy one of the most important political events of the year had taken place, the murder of Kotzebue by the radical student Karl Sand. The consequences became clear at the conference held in Carlsbad from 6 to 31 August, under Metternich's leadership, between Austria, Prussia, and the seven other largest German states. The repressive measures agreed included strict control of the universities, suppression of the student *Burschenschaft*, and the imposition of severe censorship of the press. In this way the Carlsbad conference firmly established the reactionary political climate of the next thirty years. Meanwhile in Vienna Grillparzer was again caught up in his affair with Charlotte on his return from Italy. In early October he was working out a detailed scenario for *Medea*; he resumed work on *Die Argonauten* about 26 October, and completed it on 3 November. On 2 November his publisher, Wallishausser, was ordered to remove the poem 'Campo vaccino' from his yearbook *Aglaja* because it gave offence to the church, and the ensuing furore culminated later in the month in Grillparzer's being personally rebuked, on the orders of the Emperor, by Count Sedlnitzky, the Chief of the State Police (*Präsident der Polizei- und Zensurhofstelle*), who was to remain the chief bulwark of Metternich's internal policy until 1848. Despite these developments Grillparzer pressed on with his work on the trilogy. *Medea* was begun on 8 November; a week later Grillparzer applied for three months' leave on account of 'the strain of renewed literary work' (B 190); on 27 January 1820 *Das Goldene Vlies* was finally completed, and the next month Grillparzer first conceived a plan for a drama centring on the figure of the thirteenth-century Bohemian king Ottokar (T 612). In March he wrote an essay 'Über das Wesen des Drama' (T 639), as a defence of *Das Goldene Vlies* against Schreyvogel's criticisms. But by late May his affair with Charlotte had reached its height, and on 10 July he made another application for leave, claiming 'a total disruption of the ganglionic nervous system' (B 203). On 15 July he was granted leave for two more months; the period from 16 July to 6 August he spent in Gastein. His diary for this summer includes the first mention of the Hero and Leander theme (T 320), and in late summer or autumn he drafted a plan of a dramatic treatment (T 322). Around September he also began preparatory work on the historical background to the Ottokar theme. On 4 October he was threatened with suspension of salary unless he returned immediately to his clerical post. He replied with a request for more time: 'I need time, I need peace!' (B 209). In mid-October he finished revising the text of *Das Goldene Vlies*, and the trilogy was submitted to the Burgtheater on 8 November. At this time the affair with Charlotte, which had been interrupted again by Grillparzer's trip to Gastein, reached another climax of intensity; but the following winter brought the first meeting with Kathi Fröhlich (1800–79) and her three sisters at a musical evening. It also brought Grillparzer's first reading of Schopenhauer, whose principal work *Die Welt als Wille und Vorstellung* had been published in 1819.

In contrast to Grillparzer's other two important love-affairs, his relations with Kathi, which were to last for the rest of his life, remained chaste. From the first he was fascinated by the beauty of her eyes (B 223), and their attraction is captured in a lively poem, 'Allgegenwart' (G 39), which was written in early March 1821. This was when he became engaged to Kathi – a step that did not seem over-hasty at the time (G 40), though it would later, as the engagement dragged on and grew stale.

A further important occasion for Grillparzer was the performance some three weeks later (26–27 March) of *Das Goldene Vlies* in the Burgtheater, with Sophie Schröder as Medea. 'Its reception was, perhaps justly, somewhat mixed' (SB 160). In May, two notable events signalled the new political era in Europe: on 5 May Napoleon died, and on 25 May Metternich was granted the title of Austrian State Chancellor. In Grillparzer's personal life, too, there were changes. In July or August he finally extricated himself from his affair with Charlotte; the break is marked by the poem 'Das Spiegelbild' (G 45). And at work he was transferred on 10 August to the Finance Ministry. On 1 December he probably applied for a position in the court library, but in vain: another applicant was appointed to the post in February 1822. Meanwhile, in preparation for the publication of *Das Goldene Vlies*, he worked on a preface, which he drafted in late November, and on a dedication to Charlotte ('Zueignung an Desdemona'): neither, however, was in the end included in the published edition of the trilogy.

In the course of 1821 and 1822 Grillparzer drafted his first plans for *Weh dem, der lügt!*; in January or February 1822 *Libussa* too was planned (T 981), and this plan was further shaped in early March (T 1035). On 17 March Marie Piquot, a young woman of whom Grillparzer had thought as no more than an acquaintance, died, leaving a will telling of her unrequited love for him. In April he worked on his plan for a drama *Krösus* (T 1086, 1093–4). On 8 May he applied for promotion to a permanent clerical post (as *Konzipist*) (B 243), but his application was refused on 17 May. Late in the same month, *Das Goldene Vlies* was published by Wallishausser. In August Grillparzer wrote a dramatic fragment, *Hannibal*, and in the autumn composed the plan for the story *Das Kloster bei Sendomir* (T 1245).

1823   By early spring in 1823 Grillparzer had moved from the Dorotheergasse (where he had lived since 1821) to the nearby Ballgasse. There followed his first attachment to the beautiful daughter of a Greek businessman and one of the large Greek community in Vienna, Marie von Smolenitz (1808–80). She was at the time not yet fifteen. Both Grillparzer's feeling of attraction and also his misgivings are expressed in 'Huldigungen' (G 169); and even at this early stage her powers of attraction worked also on the miniaturist Moritz Michael Daffinger (1790–1849). Between 12 February and 9 March 1823 Grillparzer composed *König*

Ottokars Glück und Ende. On 13 March he made another application for promotion (B 247), which was turned down in June. Between 15 and 23 March, having been approached with a request to provide a libretto for Beethoven, he wrote *Melusina*; he entertained no great hopes that the subject would appeal to Beethoven (*Gespr.* 316/iii), but Beethoven wrote a warm letter of thanks for the honour of his co-operation: 'I might almost say that I am prouder of this event than of any of the greatest distinctions that could be bestowed on me' (B 2086). From late April into July Grillparzer wrote out and revised a second manuscript of *König Ottokars Glück und Ende.* On 7 July he was at last promoted, being appointed *Ministerialkonzipist des Finanzministeriums*, i.e. chief clerk to Count Stadion. From the beginning of August to mid-October, he was twice at Count Stadion's estates at Jamnitz, in Moravia. Of the letters he wrote to Kathi Fröhlich from Jamnitz, one of 3 August (B 249) seems to allude to friction and disagreements between them; and though his continued general affection for her is shown in B 250–2 (23 September–4 October), after his return to Vienna it was his affair with Marie von Smolenitz that developed, reaching a stage of secret intimacy in the period from late autumn 1823 into early 1824.

In mid-October 1823 *König Ottokars Glück und Ende* was submitted to the Burgtheater, and towards the end of November a copy was submitted to the censor. In mid-January it was 1824 officially banned. In Beethoven's conversation-book Grillparzer wrote: 'No-one can understand the reason for the prohibition' (*Gespr.* 355). But later in the same month the play was read to the Empress Karoline Auguste, and the censorship question was reopened. Grillparzer meanwhile was pressing Beethoven about the composition of a score for *Melusina* (*Gespr.* 355). The early part of 1824 also saw the beginning of his intensive study of Lope de Vega, including a reading of Lope's play *Las paces de los Reyes y Judía de Toledo.* Grillparzer made his first plan for his own drama on the theme (T 1330), and began *Die Jüdin von Toledo*, writing about a hundred lines in trochaic metre. In early spring of this same year he also began to make notes on material for *Ein Bruderzwist in Habsburg*, and continued them throughout the year. Despite the loss of his influential mentor Count Stadion, who died on 15 May, publication (though not yet theatrical production) of *König Ottokar* was permitted by mid-July; and on 21 August *Die Ahnfrau* was for the first time performed in the Burgtheater.

11

In the course of the summer Grillparzer began the autobiographical poem 'Jugenderinnerungen im Grünen' (G 84, xv), though he completed only the first six stanzas. He also met the censor responsible for the ban on *König Ottokar*, and learnt that it was only a precautionary measure; asked what he had found to object to in the play, the censor replied: 'Nothing at all, but I thought to myself, "One never can tell!"' (SB 180). Towards the end of the year Grillparzer composed a scenario for Acts II and III of *Weh dem, der lügt!*; in late December approval was at last given for *König Ottokar* to be produced in the Burgtheater; and in the first weeks of 1825 Grillparzer was approached with an invitation to write a drama to commemorate the coronation of the Empress as Queen of Hungary, which was to take place on 25 September 1825.

1825

Years of crisis (1825–8)

In 1825 Grillparzer's love-affair with Marie reached its height, a source both of great pleasure – 'The first period of my love for this woman was really exceptionally delightful' (T 2020) – and of suspicion of Marie's character. This disquiet is reflected both in the short story *Das Kloster bei Sendomir*, which was largely written early in the year, and also in the 'Briefe an Marie' (T 1635–40), a remarkable series of intense, almost lyrical letters in which devoted love mingles with jealous mistrust, with the simple (and justified) fear 'that I must think you unfaithful' (T 1635). On 19 February the première of *König Ottokars Glück und Ende* took place. The text was published that same morning by Wallishausser, and immediately sold over five hundred copies. In the evening, the performance was given before a packed auditorium, with Heinrich Anschütz in the role of Ottokar, and concluded with a twenty-eight-line epilogue composed for the occasion by the poet and dramatist Johann Christian von Zedlitz. The reception was mixed. Zedlitz himself wrote a favourable review, which appeared on 14–15 March in the *Abendzeitung*; but in the *Gesellschafter* of 6 April his praise was treated with sarcasm, and a bleaker critical view expressed: 'Das Stück...sollte besser betitelt sein: Ottokars Ende ist ein Glück – nämlich für die Leser und Zuschauer; Wallishaussers Glück und Grillparzers Ende.'[1] While

---

[1] 'The play were better named "The end of Ottokar is a piece of good fortune" – that is, for the readers and the audience: Wallishausser's fortune and the end of Grillparzer.'

the arguments raged, Grillparzer turned down the commission for a coronation-piece; he had become interested in the material for his next tragedy, *Ein treuer Diener seines Herrn*, but saw that it was unsuitable for the occasion, 'since at a celebration of a queen's coronation one cannot present on the stage a revolution and the murder of a queen' (*Gespr.* 1182). The commission was taken over by Karl Meisl, who eventually provided a drama *Gisela von Bayern, erste Königin der Magyaren*; Grillparzer continued to read up the history of the Bancban story, and also made a draft sketch of the first act of another historical play, *Ein Bruderzwist in Habsburg*.

In the course of this year Grillparzer also progressed slowly with 'Jugenderinnerungen im Grünen', which he took as far as line 104. A major part of the new material (73–104) deals with his deteriorating relations with Kathi. Their differences of temperament produced constant 'Ringen, Stürmen, Weinen' (95),[1] frictions and disagreements which by the beginning of 1826, though Grillparzer held indecisively back from formally breaking off the engagement, caused him to write with clear regret of 'that relationship into which I rushed with so little thought' (T 1413). Another source of tribulation was an episode in November: together with some members of the *Ludlamshöhle* club, a club of artists and writers, he was present at a brush between Daffinger and a military policeman. A warrant for Daffinger's arrest was issued on 10 December; Grillparzer was cautioned as to possible effects on his own career, and on 15 February 1826 he was repri- 1826 manded at police headquarters. By this time he had moved into rooms in the Spiegelgasse; within the next few months the Fröhlichs were to move into the same house, one floor higher. Throughout the winter he worked at the planning stages of *Libussa, Ein treuer Diener seines Herrn* and *Des Meeres und der Liebe Wellen*, but only sporadically, and with no sense of satisfactory progress (T 1428). In February he made a start on the text of *Libussa*, but advanced only to line 275, when he broke off work; and on 10 March he began the text of *Ein treuer Diener*, progressing at this stage up to line 279. On 10 April he had what was to be his last meeting with Beethoven, at the Gasthaus 'Zur Eiche', not far from his rooms. He was in low spirits, complaining about police censorship and discontented with his writing: 'My own works afford me no pleasure'; but Beethoven appears to have

---

[1] 'Struggles, storms, tears.' See also T 1436.

tried to encourage him (*Gespr.* 437). The main centre of his social activities throughout the spring was the *Ludlamshöhle* club, of which he had become a member, at the instigation of Zedlitz, on 4 March. In mid-March he composed a poem, 'Vision' (G 59), on the illness of the Emperor, and read it at the *Ludlamshöhle* to patriotic applause. In mid-April the police raided the club, which was (apparently groundlessly) under suspicion of being a politically active secret society; on 19 April, at 6 a.m., Grillparzer's apartment was searched. The *Ludlamshöhle* was subsequently disbanded. Grillparzer satirized the affair towards the end of the month in the first act of a 'Second Part' to *Die Zauberflöte*. But his troubles continued, for the poem 'Vision', published on 20 April, angered the Empress 'because it speaks of *two* women sitting at the Emperor's bedside, whereas in fact only *she* sat up *alone* with him' (T 1438).

In July and August Grillparzer resumed and completed the lament 'Jugenderinnerungen im Grünen'. There were new tensions with Kathi (T 1662), and relations with Marie had been bitterly soured: she was with child by Daffinger. On 21 August Grillparzer left Vienna on a journey to Germany 'pour prendre congé' (T 1663); he left to escape from 'tangled affairs of the heart' (SB 180), but went despondently, 'with a sense of a complete drying-up of my poetic talent' (SB 199). Travelling by way of Prague (23–5 August), where he was reminded of his plans for the *Bruderzwist* (T 1494), he visited Dresden (where he saw Tieck), Berlin (where he met Hegel), Leipzig, Weimar and Munich. In Weimar he met Goethe on 29 September and 3 October, but with characteristic lack of self-confidence refused a further invitation: 'I was afraid of being alone with Goethe for a whole evening and, after much wavering, did not go' (SB 199). Nevertheless, Goethe's impression was favourable; on 11 October he wrote to Zelter: 'Grillparzer is a pleasant, agreeable man; we may indeed credit him with innate poetic talent...' (*Gespr.* 461/v). Early in October, Marie's child was born. In the same month Grillparzer began his cycle *Tristia ex Ponto* (G 84), conceiving it as a cycle of five poems, and writing 'Böse Stunde', 'Polarszene', 'Frühlings Kommen' and 'Der Fischer'. In the autumn he began the first full manuscript of *Des Meeres und der Liebe Wellen*, taking it to line 348 and continuing with further detailed sketches. He also resumed work on 31 October on the text of *Ein treuer Diener*, completing his first full manuscript version on 5 December. On the evening of 15 December, at the home of Schubert's friend Joseph von Spaun, he met the dramatist Eduard von Bauernfeld for the first time. Bauernfeld wrote in his diary: 'I do not know whether he liked me particularly'; but further meetings took place in the 'Silbernes Kaffeehaus' in the Plankengasse (which intersects the Spiegelgasse). This coffee-house was now a centre for meetings of writers, musicians, painters, actors and so on, and among the other regular guests was the popular actor-dramatist Ferdinand Raimund, whose comedy *Das Mädchen aus der Feenwelt oder der Bauer als Millionär* had been given its première at the Theater in der Leopoldstadt on 10 November. Bauernfeld later described the group as 'a complete Parnassus' (*Gespr.* 559). Towards the end of December Grillparzer resumed work on the text of *Libussa*. He finished the first act – which in later life he is reported to have regarded as the best of all his work (*Gespr.* 1148/iv) – and progressed in the second as far as line 655; and in December 1826 and January 1827 he also worked on revising *Ein treuer Diener seines Herrn*.

1827

In January 1827 Marie's attractions for him revived, and as soon as he had completed his revision of *Ein treuer Diener* he recommenced work on *Des Meeres und der Liebe Wellen*. It was of this stage of his work on the text that he later recalled 'that in the principal character I constantly saw before me Marie in all her then truly heavenly beauty' (T 2132). He also worked on Mariana's *History of Spain* in relation to his other projected love-tragedy; work proceeded alternately on *Des Meeres und der Liebe Wellen* and the plans for *Die Jüdin*, and in the spring he also completed *Das Kloster bei Sendomir*. On 26 March Beethoven died, aged fifty-six; Grillparzer's funeral oration ('Rede am Grabe') was spoken on 29 March by Anschütz beside the coffin, outside the cemetery. Grillparzer, Schubert and Raimund were all among the torch-bearers in the funeral procession. On 11 August Schubert's 'Ständchen' ('Zögernd leise...', G 67b), composed in July, was performed by Josefine Fröhlich, Kathi's sister, though Schubert himself forgot to turn up for the occasion.

It was now two and a half years since Grillparzer's last major work, *König Ottokar*, had been published, and on 14 August the *Wiener Zeitschrift*... printed a poem by Bauernfeld, 'An Grillparzer' (B 328), exhorting him to produce more work. In fact, in the spring of 1827 Grillparzer had made detailed plans for the *Bruderzwist* and had begun a further revision of *Ein treuer Diener*, which was finally completed at the end of August. By the time he composed his answer to Bauernfeld, 'Rechtfertigung' (G 68), in mid-September, justifying his slowness in publishing further works, his relations with Marie had reached a new crisis of jealousy and mistrust. He copied the 'Briefe an Marie' into his diary (T 1635–40) and composed the poems 'Verwünschung' and 'Trennung', expressing respectively his disillusion and his decision to make a final break from her. He also wrote more *Tristia*: 'Verwandlungen', 'Sorgenvoll', 'Freundeswort', 'Reiselust', 'Die Porträtmalerin' and 'Der Halbmond glänzet...' (G 193), which was later omitted from the cycle. On 16 September Charlotte von Paumgartten died, having on her deathbed accused Grillparzer of being responsible for her state (T 1613); and also in mid-September Grillparzer learnt finally that Marie and Daffinger were to marry. By now he had probably reached Act IV of *Des Meeres und der Liebe Wellen*; but his progress seemed discouraging (T 1605), and he resumed work on the second act of *Der Traum ein Leben*: 'Das Bunte, Stoßweise des Stoffes war eben geeignet, mir selber einen Anstoß in meiner Verdrossenheit zu geben' (SB 214).[1] And in October the manuscript of *Ein treuer Diener seines Herrn* was at last submitted to the Burgtheater.

In early November, the monument by Beethoven's grave was unveiled, Grillparzer's 'Rede am Grabe bei der Enthüllung des Denksteines' being again spoken by Anschütz. Towards the end of the year *Das Kloster bei Sendomir* appeared in the *Aglaja* for 1828; and Grillparzer made a number of notes in his diary in which he analysed himself critically under the guise of the fictional 'Fixlmüllner' (T 1610, 1618, 1652–7, 1661–3, 1673), recording shortcomings in his talent, lack of pleasure in his work, and increasing shyness about poetic self-exposure. On 30 December Marie and Daffinger married.

1828   In the first weeks of 1828, Grillparzer began the text of *Ein Bruderzwist in Habsburg*, taking it as far as line 299. On 28 February *Ein treuer Diener seines Herrn* was performed. Anschütz played Bancban, Sophie Schröder the queen, and Ludwig Löwe Otto von Meran. The Emperor was present, and the evening was highly successful (T 1623), the production being greeted 'with tremendous applause' (SB 204). The Emperor also attended the third performance on 2 March; then on 4 March Grillparzer was informed by Sedlnitzky that the Emperor wished to acquire sole ownership of the piece (which in effect would mean its withdrawal from

---

[1] 'The colourful subject-matter, with its variety and liveliness, was just what was needed to jolt me out of my low spirits.'

circulation). The following day Grillparzer wrote to Sedlnitzky, suggesting 3,000 fl. as a price for the work, but emphasizing that he would prefer it to be published and performed freely and setting out the counter-argument he had already presented orally to Sedlnitzky: that copies of the play had already been made, so that its complete withdrawal might not be practicable (B 339). On 7 March, at the fourth performance, the Emperor was once more present; and towards the end of the month his decision about 'acquiring' the play was reversed. Meanwhile Grillparzer was still working on *Des Meeres und der Liebe Wellen*, and he completed his manuscript in late autumn (though the text was revised several times in subsequent years). Notable events in Vienna in the later part of the year were the première of Raimund's *Der Alpenkönig und der Menschenfeind* on 17 October at the Theater in der Leopoldstadt and on 19 November the death, at the age of thirty-one, of Schubert, which brought to a close a whole brilliant chapter in the cultural life of the city. On his memorial stone were inscribed Grillparzer's words, emphasizing Schubert's potential and promise (rather than the substance of his achievement, the full extent of which Grillparzer could not know), but memorable in their simplicity: 'Die Tonkunst begrub hier einen reichen Besitz, / Aber noch viel schönere Hoffnungen...' (G 497, v).[1]

Last years in the theatre (1829–38)

By mid-February 1829 Grillparzer was again in frequent contact 1829 with Daffinger and his wife. In this period he returned to the work of polishing the text of *Des Meeres und der Liebe Wellen*, of which he had begun to write out a new fair copy; he was still worried by what he considered to be the over-theatrical ending (T 1709). That by the end of the month he was once again captivated by Marie's beauty is clear from his diary: on 24 February 'At Daffinger's in the afternoon. His wife very beautiful' (T 1722); on 28 February 'At D.'s in the afternoon. His wife beautiful, beautiful, beautiful' (T 1735). This brief reawakening of his feelings coincided with the rapid completion (by 25 February) of his new manuscript; a copy of it was submitted to the Burgtheater the following month. At about the same time he began detailed preparatory work on *Esther*, and in July wrote most of his fragmentary dialogue *Le poète sifflé*, in which he satirizes various

---

[1] 'Music has buried here great riches, but still finer hopes by far...'

attitudes to the theatre and adds a self-satirical sketch of an awkward and self-conscious poet. The sharpest passage is one in which the principal figure, Adèle, accuses dramatists of indecently laying bare their inmost selves – a recapitulation of what Grillparzer had himself strongly felt at the première of *Die Ahnfrau* and had expressed again in 1827 in a Fixlmüllner-note (T 1657) – and of conducting love-affairs as 'psychological experiments', exploiting them in order to gain material for their tragedies – a rehearsal of his long-standing feelings of guilt about his relations with Charlotte von Paumgartten.

1830   On 28 February and 1 March 1830 the Leopoldstadt district was severely flooded; and it was following this that the familiar figure of a begging violinist disappeared from the Gasthaus 'Zum Jägerhorn' in the Dorotheergasse – a circumstance that suggested the outline of the story *Der arme Spielmann*. What Grillparzer continued with in the spring of 1830, however, was his preparatory work on *Esther*; he also commemorated in the poem 'Begegnung' (G 73) his first meeting with the seventeen-year-old Heloise Hoechner, and attempted to incorporate this poem in a fair copy of the *Tristia* which, however, he did not complete. On 30 April *Ein treuer Diener seines Herrn* was published by Wallishausser. The summer was made notable throughout Europe by the July Revolution (27–9 July) in Paris: about that time Grillparzer began the manuscript of *Esther* and advanced as far as line 227. In the autumn he completed his first full manuscript of *Der Traum ein Leben*. Meanwhile by early August he had decided that he ought to make a complete break from Kathi: 'Certainly no change within me can be expected if this connection with F. is not ended completely' (T 1824). In December, while she was away in Milan with her sister Josefine (the singer), he moved away from the Spiegelgasse.

1831   In the second half of February 1831, he began *Der arme Spielmann*. The following month *Der Traum ein Leben* was submitted to Schreyvogel, whose report was cautiously negative (*Gespr.* 564); and on 5 April the première of *Des Meeres und der Liebe Wellen* took place in the Burgtheater, with Julie Gley as Hero. It was a failure, and work on *Der arme Spielmann* ground to a dispirited halt. Yet another entanglement with Marie, which inspired the sensuous poem 'Ich weiß ein Haar' (G 203) and brought her close to a separation from Daffinger (T 2019), probably prompted Grillparzer to leave Vienna and go on a walking tour to Ischl with three friends (Bauernfeld, the medievalist Theodor von

Karajan, and a painter, Josef Beyer) from 16 to 29 July, and after that to go on with Karajan to Gastein. There he wrote two new *Tristia*, 'Ablehnung' and 'Noch einmal in Gastein', and the first fourteen lines of a third, 'Naturszene'; and on about 26 August he had an interesting and stimulating meeting with Archduke Johann: 'If I should ever write my *Rudolf II*, this Archduke Johann will figure in it as Archduke Mathias' (T 1920). The holiday was effectively the end of his entanglements with Marie, though he remained disappointed and restless for the next two years or so and kept up occasional contact with the Daffinger household into the 1840s. What the holiday had not alleviated was either his despondency or his sense of ageing; on 26 August he wrote in his diary, 'Evening is beginning to set in' (T 1921). At the beginning of September he was back in Vienna, where a cholera epidemic had broken out in mid-August. More trouble with the censor was in store. A poem that he had written in the early summer, 'Klosterszene' (G 76), included stanzas critical of the repression of free thought (ll. 49–64), and was censored; the almanach *Vesta* for 1832, in which it was to appear, had to print a substitute poem. Grillparzer's next poems included a still more radical one, 'Warschau' (G 77). On 27 September an article by Friedrich von Gentz had appeared in the *Augsburger Allgemeine Zeitung* praising the Russian intervention in Warsaw – where on 8 September troops had finally put down the Polish insurrection of the previous year – as a preservation of political order. 'Warschau' was Grillparzer's riposte, but it was unpublishable. Also in September he returned to work on his *Tristia*, completing 'Naturszene' and adding it and the two other Gastein poems, together with the 'Schlußwort'. In October and November he completed the first act of the *Bruderzwist* and began the second; and on 13 November he applied for an appointment as Director of the State Archives. Towards the end of the year he made detailed notes on Lope's *La hermosa Ester*, and in mid-December progressed slightly on Act II of *Libussa*. On 19 December a quarrel with Kathi was followed, as usual, by an immediate reconciliation (T 1934); but the year ended in deep discontent, in a sense of having 'no foothold' (T 1931). In the political scene too the discontent continued to manifest itself, notably in the Lyon uprising of November; in the Austrian context the major signal of the political mood of the year was the publication in Hamburg of the radical *Spaziergänge eines Wiener Poeten* by 'Anastasias Grün' (Count Auersperg).

19

1832   On 23 January 1832 Grillparzer was appointed 'Archivdirektor der allgemeinen Hofkammer', but it was a distinction that filled him with misgivings. Two days later he wrote in his diary: 'Have been given the post as chief archivist and so sold the son of man for thirty pieces of silver' (T 1989). Socially, he was still mixing with Bauernfeld's circle, which in March took to meeting in the Gasthaus zum 'Stern', in the Brandstätte, and Bauernfeld later remembered his lively contributions: 'Grillparzer especially did not stint with the pearls of his mind and spirit, and when he was on good form he was always ready with the most cogent witticisms' (*Gespr.* 558). In the course of this spring he wrote the last of his *Tristia*, 'Intermezzo'; but the season also brought two sad signs of the passing of a whole cultural age. On 22 March Goethe died (though the Second Part of *Faust* was published in this same year); and in May Schreyvogel was dismissed from the Burgtheater. As from 13 May Count Czernin, the *Oberstkämmerer*, himself took over the direction of the theatre, with Deinhardstein as deputy director (*Vizedirektor*) in Schreyvogel's place. It was a change that Grillparzer lamented: the poem 'Neue Theaterdirektion' ('Thespis' altes Reich ist hin...', G 208) expresses his criticism.

In June and July he pressed on further with *Libussa*, advancing as far as line 1333. But on 28 July Schreyvogel died – dying, as Bauernfeld put it in his diary, 'of cholera or of being pensioned off'. His loss was keenly felt in literary circles, and most keenly of all by Grillparzer, who felt himself increasingly isolated. Four years after Schreyvogel's death he was to write: 'Since his death there has been *no-one* in Vienna with whom I should care to discuss artistic matters' (T 3168). By September 1832 he had grown aware that even his friendship with Bauernfeld was becoming cooler. Bauernfeld had noticed signs of this a whole twelve months previously, and had suspected Grillparzer of unworthy motives: 'He has been far less friendly towards me since I have begun to make a name for myself' (*Gespr.* 568); in fact, Grillparzer merely felt disappointed by what he regarded as Bauernfeld's frivolity and irresponsibility (T 2009). But although their mutual admiration lessened, the playwrights remained friends, and continued to see much of each other for several more years.

September saw the beginning of Grillparzer's study of Hegel (T 2010), but his work as chief archivist prevented him from getting down to creative work: 'For a whole six months now, I have completely forgotten that I am the same man who once

looked like winning a place among the leading poets of his time...'
(T 2006). On 30 September he found himself in the role of peace-
maker in a quarrel between Daffinger and Marie: the incident
prompted him to reflect on the memory of his first love of Marie,
and he concluded by summarizing her character in the formula:
'She is a child' (T 2020). By 10 October he had resumed work
on the revision of *Des Meeres und der Liebe Wellen*. Another
quarrel with Kathi was followed by yet another affectionate
reconciliation the next day (T 2024, 2026). In November he worked
on revising *Der Traum ein Leben*; in December he showed the
revised text of *Des Meeres und der Liebe Wellen* to Bauernfeld
(*Gespr.* 581, 1432), and as a result of his criticisms made a few
more small alterations. Around Christmas he resumed work on
Libussa, and finished the third act early the next year; at the
end of 1832 he also wrote a loyal poem 'Auf die Genesung des
Kronprinzen' (G 80), which, emphasizing Archduke Ferdinand's
benevolence, equated goodness with wisdom, but which was widely
misunderstood – and quickly parodied (B 396) – as a disrespectful
comment on his near-idiocy.

Early in 1833 Grillparzer composed the poem 'An die Sammlung' 1833
(G 210), a plea for the return of the inspiration of creative composure
which the pressures of life had destroyed: 'Mich hat der Menschen
wildbewegtes Treiben / Im Innersten verwirret und zerstört...'
(ll. 27f.).[1] On 27 February *Melusina* was given its first performance
in Berlin, with music by Konradin Kreutzer, and in March
Grillparzer helped Bauernfeld with ideas and advice for his comedy
Helene; but an audience with the Emperor on 10 April was
a disappointment in that after the episode of the poem 'Auf die
Genesung des Kronprinzen' his request for an increase in his
salary was fruitless. Three days later, taking stock of his life, he
wrote: 'I am 42 years old and feel like an old man' (T 2074). One
unmistakable sign of the changing times had occurred on 11 April:
the première in the Theater an der Wien of Nestroy's burlesque
Lumpazivagabundus. Another notable première was that of *Helene* in
the Burgtheater on 19 August; and by November Grillparzer was
collaborating with Bauernfeld again, drafting a revision of the
third act of *Die Bekenntnisse*. At the end of the year *Melusina*
was published by the firm of Wallishausser.

Early in 1834 the *Tristia* cycle was at last arranged in its 1834

---

[1] 'The turbulence of life about me has confused and destroyed my innermost
being...'

final order, ready for publication in the following year's *Vesta*: it was at this stage that 'Trennung', 'Verwünschung', 'Intermezzo' and 'Jugenderinnerungen im Grünen' were included. On 8 February *Die Bekenntnisse* was produced at the Burgtheater; another important première which Grillparzer attended the same month (*Gespr.* 1437) was that of Raimund's last play, *Der Verschwender*, at the Theater in der Josefstadt (20 February). On 22 March Grillparzer applied – unsuccessfully – for a post as a superintendent in the University Library (B 405). In early April he gave *Des Meeres und der Liebe Wellen* to Zedlitz to read, but was disappointed by his adversely critical reaction (T 2132). On 4 October, however, the première took place in the Burgtheater of *Der Traum ein Leben*, in a production that was to remain in the repertory of the theatre till 1904. Ludwig Löwe played the part of Rustan; and the evening was summed up by Grillparzer in his diary in the triumphant formula: 'Total success' (T 2194). A series of letters written by Heloise Hoechner (with whom his friendship had for some months been growing closer) between 7 October and 27 November show that Grillparzer had now begun strenuously to avoid her.

1835   On 24 January 1835 the appearance in the *Blätter für Literatur, Kunst und Kritik* of Bauernfeld's essay 'Kritik und Kritiker unserer Zeit' marked the opening of Bauernfeld's feud with the critic Moritz Gottlieb Saphir. An ironical paragraph by Grillparzer, 'Meine Ansicht', which appeared in the same journal on 18 February, established him as being on Bauernfeld's side against Saphir; Saphir's reply appeared in the *Theaterzeitung* on 22 February, under the same heading. In February Grillparzer wrote the first two acts of *Weh dem, der lügt!*; what interrupted him at that stage was probably the news of the death on 2 March of the Emperor. Franz was succeeded by his feeble-witted son Ferdinand, whom in a deathbed testament he enjoined to rely on Metternich. On 24 March Bauernfeld's drama *Fortunat* was performed in the Theater in der Josefstadt, and was promptly damned by Saphir in a review in the *Theaterzeitung* (26–8 March). On 9 April, in the same theatre, *Melusina* was given its first performance in Vienna. That month Grillparzer helped Bauernfeld on another play, *Bürgerlich und Romantisch*, on which he made several critical notes. Meantime his interest in Heloise was growing again (cf. G 575), and on 4 May she wrote him a letter full of enthusiasm for *Des Meeres und der Liebe Wellen* – and for himself: 'How shall

I bear it when you go away?...How fortunate those girls were who, disregarding all else and following their hearts alone, never left the man of their choice! I know I am saying too much, much too much, but I can speak no other way; not today...' (B 440). But she went too far when she wrote seven days later inviting him to join her and her sister and father in sharing a flat in the Spiegelgasse (B 441): Grillparzer characteristically took refuge in flight, and spent June in Heiligenstadt with Bauernfeld. On 7 September *Bürgerlich und Romantisch* was performed in the Burgtheater; Saphir's riposte followed on 9 and 10 September in the *Theaterzeitung*. In November Bauernfeld recorded in his diary that Grillparzer was disappearing from the circle in the 'Stern' (*Gespr.* 657); and the year ended with yet another bereavement for Grillparzer with the death on 26 December of his uncle Josef Sonnleithner.

On 24 March 1836 another comedy by Bauernfeld, *Der literarische* 1836 *Salon*, which included an open satirical attack on Saphir, was performed in the Burgtheater – for one performance only, for it was immediately banned. Saphir wrote a scathing review in the *Theaterzeitung* (26 March): 'For my part I left the theatre with one consolation: it has just been made clear to me how colossally talented I am! If it is so difficult to be witty, if it is so impossible to provoke laughter without making personal allusions, what a genius I must be!' On 30 March Grillparzer left the feud behind him as he set out for Paris: 'I must take a homœopathic cure' (T 2868). His stay in the French capital, which began on 9 April, largely failed to relieve his gloom – by the end of April he was writing that he was 'almost pleased to be leaving Paris again soon' (T 2989) – but it got off to a lively start. On 12 April he met Meyerbeer (whom he saw again later on 22 and 24 April); the next evening he saw the celebrated vaudeville actor Etienne Arnal performing; and on 14 April he met Börne: further meetings on 20 April and 9 and 10 May established 'relations almost of friendship' (SB 218). On 19 April he visited the Père Lachaise cemetery, and the grave of Abelard and Héloïse reminded him of Heloise Hoechner. He now completed, and wrote out in his diary (T 2919), the poem 'Entsagung' (G 87), which he had begun the previous year. Their close relations were now over, and in 1837 she married a Rumanian professor of engineering.

On 27 April Grillparzer had a pleasant meeting with Heine: 'I enjoyed the rare pleasure of finding common sense in a German man of letters' (T 2971). On 13 May he also met Dumas the elder;

23

but then on 15 May he left Paris for London, where he spent a month of a cold and wet early summer. A feature of his stay was his frequent theatre-going: he saw Macready at Covent Garden in *Macbeth* (23 May) and as Cassius in *Julius Caesar*, with Charles Kemble as Mark Antony (30 May); he saw Giulia Grisi at the King's Theatre in Rossini's *Gazza Ladra* (31 May) and *L'assedio di Corinto* (7 June), in Donizetti's *Marino Falieri* (9 June) and in Bellini's *Otello* (14 June); and he saw Ellen Tree in *The School for Scandal* at the Haymarket (11 June). But perhaps the highlight of his stay was a debate in the House of Commons, which he watched on 2 and 3 June and in which he heard both O'Connell and Peel speak. This too appealed to him by its theatrical quality: 'The whole thing was thrilling simply as a spectacle' ('als Schauspiel': SB 224). He left London on 16 June, and though when he arrived in Munich on 28 June it was to discover that his brother Karl, in temporary insanity, had committed embezzlement and accused himself of murder (T 3151), nevertheless in mid-August, when he was back in Vienna, Bauernfeld found him 'somewhat more cheerful' (*Gespr.* 673). But more tribulations were in store. Raimund shot himself, and died – at the age of only forty-six – on 5 September; and Grillparzer's old friend Zedlitz, who had translated Byron's *Childe Harold's Pilgrimage*, angered him by giving a copy, with a loyal dedication, to Metternich (G 614). In mid-September Grillparzer himself, by contrast, composed his satirical poem 'Für unser Glück, du edler Fürst...' (G 217) on Metternich's oppressive and restrictive policies.

1837   In early April 1837 Grillparzer was helping Bauernfeld again, this time with notes on *Der Selbstquäler* (T 3253). On 16 April Bauernfeld read the play to a circle of friends including Grillparzer, Lenau and Ernst von Feuchtersleben. This was the first meeting between Grillparzer and Feuchtersleben and the beginning of their friendship: 'Our first conversation was enough to bring about a meeting of minds,' Grillparzer wrote in his short memoir after Feuchtersleben's death; '...before we knew it we were friends.' In May 1837 he wrote the last three acts of *Weh dem, der lügt!*, and read it to Feuchtersleben and Bauernfeld on 25 or 26 June. On 6 November Bauernfeld's *Der Selbstquäler* was performed at the Burgtheater; four days later Saphir's review in *Der Humorist* dismissed the play as being thin, monotonous in plot, lacking truth to life, and uneven in its verse. Towards the end of the month Grillparzer submitted his own comedy to the Burgtheater.

On 23 January 1838 it was at last officially decided that the 1838
post in the University Library should go to an experienced
librarian, Franz Lechner. A still more bitter disappointment
awaited Grillparzer on 6 March: the failure of the première of
Weh dem, der lügt!, in which Ludwig Löwe played Leon and
Julie Rettich, the former Julie Gley, played Edrita. Bauernfeld
came to Grillparzer's defence with 'Weh dem, der dichtet!', published on 13 March in the *Wiener Zeitschrift...*; Saphir replied
in *Der Humorist* six days later with a piece entitled 'Wehe dem
Publikum, das richtet'.[1] On 31 May Grillparzer's *Hannibal* was
published in a charity *Album* edited by the journalist Friedrich
Witthauer, the editor of the *Wiener Zeitschrift...* and a member
of the 'Stern' circle; but the failure of *Weh dem, der lügt!* now
accelerated still further Grillparzer's withdrawal from that circle
(*Gespr.* 693).

Withdrawal (1838–56)

In October 1838 Zedlitz was officially appointed to a position for
which he had applied in May in the State Chancellery, working
in effect as a journalistic apologist for the Metternich régime.
Even the financial pressures on Zedlitz could not excuse this in
the eyes of Grillparzer, who expressed his criticism both in verse
(G 234) and in conversation: 'Zedlitz's crime is that having
deservedly made his name in literature he has allowed and still
allows himself to be used as the mouthpiece of those corrupt and
stupid men' (*Gespr.* 714). Towards the end of the year he revised
the end of Act I of the *Bruderzwist*, and early in 1839 he advanced 1839
as far as line 753, as well as taking *Esther* to line 760. In the autumn
he wrote the first one and a half acts of *Die Jüdin von Toledo*
(reaching line 557) and completed the second act of the *Bruderzwist*;
meanwhile (August to December) the firm of Wallishausser published *Der Traum ein Leben*, *Weh dem, der lügt!* and *Des Meeres und
der Liebe Wellen*. By mid-November Bauernfeld sadly wrote that
the 'Stern' circle had completely disbanded (*Gespr.* 713).

The summer of 1840 – which in Prussia saw the succession to 1840
the throne of Friedrich Wilhelm IV (7 June) – was spent by
Grillparzer in Döbling, where he completed the second act of
Esther. In the autumn a new society of writers, actors and artists
was founded, the 'Concordia'; Grillparzer became a member –

---

[1] Grillparzer's title: 'Woe to him who lies!' Bauernfeld's title: 'Woe to him
who is a poet!' Saphir's title: 'Woe to the public that passes judgment!'

others included Nestroy and Löwe – and attended meetings regularly. On 29 November Act I of *Libussa* was performed at a charity performance in the Burgtheater, with Löwe in the role of Primislaus and Julie Rettich in that of Libussa; and in January 1841 the act was published in a charity *Album*. But on 31 March Grillparzer's position in relation to the Burgtheater was weakened still further with the end of Deinhardstein's appointment as director. In June permission was given for the foundation of the *Juridisch-politischer Leseverein*, the most important of the liberal societies of the pre-revolutionary period (the *Vormärz*). It was granted official approval as, in effect, a library of law periodicals; but the announcement carried by the *Wiener Zeitung* on 5 December advertised it as a medium of information about progress in literature in general. Its membership was drawn from the professional classes, including high officials, clerics, lawyers, army officers; and one of its leading members was the future minister Alexander Bach.

Towards the end of the year Grillparzer took satirical stock of German literature in the dialogue 'Friedrich der Große und Lessing'; but he made no further progress on major projects until 1842 July and August 1842, when he resumed and completed *Der arme Spielmann*. In the autumn of 1842, as he told Adolf Foglár in conversation at the end of October, he planned to take up work on his uncompleted plays again (*Gespr.* 762); in fact what he did 1843 turn to in January 1843 was his final revision of the text of *Die Ahnfrau* for the publication of its sixth edition the following year. On 9 July 1843 another of the leading figures in the literary and cultural life of Old Vienna died: Karoline Pichler. On 27 August Grillparzer was seen off by the Fröhlich sisters (Kathi weeping, 'quite beside herself about the dangerous journey', T 3628) as he set off on a steamer eastwards down the Danube. The first stop was Pressburg, where he attended a debate in the Diet (28 August); from there he continued his journey to Constantinople and Greece, and only returned to Vienna on 7 November.

1844　In 1844 he applied twice for the post of court librarian: the first application, made in April, was refused on 11 June; the second, made in September, was refused in December. The appointment – to Grillparzer's bitter disappointment – went to a younger man, Baron Münch-Bellinghausen, who had been in public service since 1826 and was better known as a minor dramatist under the pseudonym Friedrich Halm. In the course of the year Grillparzer

26

also drafted a memorandum on censorship ('Über die Aufhebung der Zensur'), on which he had already made one beginning in the late 1830s. In it he rejected the arguments of the liberal extremists but supported the reform or – since good censorship was impracticable – the abolition of censorship in the literary field. The memorandum was never completed and submitted. In the winter of 1844–5 he at last returned to other kinds of writing. First, probably, came the predominantly anecdotal memoir 'Meine Erinnerungen an Beethoven'; then he composed Act III of the *Bruderzwist* and advanced in Act IV as far as line 2022. In January 1845 he also re- 1845 sumed work on *Libussa*, of which two acts were still to be written.

The question of censorship was now a burning public issue in liberal circles. On 20 February a meeting was called, with Josef von Hammer-Purgstall as host, to discuss the submission of a petition demanding relaxation of censorship. Bauernfeld read a draft version to the twenty-four people present, who included Auersperg, Karajan, Castelli, Feuchtersleben, Münch and Grillparzer. Bauernfeld was doubtful of the support of these last three (*Gespr.* 852), but the petition was finally signed by all thirty-three people, including Grillparzer, who attended the next meeting on 11 March; and further signatories within the next few days included even Zedlitz, who received special permission from Metternich. The petition was submitted on 16 March.

Though in the summer Grillparzer felt that his creative faculties were declining – on 19 June he told Foglár 'I am withering away, and indeed from *within*, which is worst of all' (*Gespr.* 863) – he continued to work on his manuscript of *Libussa*, which he finally completed in the autumn of the following year. On 8 July 1846 1846 Stifter's publisher, Gustav Heckenast, applied for rights to publish a collected edition of Grillparzer's works (B 651). He was in fact not the first publisher to make enquiries of this sort, for advances had been made in 1841 from a publisher in Mainz and in 1845 from publishers in Vienna and Stuttgart. Like the previous applicants, Heckenast was refused, but on 20 November Grillparzer sent *Der arme Spielmann* to the editor of the yearbook *Iris*, which Heckenast published. Meanwhile the signs of impending political change were growing in number: in Vienna, Bauernfeld's *Großjährig*, a society comedy satirizing the Metternich system, was produced at the Burgtheater on 16 November; in Munich, the Lola Montez scandal began in the autumn of 1846, and in mid-February 1847 1847 the Abel government fell.

In May 1847 the Austrian Academy of Sciences (*Akademie der Wissenschaften*) was founded, with Grillparzer as a founder-member. In spring or early summer he completed Act IV of the *Bruderzwist*; then from 2 to 28 September he made his second journey to Germany, travelling with Kathi Fröhlich's nephew Wilhelm Bogner to Munich, Hamburg and Berlin, where on 26 September he renewed his acquaintance with Meyerbeer. While he was away, the *Augsburger Allgemeine Zeitung* of 6 September printed part of a letter written to the editor by Stifter on 21 August, describing *Der arme Spielmann* (which he had read in proof) as a masterpiece (*Gespr.* 910). Once back from his journey, Grillparzer proceeded with the last act of the *Bruderzwist*, reaching line 2526; and that same autumn the 1848 issue of *Iris* appeared, containing *Der arme Spielmann*.

The political situation continued to deteriorate. One notable incident was the inspection of the *Leseverein* library by Sedlnitzky, who had long viewed the society as a cradle of controversy and revolution. Having enjoyed the protection of the chief minister for internal affairs, Count Kolowrat, the *Leseverein* had retained considerable freedom; and the library was found to contain a number of proscribed works, including Rousseau's *Du Contrat Social*. Grillparzer's concern at the political situation led him in December 1847 to draft a letter of warning to Archduke Ludwig 1848 (B 664) and in January 1848, after the failure of the petition on censorship, to express his apprehension in the poem 'Vorzeichen' ('Wenn sich der Untergang...', G 125); nevertheless, in the winter of 1847–8 he wrote out a final manuscript of *Libussa*, took *Esther* to line 979 (the end of the fragment), completed the last act of the *Bruderzwist* and, by February 1848, copied out and revised a second manuscript of the latter play. But then, in the wake of the Paris revolution of 24 February (which achieved the abdication of Louis-Philippe and the proclamation of a republic) and radical unrest in Budapest and Prague, revolt broke out in Vienna on 13 March. In the following seven and a half months, thousands of people were killed; nevertheless, especially at first, it was a revolution in the Viennese manner, with high spirits as well as political fervour. Later Grillparzer was to recall in his reminiscences of the year 1848: '...It was the gayest revolution imaginable. Favoured by the finest spring weather, the whole population swarmed through the streets all day long.' But the uprising achieved immediate results: not only the resignation of Metternich, who fled to England, and of Sedlnitzky, but also (on 15 March) the Emperor's promise of a parliamentary constitution and of freedom of the press. On 20 March, in Munich, the King of Bavaria abdicated. Between mid-March and mid-July Grillparzer drafted four open letters, intended as warnings to the Viennese about the dangers of disorder; and in the poem 'Mein Vaterland' (G 126), which appeared on 1 April in the first number of the new *Constitutionelle Donau-Zeitung*, he supported the new libertarian trends but added an apprehensive warning against deserting old values. On 3 April he was one of the writers who elected four representatives (including Bauernfeld and Auersperg) to attend the German national *Vorparlament* which had begun to meet in Frankfurt on 31 March; and in mid-April he denied, in the epigram G 1108, that his political views, formerly liberal, were now ultra-conservative. In the same month, however, he joined the newly-formed conservative 'Österreichischer Club'. The Frankfurt *Vorparlament*, meanwhile, broke up before the Austrian delegation had arrived; and Bauernfeld, who had played a leading role in the events throughout March, was spending April in Graz writing his political fantasy-drama *Die Republik der Tiere*. On 11 April the Emperor's confirmation of the Hungarian 'March laws' was in effect a confirmation of the revolution there, giving Hungary dominion status. On 25 April a parliamentary constitution was published in Vienna for the rest of the Empire; this was, however, withdrawn after further demonstrations on 15 May, and a new democratic constitution was proclaimed which promised a Constituent Assembly elected by universal suffrage. On 17 May the Emperor fled to Innsbruck.

On 26 May – one day after the early death of Grillparzer's young friend Wilhelm Bogner – the first barricades were erected in Vienna, and a radical Committee of Public Safety was set up, which was supported by students and workers and which was in effect to direct the revolution. The events of this month distanced Grillparzer further from the liberals (a development which he commented on with asperity in an epigram, G 1118); and the publication on 8 June, in the *Constitutionelle Donau-Zeitung*, of his loyalist poem 'Feldmarschall Radetzky' (G 128) in praise of the commander of the Austrian troops in Upper Italy established his reputation as an ultra-conservative. In real danger from extremist demonstrators, he left Vienna for the country, and from 14 June until late July he remained in Baden. There, in June, he and Bauernfeld met and discussed the political situation; Bauernfeld's diary records that they were close to quarrelling (*Gespr.* 949/i).

In Vienna the new freedom allowed the première of Nestroy's political satire *Freiheit in Krähwinkel*, a dramatic review of the revolution so far. This took place on 1 July in the recently opened Carl-Theater, which had been erected on the site of the old Theater in der Leopoldstadt. The play was an immediate success and was performed thirty-six times in three months. On 22 July the newly constituted *Reichstag* met. But there were further riots in August, and again on 6 October – the most serious and dangerous of the revolts, which aimed at ending the Austrian Empire, establishing Hungarian national independence and aligning Austria with Germany. On 7 October Grillparzer drew up his will, ordering that the 'apparently completed' pieces *Libussa* and *Rudolf II* should be destroyed. The Emperor and his family fled again, this time to Olmütz in Moravia. But the revolt was defeated. Under Prince Windischgrätz, imperial troops surrounded Vienna. Fighting began on 24 October, and became heavy on 28 October. Troops of the National Guard and the students' *akademische Legion* (both officially dissolved by Windischgrätz on 23 October) held a barricade in the Praterstraße for over nine hours' fighting. The imperial troops finally entered the centre of the old city on 31 October, completed its capitulation on 1 November, and later in the winter occupied Budapest. Censorship had already been reimposed when Schwarzenberg became Prime Minister on 21 November. On 2 December Ferdinand abdicated, to be succeeded by his eighteen-year-old nephew, Franz Josef; and in the course of November and December Grillparzer returned to dramatic writing, resuming work (after an interval of nine years) on his manuscript of *Die Jüdin von Toledo*, and completing Act II and advancing in Act III approximately to line 979.

1849 On the first day of 1849 the *Akademie der Wissenschaften* invited Grillparzer, as it was inviting all its members, to write the story of his life (the aim being eventually to publish these autobiographical sketches in lieu of obituaries). Grillparzer did not respond immediately; among the pieces he did, however, write in the early part of 1849 was an essay 'Über das Hofburgtheater'.

The political situation in Europe continued to be disturbed. On 23 March Radetzky defeated the King of Sardinia at Novara and published a bulletin the next day announcing the King's abdication. Five days later Friedrich Wilhelm IV was elected hereditary German Emperor, in an empire to exclude Austria, by the National Assembly in Frankfurt. Austria's delegates were withdrawn early in April, but when Friedrich Wilhelm declined the throne, the whole Frankfurt Assembly petered out. Also early in April Windischgrätz was forced to withdraw from Budapest, and on 14 April Kossuth was elected Governor of Hungary; but in May Russian troops entered Hungary in support of the Emperor. The Hungarian army capitulated in August, and Kossuth fled to Turkey. Meanwhile, on 27 April, Grillparzer had moved back to the Spiegelgasse, this time as a subtenant of the Fröhlich sisters. It was his last move; Kathi became in effect his housekeeper for more than twenty years – years of devotion which completed the development into an old maid of the once romantic and lively girl of the poem 'Allgegenwart'. Two more of Grillparzer's friends died in the summer of 1849: on 22 August Daffinger (of cholera), on 3 September Feuchtersleben. Also in September, Grillparzer surveyed his own career in a long melancholy diary-note (T 4025), acknowledging that, isolated in an increasingly alien world, he had failed to achieve his artistic goals, and ascribing his failure to his own character: 'an over-susceptible nature, with a tendency to hypochondria and a decided abhorrence of publicity'. In the same note he expressed the resolve that his last plays should not see the light of day during his lifetime. This was, in fact, already a modification of the instructions in his will; and a little later he undertook another revision of the *Bruderzwist*, and in December he nearly completed Act III of *Die Jüdin von Toledo*, reaching line 1126. On 26 December the Emperor signed a decree making Heinrich Laube director of the Burgtheater; and on 26 January 1850 Laube made known in the *Wiener Zeitung* his intention of **1850** reinstating Grillparzer's plays in their rightful place on the Burgtheater repertory.

In late September and October 1850 Grillparzer wrote his 'Erinnerungen aus dem Revolutionsjahr 1848', which include criticism of Bauernfeld's political attitudes, accusing him of naivety and of popularity-mongering. This signalled the final breakdown of the friendship between the two dramatists. Another memoir written in this year and the next was 'Meine Erinnerungen an Feuchtersleben'. On 16 November 1850 the first of Laube's new Grillparzer-productions, *Medea*, was performed in the Burgtheater, with Julie Rettich as Medea; and from November 1850 to January 1851 Grillparzer served Laube as one of the five judges **1851** in a competition for new comedies held by the Burgtheater: the winning entry, announced on 27 January 1851, was Bauernfeld's *Der kategorische Imperativ*. In the spring and summer of 1851 *Die Jüdin von Toledo* was completed, the last of all Grillparzer's plays; and in the autumn two more of his earlier tragedies were performed in the Burgtheater under Laube's direction: on 18 October *Ein treuer Diener seines Herrn*, with Löwe as Bancban and Christine Hebbel as the queen, and on 29 November *Des Meeres und der Liebe Wellen*, with Anschütz as the priest. Both productions were performed with great success; Grillparzer's reaction was: 'Too late!' (*Gespr.* 1495).

On 31 December 1851 the new absolutism which had replaced the constitutional freedoms nominally won by the 1848 revolution was fully re-established by a patent introducing imperial rule and 1852 reducing the role of the *Reichsrat* to an advisory one. 1852 was a year full of landmarks, signs of the changing times. *Kampl*, produced in the Carl-Theater on 29 March, was Nestroy's last full-length success. In April Schwarzenberg died suddenly. In November Cavour became premier in Turin, and in France Napoleon III was proclaimed Emperor. Early the same year, and 1853 then once more early in 1853, Grillparzer was again requested to write his life-story for the *Akademie der Wissenschaften*. In January 1853 his *Selbstbiographie* was at last begun, but he broke off work on it in May or thereabouts. Meanwhile, by April, he had shown the manuscript of *Libussa* to Laube, and in December he gave permission for the work to be performed if its success could be 1854 guaranteed; in February 1854, Laube cautiously refused to give such a guarantee (*Gespr.* 1503).

On 24 April 1854 Franz Josef married Elisabeth of Bavaria – an event which Grillparzer celebrated in an epithalamium (G 137). 1855 The following year the reactionary climate following the revolution reached a climax. After prolonged negotiation with the papacy, a concordat – which in the 1840s had been prevented by Kolowrat and the Josephinians – was signed in August and promulgated on 5 November.

1856 On 5 January 1856 another Laube production was staged in the Burgtheater: *König Ottokars Glück und Ende*, with Julie Rettich as Margarete and Anschütz as Horneck. On 17 April Grillparzer retired from the civil service, with the honorary title *Hofrat*.

Old age (1857–72)

In October 1857 the most ambitious of Laube's new productions – 1857
the whole of *Das Goldene Vlies* – was staged in the Burgtheater.
But the old order was now rapidly changing, both in Vienna, where
demolition of the walls and ramparts round the old city centre
started early in 1858, and in Austria as a whole: in the Franco- 1858
Austrian war in Italy which broke out in April 1859, the Austrians 1859
were defeated on 4 June at Magenta and on 24 June at Solferino,
and in the armistice which was signed at Villafranca on 12 July
Austria surrendered Lombardy. On 11 June, Metternich died.
On 7 November 1859 Grillparzer was given (*in absentia*) an honorary
doctorate from the University of Leipzig; and in January 1860 1860
he received a long letter from Stifter, who was under the impression
that he was celebrating his seventieth birthday and expressed his
admiration and affection (B 971). On 17 January Grillparzer
replied rather sadly about his condition: 'My literary art ("die
Poesie") has forsaken me, as music did some time ago' (B 973).
In March, talking to Wilhelm von Wartenegg, he again emphasized his feeling of growing old; he also spoke of his unpublished
tragedies, and now altogether contradicted his testamentary
instructions that they should be destroyed: 'As for anything else
I have written, they can take it when I am dead and do with it
what they will' (*Gespr.* 1088). On 29 January 1861 his brother 1861
Karl (whose family he had helped to support for many years) died.
On 8 April, in an epigram, he restated the plaint of the previous
year's letter to Stifter: 'Der Dichter liegt seit lang begraben'
(G 1656).[1] On 15 April he was created a member of the *Herrenhaus*
(the Upper House of the Austrian parliament). On 6 May the
Libussa 'Vorspiel' was introduced on to the regular repertory of
the Burgtheater.
The sense of ageing continued to grow – in November 1861 he
complained to Wartenegg particularly about weakening eyesight,
which made reading difficult, and Wartenegg noted that his
hearing was also failing (*Gespr.* 1112) – and more of his contempo-
raries died: Zedlitz on 16 March 1862, and Nestroy two months 1862
later (25 May). In August, discussing *Esther* with Emil Kuh, he
said he had left it as a fragment as the two completed acts made
a rounded whole on their own (*Gespr.* 1116); he had given a
substantial part of the fragment (1–731) to Kuh to be published

---

[1] 'The poet has long since lain buried.'

in a *Dichteralbum* which Kuh was editing and which appeared in November. By then another sign had been given of the new political order in Europe: on 8 October Bismarck had officially been appointed the Prussian *Ministerpräsident* and Foreign

1863 Minister. On 29 May 1863 Grillparzer at last made a new (though in fact still not a final) will, in which he bequeathed his literary remains to the Fröhlich sisters (B 1140). A fall in Tüffer, a spa in Styria, on 16 June of the same year further weakened his hearing; in the late autumn, however, there began a series of visits paid him by Frau Auguste von Littrow-Bischoff, which included several interesting conversations about his works. It was also in 1863, in Ulm, that Clara Ziegler first played the part of Medea, which she was to make famous throughout Germany in the 1880s. On 13

1864 December Hebbel died. A month later, on 15 January 1864, Grillparzer was made a freeman of Vienna – of a changing Vienna, whose development into a modern city was demonstrated in the

1865 opening of the *Ringstraße* on 1 May 1865 – and on 8 December 1865 another of his tragedies was reinstated in the Burgtheater: *Sappho*, with the young Charlotte Wolter in the title role. On 6 January

1866 1866 a long conversation with Robert Zimmermann included a brief discussion of how the ending of *Esther* would have turned out (*Gespr.* 1176). On 26 May Grillparzer made his final will, naming Kathi Fröhlich as sole heir of his literary remains (B 1375).

This was, however, a year overshadowed by political and military events. The Seven Weeks War broke out in early June, and on 3 July Austria was decisively defeated by Prussia at Sadowa in Bohemia. The Peace of Prague, signed on 23 August and ratified a week later, excluded Austria from the German Confederation.

1867 In 1867 the dual monarchy was established, with the Emperor of Austria as King of Hungary; the same year also saw the publication of the first book of Karl Marx's *Das Kapital*. In September 1867 Laube's directorship of the Burgtheater came to an end; and

1868 on 25 February 1868 one of the most illustrious of its former stars, Sophie Schröder, died. A few weeks later, on 21 March 1868, the most dramatic event of Grillparzer's later life took place. He was persuaded by Count Auersperg to go to the parliament to cast his vote in the Upper House ballot against the Catholic attempt to block the new liberal marriage laws. This vote amounted in effect to a repeal of the concordat (which indeed was finally cancelled in July 1870). For the only time in his life Grillparzer was a public political hero, and that evening there were cheering crowds gathered in the Spiegelgasse. Eight days later a charity performance of *Esther* was given in the old Hofoperntheater, and on 28 April the first performance in the Burgtheater followed. In May he discussed with Auguste von Littrow-Bischoff how the play would have continued had he completed it (*Gespr.* 1212), and on 22 August he himself paid one of his now rare visits to the theatre to attend a performance in Baden. In January 1869 he composed the six verses 1869 which round off the *Hannibal* scene; and this was performed on 21 February at the Hofoperntheater, under the title 'Hannibal und Scipio', in aid of the fund for the monument to Schiller in Vienna.

On 19 July 1870 the Franco-Prussian war was declared. The 1870 theatrical life of Vienna continued unabated, with Franz von Dingelstedt's reign as director of the Burgtheater beginning on 19 December; and though Grillparzer refused the firm of Wallishausser permission to issue a commemorative edition of his poems for his eightieth birthday, the occasion was celebrated in January 1871 with a revival of *Die Ahnfrau* in the Theater an der Wien. 1871 1871 was a year which saw the publication of Dostoievsky's *The Devils* and of the first volume of Zola's naturalist cycle *Les Rougon-Macquart*. But it was the war that dominated the attention of Western Europe until the defeat of France, the proclamation of Wilhelm I of Prussia as German Emperor in Versailles in January 1871 and the signing of peace at Frankfurt on 10 May. Bismarck became Chancellor of Germany, and Prussian domination of the German-speaking states was assured. Though Vienna was now a modern city, its importance was greatly diminished. The Empire of which it was the capital was in rapid decline; once the city of Beethoven and Schubert, it was now the city of the waltz; its theatres were increasingly devoted to the escapist world of the operetta. Politically and culturally, Vienna's Golden Age had already passed when its greatest tragic dramatist died on 21 January 1872. 1872

His posthumous plays were published in the same year, in the first collected edition of his works. The first to be performed was the *Bruderzwist*, which was staged by Laube in the Stadttheater on 24 September and by Dingelstedt in the Burgtheater four days later. *Die Jüdin von Toledo* was performed in Prague in November, and in the Burgtheater the following January, on the anniversary of Grillparzer's death. *Libussa* followed a year later, and in 1879 Dingelstedt at last completed the revival of his works with a successful new production of *Weh dem, der lügt!*

2-2

2

THE ARTIST

Grillparzer's conception of drama

The thematic links between Grillparzer's works – his treatment of the recurrent central motives of duty, love and ambition – are closer than any purely formal links. In 1922 Hofmannsthal even claimed in his 'Rede auf Grillparzer' that every one of Grillparzer's plays belongs to a different dramatic genre; and while this is an overstatement, certainly they are not all of a kind. He wrote love-tragedies and histories; he also wrote a ghost-play, a fantastic dream-play, a trilogy based on Greek myth, and a comedy. Moreover, he is not a dramatist who wrote within a single readily defined dramatic tradition. His work draws on and is influenced by several traditions – principally Shakespearian tragedy, German classical tragedy, the spectacular comedy of the Viennese popular theatres and the drama of the Spanish Golden Age.

Underlying his work in the various genres he attempted is, however, a consistent view of drama, which was conditioned by the theatrical life and traditions of his native city. First and foremost, he regarded drama not as literature alone, but as a *theatrical* art. His fragmentary autobiography of 1853 contains the observation: 'I was an Austrian to the core, and with each of my plays had in mind its performance – and indeed its performance in my native city. A play that is read is a book, instead of a living action' (SB 214). Since his own works were written for performance before an audience, he placed considerable weight on the audience's verdict. He wrote of the public as a 'jury' as early as 1821 (T 933), and restated this conception of its role several times in later years; and he worked into *Der arme Spielmann* an emphatic statement of his preference for the judgment of an audience over that of the critics – the view that 'the unrestrained outburst of an overfilled theatre has always been ten times more interesting, indeed more instructive, than the fabricated judgment of some literary matador, stunted in body and soul, and bloated with the blood of authors that he has sucked like a spider' (p. 39). In several places – in his diary (T 2304), in his autobiography (SB 161) and in an essay of the early 1860s, 'Zur Literargeschichte' – he argued that while the poet must not be dictated to by popular taste, he must make his work accessible and comprehensible to that common humanity which is represented in the theatre by the audience. From this concern with directness of appeal follows the belief that 'the truly dramatic is always theatrical, even if the reverse is not true' (T 3262) – that is, while sheer spectacle for its own sake does not constitute drama, nevertheless drama must have immediacy and plasticity. It is for the lack of just these essential qualities that in 1817 he criticized Goethe's two classical dramas, *Iphigenie auf Tauris* and *Torquato Tasso*, as being poetically beautiful but essentially undramatic (T 225). Goethe, and Schiller also, lacked the advantages of a metropolitan theatrical tradition; of Schiller Grillparzer was to observe that if he had had a real public and good actors he would have been an even greater dramatic poet than he was (SB 196).

By comparison with the dramas of Weimar classicism, most of Grillparzer's plays are full of stage action, including fighting and murder and suicide on the stage. In his autobiography he mentions, with some misgivings, the element of 'violence' ('das Gewalttätige') in his work, and points to the influence of the Spanish theatre (SB 214f.). This active element in his work is part of its theatricality. All his plays have a strong visual quality, and throughout his career he aimed at achieving a high degree of plasticity, which he would define in the terms 'Anschaulichkeit' and 'Bildlichkeit'. He tried not only to express emotional developments in the dialogue, but also to represent them by concrete equivalents on the stage, so that theatrical effects bring out visually the inner action. The spoken word is linked to action and gesture: he once wrote of the splendid stage effect that can be achieved by 'words and visual impression together' ('Wort und Bild zu gleicher Zeit', T 279).

His language too is exceptionally vivid; his plays are rich in metaphors and striking imagery. Examples range from the single phrase with which the coquettish Rahel turns to King Alphons for protection:

Ah, hier steht ein Mann
Mit Mondscheinaugen, strahlend Trost und Kühlung
(*Die Jüdin von Toledo* 308f.)[1]

---

[1] 'Ah, here stands a man with moonlight-eyes that radiate solace and cooling calm.'

to the extended comparison with a bird beginning to fly in which
Rustan expresses his feelings of excitement and freedom (*Der
Traum ein Leben* 661–71). There are dynamic dramatic images,
building up a sense of threat and pointing forward to tragedy.
Leander compares the light cast by Hero's lamp to a golden net
spread over the waters (*Des Meeres und der Liebe Wellen* 1112–15);
King Ahasver expounds his fear of parasitic courtiers:

> Da sind sie, da, die Feinde alles Blühns,
> Das kriechende Geschlecht, die leisen Nagens
> Anbohren jedes Blatt, bis es sich krümmt
> Mit bittrer Windung nach dem Innern zu
> Und fahl wird, hart, und stirbt...
> (*Esther* 234–8)[1]

Or again, metaphor and image may serve to sum up the whole
course of a tragedy. Ottokar sees his downfall as that of a trapped
and wounded beast, 'poisoned' by his own queen:

> Und als ich blutend heimkam aus der Schlacht,
> Goß sie mir Gift, statt Balsam, in die Wunden.
> Mit Hohn und Spott hat sie mich aufgestachelt,
> Daß blind ich rannte in das Todesnetz,
> Das nun zusammenschlägt ob meinem Scheitel.
> (*König Ottokars Glück und Ende* 2673–7)[2]

The political insight which Rudolf II's opponents have tragically
lacked is expressed in a comparison of his role in the empire to
that of the crown wheel in the works of a clock:

> ...Daß an der Uhr, in der die Feder drängt,
> Das Kronrad wesentlich mit seiner Hemmung,
> Damit nicht abrollt *eines* Zugs das Werk,
> Und sie in ihrem Zögern weist die Stunde.
> (*Ein Bruderzwist in Habsburg* 2341–4)[3]

What images such as these have in common is a typical clarity
and economy: they illuminate character and dramatic action, and
are not allowed to develop into florid decoration. What Grillparzer

---

[1] 'There, there they are, the foes of all that blooms, the creeping species
that with silent gnawing bore into every leaf until it curls in bitter coils
back upon itself and fades, grows hard, and dies...'

[2] 'And when I came home bleeding from the battle she poured not balm but
poison on my wounds. She goaded me with scorn and ridicule, so that I ran
blindly into the mortal trap that now snaps shut over my head.'

[3] '...That while the mainspring in a clock drives the movement, the crown-
wheel in its escapement is essential too, so that the movement does not
run down all at once but in its slow advance can show the time.'

strove to achieve in his language was to preserve the expressiveness and the power of German blank verse while avoiding floridness, turgidity and rant. Making this point, Professor Zdenko Škreb observes that when it is necessary, Grillparzer will completely alter the word order to give the greatest possible strength to one word; that his verse sounds bare, direct, undecorated, striking a note that is not heard elsewhere in German drama either before him or in his own time or after him.[1] Škreb's points about the directness of Grillparzer's style and the flexibility of his word order can both be illustrated by a dialogue between Edrita and Leon in *Weh dem, der lügt!*:

LEON (*nach ihrer Hand fassend*)
     Edrita!
EDRITA   Laß nur das! – Kannst du mich missen,
     Ich kann es auch. Und nun zu nöt'gern Dingen.
     Wo ist dein Freund?
LEON   Er gräbt dort an der Brücke.
EDRITA   Er gräbt?
LEON   Der Pfeiler einen sticht er ab,
     Daß ein sie bricht, wird irgend sie betreten.

                                     (1178–82)[2]

Their expressions of affection are bare to the point of being little more than hints. Edrita's reproof, then her two questions about Atalus and Leon's first answer are all extremely simple and natural in their phrasing. Then in Leon's second reply the separable prefix *ein* is brought forward from its natural position to an emphatic place at the beginning of the line, so that more weight is placed on the dramatic (and comic) image of the bridge crashing in. The economy of the whole exchange is characteristic. Grillparzer's plays do contain long speeches and monologues – passages of expository narrative, of quiet reflection, or of lyrical emotion – but by comparison with Schiller's style, Grillparzer's is very much less declamatory: Hofmannsthal rightly suggests that the un-rhetorical language of Lessing's *Nathan der Weise* is a truer fore-runner of Grillparzer's blank verse than Schiller's language which contained too much verve and show ('ein Zuviel von Schwung und Prunk').

[1] *Jb.* (3. Folge), VI, 81.
[2] Leon (*reaching for her hand*): 'Edrita!' 'Now stop that! If you will miss me, so shall I miss you. And now to more important things — where is your friend?' 'He is digging away at the bridge over there.' 'Digging?' 'He is cutting away one of the pillars: then *in* the bridge will cave when it is stood on!'

Often, indeed, Grillparzer conveys a character's feelings not in a speech at all but by a suggestive silence, coupled perhaps to a revealing gesture. The effect is more natural, and no less clear. In the final act of *Sappho*, for example, the heroine's sense of her guilt towards Phaon is brought out by the way she listens in silence to his reproaches and lowers her eyes, unwilling to meet his gaze (1703). In *Libussa* the heroine disguises herself as a servant in order to overhear Primislaus's conversation with Wlasta (1572ff.); and as he reveals his love for herself and then (in his eagerness to secure a jewel that figures in the play as a kind of talisman) proceeds apparently to flirt with Wlasta, Libussa betrays the strength of her emotion not by breaking her silence but by failing to hold her candle steady and finally throwing it down. The candle – first burning brightly, then wavering, and finally falling – appears as a visible symbol of Libussa's silent hopes. Or again in the fourth act of *Ein Bruderzwist in Habsburg*, when Rudolf II is practically a prisoner in his own castle, three characters in turn speak to him while he, chafing at the restriction of his former power, responds only with occasional gestures and speaks not a single word for nearly two hundred lines. One of the characters, a servant, is pleading urgently for a key to let physicians into the room where Rudolf's son Don Cäsar is dying; and the climax is achieved with gesture as Rudolf takes the key and then throws it away into a well in the castle grounds, effectively condemning Don Cäsar to death. Only then does he speak, with his only words in the whole scene:

> Er ist gerichtet,
> Von mir, von seinem Kaiser, seinem –
> (*mit zitternder, von Weinen erstickter Stimme*)
> Herrn! (2188f.)[1]

All the emotion is left implicit, suggested rather than declaimed; the sequence achieves its effect by just that telling combination of speech with action and gesture that Grillparzer aimed at.

The end of the previous act of the same play contains another example of this combination. The young Archduke Leopold has gained the Emperor's permission – which Rudolf has immediately regretted giving – to invade Bohemia with his army. This is a reversal of Rudolf's policy, and will make the Thirty Years War inevitable. Duke Julius of Brunswick has chased Leopold and

---

[1] 'He has been judged, by me, by his Emperor, his – (*with trembling, tear-choked voice*) Lord!'

seized him; but Leopold escapes by slipping out of his cloak and proceeds, undisguised, on his way. Julius spells out the significance of the action – the threat that has lain concealed in Leopold's manœuvring is now out in the open:

LEOPOLD (*den Mantel abstreifend, der in Herzog Julius' Hand zurück-bleibt*)
> Wie Joseph denn im Hause Potiphar
> Lass' ich den Mantel Euch, mich selber nicht.

RAMEE (*auf das Volk zeigend*)
> Herr, wenn man Euch erkennt!

LEOPOLD   Man soll mich kennen!
(*mit starken Schritten nach rechts abgehend*)
> Halt ihn zurück!

(*Ramee tritt zwischen beide.*)

JULIUS   Nun denn, es ist geschehn.
(*den Mantel fallenlassend*)
> Die Hülle liegt am Boden. Das Verhüllte
> Geht offen seinen Weg als Untergang.   (1828–33)[1]

It is characteristically at just such dramatic climaxes that Grillparzer most exploits the possibilities of stage action and accompanies it by this energetic, rather staccato language. The use made of the cloak is also characteristic: stage requisites feature centrally in many of Grillparzer's works, concrete objects – a dagger, a goblet, a picture, a jewel – that can represent some element in the dramatic situation and contribute to the effect of *Anschaulichkeit*.

The cloak is a property that he uses frequently. When Ottokar confronts Rudolf I in a richly embroidered cloak, and when Sappho wears her cloak of splendid scarlet, the garments are outward tokens not only of their positions but also of their *attitudes* as warrior-king and poetess respectively; and they form a contrast with the simple clothes in which they appear at other times, Ottokar when he is defeated, Sappho when she has turned her back on her life as a poetess. Ottokar casts aside his glittering cloak after he has been revealed kneeling before the Emperor. In this scene he has been standing with bowed head; then when

---

[1] Leopold (*slipping out of his cloak, which remains in Duke Julius's hands*): 'So, like Joseph with the wife of Potiphar, I leave my garment in your hands, but not myself.' Ramee (*pointing to the crowd*): 'My lord, what if you are recognized!' 'Let me be recognized! (*As he goes off with firm strides:*) Hold him back!' (*Ramee steps between them.*) Julius: 'So – it has happened, then. (*Letting the cloak drop*) The mask lies on the ground, and what was masked goes openly on its way, destruction incarnate.'

Seyfried von Merenberg speaks to him he starts, glares angrily, tears open the clasp on his cloak, so that it falls, and with the other hand reaches up to the back of his head and tears off his crown. Then he rushes off, shouting – his only word during this sequence – 'Fort!' ('Away!'). The minuteness with which the stage direction describes his actions is typical of Grillparzer's painstaking concern with visual effects: similarly detailed physical descriptions are given, for example, of Ottokar's reaction to the news of Rudolf's election as Emperor (*König Ottokars Glück und Ende* 1220/SD), or of the reactions of King Alphons to seeing Rahel's corpse (*Die Jüdin von Toledo* 1812/SD). The directions are meticulous because the actions are precisely conceived, intended to achieve a significant plastic effect. In throwing off his sumptuous cloak and his crown Ottokar is expressing his sense of disgrace, which he never manages to overcome, and which helps to lead him on to his final defeat. In the next act he appears wrapped in a dark cloak; and it is only after his penitence and death that Rudolf spreads his own imperial cloak over his body, as it were in restoration of his honour:

> ...Und ist von deinem Prunk und Reichtum allen
> Nicht eine arme Decke dir geblieben,
> Als Leichentuch zu hüllen deinen Leib.
> Den Kaisermantel, dem du nachgestrebt,
> Ich nehm' ihn ab und breit' ihn über dich,
> > (*er tut es*)
> Daß als ein Kaiser du begraben werdest,
> Der du gestorben wie ein Bettler bist. (2959–65)[1]

Stage action can also be revealing of fundamental qualities of character. An example involving a cloak occurs in the second act of *Ein Bruderzwist in Habsburg*. Archduke Mathias has escaped from defeat in battle wearing a long countryman's coat, and he swears he will wear no other till he has avenged his disgrace (694f.); but when a short cloak is in fact brought, he quickly changes into it, muttering that 'it really makes no odds' ('Es gilt wohl gleich', 711). The action and the words together suggest very clearly the weakness of his character, his lack of moral fibre.

The linking of the spoken text to gesture and action gives the language a gestural quality which is essentially theatrical, and

---

[1] '...And of all your splendour and riches not one poor covering is left as a shroud to wrap your body in. I now take off the imperial cloak to which you aspired, and spread it over you (*he does so*) so that having died as a beggar you may be buried as an Emperor.'

which is as distinct from the dispassionate quality, the understatements and ironies of *Nathan der Weise* as it is from the rhetoric of Schiller. Where Hofmannsthal's comparison with *Nathan der Weise* is most apt is in Grillparzer's frequent use of natural, colloquial turns of phrase, even in plays where the language is for the most part kept at a more evenly poetic level, such as *Sappho, Des Meeres und der Liebe Wellen* and *Libussa*. Grillparzer's language is written to be spoken, and is built on the rhythms and idiom of everyday speech. He once described himself as 'a Doric poet', who did not worry about formal correctness – 'I speak the language of my fatherland' (T 1625). In all his plays we meet regional verbal forms and contractions, colloquial exclamations, and particles characteristic of spoken Viennese. Though all his plays are in verse, the style is constantly escaping from the stiffness of regular lines. His works in pentameters abound in lines with extra feet. Enjambment is common: the verses obey the rhythm of the characters' thoughts and arguments rather than that of prosody. The dialogue is interrupted by pauses, as it is helped out by gestures. From Shakespeare, Schiller and above all Lessing, Grillparzer took up the device of breaking up lines between various speakers, and made the utmost use of it. Not only are his divided lines very numerous; a pentameter may be broken into as many as six parts, spoken by two characters alternately (e.g. *Die Argonauten* 1600), or it may be divided between three speakers (e.g. *Medea* 198). Joachim Kaiser writes of similar examples in *Das Goldene Vlies* as completely dissolving the pattern of blank verse. Such 'atomization' of the verse almost always occurs, as he observes, at a high pitch of tension, when the whole emotional balance of the characters is at risk. It can, for example, be designed to build up an atmosphere of tautness, sharpening a dispute and bringing it to a sudden electric climax:

MEDEA Du gehst?

JASON Ich geh'!

MEDEA Trotz allem, was ich bat, Doch gehst du?

JASON Ja!

MEDEA (*aufspringend*) So komm!

JASON Wohin?

MEDEA Zum Vlies...

(*Die Argonauten* 1462f.)[1]

---

[1] 'You are going?' 'I am!' 'Despite all my pleas, you are still going?' 'Yes!' (*Medea, springing to her feet:*) 'Come, then!' 'Where to?' 'To the Fleece...'

In *Das Goldene Vlies* especially the trick is rather overworked, and (as in the initial repetitions in the above example) the effect can often be *over*-theatrical, over-exclamatory. But in a later play such as *Des Meeres und der Liebe Wellen*, the broken line is skilfully exploited to bring out the tension and the awkwardness in the final dialogue between the heart-broken heroine and her relentlessly strict uncle, the priest (2022ff.). And the tendency to break up the line is not confined to Grillparzer's writing in iambic pentameters. It is also a feature of the four-footed lines of *Der Traum ein Leben*, where it not only helps to reduce the potential sing-song effect of uninterrupted trochees: in the rather fantastic atmosphere of this play, the exclamatory effect is highly appropriate, and the device is well suited to moments of tension. The short verse is broken into three parts at points of dispute or conflict, of tense expectation, of climactic excitement or of deep emotion.[1] It can even be broken up into four parts: for example, to highlight a clash of conflicting willpower between Rustan and Zanga (2244). And it is with essentially the same device – even though the separate parts of the line are not split up alternately between different speakers – that Grillparzer builds up in a series of probing, jabbing, bullying questions to the climax in which Rustan is accused of regicide by the hitherto dumb Kaleb:

RUSTAN   Jener? Der dort? Dieser?
DER ALTE KALEB   D—U!

                                     (2280)[2]

An earlier example of the quartered line also comes at a moment of accusation:

KÄMMERLING   Herr—
KÖNIG   Du zögerst?
KÄMMERLING   Wag' ich's?
KÖNIG   Sprich!
           Wen zeiht man des Mordes?
KÄMMERLING   Dich!

                                    (1359f.)[3]

And here not only is the tension built up by the rapid crossfire of question and temporization: the dramatic effect is still further enhanced by the emphatic rhyme in the following line.

---

[1] E.g.: (conflict) 1349, 1637f., 2069; (expectation) 69, 74; (excitement) 411, 1060, 2529; (emotion) 611, 882, 1067, 1098, 2289, 2374, 2677, 2706.
[2] 'That man? Or that man? This man?' ' – YOU!'
[3] Attendant: 'Sire – ' King: 'You hesitate?' 'Dare I?' 'Speak! Who is being accused of the murder?' 'You!'

With their rich visual effects, their abundance of stage action and their emphatic language, Grillparzer's plays are exciting works. The appeal they make is the very opposite of the intellectual appeal of the literary drama of ideas. Grillparzer knew that art is not an intellectual process, but belongs to the realm of the emotions and the imagination ('die Empfindung', T 4115). In 1837, in an essay on the popular dramatist Ferdinand Raimund (whose work depends in high measure upon visual effects in theatrical performance), he singled out the best of Raimund's plays, *Der Alpenkönig und der Menschenfeind*, as an illustration of the truth 'daß nicht in der *Idee* die Aufgabe der Kunst liegt, sondern in der *Belebung* der Idee' and – a corollary – 'daß die Poesie Wesen und Anschauungen will, nicht abgeschattete Begriffe'.[1] Shortly after this he noted in his diary that the very basis of 'die Poesie', by which he means all imaginative creative writing, consists in image and metaphor (T 3310), and summed up the essential spirit of imaginative writing as combining 'the profundity of the philosopher and a child's delight at colourful pictures' (T 3316). His own works show this combination of the aesthetic sense and profundity of insight; but in his case the profundity does not take the form of 'neatly outlined abstractions'. Rather it informs his exploration of character: it is revealed in the subtlety of his depiction of human motivation and reaction, by which he achieves the effect of 'strict causality' that he regarded as essential to drama (T 639). It was with some ruefulness that in later life he observed how people were always looking for 'ideas' in his plays (*Gespr.* 1176); works of art are not mere vehicles for ideas, and imaginative writing cannot consist merely in the development of some general or philosophical idea. As early as 1817 Grillparzer noted: 'No true *poet*, producing a masterpiece, has ever started out from a general idea' (T 200). Later he would put it less dogmatically: in 1834 he wrote in his diary that a drama might well be based on an idea, on one condition – '...provided that the author is conscious of a great quickening power, like Calderón perhaps' (T 2175). This 'quickening power' is always the all-important criterion, the power that can transform the mere idea into the life of art. He never changed his view that drama must never be reduced to a medium for propounding philosophical or

---

[1] '...that art is not concerned with an *idea*, but with giving *life* to the idea; that literature is concerned with beings and things as we perceive them with our senses, not with neatly outlined abstractions.'

political ideas. Nor should it be reduced to a medium for didacticism. On this point he could concur fully with Goethe: '"A true artistic presentation does not have a didactic aim," Goethe says somewhere, and any artist will agree with him. The theatre is not a house of correction for rascals...' (T 639).

In several respects Grillparzer's work is very modern: in the detailed psychological accuracy of his characterization (especially of his heroines, but also of male figures such as Ottokar and Rudolf II); in the way his characters do not declaim but betray their feelings; in the association of their shortcomings with their circumstances and environment, whether corrupting or over-protective;[1] in the profound historical insight of his last tragedies. In other respects he seems very much a figure of his own time: in the rather stagy language of some of his early plays; in his romantic belief in inspiration; and also in the strong insistence on duty in his works. To say that his plays are not fundamentally didactic does not mean that they have no moral purport (similarly, to say that they are not plays of ideas does not mean that they are devoid of ideas). On the contrary, his plays warn against the dangers of materialism, of ambition, of selfishness, and of yielding to excess of passion. Particularly in his late twenties – at the time when he first conceived his plan for *Der Traum ein Leben* and when he wrote the trilogy *Das Goldene Vlies* and the essay 'Über das Wesen des Drama' – he clearly placed unusual weight on the moral element in drama; and throughout his career there is a consistently strong emphasis in his characterization on problems of moral responsibility. Moreover, one of the features of his work that can at first seem alien to English readers is his tendency to round off his plays with some kind of moral summary – a tendency derived mainly from indigenous Austrian influences, including the popular stage, and strengthened by his reading of Spanish drama. But most commonly these conclusions are not just brief preceptive morals: rather the central characters look back over the action, taking stock of it and drawing the lesson from it; the tone is elegiac rather than moralistic. Grillparzer once described himself as 'an elegiac character' (T 1617); and indeed the note of quiet retrospective sadness is one of the most distinctive characteristics

---

[1] Thus Jaromir in *Die Ahnfrau* (1892ff.) and Otto von Meran in *Ein treuer Diener* (1220–7) try to exonerate themselves, and the failings of Ottokar and Alphons are explained by Rudolf I and Garceran respectively (*König Ottokar* 1881–3; *Die Jüdin von Toledo* 851 ff.).

of his verse. Characters who make elegiac speeches reviewing their tragedies include Sappho, Ottokar, Bancbanus (the hero of *Ein treuer Diener seines Herrn*), and Alphons in *Die Jüdin von Toledo*. It is also true, however, that the moral attitudes maintained in these conclusions are characteristically strict; so too is the emphasis placed on duty, in contrast to personal motives such as ambition or love, throughout the plays. This severity is embodied in the representatives of duty such as Rudolf I in *König Ottokars Glück und Ende*, the priest in *Des Meeres und der Liebe Wellen*, Bishop Gregor in *Weh dem, der lügt!* and the queen in *Die Jüdin von Toledo*. The danger – which, as we shall see, Grillparzer does not always avoid – is that these figures may appear either formidably harsh or else rather woodenly pious. Moreover, a heavy moral emphasis can detract from the purely tragic effect of a play; this point will be discussed more fully in connexion with *König Ottokars Glück und Ende* (see pp. 111–13, below).

There are various factors underlying the strict insistence on duty. It has been interpreted, for instance, as a symptom of the whole social climate of Metternich's Austria, a feature of the *Biedermeier* age (though this normative label is seriously inadequate in that the resignation in Grillparzer has none of the contentedness of the authentic *Biedermeier* mood). It was, no doubt, bulwarked by Grillparzer's long admiration of Kant. But while in part it reflects the philosophic and social background of his age, its deepest origins are to be found rather in an element of Grillparzer's own experience, his gnawing sense of his supreme duty to his art.

Die Ahnfrau

Grillparzer was not one of those poetic geniuses who dazzle the world with their brilliance while they are still in their teens. Even the first three of the plays by which, as a young man, he established his reputation contain undeniable inequalities; and indeed he was over thirty before he fully mastered the dramatic medium.

His *juvenilia* were no more than promising. The most ambitious undertaking of his youth was the long tragedy *Blanka von Kastilien*, which was heavily influenced, in subject and in language, by Schiller's *Don Carlos*: rejected by the Burgtheater, it was not given its first performance until 1958, when it was staged in Vienna – an experiment that is unlikely to be repeated. In treating the theme of loyalty to a dubious cause, and a conflict between

loyalty and love, it anticipates *Ein treuer Diener seines Herrn*;
but the verse has a rhetorical, almost operatic quality which is
quite unlike Grillparzer's later manner. The following rather
melodramatic passage from the last act, for example, with its
final refrain-effect, surely reads like part of an operatic duet:

FEDRIKO   An meine Brust! Mein Weib! – Jetzt wieder mein!
           Von Gottes Hand mir selber angetraut!
           Nun mag der Tod uns immerhin erscheinen,
           Er trennt uns nicht, er kann uns nur vereinen!
BLANKA (*an seinem Halse*)
           Er trennt uns nicht, er kann uns nur vereinen!   (5035–9)[1]

If Grillparzer's prospects as a dramatist were uncertain, his
ambitions were clear. Although the feelings of inadequacy and
unworthiness that he had caricatured as early as 1808 in *Das
Narrennest* recurred frequently throughout his creative life, he
showed great single-mindedness about the actual nature of his
vocation. He grew in fact to identify himself wholly with his
poetic mission, to dedicate himself wholly to his art, to claim for
it absolute authority in his life and thought. 'For me there has
never been any truth other than literary art', he wrote in his diary
in 1827 (T 1614). Six years earlier he had admitted to Altmütter
his 'limitless striving after art and all that belongs to art' (B 223),
and a diary-note of 1826 testifies to his complete submergence in
his poetic vocation: 'This much is certain: if ever the poet in me
goes overboard, I shall send the rest of me with him' (T 1424). In
1833 again he wrote of 'die Poesie' as 'the aim of my life' (T 2074).

In the light of his consistent devotion to his poetic and dramatic
ambitions and ideals, it is all the more curious that his first great
success, the work which first made him famous, might not have
been written at all without the encouragement of Josef Schreyvogel.
Moreover, once he had been cajoled into writing it, Grillparzer
bore each act to Schreyvogel for criticism and revised the text
thoroughly with his assistance. The second version was nearly
five hundred lines longer than the original, but it was cut for its
performance in January 1817.

The *Ahnfrau* of the title is the ancestress of the noble house of
Borotin, who was killed by her husband for infidelity and whose
spirit has been doomed to wander, in expiation of her sin, till all

---

[1] 'Come to my breast, my wife – now mine once more! Entrusted to me
alone by God's hand! Now death can appear to us if it will: it will not
divide us, it can only unite us!' Blanka (*clinging to him*): 'It will not divide
us, it can only unite us!'

her descendants are dead. Only one branch of the family now survives, and she haunts their castle. Accordingly – as Carlyle put it – 'she is heard, from time to time, slamming doors and the like, and now and then seen with dreadful goggle-eyes and other ghost-appurtenances, to the terror not only of servant people, but of old Count Borotin, her now sole male descendant'.[1] The Count's only daughter, Bertha, has fallen in love with a stranger, who has rescued her from bandits in the forest. This stranger, Jaromir, is a robber chief; but he is also the Count's son, Bertha's brother, who was kidnapped when he was a child and was believed to be dead. In a battle at night against the robbers, the Count is killed by Jaromir himself with the very dagger with which the ancestress too was murdered. Bertha dies, either of grief or else possibly of poison (she is intending suicide when she collapses at the end of the fourth act); and finally, in the ancestral vault, Jaromir mistakes the ghostly ancestress for Bertha and dies in her embrace. Thus all the Borotins are dead, and the guilt of the ancestress is expiated at last.

In his autobiography (SB 117) Grillparzer mentions two sources for this action: the story of the eighteenth-century French robber Louis Mandrin, from which he derived the motif of Bertha's love for a noble robber; and a 'popular tale' – probably a translation of part of M. G. Lewis's famous Gothic romance *Ambrosio or The Monk* (1795) – which provided the motif of Jaromir's mistaking the ghost for his real beloved. He also admits that his treatment of the whole horrifying subject betrays the influence of Calderón's *La Devoción de la Cruz* (SB 120). In particular he regarded Calderón's octosyllabic line as having influenced his choice of metre (the trochaic dimeter). But two further important influences were at work closer at hand. One was the current vogue of romantic fate-tragedies, the heroes of which succumb amid melodramatic effects to a terrible fate hanging over them or their family. *Die Ahnfrau* shows striking similarities with plays of this genre. The use of the 'fateful' dagger, for example, is reminiscent (as contemporary reviewers quickly noticed) of Zacharias Werner's play *Der vierundzwanzigste Februar*, which had been published only the previous year; and in treating a hero who returns home from afar and unwittingly fulfils his destined 'fate' by killing a member of his own family, the action is similar in outline to that of another

---

[1] Carlyle, *Collected Works*, vol. VII (*Critical and Miscellaneous Essays*, II) (London, 1869), p. 127.

recent work, *Die Schuld* by Adolf Müllner, which Grillparzer certainly knew (T 216) and which is also written in trochaic verse. Overlapping with and colouring this influence was that of the spooky comedies (*Geisterstücke*) of the popular Viennese stage, the main action of which normally treated the liberation of a ghost from the restless wandering with which it has had to expiate some crime. There had been a vogue for plays of this kind at the end of the eighteenth century and in the first years of the nineteenth. Grillparzer's own early comedy, *Das Narrennest*, includes a reference (scene 5) to two of the best-known *Geisterstücke* by the popular dramatist K. F. Hensler, *Der alte Überall und Nirgends* (1795) and *Die zwölf schlafenden Jungfrauen* (1797). Grillparzer saw the latter play in about 1800 and still remembered it vividly in later life (SB 72).

Grillparzer's own rueful view of the material of *Die Ahnfrau* as seeming 'at best suitable for the popular theatres' (SB 118) and his reference to the first version of the work as a 'ghost tale' (SB 122) suggest that he himself principally felt the kinship of his work with the popular *Geisterstücke* of his boyhood; but what the critics saw in the finished piece was a fate-tragedy. Hebenstreit published a sharp review in the *Modenzeitung*, together with the essay 'Gegen die romantische Schicksalstragödie' by Alois Jeitteles (1794–1858).[1] Jeitteles, who is better known to posterity as the author of the lyrics of Beethoven's song-cycle *An die ferne Geliebte*, did not mention either *Die Ahnfrau* or its author by name at all: he began his essay by making the Romantic distinction between Fate as the basis of ancient tragedy and Providence as the proper basis of modern tragedy, and from this viewpoint he attacked fate-tragedy as a genre for its fatalism and general incredibility. Grillparzer had already rejected the idea of Providence as a criterion (T 176), on the grounds that it is inconsistent with the tragic effect. But it was not Jeitteles' actual argument that most rankled, for Grillparzer himself was not an adherent of the fate-tragedy. There, indeed, was the rub, for in the adjacent review Hebenstreit criticized *Die Ahnfrau* specifically as 'an aberration of a poetic mind, arising from false conceptions of the nature of tragedy'. In this way Grillparzer found himself publicly relegated to the status of a mere fate-dramatist.

Over the years he placed the blame for this on Schreyvogel's influence. As early as May 1817, reacting to a critique of the play by Müllner, he insisted 'that the *Ahnfrau* in its present form is

---

[1] Both pieces are reprinted in *Wke.* I/14, 225–9.

not *my Ahnfrau*' (T 223). And half a century after the first production he still blamed Schreyvogel for having made him 'ruin'
his play: 'I am not sorry that I wrote it – but I *am* sorry that
I ruined it by a revision which Schreyvogel talked me into and
which broke the logic of the play and spoilt it' (*Gespr*. 1189).

While public reaction to the play was clearly very different from
what Grillparzer had intended, his claim that Schreyvogel's
influence had spoiled the play is not justified; nor does his later
denial that he had made use of the idea of Fate at all (SB 125)
square with his attitude at the time. In 1817 in an essay 'Über
das Fatum' he attempted to define the scope and significance of
the idea of 'Fate' in the context of modern drama, and he laid
emphasis especially on its vagueness: it serves only as an eery
atmospheric effect, suggestive of some 'dark presentiment'. It is
precisely this atmosphere of grim foreboding that characterizes
the romantic fate-tragedies of such writers as Müllner; indeed
Grillparzer admits, 'It was in this way that Müllner used the
idea of Fate', and adds, 'I flatter myself that I too have used it
in this way, and the effect which it has had even on the educated
part of the public strengthens my opinion.' The other argument
that he was later to advance is that what the outcome of *Die
Ahnfrau* involves is the sin of the fathers being visited upon a
later generation: '...You have before you an act of mysterious
justice instead of Fate' (SB 126). Either this is mere quibbling, or
it implies the idea of a hereditary (and destructive) evil working
itself out within the family. Yet in 1817, when Müllner in his
critique suggested that the 'basic idea' of the work was intended
to consist in 'the moral hereditary disease which is transmitted
in stock of criminal origin' (T 222), Grillparzer rejected his interpretation and insisted 'that in this play, according to its original
design, there was never any question of the realization of an
abstract general idea' (T 223). The idea of an inherited evil, then,
was *alien* to Grillparzer's original conception of his play. Indeed,
the whole motif of illegitimacy, on which the dramatic expression of
the idea depends, was introduced only at Schreyvogel's suggestion;
in the first version, the ancestress was killed in punishment for
a single act of infidelity (first version, 456–62),[1] and the present

---

[1] The standard text of the work is that of the last edition prepared by
Grillparzer, which was published in 1844. This is given in *Wke*. I/1, 7–148.
All line references are to this text, except where it is explicitly stated that
they are to the first edition, which is given in *Wke*. I/1, 149–256.

members of the family were explicitly of Zierotin [= Borotin] stock (first version, 474).

The comments that Schreyvogel wrote on Grillparzer's manu- script are given in the notes to the first volume of the Sauer/ Backmann edition of Grillparzer's works (pp. 418–29). They show that he wanted alterations of four kinds. First, he suggested that the play be cast in five acts instead of four; accordingly, Act III was divided. Secondly, in several notes he suggested a revision of the text to achieve a greater liveliness in the dialogue. Thirdly, he suggested various detailed modifications in the characterization and sought to heighten the dramatic tension as a result: one note of this kind led to the introduction in Act II of the exchange between Jaromir and the Captain of the troops searching for him, and Jaromir's defence of the robbers (1255–1339). Fourthly, in the most important of Schreyvogel's points, he suggested that the involvement of the ancestress in the fate of the family should be more satisfactorily motivated, so that the whole action could be given a deeper significance and the ancestress herself become a truly tragic figure. In accordance with his specific proposals to implement this closer association of the ancestress with the characters of the play, it is made clear in the final version not only that she was killed for infidelity but that they are her illegitimate descendants, 'the fruit of sin' (538), and that she is condemned to roam until they, the offspring of her infidelity, are dead. Her own interest is now closely involved in their downfall, and also, conflictingly, in their well-being since she is explicitly their direct ancestress: she is introduced in the third act (2094ff.) to warn Bertha and Jaromir as he takes the dagger. This is again an emendation made at Schreyvogel's suggestion, though the actual entry takes place some eighty lines later than he suggested.

In 1860, discussing the play with Wilhelm von Wartenegg, Grillparzer sought as usual to dismiss the idea that it could be called a fate-drama, and claimed that at heart it was a play about a fateful love, in which the ancestress served only as a poetic device to heighten the atmosphere but was in fact irrelevant to the main action: '"Not a fate-tragedy!" he cried, "I didn't want to write one and I didn't write one. The whole thing can stand even if one removes the ancestress. A girl loves a young man without having any idea who he is: finally she learns everything. That can stand without the ancestress – but without her Jaromir is just an ordinary robber. With the ghost everything takes on a different colour; I like that – it is the kind of poetry with which we grew up...'' (*Gespr.* 1088). While it is true, as we have seen, that at the time of the performance of *Die Ahnfrau* Grillparzer regarded the fateful trappings of the play primarily as a means of heightening the atmosphere, such a reduction of the plot to a love-story is a considerable oversimplification – a striking example of his tendency, in the conversations of his later years, to talk of the subjects of his plays in terms of very simple human situations, with a minimum of abstract 'ideas'. In fact, in itself the presence or absence of the ghost could make no difference to Jaromir's basic character (though it does affect the presentation of his character); and the ancestress is *not* inessential to the story even in the first version, since Jaromir meets his death in her arms. On the other hand, it is true that the revisions exacted by Schreyvogel increased the role of the ghost considerably, and gave it a dominant importance which clearly did not accord with Grillparzer's own conception of his play.

One result of the closer association of the ghost with the fate of her descendants is that the essential villainy of Jaromir's character is more subtly suggested – an important addition in a play in which the characterization otherwise has little depth and detail. The sin which is the whole premise for the ghost's existence is revealed in him as a taint of character, so that his fate, as externalized in his final deathly union with the ghost, appears not as something arbitrary (here is a distinction from *Die Schuld*) but as being related to his own character and will. His situation is summarized by Bertha in the line 'Unglück, ach, *und* Freveltat' (2182):[1] with the evil fate hanging over him there is combined his own corresponding evil. He himself attempts to distinguish between his intention and his fateful achievement:

> Ja, der Wille ist der meine,
> Doch die Tat ist dem Geschick...
>
> Unsre Taten sind nur Würfe
> In des Zufalls blinde Nacht...
>
> Meinen Wurf will ich vertreten,
> Aber das nicht, was er traf! (2997f., 3003f., 3007f.)[2]

---

[1] 'Misfortune *and*, alas, wickedness.'

[2] 'Yes indeed, the will is mine, but the deed belongs to Fate...Our actions are as dice thrown into the blind night of Chance...I will defend my throw, but not how it fell!' But *Wurf* and *treffen* have a double sense: the last two lines also mean 'I will defend my throwing of the dagger, but not what it struck!'

The dissociation of intention and responsibility in this is indicative of his villainy; but in any case, precisely because his fate is dependent on his character, the distinction he tries to make is an unclear one: by his (conditioned) 'will' he himself increasingly achieves the evil that runs through his whole family, and his final embrace of the ancestress represents his complete submergence in this inescapable fate. In the final version, his evil character is also revealed in his extortion of Bertha's consent to flee with him (2014–27) and in his incestuous addiction to his lust for her. In the first version, however, his nature is painted still blacker, for he is egregiously dishonest both towards her and towards her father: not only does he conceal his identity, he also gives a long and elaborate account of fictitious noble origins (first version, 935–65), which in the final version, at Schreyvogel's objection to his complete lack of any sense of truthfulness, is deleted and replaced by a short exchange between himself and the Count, shorn of details (1113–22). In both versions he later protests that he did not deceive them from choice (first version, 1431; final version, 1816); but that is said when his secret is already out, and so carries little conviction. In the first version especially, this deceitful trait in Jaromir must inevitably cast doubt on the genuineness of his affection for Bertha, despite his pointed insistence – strategically placed just before his proposal that they should flee together – that even a robber has human feelings (first version, 1486; final version, 1870). That his deception is much more lightly glossed over in the final version is a romanticizing touch inconsistent with Schreyvogel's other suggestions.

In general, in keeping with the greater emphasis on the idea of Fate, one of Schreyvogel's main concerns was to increase the atmospheric power of the play. It was his suggestion, for example, that Act II should be concluded 'with a monologue full of foreboding'. The result is Bertha's long speech (1515ff.) about her love and about the fear and unhappiness born of love; and the act now ends on a very sensational note as Bertha, hearing shots outside and also sensing the presence of the ghost, cries out fearfully for Jaromir's protection, only to discover his flight:

> Weh mir! – Weh! – Ich bin allein! –
> Ha, allein? – Was streifte da
> Kalt und wehend mir vorüber! –
> Bist du's, geist'ge Sünderin? –
> Ha, ich fühle deine Nähe,

Ha, ich höre deinen Tritt!
(an der Türe von Jaromirs Gemach)
Jaromir, wach auf, wach auf!
Schütze deine Bertha! – Jaromir!
Nur ein Wort, nur einen Laut,
Daß du wachst, daß du mich hörst,
Daß ich nicht allein! – Bei dir! –
Schweigst du? – Ha ich muß dich sehen,
Dich umfangen, dich umschlingen,
Sehen, fühlen, daß du lebst.
(Öffnet die Türe und stürzt hinein. Es fällt noch ein Schuß.)
(Heraustaumelnd)
Haltet ein! O haltet ein!
Alles leer! – das Fenster offen!
Er ist fort! – ist tot! tot! – tot!   (1591–1607)[1]

Similar alterations for which no notes by Schreyvogel have survived but which were made by Grillparzer after consultation with him include the lines about the symbolic function of the dagger which Bertha speaks immediately before the warning appearance of the ghost:

> Als ein Zeichen hängt er da
> Von dem nächtlichen Verhängnis,
> Das ob unserm Hause brütet.
> Blut'ges hat er schon gesehn,
> Blut'ges kann noch jetzt geschehn!   (2090–4)[2]

Also new are the further reference to Fate in line 2522, the fatalistic passage 2544–65 in the Count's dying speech, and the final triumphant speech of the ancestress, 'Nun wohlan, es ist vollbracht...' (3299ff.).

Schreyvogel was a discriminating critic, and several passages escaped substantially unscathed, including Bertha's dying speech (2598–2646) and – even though at the first reading he found the last act 'too gruesome and altogether formless still' (*Gespr.* 52) – the first part of the last act (2647–3183), in which Jaromir returns

---

[1] 'Woe is me – I am alone! What, alone? – What brushed past me then, cold and fluttering? Is it you, ghostly sinner? Ah, I feel that you are near, I hear your step! *(At the door to Jaromir's room)* Jaromir, wake up, wake up! Protect your Bertha! Jaromir! Just one word, just one sound, to show that you are awake and that you hear me, that I am not alone, that you are near! – You are silent? Oh, I must see you, hold you, embrace you, see and feel that you are alive! *(Opens the door and rushes in. Another shot rings out. Bertha, staggering out:)* Stop! Oh stop! – All empty! The window open! He is gone! He is dead! Dead! – Dead!'

[2] 'It hangs there as a symbol of the dark fate that hangs over our house. It has already seen bloody deeds – bloody deeds can happen now again!'

and protests that the tragedy is the work of Fate. And if Schrey-vogel was an astute mentor, Grillparzer was no less alert, and was able to defend his work where necessary against Schreyvogel's objections. Jaromir's admission that he is an outlaw (1802–2064) remains substantially unchanged from the original text (1417–1678), despite Schreyvogel's note that it should be recast. Grillparzer resisted Schreyvogel's suggestion that the ancestress might be introduced, unseen by Bertha and Jaromir, to witness their confession of their love; and he also resisted the suggestion that after winning Bertha's promise to flee with him Jaromir should leave the stage. Similarly, the splendid scene in which Bertha hears of her father's wound and betrays the fact that her prime concern is for Jaromir's safety (2160–2293) remains substantially unchanged from the original text (1731–1863), despite Schreyvogel's criticisms.

In short, the revision was the result of the creative interplay of two imaginative minds; and granted Schreyvogel's conception of the play as a fate-drama there can be no doubt that the revision he inspired greatly strengthened its atmospheric power. It may be, however, that in the preparation of the text for production the emphasis on 'atmosphere' was overdone, with the introduction of somewhat melodramatic effects. When the ancestress first appears to the Count, for example, she is described in Grillparzer's original manuscript simply as 'appearing beside the chair of the sleeping Count and sadly bending over him' (first version, SD/292). In the revised version the scene is described in a long stage direction (which was in fact not cut down again by Grillparzer until his final revision of the text in 1843):

Die Uhr schlägt die achte Stunde. Bei dem letzten Schlage verlöschen die Lichter; ein Windstoß streift durchs Gemach; der Sturm heult von außen, und unter seltsamen Geräusche erscheint die Ahnfrau, Berthan an Gestalt ganz ähnlich, und in der Kleidung nur durch einen wallenden Schleier unterschieden, neben dem Stuhle des Schlafenden und beugt sich schmerzlich über ihn.[1]

And the ending of the stage version was also given added colour with a description of the ancestress's return to her tomb:

[1] 'The clock strikes eight. At the last chime the lights go out; a gust of wind blows through the room, the storm howls from without, and amid strange noises the ancestress, in appearance exactly like Bertha and in dress distinguished from her only by a billowing veil, appears by the chair of the sleeping Count and sadly bends over him.'

Ferne Musik erklingt. Das Innere des Grabmals erfüllt blendender Glanz, in welchem sich die Ahnfrau, die Hände gen Himmel gehoben, unter sanften Akkorden verklärt.[1]

Effects of this kind could be exploited to the full in the Theater an der Wien, where the première took place and which was associated particularly with spectacular popular productions making use of lavish scenic effects.

The production of *Die Ahnfrau* appeared to Grillparzer to deal a severe blow to his hopes of establishing himself as a serious dramatic poet. These hopes were indeed reflected in the play itself; for it is on his ambitions, and on the doubts that went with them, that he drew in his conception of the central character. Jaromir is ambitious:

> Ei, bei Gott, ich bin ein Mann!
> Ich vermag, was *einer* kann! (822f.)[2]

– a motif of determined self-assertion that is echoed in a piece written shortly after, the first act of *Der Traum ein Leben*, in the resolve of the ambitious Rustan:

> Was ein andrer kann auf Erden,
> Ei, bei Gott! das kann ich auch. (276f.)[3]

But Jaromir was also conceived as an essentially unworthy hero. He is dishonest – a motif which corresponds to Grillparzer's earlier and typically atrabilious suspicion of a tendency in himself to wilful deception, an 'inclination towards, even pleasure in, lying' (T 17); this is a recurrent motif in his works, and the essential evil of untruthfulness is finally given its most uncompromising expression in *Weh dem, der lügt!* 119–21. Jaromir's sole excuse for his past conduct lies in his upbringing and environment (1892–1907): as an outcast (1873), he is doomed by circumstance – and Fate – to fall short of his own hopes and of any ideal standards, as Grillparzer felt himself doomed to fall short of his literary goals. In the poem 'Jugenderinnerungen im Grünen' Grillparzer devotes one stanza to summarizing the subjects of the first four of his plays to be performed and published:

[1] 'Distant music. The inside of the tomb is filled with dazzling radiance in which the ancestress, her hands raised towards Heaven, is transfigured, while soft chords are heard.'
[2] 'Ah, by Heaven, I am a man! I can do what anyone can!'
[3] 'Whatever another can achieve on earth – by Heaven, I can do the same!'

GRILLPARZER

> 'Den Armen, dem sich ab ein Gott gewendet,
> Des Dichters blendend, trauriges Geschick,
> Wie das Gemüt im eignen Abgrund endet,
> Der Erdengröße schnellverwelktes Glück.'   (121–4).[1]

The first line of this stanza describes Jaromir, 'the wretch from whom a God has turned away'. The whole characterization of his part is informed by a fateful gloom which reflects Grillparzer's lack of self-confidence at this stage of his life and especially his forebodings concerning his ability – and his worthiness – to fulfil his aspirations as a dramatic poet. In this respect Jaromir is an equivalent, in far more sombre colours, of the earlier figure Seraphin Klodius Storch.

And despite its success at the box-office, the reception of his play was not of a kind to reassure him. One effect its success had, for example, was to stimulate a vogue in the popular theatres for burlesque ghost-plays (*Gespensterpossen*), one of the first of these being Karl Meisl's parody *Die Frau Ahndl*, which caricatured the villainy of Jaromir, debunked the sentiment of Bertha, and burlesqued the use of howling winds as a stage effect accompanying the appearance of the ancestress. Grillparzer had at last drawn attention to himself. But he had done so with a sensational kind of success; he had done it only with considerable help from Schreyvogel; and he had done it with a work which still – as he quickly saw – was immature and unworthy of him: 'That...in every respect premature creation', he described it to Müllner in January 1818 (B 98). To be parodied in Leopoldstadt and to have the subjective emotional content of his work taken in the salons as the outpourings of a fate-dramatist was far from being the kind of effect he had aimed to create, and the potential affinities in mood and metre between *Die Ahnfrau* and the dream-play (*Der Traum ein Leben*) which he was planning can only have deterred him from proceeding with work on the new project. Although he eventually began to compose the text in September 1817, he abandoned work on it as soon as casting difficulties arose in the following month, and did not take it up again for a decade.

[1] 'The wretch from whom a God has turned away; the dazzling, sad destiny of the poet; how the feeling heart ends in its own abyss; the fast-withered fortune of earthly greatness.'

Sappho

While on the one hand Grillparzer's self-doubts were inevitably sharpened by what he saw as the universal misunderstanding of *Die Ahnfrau*, on the other hand he was all the more determined that his next play must prove his stature as a serious dramatic poet. He subsequently discussed its genesis at length on three occasions: in a draft of a letter written to Müllner early in 1818 (B 104); in a conversation with Adolf Foglár in 1846 (*Gespr.* 880); and in the *Selbstbiographie*. These three passages are much more consistent and more helpful than his various statements on *Die Ahnfrau*. They explain that he resolved to avoid the 'purely subjective outbursts' (B 104) which had given *Die Ahnfrau* its sensational appeal and to demonstrate his poetic gifts in a form that would allow him to exercise the classical virtue of restraint. In searching for a new subject, he regarded simplicity as having a pre-eminent importance dictated by his artistic aim: that of avoiding both all undisciplined emotionalism and also the extravagant stage effects and sensational plot of the fate-tragedy. He was determined to prove that he was capable of creating his effect 'purely by the power of poetry' (SB 127). When the advocate Joël suggested to him in June 1817 that he should provide his friend the composer Josef Weigl with a libretto on the subject of the ancient Greek poetess Sappho, Grillparzer at once thought of the subject in terms not of an opera, but of a tragedy: 'He mentioned Sappho. I immediately replied that it might make a tragedy too. He objected that too little happened for that' (SB 127). That the story should be uneventful by comparison with the theatricality of *Die Ahnfrau* corresponded exactly to Grillparzer's plans; by that very evening he had thought out his scenario, and two days later he began work on the text, writing in iambic pentameters, the standard metre of German classical drama. In under four weeks he finished the whole play, which immediately made on Schreyvogel just the kind of 'poetic' impression that Grillparzer had hoped for (*Gespr.* 71). The first two acts contain a number of allusive echoes of the extant fragments of Sappho's poetry, and a translation of her ode to Aphrodite forms the closing scene of the first act – its inclusion as a monologue being determined, so Grillparzer told Müllner, by his resolve that the critics should not be able to say that his tragedy was without any trace of the spirit of the historical Sappho.

While Grillparzer's own accounts of the genesis of the play mention no other sources, several possible literary influences have been suggested, and two in particular have recently received some critical support. One is Mme de Staël's novel *Corinne* (1807), which tells the story of the unhappy and finally fatal love of a poetess. That Grillparzer may have been influenced by this work is a suggestion that has repeatedly been made since his own time – indeed, the one reservation in Byron's eulogy of the play was that it was 'too Madame de Staëlish, now and then' – and one recent critic has even designated it as his principal source. But while it is true that Grillparzer read *Corinne* in 1816, he did so with little pleasure (T 169); and any claim for its direct influence over and above general reminiscence and stimulus, which he himself conceded (*Gespr.* 512), runs counter to his explicit denial in later life that it had served him as a source (*Gespr.* 1185). Another theory, prompted by the similarity of Melitta's name to that of Melite, the heroine of an early version of Hölderlin's novel *Hyperion*, is that Grillparzer may have read this fragmentary version (which had been published in Schiller's *Thalia* in 1794) when he was working on his Greek in the court library in 1813 and that he may subsequently have drawn on it in *Sappho*. This possibility of a link between Hölderlin and Grillparzer is intriguing, in view of certain other affinities in their works, but it is unconvincing; for what Grillparzer worked on in the library was the Greek *language* (SB 113f.), and there is no evidence at all among all his copious essays and notes that he ever read *Hyperion* or, indeed, anything else by Hölderlin. Again, it may be that Goethe's *Tasso* served him as a model of a classical treatment of *le malheur d'être poète* (a phrase Grillparzer used in the letter to Müllner to describe the subject-matter of *Sappho*). But it is striking how even when he was attempting a work of classical simplicity Grillparzer's theatrical sense, conditioned by the visual richness of Viennese stage tradition, led him to introduce around the three central characters not only Rhamnes but a number of other figures – the crowd who welcome Sappho in the first act, servants and slaves, and the peasant of the last act – so that the action has extra variety and the central drama is set against a background of everyday life such as is absent from the much more strictly stylized classicism of Goethe's play. Moreover, the central problem in *Tasso* – that of privileged genius romantically at odds with the practical demands of society – is very different from the tragic situation in *Sappho*.

'In the catastrophe,' so Grillparzer wrote to Müllner, 'Sappho is a woman in love, jealous, and distraught with passion...' In the course of the play she learns, as so many of Grillparzer's heroines do, the bitter power of love; she comes to know the very agony which (so she tells Phaon) she wants to spare Melitta:

> ...die Erfahrung,
> Wie ungestillte Sehnsucht sich verzehret,
> Und wie verschmähte Liebe nagend quält.   (774–6)[1]

In his autobiography, answering the criticism that the play portrays the woman in Sappho rather than the poet, Grillparzer emphasizes the warmth and reality of her feelings: he 'wanted to have Sappho fall victim to a true passion' (SB 130f.). She reacts to the disappointment of her hopes with tragic emotional violence because her love is, as Rhamnes observes, 'without limits' (1801): she herself warns Phaon that she is a creature of excessive emotion (126f.). But Grillparzer conceived this excess of feeling as being associated with her poethood; he believed that emotional intensity is natural to the creative artist and is what the intensity of his art springs from. This is the sense of his argument in the letter to Müllner that the verisimilitude of the tragedy depends to a large extent on the fact that Sappho is a poetess: psychologically, her stature as a poetess both implies and depends on a strength of feeling sufficient to induce her tragedy.

The letter to Müllner also emphasizes that in her jealous passion Sappho is 'a woman who loves a *younger* man'. In ancient Greece the story of her fatal love for Phaon was treated not in tragedy but in Attic comedy; and disparity in ages is in fact a traditional comic subject (though comedy often has the roles reversed and shows the deception of an old man by a younger woman, as in *L'Ecole des Femmes* or the adventures of Pantalone in the *commedia dell'arte*). But there is no such thing as a 'comic situation' or a 'tragic situation', in absolute terms: a situation in itself is merely the raw material of drama, and the effect springs from its treatment. Thus a subject may be treated comically or tragically according to the viewpoint of the dramatist, according to whether he plays on or distances the emotional potential of the situation. Inherent in any disparity in ages is an element of insecurity, of imbalance, which may lend itself to comedy if its practical consequences

---

[1] '...the experience of how unappeased longing consumes itself, and how love that is spurned gnaws and tortures.'

(the apparently incongruous *behaviour* of the characters, rather than their feelings) are concentrated on, but which may also lend itself to tragedy when attention is focused on the *emotions* engendered. One of the problems in stage productions of *Sappho* is that the gap in age between Sappho and Phaon must be brought out clearly, but must not be so exaggerated as to make her situation seem (comically) grotesque. In 1818 Sophie Schröder, whose performance Grillparzer regarded at the time as an interpretation of penetrating accuracy (*Gespr.* 154), was in her late thirties, old enough to highlight the contrast with Phaon and Melitta; at the same time, while she was not a beauty – Grillparzer once described her as being 'of repellent ugliness' (*Gespr.* 1190) – nevertheless on the stage she was still able to radiate emotional vitality. It is just this balance that must be struck in performance: love is still within Sappho's grasp, but her sense of ageing lends an unconscious urgency to her grasping. Even in the first act she is not fully confident in her love, she doubts that she can match Phaon's youthful vigour (370–2); her awareness of the contrast between her own experience and his inexperience raises still further doubts, and uneasily she acknowledges that she has still not reached the magic land of complete happiness in love (381–97).

Together with the disparity in age separating Sappho from Phaon goes a still wider disparity in character and calling. The problematic nature of her *malheur d'être poète* is made clear at the very start of the play, when, returning in triumph to Lesbos, she presents Phaon to the jubilant people of the island as one who is destined to draw her out of the remoteness of her life as a poetess:

> Er war bestimmt, in seiner Gaben Fülle,
> Mich von der Dichtkunst wolkennahen Gipfeln
> In dieses Lebens heitre Blütentäler
> Mit sanft bezwingender Gewalt herabzuziehn.
> An seiner Seite werd' ich unter euch
> Ein einfach stilles Hirtenleben führen... (89–94)[1]

In loving Phaon, then, she is aspiring to a humble everyday life ('ein stilles Hirtenleben') diametrically different from her life as a celebrated poetess. Unlike Goethe's Tasso, she is *attracted* by the very limitations that distinguish her fellow-beings from

---

[1] 'In the abundance of his gifts, he was destined to draw me down, with gently compelling power, from the peaks of poetry amid the clouds into the happy flowering valleys of this life. At his side I shall lead among you a simple, peaceful pastoral life...'

herself: she sees them not as limitations but as a source of happiness. Henceforth she is resolved to sing 'only in praise of peaceful domestic joys' (96). Her desire for the simple contentment of affectionate domesticity springs from dissatisfaction with her celebrity – fame and ambition, she tells Melitta, do not bring happiness (398f.) – and from a sense that its rewards are barren. This barrenness she sees as symbolized in her oppressive laurel wreath:

> Kalt, frucht- und duftlos drücket er das Haupt,
> Dem er Ersatz versprach für manches Opfer.   (273f.)[1]

The basis of her discontent, then, is a sense of 'sacrifice' arising from the isolation that her poethood entails. What she does not recognize, though the society around her does, is that because her gift is an extraordinary, even a divine one, it imposes an exclusive duty and inevitably sets her apart from her fellows. None of the other characters in the play looks on her otherwise than as a great poetess; in their eyes – that is, in the eyes of the world – she is not only different from but also 'above' them. Her relations with Phaon, far from completely breaking down her isolation, make it most painfully manifest: her attempt to bridge the disparity of position and stature between them creates what all the world must recognize – Rhamnes' immediate reaction of shocked incredulity shows this (302) – as an impossible situation. It is not merely a question of rank, for she is able to present him to the people of Lesbos as well-born (72); but nevertheless she appears superior. This is clear from their very first entrance side by side – Phaon simply clad, Sappho richly, with a golden lyre in her hand and her laurel wreath on her head. She addresses him lovingly, 'Geliebter' (128); he replies with veneration, 'Erhabne Frau' (130). He is bewildered by his good fortune in being raised from obscurity by that 'exalted woman' (155), whose 'exalted divine image' (164) he has always revered. However fervently he expresses his admiration, he still returns to his sense of surprise and confusion because of the disparity between them:

> Wer glaubte auch, daß Hellas' erste Frau
> Auf Hellas' letzten Jüngling würde schauen!   (255f.)[2]

---

[1] 'Cold, without fruit or scent, it presses on my head, after promising to compensate for many a sacrifice.'
[2] 'Who would have thought that the most important woman of Hellas would glance at Hellas' least important youth!'

It is precisely because Phaon honours her celebrity rather than loving her person that at the end of the first act Sappho speaks her hymnic prayer to Aphrodite to promote her love. Although she comes to realize that before her involvement with Phaon she never truly knew either the joys or the sorrows of the ordinary world (1274f.), at this stage she still thinks of herself as having experience of love, including its disappointments (120–2). Nevertheless she knows that her love for Phaon is something exceptional, unique and vitally important for her:

> Nur *eins* verlieren könnt' ich wahrlich nicht,
> Dich, Phaon, deine Freundschaft, deine Liebe! (123f.)[1]

Under the spell cast by this love, it is no longer art that she views as the goal of her aspirations, but 'life' (which here means a whole-hearted involvement in human relations): 'Und *leben* ist ja doch des Lebens höchstes Ziel!' (270).[2] It is by contrast with 'life' that art seems fruitless (273f.); indeed, Sappho argues that art is dependent on 'life' for its very existence:

> Und ewig ist die arme Kunst gezwungen,
> Zu betteln von des Lebens Überfluß! (276f.)[3]

As she speaks these lines, she reaches out her arms towards Phaon, and the gesture clearly reveals that it is as a woman rather than as an artist that she needs his love. Her actual argument implies that there is no discrepancy between her needs as an artist and what she believes to be her needs as a woman; but in fact there is a radical discrepancy, that 'contrast between art and life' which Grillparzer defined as an element in the play in the letter to Müllner. In the same letter he also observed: 'Phaon and Melitta are on the side of life.' A victim of the attraction of a 'life' which is alien to her nature, Sappho deceives herself about her nature and her whole relation to her art; she is the first of a long line of major characters in Grillparzer's plays whose tragedy is a tragedy of self-deception. When, in her appeal to Phaon, she talks of Lethe, the river of oblivion (285), the reference betrays her position as illusory, dependent on her forgetfulness of her true responsibilities; under the influence of love, she allows her thinking about her art and about her attitude

---

[1] 'There is only one thing I could truly not bear to lose – you, Phaon, your friendship, your love!'
[2] 'And *living* is the highest goal of life!'
[3] 'And art in its poverty is eternally compelled to beg from life's plenty!'

to it to become blurred. In Act III, for example, she speaks of art first in terms of inspiration (this is the sense of her allusion to the spring of the Muses, 'Aganippe', 942), but then in terms of fame (954); earlier, when still wholly dazzled by her hopes of happiness with Phaon, she warns Melitta how dangerous it is for anyone to be lured by ambition from his or her proper place:

> Weh dem, den aus der Seinen stillem Kreise
> Des Ruhms, der Ehrsucht eitler Schatten lockt. (398f.)[1]

Precisely because she is dazzled by love, this is put partially; the real truth (which her warning conceals, because at this stage she cannot acknowledge it) is that her proper role is that of a poet, and her duty to her calling cannot be dismissed in terms of worldly 'success'. But nor does she see that in pursuing her new ideal she is not only renouncing her poetic isolation but betraying her art itself. When she talks of exchanging the laurel for the myrtle and of singing only of 'peaceful domestic joys', it may seem (as Vordtriede has suggested) that she is thinking of composing nothing more than lullabies or songs on domestic themes, for which no laurels are to be won; but when later she speaks of the interdependence of art and life (280–3) it is clear that what she is – quite in vain – hoping to do is to have the best of both worlds. Whereas the service of art is ideally a selfless duty, her pursuit of happiness and fulfilment is in fact selfish; this is brought out by the way she fails to hear Rhamnes' questions in the second scene of Act IV, and remains absorbed in her consideration of the ungrateful lovers (1244ff.). But since the 'fulfilment' she pursues is illusory, and is not her true fulfilment, in her selfishness she jeopardizes her whole integrity of character, and finds it again – just as the king in *Die Jüdin von Toledo* will 'find himself' again (1440) – in returning to her duty, symbolized in the lyre (1912ff.).

Phaon's appeal to her is as a figure of youth, 'Geschmückt mit dieses *Lebens* schönsten Blüten' (372) [my italics].[2] It appears that in early Burgtheater performances Phaon was played as something of a churl; in September 1831 Costenoble weighed up an actor's performance in the part against what he remembered as 'Grillparzer's lout' ('der Lümmel Grillparzers'). Indeed in Act IV Sappho herself refers to Phaon as uncouth ('der Rauhe', 1281).

---

[1] 'Woe to him who is tempted out of the peaceful circle of his own kind by the hollow shade of fame and ambition!'

[2] 'Adorned with the loveliest blooms of this life.'

But this is said in a vengeful spirit, when what she sees in him is the destroyer of her hopes. In fact, while he has the strength and vitality of youth, Phaon is portrayed as more than a mere lout; though he is not an artist, he is appreciative of art. It is, perhaps, not mere modesty that makes him query Sappho's very sanguine assessment of his gifts (77–81); nevertheless, he has played the lyre himself (162f.), and the eloquence with which he expresses his admiration of Sappho (191–201) is far from the language of loutishness.[1] But the qualities of his youth which most stand contrasted to Sappho are his directness and his naivety and it is these qualities which emerge most strongly from the central scenes as the climax of the love-conflict builds up. The dramatization here has already that plasticity of action which was increasingly to become a hallmark of Grillparzer's style: first the scene (II, 4) in which Melitta, wearing on her breast the rose Phaon has given her as a token of friendship, wants to pluck one for him, chooses one above her reach and then, stretching to bend the branch so that Phaon can cut the flower, slips – into his arms; whereupon he quickly kisses her and Sappho enters to find her in his arms. Then the opening scene of the third act (one of the first scenes Grillparzer visualized to himself when planning the play) in which Sappho sees Phaon sleeping innocently and rouses him with a kiss on the brow, only for him to awaken not with her name on his lips, as she has hoped, but with Melitta's. And in his utter naivety he now makes no attempt to conceal from Sappho that the face of smiling innocence of which he has dreamt was Melitta's, but confirms it in surprise:

> ...Wer sagte *dir*,
> Daß sie es war? – Ich wußt' es selber kaum! (922f.)[2]

It is precisely in this naivety that Melitta's character most closely matches his. In her case it is revealed most vividly later in the third act, when she appears dressed with care, and with roses in her hair and at her breast – celebrating, as she tells Sappho, a day that is happy because the poetess has returned, and for another reason, which she herself cannot define: 'Ich weiß nicht recht, doch fröhlich bin ich' (1034).[3] Sappho has already sharply

---

[1] In this appreciativeness he is like Antonio in Goethe's *Tasso*, the representative of practicality who eulogizes the poet Ariosto at the end of Act I. In neither play is the poet surrounded by Philistines.

[2] '...Who told *you* that it was she? – I scarcely knew it myself!'

[3] 'I hardly know why – yet I am indeed happy.'

warned Phaon that Melitta is 'not of high intellect – of moderate gifts' (756), and Grillparzer's own comments both in the letter to Müllner and in later conversation (*Gespr.* 1176) very clearly confirm that this is indeed how he conceived her. She contrasts with Sappho not as a *positive* opposite to Sappho's restless and intense character, but rather as negative to positive; she is no more than the 'sweet girl of placid disposition' ('das liebe Mädchen mit dem stillen Sinn') as which Sappho describes her (755), and represents an ideal only to the very limited extent of her sensual simplicity. Her quality of the 'stiller Sinn', which Sappho so clearly lacks, is precisely what Phaon singles out to praise as 'the finest attribute of woman' (1143); but she herself is still only at that stage of development where she is leaving girlhood behind her and blossoming into womanhood. Sappho, returned from Olympia, finds her changed, hardly recognizable (339–45). In the sense that Grillparzer portrays in her the birth of love from initial innocence, she has been seen as a forerunner of Hero; but the characterization is not deep. Melitta was, indeed, introduced into the story by Grillparzer in the first place out of dramatic necessity: she is simply the 'other woman', to borrow a term he himself used in 1866 when discussing the motivation of Sappho's death: 'Sappho leaps into the sea because Phaon does not return her love; that could have no more cogent reason than that he loved another woman, and that's all there is to it' (*Gespr.* 1185). Her victory over her mistress is established at the end of the third act, in another scene of striking theatrical vividness, where Melitta finally yields her rose, only for Phaon to seize it, restore it to her, and lead her off, leaving Sappho with arms outstretched and eloquently empty. The irony is that when Melitta in her virginal modesty had not so much as looked at Phaon (335–7) it was Sappho herself who first demanded that she should admire him (322ff.). Melitta, lonely, homesick, and deprived of affection (560ff.), is quickly vulnerable to Phaon's advances; and if in the following act Phaon displays his naivety in his scene with Sappho, his perceptions are much keener with Melitta. His eye for his opportunity is much sharper too: his claim to be, like her, homesick (595f.) is plainly a fabrication, bearing no relation to the rapt excitement which he has in fact shown at the beginning of the act – an excitement so complete that he has forgotten his parents altogether (497f.).

In the course of the play both Phaon and Sappho attain a new self-knowledge, and with it a new self-possession. Phaon's very involvement with Sappho is a denial of his true nature, and he himself betrays something of the falsity of his position in his explicit wish that he could be something other than what he is:

> O könnt' ich doch mein ganzes frühres Leben
> Umtauschend, wie die Kleider, von mir werfen,
> *Besinnung* mir und Klarheit mir gewinnen,
> Um ganz zu sein, was ich zu sein begehre!   (315–18)[1]

In the third act he admits to Melitta that he was once bemused by the magic of Sappho's lyre, and that it is only since knowing her (Melitta) that he has become himself again: '*Dein* Anblick erst gab mich mir selber wieder' (1173).[2] And whereas Sappho has at first despised the laurel as barren (272), she learns to see it as the evergreen symbol of immortal life (1280). Phaon – in an echoing variant on Arkas' line in the second scene of Goethe's *Iphigenie*, 'Bedenke, was du tust und was dir nützt' – pleads with her: 'Bedenke, was du tust und *wer du bist*!' (1784) [my italics];[3] and she achieves exactly the insight for which he asks: 'Ich suchte *dich* und habe *mich* gefunden!' (1960).[4] The process is in the most literal sense one of disillusion. At first she saw Phaon 'drawing her down' into a life of blossoming happiness, 'in dieses Lebens heitre Blütentäler' (91f.); later she sees him as having 'drawn her down' into a wasteland, 'in die öde Wüste' (1283). It is a bitter experience; but in this way she wins through to being true to herself – to her true self: she learns to set the poet in herself above the lover. Having in effect denied her calling and having subsequently lost all her control over the passionate nature that fired her art as well as her love, she finally reaffirms, by her renunciation of Phaon, the paramount claims of her real duty. As early as Act III she has learnt to bemoan that she has ever deserted that poetic eminence for which she was properly destined (946ff.):

> Dort oben war mein Platz, dort an den Wolken,
> Hier ist kein Ort für mich, als nur das Grab.

[1] 'If only I could change and cast away, like clothes, the whole of my earlier life, and so achieve calm and clarity of mind to become wholly what I long to be!'
[2] 'The sight of *you* first restored me to myself.'
[3] Arkas: 'Consider what you are doing and what is to your advantage!' Phaon: 'Consider what you are doing and who you are!' This plea corresponds rather to Antonio's last words in *Tasso*: 'Erkenne, was du bist!'
[4] 'I sought *you*, and I have found *myself*!'

Already she perceives that her misery has been a direct result of abandoning her lofty solitude cut off from that 'simple pastoral life' for which she misguidedly longed:

> Wen Götter sich zum Eigentum erlesen,
> Geselle sich zu Erdenbürgern nicht... (948f.)

She recognizes that it is not possible for her to have the best of both worlds:

> Von beiden Welten *eine* mußt du wählen,
> Hast du gewählt, dann ist kein Rücktritt mehr!
> (952f.)[1]

In Act V at last, after her further experiences of jealousy, rage and finally shame, she is ready to act on her insight. To be true to her art she must renounce her desire for the attractions – the distractions – of 'life' (as embodied in her love for Phaon); and she thanks the gods for the lesson that the poet is a being chosen, or condemned, only to sip at the draught of life:

> Ihr habt der Dichterin vergönnt, zu nippen
> An dieses Lebens süß umkränzten Kelch,
> Zu nippen nur, zu trinken nicht. (1995–7)[2]

Her self-immolation at the end of the play comes after her reassumption of her cloak, lyre and laurel wreath, which, by their contrast with her simple dress in the love scenes, visibly represent her new spirit.

Sappho is still in several respects an immature work. Where it particularly shows high promise is in the verse: Zacharias Werner was so deeply impressed that he compared it to Goethe's verse in *Iphigenie* (*Gespr.* 1552). The composition shows skilful control of the devices of rhetoric, as in the effective use of repetition either of whole lines (113, 122) or of constructions building up a climax within a single sentence (48ff., 1705ff.), the device of anaphora. It also shows already Grillparzer's characteristic flexibility in the use of the pentameter: the regularity of the metre is broken up by, in all, nearly sixty four-foot or six-foot lines, and especially in the scenes II, 4–5 the dramatic tension is built up

[1] 'My place was up there, up amid the clouds; there is no place for me here except the grave. Whoever has been chosen by the gods must not consort with people of this earth...You must choose *one* of the two worlds, and once the choice is made there is no going back!' (946–9, 952f.)

[2] 'You have allowed your poetess to sip at the sweet garlanded cup of this life, but only to sip, not to drink.'

with the use of short sentences and the splitting of lines between speakers.[1] In longer speeches, too, there are passages which show Grillparzer's command of variations of rhythm. One good example of the strength and range of his writing is provided by the opening scene of the fourth act. It is a setting full of atmosphere: in the moonlit silence Sappho is alone with her sorrow:

> Still ist es um mich her, die Lüfte schweigen,
> Des Lebens muntre Töne sind verstummt,
> Kein Laut schallt aus den unbewegten Blättern,
> Und einsam wie ein spätverirrter Fremdling
> Geht meines Weinens Stimme durch die Nacht.
>
> (1196–1200)[2]

As well as the musical play on soft *sch* and *l* sounds, the verse has an evenness and smoothness in keeping with the mood; then her sorrow sharpens to despair as she reflects on the most heinous crime of all, ingratitude, and now the long lines are broken up in emphatic exclamations, the evenness of the verse makes way for a powerful staccato effect:

> Doch kenn' ich eins [*scil.* ein Verbrechen], vor dessen
>   dunkelm Abstich
> Die andern alle lilienweiß erscheinen,
> Und *Undank* ist sein Nam'! Er übt allein,
> Was alle andern einzeln nur verüben,
> Er lügt, er raubt, betrügt, schwört falsche Eide,
> Verrät und tötet! Undank! Undank! Undank!
>
> (1213–18)[3]

Elsewhere, however, the verse shows traces of unsureness: as is perhaps only to be expected in a relatively inexperienced writer who had just veered from the exciting rapidity of four-footed trochaic lines to the much more measured rhythms of iambic pentameters, Grillparzer had not yet gained full control over his style. Symptomatic of his insecurity are, for example, a number of weak conceits, such as Phaon's comparison of Sappho's dress to a stream (225–7) and Sappho's comparison of Melitta's affection

---

[1] E.g., 644f., 685–7, 714–18.

[2] 'Around me all is quiet, the breezes still; the cheerful sounds of life are hushed, the leaves are motionless and make no noise – and my weeping sounds through the darkness, lonely as a stranger lost at night.'

[3] 'But I know one crime, in contrast to whose blackness all others seem lily-white, and *ingratitude* is its name! Alone it does what all the others only do singly: it lies, it robs, deceives, it swears false oaths, betrays and kills! Ingratitude! Ingratitude! Ingratitude!'

to a snail, as being equally shy and quick to withdraw back into its shell (761ff.) – a weak comparison because in all its other connotations it is grotesquely unsuitable. Or again in Act IV Phaon encourages Melitta with an image, 'Die Hand des Bräutigams hält dich umschlungen!' (1463)[1] which (owing to the substitution of *Hand* for *Arm*) clearly does not work.

There are, moreover, serious improbabilities in the working out of the plot. Böttiger pointed out to Grillparzer that it was simply not possible for a Greek poetess to draw a dagger on her slave, as Sappho does on Melitta near the end of Act III (B 103); equally improbable – and more important dramatically, in that the development of the plot depends on it – is the sequence in which Sappho sends for Melitta with the intention of having her shipped off to Chios, and then, when she appears, fights shy of facing her, with the result that Phaon is able to rescue her and escape with her himself.

It is, however, the conclusion that raises the most fundamental critical questions. There is clearly a symbolical sense in which Sappho's literal renunciation of life represents her renunciation of Phaon, and of the attractions of 'life' in the terms of her own dilemma. But this symbolical reading does not answer all the problems concerning the motivation and implications of Sappho's death at the more realistic level of characterization. In particular it does not answer the problem of why Sappho looks forward to death as her 'final *reward*' from the gods (2002).

When, having embraced Phaon and Melitta and united them, with her blessing, on the altar of Aphrodite, she remounts the Leucadian rock and throws herself down into the sea, she does so quite explicitly in expiation of her guilt in life: 'So zahle ich die letzte Schuld des Lebens!' (2027).[2] It appears, then, that her 'reward' lies in expiation; but as the final curtain falls we are told by Rhamnes that she has accomplished something else, that she has returned to her true sphere:

> Es war auf Erden ihre Heimat nicht –
> Sie ist zurückgekehret zu den Ihren![3]

Here Rhamnes is, perhaps, partly echoing the arguments of Sappho and Phaon, who have both made the point that she does

---

[1] 'Your sweetheart's hand embraces you!'
[2] 'Thus I pay my final debt in life!'
[3] 'Her home was not on earth – she has returned to her own kind!'

not belong to the world of ordinary mortals (957, 1726–8); and in any case he is perhaps not the best judge. There is a revealing exchange in the very first scene of the play, when Sappho is approaching. Rhamnes urges her slave-girls to join in the rejoicing – '...So freut euch doch! / Seht ihr den Kranz?' Melitta replies 'Ich sehe Sappho nur!' (23f.).[1] In contrast to Melitta's uncomplicated delight, which is engagingly characteristic of her naivety, Rhamnes' reaction is one of pride; and what he dwells on is the sign of Sappho's poetic eminence. This pride underlies his unswerving loyalty to her throughout the play, and is clearly an element in his final phrase-making solemnity. As a concluding line rounding off the play, the phrase is, moreover, something of a cliché: the idea that the poet is at home with the gods of Olympus is a common one in eighteenth-century poetry. Nevertheless, the fact that Sappho's death is set against a sunrise, as opposed to a sunset (1977), further suggests that it is meant to be seen as a positive decision, a step into a new life.

Nowhere in the play, however, does she suggest that death will literally bring her immortal union with the gods. While she regards herself as having been chosen by the gods and as belonging to them (948), and as serving them as their priestess (2008), she is still only a mortal: the only immortality she enjoys is that of her art, which she acknowledges (1226–8) and thanks the gods for granting her (1989–94), and which Rhamnes too emphasizes (1835ff.). Her death, then, *must* have a solely symbolical sense: it can signify only her acceptance of the artist's need to cut himself off from 'life' in the special sense of the attractions of love. A representative reading in this spirit is offered in a recent commentary by Professor Kokyo Morikawa: 'For the sake of art she must forgo love and life. Her death is not expiation; it is renunciation.'[2] While we have seen that her death *is* conceived as an act of expiation, we may agree that it is – also – a renunciation; but in what positive sense can this renunciation be said to be made 'for the sake of her art', when she is cutting off her artistic career? When in Act III she recognizes the hopelessness of her situation and says that her true place was above, that the only abode earth can offer her is the grave (946f.), it is clear that she regards the grave as something negative, an ending and an

---

[1] Rhamnes: 'Rejoice, then! Do you see the laurel wreath?' Melitta: 'I only see Sappho!'

[2] *Jb.* (3. Folge) VI, 108.

escape, with nothing of the achievement which might justify her talk of expiation, and no promise of anything that can justify her rejoicing in the prospect of joining or rejoining the immortals. As a symbolical gesture her death is no answer to problems which, arising from her relations with Phaon, have been posed and experienced not merely in symbolical terms but emotionally. At that level, she chooses death as the only escape from an emotional crisis – she explicitly wants to escape from the mockery that she would have to face if she lived on (2008–10) – and it is specious for her to speak of her work as completed (2001). As a conclusion to the tragedy either of a creative artist or of a victim of jealous passion, her leap from the Leucadian rock can only be read as an act of despair, and the suggestive sunrise against which she leaps seems only a misleading melodramatic effect.

If this treatment of the ending of the Sappho legend is unsatisfactory dramatically, it is hardly more satisfactory as a working out of Grillparzer's own view of the position and duty of the poet. For though he embarked on *Sappho* with the aim of achieving classical objectivity, in the event his presentation of the heroine's initial *malheur d'être poète* corresponds to and reflects his own brooding discontent in 1817, when after the disappointing reception of *Die Ahnfrau* the rewards of his artistic vocation seemed no compensation for the isolation that he felt it imposed; the same feeling was still strong a year later when in the poem 'Abschied von Gastein' (G 18) he wrote of his art as

> Was Gott mir gab, worum sie mich beneiden,
> Und was der Quell doch ist von meiner Pein.[1]

Despite his plans of objectivity, in fact, *Sappho* developed into a treatment of a subjective dilemma centring on the precarious balance, in 'des Dichters blendend, trauriges Geschick', between the rewards of achievement and the harsh deprivation consequent upon duty; and as a conclusion to Grillparzer's own perception of this 'contrast between art and life' Sappho's death is no kind of a solution – in comparison, even Tasso's problematic reconciliation with Antonio is positive and realistic. If, however, Grillparzer's dramatic exploration of the contrast of priorities still lacks clarity in *Sappho*, and if Sappho's death in particular is obscure in its implications, nevertheless her intention – the final

---

[1] 'What God gave me, what they envy me for, and what is nonetheless the source of my suffering.'

subordination of personal inclination to the standards of duty –
reflects Grillparzer's own consistent attitude to his art. And the
values and motives involved in the action – love, duty and (still
a secondary element here) ambition – are the same motives which,
extended to wider fields than the problems of poethood, are the
principal recurring motives of his work. In varying combinations,
they are central in all the greatest of his dramas.

Melusina

Of the works Grillparzer completed in the next few years, the
one that thematically has the closest kinship with *Sappho* is the
libretto *Melusina*, a minor work which was written in 1823 for
Beethoven. In the event, Beethoven never composed music for
it. In 1823 he finished his Ninth Symphony, and he was about to
embark on his last seven great string quartets; and by comparison
with conceptions of such profundity, *Melusina* must have seemed
slight and trivial. For in form and spirit it is far removed from
the classical style of *Sappho* (and of *Das Goldene Vlies*): it is
essentially a *Zauberspiel* in the manner of the Viennese popular
stage, with dancing, spectacular scenic effects and a comic servant
in the manner of Hanswurst. Its most direct model in the popular
theatre is K. F. Hensler's famous comedy *Das Donauweibchen*
(1798), which in a similar knightly milieu treats a local variation
of the Melusina legend, with a knight (Albrecht) caught between
the love of the water-nymph Hulda and his mortal beloved. Both
in form and in subject, then, Grillparzer's libretto is rooted in
popular tradition; but his treatment makes of the theme a romantic
allegory of the relation of man to an absolute ideal.

That the figure of Melusina has a symbolical significance is
suggested in the first speech of the knight Raimund. Raimund
suspects that she is insubstantial, a projection of his own un-
realizable longings or aspirations (26–30). He knows, however,
that what attracts him is a 'high power' (42), just as in *Das
Donauweibchen* Albrecht sees Hulda not as an infranatural spirit
but as 'a supernatural being' (Second Part, II, 10). Raimund's
servant (Troll), on the other hand, believes he must be 'bewitched'
(112), and his beloved (Bertha) and her brother believe that he
is in contact with 'the powers of darkness' (292). Melusina's
enchantment is evil in their eyes in the first place because it
conflicts with Raimund's attachment to Bertha: Troll reproaches

him with his neglect of her, and also with an apparent falling-off of his natural vitality and high spirits:

> Sie sieht nur Euch, Ihr aber seht, weiß Gott, was. Immer hier herum, an diesem alten Brunnen. Ich glaube, Ihr seid behext. Einst wart Ihr so munter, nun seid Ihr traurig geworden. (110–13)[1]

And indeed, while Melusina promises Raimund that her love will bring him rewards, she warns him explicitly that it will also involve many deprivations (159f.). She lists these deprivations: human contact, wine and food, entertainment (160–5) – in short, the pleasures of the world.

The rewards that she can offer him at this high cost afford insight into her symbolical role, into the nature of the human aspirations she represents. In the first place she offers him a new clarity of perception and profundity of vision (177f.): the characteristics, that is, of contemplation and imagination. Later, seeking to beguile Raimund into believing in no other enticement in the world but herself, she calls on the art of poetry to serve her (393ff.). Still later she recounts to Raimund what her love has indeed provided: vision, knowledge and art – 'the infinite kingdom of the arts' (425). Her realm, then, emerges clearly as one of imaginative art, her power being associated specifically with the art of poetry. In this realm, however, Raimund finds that he is not satisfied by the imaginative life: he longs for activity (428).

The conflict of interests and standards here is absolute. For Melusina this practical urge is destructive of all she stands for: '*Be* active,' she tells Raimund, 'destroy me!' (430). In the eyes of the practical world, as represented by Bertha's brother, Raimund's longing for Melusina is something that undermines activity – it is, he tells Raimund, 'the grave of all energy' (799), and this is the second reason why to him Melusina's enchantment is something evil. It is because Raimund is himself a knight, with origins and obligations in the world of practical action and achievement, that he cannot devote himself fully to Melusina's realm, and that its rewards do not satisfy him.

Nevertheless, despite his dissatisfaction with his experience of Melusina's realm, Raimund long refuses to give up the magic ring which she has given him. His preservation of this ring is an agreed signal of his continued love for her, and by turning it

---

[1] 'She sees only you; but what you see, goodness only knows! Always around here, at this old well – I think you are bewitched! Once you were so gay, now you have become sad.'

on his finger he is able to summon her to his view (184f.) – a use
of a talismanic ring which is derived from a similar motif in the
second part of *Das Donauweibchen*. Raimund preserves the ring
in order to conjure up Melusina with 'formative power' (780);
when he finally does give it up, he discovers that what he has lost
is the only thing worth living for, and he is willing to give up his
life to recover it (908). He follows Melusina into his death, and in
final apotheosis he ascends through clouds to her heavenly throne.

The moral of the piece is summed up – again, the technique is
reminiscent of the simple pattern of popular comedy – in a monitory
final chorus:

> Wem sich höhre Mächte künden,
> Muß auf ewig sich verbünden
> Oder nahen mög' er nie,
> Halben Dienst verschmähen sie.[1]

This warning against the consequences of 'half-service' corresponds
to a fundamental part of Grillparzer's own conception of his duty
as a poet. Four years later he accused himself in very similar
terms of having only half-devoted himself to his art, and of
having been rewarded in return with only the half-achievement
that was his just desert:

> Halb gab ich mich hin den Musen,
> Und sie erhörten mich halb;
> Hart auf der Hälfte des Lebens
> Entflohn sie und ließen mich alt.   (G 193)[2]

That anything but total and unwavering dedication to a high
vocation is disastrous – specifically, that art has an absolute claim
on those who are chosen to its service – is exactly the lesson that
Sappho learns. It is a life of complete devotion to art (devotion
such as *Sappho* and *Melusina* affirm) that is reviewed ironically
in the best-known of Grillparzer's prose writings, the short story
Der arme Spielmann.

Der arme Spielmann

Der arme Spielmann, the last completed work that Grillparzer
published in his lifetime, is the only other of his works in which
the central character is actually an artist. It is also the only one

---

[1] 'The man to whom higher powers reveal themselves must commit himself
to them for ever, or let him never draw near to them: they scorn half-service.'
[2] 'I half devoted myself to the Muses, and they half answered me: half-way
through my life they fled and left me old.'

of his works that is set in the Vienna of his own times. The city
as a whole, indeed, is what the text begins with: Vienna in July.
From there the focus narrows, first to the popular festival in
Brigittenau (which lay by an arm of the Danube, to the north
of the centre of the city), and then to the central figure, the
mendicant fiddler who stands playing 'with a smiling, self-
approving expression' (p. 40) as the crowds pass by. A few lines
later this picture of his manner of playing is enlarged: '...he was
belabouring an old much-cracked violin, beating time not only
by raising and lowering his foot, but also by a corresponding
movement of his whole bent body.' The picture the narrator
presents – the fiddler bobbing in time with the music, so that his
whole frame seems to gesture in lone accord with what he is
playing – is a comic one; and it helps to set the mood for the
whole portrait of Jakob, a portrait of 'so much artistic zeal with
so much ineptitude' (41).

For the tone adopted by the narrator in the opening pages is
a strongly ironic one – an irony which seems to set him as much
apart from the background of festivities as Jakob himself. He
ironizes as 'anthropological voracity' (41) his fascinated interest
in the fiddler; but his self-irony does not mask the perceptiveness
of his insight, and gradually the significance of his subject emerges.
That the fiddler wends his way homewards in the opposite
direction to the crowds as they arrive for the fair not only
suggests an unexpected moral independence, but seems physically
to exemplify, at the lowest possible level, the solitary nature of
the artist's lot. Jakob leaves, the narrator tells us, 'as a man going
home' (41); and this is meant not only in its physical sense, for
Jakob is also returning to his spiritual home – what he is going
to do is to devote himself to his music, in solitary improvisation.
In his room, where the narrator visits him a few days later, the
conscientious apartness of his lot is further symbolized by the
chalk line which divides his meticulously ordered half of the room
from the rank disorder of the other half (48).

The life-story Jakob has to tell is one not only of music but
also of love, and the two threads are joined in the last view the
narrator has of him, playing in rapt absorption the melody sung
by Barbara, whom he loved and lost. But he is reluctant to tell
his story: 'I have no story', he says (50). The reticence and
discretion with which he talks of his past life distance us from
the events and feelings in it; so too does the fact that his narrative

is as it were filtered through the ironic viewpoint of the narrator, which the opening sequence has established. In the body of the story the narrator's voice unobtrusively but repeatedly interrupts, warding off too great an empathy on the part of the reader. By the interaction of the two voices we are allowed to see the absurdity as well as the tragedy in the story of the fiddler's love of Barbara and of his music; the laconic manner of both tellers prevents the story from descending either to the ridiculous or to the sentimental. The ultra-pathetic is told without sentimentality; irony and pathos are in perfect balance.

The pathos of Jakob's failure lies in the disparity between his intentions and his achievements. The earliest important example in his everyday life is his disgrace in a recitation exercise at school, which estranges his father from him (52): looking back at his father's death, he comments: 'I hope one day to see him again in that place where we are judged according to our intentions and not our deeds' (65). At work his slowness, a result of over-conscientiousness, is taken as slackness (53) and his courtesy to Barbara is taken as philandering, so that he gains the reputation of being negligent and dissolute. His hesitancy in approaching the shop where Barbara lives appears so suspicious that he is apprehended as a thief by her father (61). His attempt to set himself up in business, based on an unpractical idea for a music-copying service, ends in his being cheated and brought to the edge of financial ruin. Equally, his performance as a musician falls short in practice: he enjoys a rich aesthetic life within his imagination, but cannot transform this inner beauty into sounds of beauty, whether in improvisation or in playing the classics. The disparity is suggested by the narrator, seeing him play from sheets of music, 'which doubtless recorded in perfect order what he rendered with such total lack of coherence' (41).

In love too Jakob's visions are cheated by reality. Though he tells his story unsentimentally, we learn from the narrator that both the sound of Barbara's song and the memory of her kiss can still bring tears to his eyes (54, 69): but while Barbara is sometimes kind to him, and understanding – she alone understands the good will of his intentions, his 'honest heart' (70) – the picture we are given of her is not a winsome one. She is mousy and pockmarked when young, and when she is old the narrator confirms that she looks as though she can never have been beautiful. Her reputation in the office where Jakob works is that she is coarse and that there is no good in her. Jakob himself observes her ill-temper. At home her behaviour is loud and vulgar. She is rude to customers; to Jakob she is cold at first, later she scolds him in the shop and mocks him in front of customers. The affection Jakob feels for her is inspired less by her unprepossessing real self than by the simple song she sings which captures his imagination. And even the song is, to the narrator's ear, 'not at all distinguished' (54). Jakob's hopes of happiness centre on illusions, on the constructions of his own imagination. Moreover the hesitancy with which he approaches Barbara at her home – first his dithering worry about displaying 'discourteous importunity' (60), then his trembling outside the shop – is evidence that he is too timid and unpractical ever to be able to grasp happiness in human relations. The most grotesque disparity between his intentions and his actual achievement in this sphere lies in the incident when at last he takes courage enough to kiss Barbara, but only through the glass pane of a closed door (69). He seems to fight shy of the sensual – even in old age his disapproval of the popular tunes played by most street musicians is based partly on the suspicion that they serve to revive 'the memory of the pleasures of dancing or other disorderly amusements' (44) – and it is characteristic that his attempt to return Barbara's impulsive kiss is made only when both his attempt and any further response on her part are physically impossible. And yet, despite the utter practical inadequacy of this reaction to her original kiss, the day remains for him a day of supreme happiness, the most blissful of his life (70).

The hardest day, by contrast, is the day of her farewell from him (75). It is the day on which for the first time she addresses him with the intimate *du*; but the feeling with which she parts from him is one of pity, '...And yet I'm sorry for you.' Bowing to practical necessity, she is at last doing what she says she has tried to resist having to do: she is marrying into 'the rough folk', where by character and upbringing she clearly belongs. Practical necessity has no place for so ineffectual a creature of the imagination as Jakob: Barbara has made this clear earlier in her plea, 'Give up your music-making and put your mind to practicalities!' (72).

Shy, unpractical, and ill-fitted to the world of his fellow-men, Jakob *cannot* do as Barbara demands; and having failed in the school of 'practicality', he devotes himself wholly to music. His first rediscovery of his violin, which he remembers as another of the happiest events in his life (53), took place when all his diligence in the office gained him a reputation for idleness; and so again now, having proved his incapability of achieving happiness in practical life, he devotes himself to his art as his sole consolation. He begins by studying the works of the classical masters. Even as an old beggar he practises and honours them still. But his playing is a means to an end, the recapturing of the divine ideal he glimpses within his imagination. Of other musicians he observes: 'They play Wolfgang Amadeus Mozart and Sebastian Bach, but no-one plays the Good Lord himself' (55). Jakob – in his imagination – 'plays the Good Lord', and he speaks of his solitary improvisation as 'prayer' (44). When he first rediscovers the violin its sound seems to him like divine inspiration: 'And then, Sir, when I drew the bow across the strings, it was as though God's finger had touched me' (54); and the structure of fugue and counterpoint he regards as 'a whole heavenly edifice' (55). When he plays the effect is inebriating, it is as though the very air around him were 'pregnant with intoxication' (54); and this sense too seems a part of the divine inspiration: 'Speech is necessary to man, as food is; but drink too ought to be kept pure, for it comes from God' (55).

His devotion to music, then, is not a romantic sacrifice of the fruits of 'life', nor is it only a means of solace: it is a pure and whole devotion, and utterly serious. Even as an unregarded street-fiddler he persistently upholds the dignity of his art. He refuses to pander to popular taste: he plays serious music and turns his back on the crowds at the *Kirtag*. He insists that he is not a mere beggar; and something of his artist's pride is brought out plastically in his insistence that money given him must not go straight into his hand but must be placed, like a well-earned tribute, in his hat (42f.). He regards the money he receives as an 'honorarium' (45).

The moral integrity and the idealism that inform the fiddler's life are finally made manifest in his death. We learn of this at the end of the *Novelle*, when we are back in the narrator's account that frames Jakob's own story. He has lost his life in the floods – not by drowning, but as a result of rescuing children and then plunging back into the waters to save his landlord's money, so that he has died of cold. His final action reveals the true motives and intentions of his life: he has given up his life in selfless service of humanity, despite the ingratitude and intolerant impatience he has met from humanity throughout his life. The humane reward, redressing the injustice of a lifetime, lies in Barbara's memory of

him, her true affection and appreciation symbolized in her refusal
to part with his violin, which – tearfully – she treasures and locks,
defensively, in a drawer.

Her husband, one of the 'rough folk', would have been willing
to sell it: Barbara's firm independence, her indifference to 'a few
Gulden more or less', proves at the last that Jakob's life has not
been totally without influence on the world around him. By the
artistic standards of his own vocation, however, neither the
practical achievement for which he dies nor Barbara's memory
has redemptive value; for while the depth of his moral integrity,
which is an essential factor in the quality of his *life*, most conspicuously informs his devotion to his music, nonetheless his
performance as a musician is lamentably inadequate. From the
very outset of his would-be professional career, his playing finds
no appreciation, and though in Brigittenau he is competing with
other beggars whose standard of musicianship (as the narrator
makes very clear) is painfully low, they make more from their
efforts than he does, and indeed play better. For 'what he played
seemed to be an incoherent sequence of notes without tempo or
melody' (41). When he obliges the children who demand waltzes
from him, they cannot tell what he is playing. He blames the
faulty discrimination of the children, saying that they 'have no
ear for music'; and in an age which demands nothing but waltzes,
public taste may well seem suspect to him. But the narrator,
speaking as a dramatist, has already affirmed the value and
validity of the judgment of the general public (39); and by any
such objective criterion, the truth is that as a violinist Jakob is
incompetent. His waltzes are unrecognizable because they are
badly played – so badly that the narrator is dumbfounded to
hear of his evenings of improvisation:

Wir waren beide ganz still geworden. Er, aus Beschämung über das
verratene Geheimnis seines Innern; ich, voll Erstaunen, den Mann von
den höchsten Stufen der Kunst sprechen zu hören, der nicht imstande
war, den leichtesten Walzer faßbar wiederzugeben.   (43)[1]

The emphasis here is *not* placed on *faßbar*, to suggest – pathetically
– a mere failure of communication or of comprehension; what he
plays does not only *seem* a mere jumble. What is stressed, distancing

---

[1] 'We had both become quite silent: he, from embarrassment at this inmost
secret that he had betrayed; I, astonished at hearing a man speaking of
the heights of art who was not able to give a recognizable rendering of the
easiest waltz.'

us from the emotional implications of the fiddler's confession, is the narrator's astonishment, the incongruity in the situation. And indeed, as the narrator discovers at first hand, Jakob's improvisation is a 'hellish concert' (48); and his grotesque lack of natural musicianship is further brought out in the wonder with which he learns of Barbara's ability to sing the melody of her song by ear (59).

In the portrait of Jakob as an artist there is much of Grillparzer himself. The point is not that Grillparzer too loved music – he played the violin occasionally in boyhood (SB 97), and used later to improvise on the piano (*Gespr.* 58) – but that some of his deepest attitudes and experiences are ironically reflected in Jakob. Even the fiddler's reluctance to tell his story is akin to his own dislike in his mature years of exposing his inner self, which is attested in his diary (T 1656) and in verse (G 105); and if Jakob's reluctance rests psychologically on the failure of his efforts both in music and in love, this too corresponds to a side of Grillparzer, who once wrote towards the end of the 1840s, 'It makes me sad that everything I do in life is a failure' (T 4026). His keen awareness of the disparity between ideas and achievements is attested in epigrams both early in his career (G 2) and – with rueful retrospection – in the 1860s (G 1688); and if it is interesting to see this awareness reflected in the delight with which at one stage he used to play an old stringless piano without any sense of missing the sound (SB 98f.), it is still more interesting that on one occasion in his youth, before he had written any of his tragedies, he related it specifically to dramatic writing – 'I should like to be able to write a tragedy in *thoughts*. It would turn out a masterpiece!' (T 45) – and that it remained with him at the peak of his creative career: 'I always lived in my dreams and projects, but proceeded only with difficulty to executing them because I knew that I should never do it to my satisfaction' (SB 214). For Jakob's 'music-making' serves as a symbol for all art, including dramatic art; and if Jakob aspires to 'play the Good Lord', so Grillparzer once wrote proudly of himself as 'a poet of ultimate truths' ('ein Dichter der letzten Dinge': G 1310, ii). Jakob's sense of the intoxicating quality of music corresponds to his own conception of poetry, as opposed to prose: 'Prose is man's food, poetry is his drink, which does not nourish him but invigorates him' (T 3493 [1839]).

Hence the quick and persistent interest taken in Jakob by the dramatist narrator of *Der arme Spielmann*. For it is not only through Jakob's voice that this *Novelle* is a confessional work.

Both the story-tellers – the intellectual artist and the imaginative artist – are fictional characters, but their roles correspond to a division that Grillparzer recognized in himself:

In mir nämlich leben zwei völlig abgesonderte Wesen. Ein Dichter von der übergreifendsten, ja sich überstürzenden Phantasie und ein Verstandesmensch der kältesten und zähesten Art. (SB 135)[1]

The imaginative artist tells his story, and the ironic narrator adds his suggestive, occasionally even caustic, comments, implying a cumulative judgment on the artist's achievement, which he sees sympathetically but with realistic clarity.

Grillparzer recognized the paramount importance of emotion and the imagination in creative art; his intellect did not usurp the place of the imagination in his own dramatic writing, but was exercised in his wide reading, refining his taste and sharpening his critical sense. The late Fred O. Nolte, a distinguished American critic, has written that 'in the catholic, delicate appreciation of things poetic and artistic, Grillparzer is not impossibly the most patiently and sensitively cultivated mind in the whole range of European letters'. And all his patiently nurtured aesthetic sensibility was constantly directed critically at his own work: by the 1820s he was already a victim of 'the most merciless self-criticism' (SB 214). While he was also capable of assessing himself soberly as the first among the successors of Goethe and Schiller (SB 201), and while this is indeed not an immodest assessment, what he dwelt on most constantly in his works was not so much the positive achievement as the degree of failure; he could not compare his work with all his reading of Calderón and Lope, of Shakespeare, of Goethe, and of the ancients, without feeling his shortcomings. In short, this naggingly self-critical self, the 'intellectual' in him, judged his work by the highest standards there are, and found it wanting: and his fears of shortcomings are reflected – ironically yet affectionately caricatured – in the total artistic failure of the poor fiddler Jakob, who cannot reproduce his classical models, and to whom the art which is his sole solace and lasting ideal in life can never offer rewards to match the pinnacle of happiness afforded by love – a happiness whose fleetingness is represented in Barbara's single kiss, but which is yet remembered as bringing the 'most blissful day' of his life.

---

[1] 'There are in me two completely separate beings: a poet of the most overweening, even precipitate imagination, and an intellectual of the coldest and most unyielding kind.'

3

AMBITION

Das Goldene Vlies

In the preface to *Das Goldene Vlies* which Grillparzer composed
in November 1821, he wrote that it was impossible for a writer
to escape the spirit of his own age; that in his age writers too
rapidly lost that 'certain innocence of mind' that was essential
for creative work, and turned to reflection, with the result that
in the search for deeper motivation and 'higher guiding principles'
they fell victim to formlessness; and that this point applied to
himself in respect of his trilogy. A significant indication of the
uncharacteristically 'reflective' nature of the work is that while
he was still engaged on its composition Grillparzer was able to
define its theme or basic idea in a generalized formula, which he
borrowed – misquoting slightly – from Schiller's *Wallenstein* trilogy:

> Das eben ist der Fluch der bösen Tat,
> Daß sie, fortzeugend, [...] Böses muß gebären.[1]

He wrote these lines over his scenario for *Medea* in early October
1819, and later in the month, when he was completing *Die
Argonauten*, he wrote a memorandum reminding himself that the
whole work was no more than a realization, or enactment, of the
idea expressed in them.

Grillparzer's concern with this idea conditioned the form of
the work. In comparison with Euripides' *Medea*, which he read
in 1817 and again in 1819, or, among modern treatments of the
theme, with Corneille's *Médée*, one of the most striking differences
lies in the breadth of the material that Grillparzer's version takes
in. Euripides and Corneille both begin as Jason is about to marry
Creon's daughter; Grillparzer does not reach this point until the
second act of the final part of his trilogy. While his first plan
was to write only a *Medea*, he conceived Medea's tragedy as the
culmination of a whole series of events beginning with her father's

---

[1] 'This is the curse of every evil deed, / That, propagating still, it brings
forth evil' (Coleridge's translation). See *Wke.* I/17, 301.

capture of the Golden Fleece and murder of Phryxus. To dramatize the whole chain of cause and effect involved treating the story in three distinct parts: the Phryxus episode (in *Der Gastfreund*), Jason's wooing of Medea and his recapture of the Fleece (*Die Argonauten*), then the tragic finale in Greece four years later (*Medea*). In this finale we see fulfilled the revenge which Phryxus was promised by Apollo in the cryptically oracular formula 'Take victory and vengeance!' ('Nimm Sieg und Rache hin!') in the course of the vision which first inspired him to set out for Colchis. Looking back on his murder, Medea warns her father how a single commitment to evil develops into a whole chain of evil consequences from which there is no escape:

> Kein Mensch, kein Gott löset die Bande,
> Mit denen die Untat sich selber umstrickt.

> (*Die Argonauten* 131f.)[1]

The long chain-reaction of evil and suffering draws in not only the guilty but those of good will, like Aietes' son Absyrtus and Kreusa, the daughter of the King of Corinth. This presentation of the inevitability with which evil engenders evil has, as Grillparzer saw, fatalistic undertones; not in the sense of the spooky atmospheric fatalism of *Die Ahnfrau* – 'There is no question of *Fate* here', he noted in anxious self-defence in the memorandum of October 1819 – but in the sense that we see the main characters of the work fashioning their own fate, from which they can never extricate themselves. The idea is a recurrent one in Grillparzer. It is expressed – albeit sophistically – by Jaromir in his argument that human actions are only 'Würfe / In des Zufalls blinde Nacht'; the same image is used in *Libussa* by Wlasta: 'Der Wurf geworfen, fällt das Los – und trifft' (2287);[2] in the same play, Primislaus sees this chain of causality running throughout human history: 'Im Anfang liegt das Ende' (1435).[3] The past is irredeemable, and this Medea discovers by harsh experience. For at the beginning of the final play in the trilogy, when she is longing to adapt herself completely to the life of Jason's homeland, she buries a chest full of her magic paraphernalia, in a conscious attempt to bury her past: the past is to be 'wafted away', with Colchis and its gods (*Medea*, 49–51). Her nurse, Gora, who cannot forgive her for her desertion of Colchis, sees the growing gulf between

---

[1] 'No man and no god can loose the bonds in which wickedness ensnares itself.'
[2] 'Once the die is cast, it cannot be undone.'
[3] 'In the beginning is contained the end.'

her and Jason as a just consequence, the proof that the actions of the past live on, wreaking their own effects and ineradicable from the mind:

> Grab ein, grab ein die Zeichen deiner Tat,
> Die Tat begräbst du nicht! (109f.)[1]

Medea faces, then, the dread possibility that the past can never be extinguished:

> So wär' denn immer da, was einmal da gewesen
> Und alles Gegenwart? (113f.)[2]

At the time she disputes the idea, but later she has to acknowledge its truth: the past lives on within herself, for example, in her memory of her past position, which, she tells Kreusa, contrasting it with her present humiliation, can never be forgotten (699). And Jason too, also talking to Kreusa, dwells on the contrast between his proud position before the Argonauts set off, surrounded by the admiration of the celebrating people of Corinth, and his present position, unrecognized or ignored in the same streets (*Medea* 795–816). The only possible escape from such memories would, as he says, be to unmake the past (821ff.), which he knows to be impossible. His past – both his triumphs and his wrongs – lives on within him, and breaks his spirit, as he later admits to Medea:

> ...Erinnrung des Vergangnen
> Liegt mir wie Blei auf meiner bangen Seele,
> Das Aug' kann ich nicht heben und das Herz.
> (1525–7)[3]

The evil of the past acts as a curse upon the future; and as though in demonstration of this theme, the action of the three parts of the trilogy is linked by curses. At the end of *Der Gastfreund*, Phryxus curses Aietes as he dies, and prays for revenge, which he associates with the Fleece for which Aietes has murdered him:

> Und dieses Vlies, das jetzt in seiner Hand,
> Soll niederschaun auf seiner Kinder Tod! (491f.)[4]

One of Aietes' children, his son Absyrtus, dies in *Die Argonauten*; the other, Medea, lives on but faces at the end of the trilogy a

---

[1] 'Bury deep the tokens of your deed! – You will not bury the deed.'
[2] 'So what has once been must exist for ever, and all is present?'
[3] 'Memory of the past lies like lead upon my anxious soul; I cannot raise my eyes or lift up my heart.'
[4] 'And that Fleece, now in his hands, shall look down on his children's death!'

misery which, she says, is worse than death (*Medea* 2312f.) – a state of emptiness, humiliation and shame which is the fullest realization of the second curse, that spoken over her by her father when she opts to follow Jason:

> ...Nicht sterben soll sie, leben;
> Leben in Schmach und Schande; verstoßen, verflucht,
> Ohne Vater, ohne Heimat, ohne Götter!
>
> (*Die Argonauten* 1361–3)[1]

To this curse Jason refers back in the *Medea*, admitting that it seems to be working still (*Medea* 749); and when it is wholly fulfilled, Medea again recalls it as she nurses her thoughts of revenge, banished and alone, 'shunned like a beast of the wild' (2112) but, as Aietes foretold, 'not dead – alas!' ('leider nicht tot', 2114).

Throughout all these events the constant centre of interest is the fateful Fleece. In the 1819 memorandum Grillparzer observed that it stood as a symbol of the main theme, 'accompanying' the events but not causing them. In 1821, in a diary note, he called it the 'intellectual centre' of the work, and redefined its symbolical significance: it should be seen to stand as 'a physical symbol of all that is desirable, and greedily sought, and wrongfully gained' (T 1241). And this was the conception that he adhered to in the autobiography, where the Fleece is described more succinctly as 'a physical symbol of wrongful possessions' (SB 134). This is a more satisfactory formula than that of 1819; for as a symbol of the desirable material possessions which men commit evil to acquire, the Fleece clearly does provoke the events of the play, acting as a catalyst to the passions or the acquisitiveness of successive characters who are subsequently either killed or left in tragic emptiness: Aietes, Jason, Kreon. But even the later definitions are inadequate. They are not, for example, appropriate in relation to Phryxus; for while he may have done wrong in removing the Fleece from Delphi in the first place he did so not out of personal acquisitiveness, but in interpretation of a divine vision – even if there was an element of personal ambition in his attempt to fulfil the promise of 'victory and vengeance'. Even after Aietes' crime the Fleece is not merely a symbol of unjustly gained possessions; for in the course of the action it develops other, wider connotations. In the final act of *Die Argonauten*,

---

[1] '...She shall not die, but live: live in disgrace and shame – cast out, accursed, without father, without country, without gods!'

when Jason displays it to Absyrtus, it serves as a sign of Medea's
betrayal, and not only seals her estrangement from her family
but contributes to the motivation of Absyrtus' suicide. And in
Act IV of *Medea*, when Medea promises it to Kreon with the
ominous assurance that he will receive what is his 'due' (1952),
it is clearly being used as a symbol of retribution, as foreshadowed
in Phryxus' curse. The Fleece itself embodies the sense of that
curse: it stimulates the selfishness of mankind, it brings disaster
to its wrongful holders, it is an instrument of the final tragedy,
and its survival at the last will bring Medea to Delphi in search
of divine judgment.

By tracing the whole history of the curse, Grillparzer laid
himself open to the charge of formlessness that he levelled against
himself in the unpublished preface. In his autobiography he
called the trilogy a 'monstrosity' (SB 159); and, illustrating his
point by reference to *Wallenstein*, he condemned the form of the
trilogy from the dramatic point of view:

Einmal ist die Trilogie oder überhaupt die Behandlung eines dramatischen
Stoffes in mehreren Teilen für sich eine schlechte Form. Das Drama ist
eine Gegenwart, es muß alles, was zur Handlung gehört, in sich
enthalten. Die Beziehung eines Teiles auf den andern gibt dem Ganzen
etwas Episches, wodurch es vielleicht an Großartigkeit gewinnt aber an
Wirklichkeit und Prägnanz verliert... (SB 135)[1]

The criteria implicit in this argument are characteristic of Grillparzer's view of drama. He recognized that in ancient Greek drama
a 'predominance' of 'description and narration' over action was
historically inherent in the dramatic tradition (T 2149); but the
same is not true of modern treatments of ancient subjects. And
while *Das Goldene Vlies* contains some impressive scenes, it would
be idle to deny that by Grillparzer's own criteria his criticisms
of the weakness of the trilogy form apply aptly to it. Much of the
story of the first two parts is essentially epic material, and its
treatment inevitably involves long passages of narrative. The
principal example in *Der Gastfreund* is Phryxus' story of his
bringing of the Fleece (270ff.). In *Die Argonauten* the climax of
the legend, Jason's encounter with the dragon that guards the
Fleece, has to take place off stage, while on stage Medea is left

---

[1] 'In the first place, the trilogy form, or any treatment of a dramatic subject
in several parts, is inherently a bad form. Drama is an action in the present,
it must contain within itself everything that is part of the action. To relate
one part to another is to give the whole an epic quality, which may perhaps
make it gain in grandeur but which makes it less realistic and less telling...'

exclaiming in horrified suspense (1557–74); and when Jason emerges triumphant, he then rehearses his adventure in a purely narrative speech (1586–96). In relation to the tragedy of the *Medea*, all the action of these first two plays is pre-history, four years past, causally connected with the events of the *Medea* but not dramatically part of them. Its place in Euripides and in Corneille is in expository speeches, spoken by the nurse and Jason respectively, in the opening scenes. In Grillparzer's *Medea* too Jason recapitulates the story of the Argonauts to Kreon (429ff.). By the criteria of drama that is enough, and the *Medea* has taken its place in the classical repertoire of the German theatre, independent of *Der Gastfreund* and *Die Argonauten*. A mere speech of exposition does not, however, satisfy the demands of analytical 'reflection', it is not enough to develop the underlying ideas of the work. The truth is that the demands of drama and 'reflection' were by Grillparzer's standards irreconcilable, and it is his recognition of this that he expressed in his preface of 1821.

The first two plays of the trilogy are rarely performed. They include what is, dramatically, some of Grillparzer's weakest writing, and the verse reflects the lack of dramatic life: it is at times stilted, at times melodramatically exclamatory, and often artificial in the short lines used to distinguish the speech of the Colchians from that of the Greeks. Where the action does spring into dramatic life is, significantly, in the scenes between Jason and Medea in *Die Argonauten*, particularly the wooing-scene in Act III: it comes to life, that is, not in treating Jason's adventures, which are strictly epic material, but in the interplay of characters, which is the stuff of drama. The dramatic effect of the whole trilogy is founded on this interplay between the two incompatible principal figures; but Jason is too reprehensible to be a tragic hero, while Medeä, however cruelly driven to her final atrocity, inevitably forfeits sympathy with her vengeful murder of Kreusa and her stabbing of her own children.

Jason's lack of moral stature is most clearly demonstrated in his wooing of Medea, which is cynically calculated as a means towards the capture of the Fleece. Even when declaring his love, he himself admits to a certain dispassionateness, a sense that he is standing outside himself, not committed but observing: 'Ich selber bin mir *Gegenstand* geworden' (*Die Argonauten* 1196).[1] It is this that justifies Medea's later charge that he made love to her

---

[1] 'I have become an *object* to myself.'

to further his ambition, that she was a mere tool, serving his selfish purpose (*Medea* 635f.), and also the repeated charges of hypocrisy that Gora levels against him in the third and fourth acts of the *Medea*. Were Medea not blinded by love, she would have recognized Jason's character from his behaviour towards her from the first. When he has declared his love for her and she tries to escape, he holds her by force, forces her on to her knees and proclaims himself her 'master' (*Die Argonauten* 1229). He then tries to bully her into an admission that she loves him, repeating over and again that she does so (1256ff.), challenging her to deny it, cajoling her into saying it herself. Later, presenting her to the Argonauts, he himself rips off her sorceress's veil, brushes aside her protests (1401–3), and at once (clearly *using* her love for his own acquisitive interests) demands that she direct him to the Fleece. Again he brushes aside all her protests; and when she threatens to kill herself, he makes it plain that the ambition to which he is committed is more important to him than her very life: 'Mein Höchstes für mein Wort und wär's dein Leben!' (1504).[1]

Once he has actually captured the Fleece, it appears, when he is challenged by Absyrtus, that he would be willing for Medea to remain in Colchis if she chose to (1703). In this same scene he also shows that he is not just boastful – this has been clear from the first – but boastful beyond his achievements. It is Medea's potion that has lulled the dragon; but it is Jason who is quick to assume the public credit: he tells Absyrtus that he is 'used to fighting dragons' (1718). When Absyrtus throws himself into the sea, Jason's complete lack of moral sense is evident in the way he at once disowns any responsibility for the incident, and blames it on Aietes:

> Die hohen Götter ruf' ich an zu Zeugen,
> Daß *du* ihn hast getötet und nicht ich! (1755f.)[2]

In the inauspicious life she shares with him in the years separating the second and third plays of the trilogy, Medea, despite her continuing love for him, learns to see through Jason's unscrupulous egoism, and she condemns it roundly to Kreusa:

> Nur *er* ist da, *er* in der weiten Welt,
> Und alles andre nichts als Stoff zu Taten. (*Medea* 630f.)[3]

---

[1] 'For my word I will stake my all – even your life!'
[2] 'I call the gods on high to witness: it was *you* who killed him, and not I!'
[3] 'Only *he* exists, only *he* in the whole world, and all else is merely fodder for his deeds.'

Jason shows his selfishness in its worst light to Kreon. First he tries to excuse himself for ever having involved himself with Medea, arguing in self-defence that in Colchis 'the measure of all things was lost' (*Medea* 446). Later he applauds her banishment; as a punishment for her part in the death of King Pelias it is indeed, he says, mild:

> Denn wahrlich, minder schuldig doch als sie,
> Trifft mich ein härtres Los, ein schwerers.
>
> (*Medea* 1327f.)[1]

His uppermost feeling, that is, is one of self-pity; for Medea he has no consideration, but takes refuge in a piece of flagrant sophistry: 'Sie zieht hinaus in angeborne Wildnis' (1329).[2] This is sophistry because it equates two quite separate, and for Medea very different, senses of the word 'Wildnis'. In fact the island of Colchis from which she came, and in which she was a powerful princess, is very far from being comparable to the abject disgrace of banishment from Corinth, to which Medea's own word, 'Elend' (2136), implying the wretchedness of exile, is much more applicable. But Jason rejects her pleas to him and supports her banishment, with a shamelessness that Medea herself comments on (1405); he defends himself as merely shrinking back from atrocity (1410) and does not acknowledge his own role in stimulating Medea's erratic conduct – a role which in her eyes, we know, is so fundamental that he seems the 'originator and sole cause' of her deeds (1070). And when Medea charges him with his responsibility towards her, he again shakes off any blame for deserting her, just as he shook off all blame for her brother's death. The fault, he says, is her own:

> MEDEA Mein Vaterland verließ ich, dir zu folgen.
> JASON Dem eignen Willen folgtest du, nicht mir.
> Hätt's dich gereut, gern ließ ich dich zurück!
>
> (*Medea* 1564–6)

To admit that he would have left her behind – after gaining the Fleece – is callous; to claim that it was her 'will' to follow him is dishonest, for he had to break down her resistance, and at the last she would gladly have stayed on Colchis (*Die Argonauten* 1703)

---

[1] 'For truly, though I am less to blame than she, mine is the harsher, harder fate.'
[2] 'She is going out into her native wilderness.'
[3] 'I left my homeland to follow you.' 'You were following your own will, not me. Had you regretted it, I should gladly have left you behind!'

were she not driven by love for Jason and had she not already irrevocably severed her links with the island by her (reluctant) assistance of him in the capture of the Fleece. To such facts Jason pays no heed: he blames her, and then proceeds to blame the Amphictyonic edict:

> Ich verlass' dich nicht,
> Ein höhrer Spruch treibt mich von dir hinweg.
>
> (*Medea* 1569f.)[1]

He uses the political edict as a shield to hide behind, a means of wriggling out from under his moral responsibility, with which Medea is confronting him.

By contrast with Jason, Medea is portrayed as having a much more acute moral awareness. One of the many notes Grillparzer made during his work on the trilogy towards the end of 1819 reads: 'Never forget that the basic thought of the last play is that after leaving Colchis Medea *wants* to be *faultless*, but cannot be.'[2] This note, while not really summarizing the 'basic thought' of the *Medea*, comes to grips with one of the most fundamental problems he faced: how to show Medea in the first two plays as being sufficiently uncivilized and as having sufficiently violent passions to motivate her murder of Kreusa and the children in the final play, while yet retaining our sympathy for her as a tragic heroine in a modern drama. He attempted to solve this difficulty by two expedients. First, he radically altered the traditional character of Medea, making her appear morally superior to the other Colchians, abandoning the gruesome legend that it was she who killed Absyrtus and then strewed the pieces of his body over the seashore to halt Aietes' pursuit, and also throwing a veil of imprecision over the details of the death of Pelias; far from being simply a barbarian sorceress, Grillparzer's Medea is wise, strong in character and outraged by her father's treatment of Phryxus. Secondly, Grillparzer emphasized as strongly as possible the general contrast between Colchis and Greece, partly by his use of different metres. From the first, as he recalled in the autobiography, he saw this contrast as being of central importance, and involving a basic contrast in atmosphere between the first two plays and the last: 'The first two parts had to be kept as barbaric and romantic as possible, precisely to bring out that difference between Colchis and Greece on which everything turned'

---

[1] 'I am not deserting you: a higher judgment is driving me away from you.'
[2] *Wke.* 1/17, 300.

(SB 136). In *Die Argonauten*, Jason makes this contrast in the wooing scene itself:

> Ich ein Hellene, du Barbarenbluts,
> Ich frei und offen, du voll Zaubertrug...
>
> (*Die Argonauten* 1204f.)[1]

He speaks of Greece as a land of light, in contrast to the dark of the island, and depicts it as an ideal country full of the spirit of friendship (1237–42). Medea has previously heard Phryxus too speak with pride of the beauty of Greece (*Der Gastfreund* 263); and it follows from her superiority to the other Colchians that she is drawn to it. Once she is there, however, she finds that a great gulf separates her from the Greeks; and this is brought out repeatedly in the first two acts of the *Medea*. She admits that she is not used to the customs of Greece: and it is for that reason, she says, that the Greeks despise her (*Medea* 400–3), degrading her who was by birth a princess. Both her endeavour and her failure to assimilate the culture of her adopted home are crystallized in her attempt to learn a favourite song of Jason's to sing to him. When first we see Kreusa trying to teach her to play the harp, Medea feels that it is hopeless, that what her hand is used to is not playing musical instruments but hunting with a spear (587f.). Then when she does try to sing for Jason, she has to beg for his attention with fearful insistence: 'Jason, ich weiß ein Lied';[2] when she fails, breaking down at the very beginning of the song (906f.), her tears bring out the depth of her suffering at the humiliation she is going through in Greece – a humiliation which is partly caused, as in this episode, by her own struggle to gain acceptance, but which still imposes an intolerable strain. When Jason asks Kreusa to sing instead, all Medea's self-restraint breaks, in a violent eruption of her natural feelings. She expresses her emotion in one of those highly theatrical gestures that are characteristic in Grillparzer, snatching up the lyre that symbolizes the culture of Greece, crushing it in her hands and throwing it at Kreusa's feet (*Medea* 924). It is the moment at which all that part of her character breaks out – all her 'barbarian blood' – which she has vainly sought to bury as belonging to the past.

The character in whom this past is articulated is Gora, Medea's companion since the very beginning of the trilogy. In the *Medea*

---

[1] 'I a Greek, you of barbarian blood; I free and open, you full of treacherous magic...'

[2] 'Jason, I know a song' (863, 874, 877).

the occasional use of shorter metres in scenes between Medea and
Gora effectively brings out, by the contrast with the pentameters
spoken by the Greeks, their strangeness in the alien land; as the
work builds up towards tragedy, both the third and fourth acts
begin with scenes of this kind, in which the shorter metres are
used, and Medea returns to them at the climax itself at the end
of Act IV. In the first of these scenes, that at the beginning of
Act III, Medea, despairing, thinks of suicide, and then of dying
together with her children, as a means of avenging herself on
Jason (1230–4). When she thinks of killing Kreusa instead, she
at once tries to resist the idea (1238–41); but Gora takes over,
spurring her on to vengeance by recounting the dreadful fates of
a series of other legendary heroes (1252ff.). At this stage Medea
remains undecided, pinning her hopes on a last confrontation
with Jason. She fails to change his attitude, but he allows her
to take one of their children into exile with her. The children
have been her one source of consolation from the outset of the
Medea, and she has clung to their embrace when left alone with
them (362f.); now when they are brought to her, the sight of their
preference for Kreusa comes as an annihilating defeat, the ultimate,
intolerable humiliation:

> Ich bin besiegt, vernichtet, zertreten,
> Sie fliehn mich, fliehn!
> Meine Kinder fliehn! (1710–12)[1]

It is this thought of the children that returns to her at the beginning
of the next act, prompting on the one hand a sense of despair
about her whole life (1798–1802) and on the other hand renewed
thoughts of revenge, which she comes finally to contemplate with
a horrible delight:

> Entsetzliches gestaltet sich in mir,
> Ich schaudre – doch ich freu' mich auch darob.
> (1851f.)[2]

The compound motivation for the destruction of her self-control
is complete: the selfish injustice of Jason, the successive humili-
ations of her life in Greece, her jealousy of Kreusa, the loss of
her children. But however well motivated, her actual crime
cannot be seen as anything but an inhuman atrocity, which repels

---

[1] 'I am defeated, annihilated, crushed – they shun me, shun me! My children shun me!'

[2] 'A terrible thought is taking shape in my mind; I shudder – and yet I also
rejoice at it.'

our sympathy. Moreover, to the last she does not repent her act, but instead laments the whole tragic sequence that is life itself:

> Nicht traur' ich, daß die Kinder nicht mehr sind.
> Ich traure, daß sie *waren* und daß *wir* sind.　　(2324f.)[1]

These lines sum up that recognition of 'das Nichtige des Irdischen', the emptiness of all earthly things, which in the essay 'Über das Wesen des Drama' Grillparzer defined as belonging to the essence of tragedy.

While Medea's conception of the universal tragedy of human existence is securely founded on her experience in association with the Golden Fleece, so that her final plight may be said to embody the lesson or moral of the trilogy, nevertheless her crime and her subsequent attitude of desolation rather than repentance together make her an unsuitable vehicle for the expression of the moral. In real life we could not stomach moralizing from a person who had committed an atrocity such as Medea's, and still less from one who remained unrepentant; and the same is true in the work of art. Yet in the final scene Grillparzer has Medea confront Jason and expound to him in a long speech the moral of the events they have lived through. This misjudgment may be attributed in part to Grillparzer's overestimation, at this stage of his career, of the moral function of tragedy: in the essay 'Über das Wesen des Drama' one of the essential characteristics he ascribed to tragedy was that it should show that every disruption of the eternal order of right ('das ewige Recht') must be brought to nought. This moral element appears, however, to have been further inflated by a subjective element of self-recrimination; for just as Jason has been accused by Medea of making love to her out of selfish ambition, so Grillparzer accused himself (most openly in *Le poète sifflé*) of having wronged Charlotte von Paumgartten, the dedicatee of the trilogy, by deliberately holding her love and coldly observing it, exploiting it for the benefit of his art. He saw himself as having undermined her happiness, yet felt too that his ambitious artistic project – the completed trilogy – fell far short of his hopes. With all these subjective undertones, the moral takes on an accusing urgency that overrides strictly dramatic considerations, and it is hammered home as Medea tells Jason again that he is at fault for their plight (2314f.): he has

---

[1] 'I do not grieve that the children are no more. I grieve that they ever *were*, and that *we are*.'

deserved the unhappy lot that has now befallen him (2327), for he has overreached himself (2331) and must now bear the suffering that is the consequence (2342ff.). Her own suffering, she tells him, is still greater (2346) – a reversal of the point earlier made by him to her, and no more convincing. She is taking the Fleece back to Delphi, and there she will submit her fate to the judgment of Apollo; meanwhile she shows it to Jason as a symbol of the vanity of human desires, a symbol of the gain and the glory which he sought but which are without substance, and she reminds him that though his illusion is shattered, its consequences still face them both:

> Erkennst das Zeichen du, um das du rangst?
> Das dir ein Ruhm war und ein Glück dir schien?
> Was ist der Erde Glück? – Ein Schatten!
> Was ist der Erde Ruhm? – Ein Traum!
> Du Armer! der von Schatten du geträumt!
> Der Traum ist aus, allein die Nacht noch nicht.
>
> (2364–9)[1]

While the prospect she holds out is the dark 'night' of expiatory suffering (2373f.), this whole final scene, like the final scene in *Sappho*, is played against a sunrise, and similar objections arise: the contrast with the darkness of the previous act is at odds with the position which the central figures in fact face. Medea tells Jason that the night of their suffering is not over; and her bleak moralizing prescription, in the last lines of the play, of atonement through suffering, gives no positive hope for the future, either in practical or in moral terms, such as the sunrise behind her might suggest. If her moralizing is unacceptable, so the scenic effects accompanying it are at the least suspect.

The theme of the vanity of ambition was a rich one for Grillparzer, but he had yet to realize its full dramatic potential. He did this, abandoning the trilogy form, in two very different plays. In *König Ottokars Glück und Ende* he explored in depth a character as ambitious as Jason but portrayed with a wider humanity, the moral issues being represented in the main dramatic conflict and the whole action of the play demonstrating the consequences of

---

[1] 'Do you recognize the prize for which you struggled, which meant fame to you and promised happiness? What is earthly happiness? A shadow! – What is earthly fame? A dream! You poor creature, who dreamt of shadows! The dream is over, but the night is not.'

Ottokar's ambition on his peoples as well as on himself and his court. In *Der Traum ein Leben* he adopted a much more stylized convention, that of the *Besserungsstück* of the Viennese popular stage, and used it to explore in the monitory dream-adventures of the central figure the potential consequences of ambition for him as an individual.

König Ottokars Glück und Ende

One of the first notes Grillparzer wrote in his diary when he was beginning work on *König Ottokars Glück und Ende* reads simply: 'Overweening pride (*Übermut*) and its downfall. King Ottokar' (T 612, February 1820); and it is well known that his work on the tragedy (and on his plan for a drama *Krösus*), by absorbing his interest in the theme of the vanity of ambition, was one of the principal reasons for the long gap in his composition of *Der Traum ein Leben*, the earliest of his mature plays to be based on this theme. The actual composition of *König Ottokars Glück und Ende* in February and March 1823 was preceded by long research into the thirteenth-century background – by 'prodigious study of everything I could get hold of on Austrian and Bohemian history of that period' (SB 166). Aspects of the play and its genesis on which modern critics have in the main concentrated include: first, the freedom with which Grillparzer has treated his historical material;[1] secondly, the role of the Emperor, Rudolf, as the defender of the just cause of political order or of some wider standard of absolute right; thirdly, the apparently unheroic nature of Ottokar's repentance; and fourthly, the question of the extent to which Ottokar's character reflects that of Napoleon – this last being prompted by Grillparzer's admission of his interest in a 'distant similarity' between the fates of Ottokar and the Emperor of the French (SB 166). Particularly the first three of these approaches are suggestive and rewarding; but as a starting-point to an appreciation of the finished tragedy as a whole a further fundamental question arises: to what extent *is* it still essentially a study of the vanity of ambition, of 'overweening pride and its downfall'?

After his first defeat, Ottokar's career is seen in just such simple proverbial terms – 'Pride comes before a fall' – by the mayor of Prague (2050); but the mayor is an unimaginative figure, and his

---

[1] For a summary of the historical background, see the edition of the play by L. H. C. Thomas (Oxford, 1953), Introduction, pp. xvi–xxii.

97

trite comment is made unimaginatively. The play as a whole is not intended merely to present any such platitudinous moral. Nor is it just a single character-study, for essentially the action presents a contrast and a struggle: between Ottokar, whose goal is the imperial crown, and Rudolf von Habsburg, who is elected to that crown. In the latest Burgtheater production, which was given its première in December 1965, nearly all the loyalist cheering for the Habsburg cause was omitted. This is a case of political touchiness in modern republican Austria outweighing artistic considerations; it is not merely a sycophantic (and hence outdated) rounding-off when the play ends – and always ought to end – with cries of 'Habsburg for ever!' For Rudolf is in the play everything that Ottokar should be and is not. Ottokar is still the hero, in the sense that he is the central character: whereas Rudolf does not appear at all in the second and fourth acts, Ottokar is central in the first act in his power, in the second in his sudden discomfiture, in the third in his submission, in the fourth in his humiliation and the upsurge of his murderous rebellion, and in the fifth in his repentance and death. But when he flouts first the rights of his queen, Margarete, and then the authority of the empire, it is Rudolf's active opposition that he has to face, and it is to Rudolf's standards that his actions stand in constant contrast.

Rudolf is a pious figure, and so consistently in the right that his character can seem flat and wooden, at least on the printed page (in performance the sheer fact of physical presence always tends to lend the role substance and colour). Unlike Ottokar, he has never been exposed to the corruption of material power. His concern with the proper rights of the empire antecedes his election (375–7); and as Emperor he is able to tell Ottokar during their confrontation in the third act that he has set personal ambition behind him (1911). His conception of kingship is based on the ideal of service, and he enters battle as a crusader for a divine cause:

> Nun vor, mit Gott! und Christus sei der Schlachtruf!
>
> (2749)[1]

He himself makes explicit his exemplary stature and function:

> Was sterblich war, ich hab' es ausgezogen
> Und bin der Kaiser nur, der niemals stirbt.   (1789f.)[2]

[1] 'Advance, with God! And let Christ's name be our battle-cry!'
[2] 'I have shed all that is mortal in myself, and am simply the Emperor, who never dies.'

AMBITION

That Ottokar, like Sappho, is shown as falling short of an absolute ideal, and that this is the *moral* core of his tragedy, is in keeping with a recurrent tendency in Grillparzer's dramatic work; and since Grillparzer's choice of, and approach to, the subjects of his works was always subjective (his treatment of the motive of ambition, for example, to a significant extent reflects a critical attitude to his own aspirations as a dramatic poet), this also suggests that the absolute values which Rudolf represents and against which Ottokar offends should not necessarily be interpreted literally as being confined to the essentially imperial and religious terms in which Rudolf states them. Certainly his use of the words 'God' and 'Christ' does not imply that his representative role was conceived by Grillparzer as having an essentially religious significance.

Grillparzer's freethinking approach to religion (in any orthodox sense of the term) may be illustrated from a diary note of 1828: 'It is highly probable that there is a centre and complex of divinity, even a force which disposes and creates – to which, however, we perhaps come closer if we say "There is *no* God" than if with our human comprehension we say "There *is* a God"' (T 1681). That he was still an unbeliever nearly thirty years later is clear from his epigrams (e.g. G 1513). In old age he insisted in conversation that he had never been an atheist or anti-religious (*Gespr.* 1201), and once he even remarked that he was actually beginning to grow religious. But even then his attitude was still very far from one of conviction: he observed that neither belief nor disbelief could be based on proof, but at least the former had the merit of being comforting (*Gespr.* 1247). And his attitude to the institution of the Christian church in particular is summed up in an epigram of 1857:

> Mit drei Ständen habe [ich] nichts zu schaffen:
> Beamte, Gelehrte und Pfaffen.   (G 1526)[1]

The significance of the word 'God' in Grillparzer is best explained in a diary-note of 1820 (T 641). The gods of the ancients, he notes, are not to be compared with the modern divinity, because they were not supreme, but subordinate to 'the eternal Law':

Die Götter waren nicht das Höchste; über ihnen stand das ewige Recht. Das haben wir personifiziert und nennen es: Gott.[2]

[1] 'There are three classes I have no truck with: officials, academics and clerics.'
[2] 'The gods were not supreme: above them was the eternal Law. That we have personified, and we call it "God".'

In a way that is highly characteristic of the moral emphasis in Grillparzer's work, the idea of God means a supreme standard of law and of right. It is this *moral* standard that Rudolf I invokes, 'personified' in the name of the deity; and the same is true also of Gregor in *Weh dem, der lügt!* and of Rudolf II in the *Bruderzwist*. Rather as Goethe uses 'the clearly outlined figures and conceptions of the Christian church' in the final scene of *Faust* as a conventional structure of reference to represent wider 'poetic intentions'[1] so too Grillparzer symbolizes the idea of the highest duty (in whatever sphere) in the devotion of the two Emperors and the bishop to their Christian ideals. In Gregor's case it is an idea inherent in his episcopal office; in the case of Rudolf I (as also in the case of Rudolf II) it is inherent in his historical position as elected ruler of the Holy Roman Empire. Against Rudolf's positively conservative role as defender of the order of the empire, which he is prepared to represent against any odds (1779–84), Ottokar stands as a destructive counterpart, endangering the political continuity embodied in the house of Habsburg.

The contrast between the standards of the two rulers is made in the first act, as in successive scenes we are shown Rudolf's sympathy and obedience towards Margarete of Austria and then the brusqueness with which Ottokar treats her. The measured account that she gives to Rudolf of her marriage to Ottokar (206ff.) brings out both the pathos of her situation and her own dignity; and it is from the point when he dissolves this marriage – which, as Margarete makes clear, he does primarily so that he can remarry in the hope of an heir (256–65) – that fortune deserts Ottokar, and his star wanes as Rudolf's ascends. That in 1820 Grillparzer also used the key phrase 'the eternal Law' in relation to tragedy, when he wrote that tragedy has essentially to show that 'every offence against the eternal Law must be brought to nought' (T 639), is perhaps a suggestive pointer to the moral pattern of this play, as well as of the trilogy. Margarete is insistent that Ottokar is acting unjustly towards her (237), and she foresees his downfall:

> Er soll vor Unrecht sorglich sich bewahren;
> Denn auch das kleinste rächt sich...   (380f.)[2]

[1] J. P. Eckermann, *Gespräche mit Goethe in den letzten Jahren seines Lebens (1823–1832)*, entry dated 6 June 1831.

[2] 'He must guard carefully against committing injustice, for even the least injustice will avenge itself...'

The fact that his downfall arises directly from his repudiation of his queen (a significant reshaping of history on Grillparzer's part) concentrates our attention on the way that Ottokar is himself unknowingly sowing the seeds of his inevitable tragedy, and is doing so in the very sphere of action – a sphere in which personal and political motives intertwine – where his seeming ruthlessness has been most sharply contrasted with Rudolf's gentleness and loyalty. Ottokar protests that his dissolution of his marriage is not prompted by mere self-seeking; but clearly it *is* largely motivated in the first instance by ambition, whether that ambition be for himself or, as he claims, conceived as patriotic service of his people (508–20). The unity of motivation in Ottokar's personal and political life is suggestively underlined by the main (political) action: his unjustified pursuit of the imperial crown after Rudolf's election brings him in the final act to the scene where, in defeat, he kneels in repentant prayer by Margarete's coffin: the action has come full circle, his wrong is avenged, he has come to the truth when it is too late. Later, taking stock of his achievements, he acknowledges that his downfall is deserved:

> Ich hab' nicht gut in deiner Welt gehaust,
> Du großer Gott!...

He acknowledges that he has achieved not good, but the evil of destructiveness:

> ...Wie Sturm und Ungewitter
> Bin ich gezogen über deine Fluren...   (2825–7)[1]

He has in short been misled by his dreams of being a second Charlemagne, 'ein zweiter Karl' (1182); he has been misled, like Jason in *Das Goldene Vlies* or Rustan in *Der Traum ein Leben*, by his selfish will; and the link between his disastrous ambition and the first fateful step of faithlessness is re-established when finally, after his murder, his corpse lies beside Margarete's coffin.

It was probably not long after the première of *König Ottokars Glück und Ende* that Grillparzer wrote that Shakespeare was 'tyrannizing his mind' (T 1407); and indeed Shakespeare's influence is particularly strong on this work. One result of this is a richness and liveliness of characterization in the secondary roles, such as Grillparzer had achieved in none of his previous dramas. In its structure, moreover, *König Ottokars Glück und Ende* is essentially

---

[1] 'Oh Lord above, I have not lived a good life on thy earth! Like storm and tempest I have swept across thy plains...'

a history in the Shakespearian manner, and of course its subject-matter is as important in the history of Austria – indeed of Germany and vast stretches of eastern and south-eastern Europe – as the material of any Shakespearian history is to an English audience; for Rudolf's election as 'German King' brought the crown for the first time to the Habsburgs, who later were Emperors, with only one brief interval in the mid-eighteenth century, from 1438 onwards, and who remained the rulers of the Austrian Empire until its dissolution after the First World War.

That Grillparzer took Shakespeare as his model may also be seen in the treatment of Ottokar's decline, which is reminiscent of *King Lear*, in two scenes particularly: in the fourth act, when Ottokar finds himself deserted by all but his faithful chancellor (2261), as Lear is left with his Fool; and in the fifth act, where Lear's pathetic dependence on Albany to undo his button is matched by Ottokar's turning to his servants for a cloak, with a wild laugh that degenerates into a raucous cough: ''s ist kalt! Hat niemand einen Mantel?' (2584)[1] – a moment as succinctly revealing of the reduction of pride to abject dependence as Medea's plea 'Jason, ich weiß ein Lied'.

As a history, *König Ottokars Glück und Ende* gains much of its effect by the breadth of its canvas, with a sub-plot running parallel with the main plot. But this widening of scope does not undermine the unity of the play. Both actions start with the rejection of Margarete and lead to Ottokar's humiliation at the hands of Zawisch von Rosenberg. When he dissolves his marriage with Margarete he chooses as his new queen not Zawisch's niece Berta, as the Rosenbergs had hoped, but Kunigunde of Hungary. The Rosenbergs conspire to gain revenge. Zawisch hints at his vindictive intentions in the first act (182f.); and from then on he feeds Ottokar's ambitions, inflates his illusions, and so spurs him on to disastrous self-assertion.[2] Ottokar is in effect led on to disaster by his own self-conceit, which Zawisch sedulously cultivates. Early in Act iii, for example, the chancellor frankly warns Ottokar that he is losing his war against Rudolf. Ottokar will not believe him:

> KANZLER Herr, es steht schlimm!
>
> OTTOKAR (*auf und nieder gehend*) Es steht sehr gut!   (1427)[3]

---

[1] 'It's cold! Has no-one a cloak?'
[2] See ll. 767ff., 1518ff., 2195–7.
[3] Chancellor: 'The position, Sire, is grave!' Ottokar (*walking to and fro*): 'It's very good!'

The chancellor lists his evidence: disease and hunger among Ottokar's troops; armies in retreat; the enemy closing in (1428–46). And then Zawisch recharges all the king's illusions of grandeur and military superiority (1526–42). That Ottokar is completely taken in by Zawisch's plausible encouragement in spite of all the real evidence is proved by his willingness to meet Rudolf; and it is precisely here that Zawisch finally achieves his political revenge when, in one of the most visually dramatic of all Grillparzer's scenes, he cuts the ropes of the tent in which Ottokar is kneeling before Rudolf, and so exposes to the whole camp the humiliating spectacle of Ottokar in defeat. Traditionally this exposure was instigated by Rudolf. This is the case, for example, in Lope de Vega's play on the same subject, *La imperial de Otón*. When Grillparzer read this work in the early 1850s he found that the integrity of Lope's Rodulfo was compromised by precisely this motif – indeed, Lope's Otón makes the point himself, saying in the final act that the episode has revealed the Emperor as a man without honour. It is, by contrast, symptomatic of Grillparzer's exemplary characterization of Rudolf that he avoids involving him in any such trickery and transforms the episode into a climax in Zawisch's revenge. Throughout these political developments, moreover, Zawisch is gaining personal revenge by his calculated wooing of Kunigunde. With his elegance and spirit he presents an obvious contrast to Ottokar, whom the hot-blooded young queen despises as an old man; having spurned Margarete because (among other reasons) she is too old, Ottokar is now himself deceived by a girl who finds him 'as grumpy as an old man' (981).

The two plots link in the fourth act. The picture of himself kneeling before his victorious rival haunts Ottokar: 'Ich kann nicht knieen sehn!' (2454);[1] and Kunigunde taunts him with it, contrasting him with Zawisch:

KÖNIGIN   ...Rosenberg!
ZAWISCH   Erlauchte Frau!
KÖNIGIN   Habt Ihr schon je gekniet?
                Vor Frauen nicht – vor Männern schon gekniet?
                Um Sold, um Lohn, aus Furcht, vor Euresgleichen?
ZAWISCH   Ich nicht.
KÖNIGIN   Und würdet's nie?

---

[1] 'I cannot bear to see anyone kneel!' He has also dwelt bitterly on the memory of his public humiliation in ll. 2283–6 and 2332f.

ZAWISCH   In meinem Leben!
KÖNIGIN   Er aber hat's getan! vor seinem Feinde,
              Vor jenem Mann gekniet, den er verachtet...

$$(2169–75)[1]$$

Here the political humiliation is being combined with sexual humiliation; and it is finally the sexual element that leads Ottokar to his last defeat. For it is Kunigunde's taunts that seduce him to make his last attempt to free himself from what she presents as his shame:

> Solang Ihr Euch nicht von der Schmach gereinigt,
> Betretet nicht als Gatte mein Gemach!   (2404f.)[2]

And so Ottokar goes to war under the pretext of salvaging his 'honour' (2407). It is a hollow pretext, for at the political level this is the very conception of honour that he has heard Rudolf condemn as vain (1893), and at the personal level, as he later admits (2672), Kunigunde has already compromised his honour with Zawisch.

Kunigunde was originally designed as a secondary figure, included because of the dramatist's need to externalize the motivation for Ottokar's rejection of Margarete: she was, that is, to be merely the 'other woman', like Melitta in *Sappho*. In fact, however, from her first entrance she stands out as a well-delineated character, spirited in manner, caustic in comment, and speaking (as Wells has observed) in a staccato style of speech which contrasts with the slower, more reflective style of Margarete and so underlines the whole contrast in character between them. The expansion of Kunigunde's role involves a considerable deepening of the psychology of the piece – for no mere 'other woman' could credibly taunt the king to the point of making him set aside all his very real scruples (2397–2400) about the ravages and dangers of the war he is being forced into unleashing; and while the play is lengthened in the process, still (as we have seen) Grillparzer maintains an intricate unity. Nor is this unity of subject-matter essentially impaired by the further subsidiary action which culminates in Ottokar's death. This is an off-shoot of the political

---

[1] Queen: '...Rosenberg!' 'Your Majesty?' 'Have you ever knelt – not to a woman: have you ever knelt to a man? To your equal, for money, for reward, from fear?' 'Never.' 'And you never would?' 'Not as long as I live!' 'But *he* did! He knelt to his enemy, to the very man he despises...'

[2] 'Until you have purged yourself of this dishonour, do not enter my room as my husband!'

action, in which we follow up a single example of the suspicion and injustice to which Ottokar's ambition drives him and are shown their consequence, Seyfried Merenberg's avenging of his father.

König Ottokars Glück und Ende is, as Grillparzer's contemporary Josef Karl Rosenbaum wrote in his diary, 'a masterpiece – but too long' (*Gespr.* 401/iii). It is the longest of all Grillparzer's plays, and it was quickly recognized that some cuts have to be made in the text for performance. One of the scenes most frequently omitted is the opening one of Act III, which shows the arrest of Merenberg. This action prepares the basis for the motivation of the eventual murder of Ottokar; but since we see Merenberg again as Ottokar's prisoner in Act IV, there is no need for his actual arrest to be shown. The real purpose of the scene is atmospheric: by affording a glimpse of Merenberg's life it illustrates qualities of simple peacefulness which are diametrically opposed to Ottokar's bearing and way of living but which are essentially the qualities defended by Rudolf as the leader of the Austrians. Thus the scene enlarges on, and gives background to, the central conflict; but as an atmospheric episode it is not strictly necessary to the economy of the play, and indeed its inclusion makes for a rather episodic effect. Later in the same act, the sequence including Horneck's eulogy of Austria (1665–1717) is also dispensable dramatically, though it is never omitted in any Austrian production. Apart from these two scenes, however, the process of deletion is a very difficult one, precisely because – as Fuerst rightly stresses in his analysis of the work as a stage play – the various strands of the action are so closely linked. Grillparzer was never lavish with self-praise, yet even he was satisfied with the general design of the action of *König Ottokars Glück und Ende*: 'I had to admit that the construction was excellent' (SB 167); and in the late 1850s, according to Helene Lieben's account, he still regarded it as his best play (*Gespr.* 1066).

At the centre of this complex action is a complex hero. For Ottokar is not a victim of *mere* ambition; he is not merely led (as Rudolf suggests) by a 'vain craving for glory' (1893). The initial impression he makes in the first act is one of arrogance: he is inconsiderately tactless both towards his subjects (395ff.) and towards his queen (524) and heartless about one of his own kinsmen whose death has brought him more lands (668–75). As a result, when he protests that his conquests have been made not for his own sake but for that of the land he rules (497–501), and that his divorce is similarly dictated by the needs of his people and his nation (506–15, 592–5), we disbelieve it, we assume it is mere sophistic rationalization. Rationalization it is; but not sophistry, for it is a rationalization that Ottokar himself has grown to believe in; it is the belief that sustains him in his struggle, lends him his stature as a ruler and finally his Lear-like pathos in defeat. Ottokar is absolutely consistent in his conviction that his actions as a ruler are performed in the interests of his people. He believes that he has bettered the lot of his territories – a conviction that makes their defection to Rudolf all the more bitter a pill (1946f.). He believes that when first he makes peace with Rudolf it is to save the lives of innocent subjects (2390f.). When he senses that he is about to face divine judgment, he prays that at least his people be spared: 'So triff mich, aber schone meines Volks!' (2862). Moreover, the people around him know that he is no mere selfish tyrant. For Seyfried Merenberg, his eventual murderer, he is at the outset a figure to be admired, '...so ein Herr, ein Ritter, so ein König' (16);[1] he has been a model of chivalry and honour (19f.; 2896f.). For his chancellor, who does not escape the harshness of his temper (1234/sd), his stature is nevertheless comparable to that of the Emperor himself: 'zwei Herrn, so hoch, so würdevoll' (1502).[2] When Rudolf is pleading for his submission, his final argument – presented not as cajoling flattery but following an earnest request that Ottokar set aside all self-deception (1879) – takes the form of an appeal to his real sense of duty to the country and people he rules:

> Ihr habt der Euren Vorteil stets gewollt;
> Gönnt ihnen Ruh', Ihr könnt nichts Beßres geben!
> (1927f.)[3]

When Ottokar is played as a wholly selfish tyrant, a braggart, arrogant and cruel and nothing else (as he was in the 1965 Burgtheater production, and as he often is), these passages make no sense; and the Ottokar of the second half of the play seems a quite different character from the Ottokar of the first half. Even Professor Walter Silz, who in a perceptive analysis of Ottokar's role discounts any view of him as a mere blustering and brutal

---

[1] '...so fine a lord, so fine a knight and king!'
[2] 'Two lords so noble and so full of majesty.'
[3] 'You have always worked for the good of your people: grant them peace, you can give them nothing better!'

tyrant and recounts in detail his good and admirable qualities, writes of a 'change and break in his character' and argues that 'there is too great a gap between the arrogant triumphator of Act I and the crushed and contrite individual of Act v'. In performance, the danger is that Ottokar's remorse will appear not as conscientious insight but as mere weakness. This seems to have been the effect at the première in 1825, to judge from Costenoble's diary-note: 'At the end the mighty hero declines into pitiful weakness' (*Gespr.* 401/ii). Similar comments may be found among reviews of the 1965 production.

In the text, however, Ottokar is consistently portrayed as a victim of his own self-confident enthusiasm, which has fed his capacity for self-deception. One indicative scene fairly early in the play is that in which news of Rudolf's election arrives. Ottokar is boastfully planning the dispositions he will make when he becomes Emperor:

OTTOKAR (*hat unterdessen den Gesandten den Brief gewiesen, mit dem Finger einzelne Stellen bezeichnend*)
> Die müssen fort – seht, der! –
(*Bei der ersten Rede des Kanzlers horcht er, in derselben Stellung bleibend, nach hinten hin in höchster Spannung. Als jener den Namen Habsburg nennt, fährt Ottokar zusammen; die Hand, mit der er auf den Brief zeigt, beginnt zu zittern; er stottert noch einige Worte.*)
> und der – muß fort!

$$(1220)^1$$

In his self-confidence he cannot at first believe what he hears: it is as though he refuses to take it in, and goes on planning. Then his hand sinks down and he stands for a moment, staring, fixed in the graphic posture of despondency; but then he pulls himself together, strides off to his room, and returns shortly to proclaim that on the following day his whole court will go hunting. Leading his followers off to prepare for the chase he displays (as Miss Margaret Atkinson has observed) 'a noisy self-confidence which is emblematic of his noisy self-confident way of embarking on ambitious schemes'. Some of his 'noisiness' is, no doubt, bravado, but at this stage his self-confidence and his determination

---

[1] Ottokar (*has meanwhile shown the letter to the messengers, pointing with one finger to particular passages*) 'They must go – look, *he* must!...' (*As the Chancellor first begins to speak behind him he listens tensely, without moving. When the Chancellor pronounces the name "Habsburg", Ottokar gives a start; the hand with which he is pointing to the letter begins to shake; he stammers out a few more words:*) 'And he...must go!'

are still quite genuine. It is precisely his self-confidence that leads him to defiance and, ultimately, defeat, to the position where finally he himself is hunted down by Rudolf's troops. Yet still, as in the scene just discussed, he clings to his illusion, he clings – against all the evidence that he is the quarry – to the belief, or at least the pretence, that he is the hunter:

OTTOKAR	Wie heißt der Ort hier?
DIENER	Götzendorf, mein König.
OTTOKAR	Der Bach?
DIENER	Die Sulz.
OTTOKAR	Ich dacht', ich wär' in Stillfried.
DIENER	Wir ritten gestern durch in dunkler Nacht.
	Jetzt liegt der Kaiser drinnen.
OTTOKAR	Nun, Gott walt's!
DIENER	Ihr solltet dort ins Haus gehn, gnäd'ger Herr!
OTTOKAR	Und daß mir niemand angreift, bis ich's sage!
	Ich hab' ihn hergelockt in diese Berge
	Mit vorgespiegelter, verstellter Flucht.
	Dringt er nun vor: die Mitte weicht zurück,
	Die Flügel schließen sich – dann gute Nacht, Herr Kaiser!
	Ich hab' ihn wie die Maus im Loch! Ha, ha!

$$(2573–83)^1$$

The first sign that Ottokar is gradually developing out of this obstinately ingrained conceit is given, in a way characteristic of Grillparzer's theatrical style, not only in words but in symbolic action, when Ottokar kneels by Margarete's coffin (2677/SD), adopting voluntarily at last that symbolical posture of humility which has rankled so long as a posture of humiliation.

But that the Ottokar of the first act and the Ottokar of the last act are one and the same character, the one the product of the other's error, is the point enforced by the construction, the beginning and ending with Margarete; and the truest epitaph for Ottokar is spoken by his chancellor: 'O Herr! du mein verirrter, wackrer Herr!' (2956). Ottokar is *verirrt*, he is tragically enmeshed in his own wrong; but at heart he is *wacker*, he is a valiant and

---

[1] 'What is this place called?' Servant: 'Götzendorf, your Majesty.' 'And the stream?' 'The Sulz.' 'I thought I was in Stillfried?' 'We rode through yesterday at dark of night. Now the Emperor is there.' 'Well, God's will be done!' 'You ought to go into the house over there, my lord.' 'And no-one is to attack until I say! I have enticed him into these mountains by feigning, pretending to retreat. Now when he thrusts forward, our centre will fall back, the flanks will close in – and then good night to the Emperor! I've got him like a mouse trapped in his hole! Ha, Ha!'

upright servant of a 'duty' conceived in pride but conceived nonetheless as a duty. The key to his whole character lies in his final self-analysis (2825ff.):

> Ich hab' nicht gut in deiner Welt gehaust,
> Du großer Gott!...

Here Ottokar has finally reached the point of honest self-knowledge. He perceives that he has stormed destructively over the lands he should have ruled in peace, and he is full of self-reproach and self-accusation:

> Wer war ich, Wurm? daß ich mich unterwand,
> Den Herrn der Welten frevelnd nachzuspielen,
> Durchs Böse suchend einen Weg zum Guten![1]

And now the self-accusation is at the same time a self-defence: he has done wrong, but in a good cause, the cause of the people whom he has always believed himself to be serving; his earlier protestation – 'Für wen hab' ich's getan? Für euch!' (501)[2] – was not hollow. And if when these words were delivered Ottokar seemed arrogant and self-willed, that arrogance was not merely cold and careless, it was what the chancellor calls 'Raschheit' (2493) – a term used also by Rudolf (1862) and by Merenberg (2430). It was, in other words, an unpremeditating pride felt for his nation as well as for himself (cf. 498). He is not the only one of Grillparzer's characters to be both *rasch* and *wacker*, for Garceran too '...ist wacker, obgleich jung und rasch' (*Die Jüdin von Toledo* 238); indeed, *rasch* is the normal word used in Grillparzer's plays to refer indulgently to the impetuosity of youth: Kreon is willing to forgive Jason's actions in Colchis as those of 'ein rascher Knabe' (*Medea* 1347), and Rudolf II speaks half-affectionately of his nephew Leopold as 'ein verzogner Fant, / Hübsch wild und rasch, bei Wein und Spiel und Schmaus' (*Bruderzwist* 512f.).[3] As well as being impetuous, Ottokar is, obviously, ambitious: he longs for political greatness for himself (608–13, 683, 1182), he thinks of his territories as belonging to himself (1296, 1305). But what is equally important is that he does not recognize this ambition in himself, so that in the motivation of his actions pride

---

[1] 'Worm that I am, who was I that I should have presumed sinfully to imitate the Lord of earth and sky, seeking through evil a way to good!'

[2] 'For whom have I done it? For you!'

[3] Garceran 'is gallant, although young and impetuous', Jason 'an impetuous youth', Leopold 'a spoilt coxcomb, wild and impetuous in his wining and gaming and feasting'.

and service are mingled, ambition blends with what he feels to be his sense of duty. Even at the end he wants to protest his real innocence:

> Geblendet war ich, so hab' ich gefehlt!
> Mit Willen hab' ich Unrecht nicht getan!

If this were hypocrisy, if this were protesting too much in the face of conscious guilt, his final admission would be a *volte-face* of character, and it is not that; it is a moment of insight, when he suddenly pierces through his own rationalizations:

> Doch, einmal, ja! – und noch einmal! O Gott,
> Ich hab' mit Willen Unrecht auch getan!   (2863–6)[1]

This is not pretence, nor is it a reversal of character: it is the workings of honest, bitter, self-punishing recollection. When, by contrast, Grillparzer's previous ambitious hero, Jason, takes stock of his life in the second act of *Medea*, he admits that he has forfeited his own self-respect, he admits that he has done wrong; but – lacking Ottokar's moral courage – he insists that it has happened independently of his intention (763–71). It is Ottokar's integrity that also stands out in a comparison with the Shakespearian passage which his accusing self-contradiction echoes, the scene on Bosworth Field in which Richard III is afflicted by 'coward conscience' (*Richard III* v, 3). Richard asks 'Is there a murderer here? No. Yes, I am.' But he is ready to contradict himself again as quickly and eager to acquit himself:

> ...Alas, I rather hate myself
> For hateful deeds committed by myself!
> I am a villain; yet I lie, I am not.

Though he then yields again to the 'thousand several tongues' of conscience, when the time for action approaches he is soon dismissing his 'babbling dreams' and decrying conscience once more as 'but a word that cowards use'. He too lacks the resolute moral courage that gives Ottokar, even in defeat, the stature of a true tragic hero.

If Ottokar's good will has often escaped critics, it is surely partly because he is presented in the framework of so extreme a contrast with the invariable goodness and rightness of his chief antagonist – a contrast that Grillparzer only heightened by such

---

[1] 'I have been dazzled, that is how I have erred! I have not done wrong with intent! – Yet once – I did! And then once more! Oh God, I *have* done wrong, with intent!'

divergencies from his source-material as the association of Ottokar's decline with his repudiation of Margarete and the dissociation of the Emperor from the cutting of the tent-cords. This central contrast tends to focus our attention on the morality of Ottokar's position, as opposed to the subtleties of his motivation; and when the presentation of character is distinctively coloured by so strong a moral emphasis, the artistic danger is that to the uncommitted spectator or reader the dramatic conflict may seem slanted. Thus Silz, commenting on Rudolf's 'ideal character', argues that it is detrimental to the balance of the play because 'our interest and sympathy, contrary to the playwright's intent ..., go with Rudolf' so that 'Rudolf...detracts from the hero's effect all through'. Much must depend here on the emphasis achieved by production and acting; and it is true that there have been productions of the play (Laube's revival in the late 1850s appears to have been a case in point) which have allowed Rudolf's role to seem the dominant one. In fact, Rudolf is too simple a character – pious to the point of self-righteousness – to sustain such prominence, and to accord it to him is to give too much weight to the moralistic element in the play; nevertheless, the standards he represents *are* those by which the central character comes to judge himself in the final shedding of his self-delusion.

The process of emerging from self-delusion into a fuller moral self-awareness is a recurrent pattern in Grillparzer's plays; it characterizes the development of Sappho, Rustan, Alphons and Mathias as well as Ottokar. Clearly the idea of attaining a condition of insight and certainty presupposes a moral order whose rightness – 'the eternal Law' – is unchallengeable: right and wrong are open to 'recognition', and are clear, finally, to the characters themselves. Hence their ability to follow up their catastrophe with elegiac reviews of the course of events and to express their perception of 'the emptiness of all earthly things'. Formally, the result is a striking example of how the influence of Austrian and Spanish dramatic traditions seems to be superimposed on the manner of Shakespearian and classical traditions; but while a moral summary is conventional in the (indigenous) form of *Der Traum ein Leben*, it is unorthodox in tragedy.

Grillparzer's basic conception of tragedy was not unorthodox; he regarded the intention of a tragic action as being to induce in the spectator or reader the classic cathartic reaction of pity and fear:

Das Tragische, das Aristoteles nur etwas steif mit Erweckung von Furcht und Mitleid bezeichnet, liegt darin, daß der Mensch das Nichtige des Irdischen erkennt; die Gefahren sieht, welchen der Beste ausgesetzt ist und oft unterliegt; daß er, für sich selbst fest das Rechte und Wahre hütend, den strauchelnden Mitmenschen bedaure, den fallenden nicht aufhöre zu lieben, wenn er ihn gleich straft, weil jede Störung vernichtet werden muß des ewigen Rechts. Menschenliebe, Duldsamkeit, Selbsterkenntnis, *Reinigung der Leidenschaften durch Mitleid und Furcht* wird eine solche Tragödie bewirken.   (T 639)[1]

For this tragic effect to be achieved, it is essential that the moral emphasis – the absolute condemnation of ambition in Jason and Ottokar, or the emphatic association of love with wrongfulness and guilt in *Des Meeres und der Liebe Wellen* and *Die Jüdin von Toledo* – must not become so dominant as to inhibit our 'pity' and 'love' for the chief characters. In *Des Meeres und der Liebe Wellen*, and also in *Ein treuer Diener seines Herrn*, the virtue of duty is in fact challenged by inclination and emotion that are not selfishly destructive but honest and mature; the balance of the dramatic action is evenly weighted and the implications of the tragic situation open. In *Des Meeres und der Liebe Wellen*, both Hero and the priest are by their own standards in the right; in *Ein treuer Diener* Bancbanus, a figure of unmistakable goodness of intention, is caught between two opposed claims (that of the king, who imposes his task, and that of the rebels who defy him) which are equally wrong. Both these plays move us to experience the full effect of pity and fear for the innocent victims of true tragedy. *Die Jüdin von Toledo*, on the other hand, presents a close parallel to *König Ottokars Glück und Ende*. Just as Ottokar is tragically dominated by ambition (which he rationalizes as belonging to and consistent with his duty), so Alphons is led to disaster because his moral nature is dominated by the passion of love. Like Ottokar, Alphons is a being of noble potential, capable of achieving recognition of his errors. But both figures act wrongly, and are contrasted to antagonists who act in accordance with ideals of duty; and this extreme moral contrast must tend

---

[1] 'The tragic effect, which Aristotle defines somewhat rigidly as the arousing of pity and fear, lies in our recognizing the emptiness of all earthly things, in our seeing the dangers to which the best of men is exposed and often succumbs, and – while ourselves holding fast to right and truth – pitying our stumbling fellow-man and continuing to love him as he falls, though also condemning him, since every offence against the eternal Law must be brought to nought. Such a tragedy will induce love, tolerance, self-knowledge, and a purging of the passions through pity and fear.'

(in varying measure, depending on the production and acting) to dull our perception of the fact that Ottokar and Alphons are each, potentially, 'der Beste' – each a good man, as Aristotle requires tragic characters to be. To this extent the effect of these particular works diverges from what is traditionally understood by the effect of tragedy, in the most exact sense of the term.[1]

Yet both plays are richly effective in other respects. *König Ottokars Glück und Ende* in particular is a many-sided work. It is a study of kingship, just and unjust; it is a work of patriotic imperialism, the national drama of Habsburg Austria; but above all it is a character-study in depth of the tyrant-hero on whom the separate but connected threads of the intricate action centre. We see his fateful injustice and its consequences in his relations with the two queens, with the Merenbergs, and with Rudolf. The depiction of his character is enhanced in depth and subtlety by the variety of separately developing situations in which we are shown his actions and their effects. And it is above all in the subtlety of the characterization, in which the dividing line between rightful and wrongful motivation is blurred by self-deception, so that faithlessness can seem justified and ambition selfless, that the play has outgrown the original formula – the simple action of a morality – 'overweening pride and its downfall', while yet presenting in its complex unity a portrait of the disastrous consequences attendant upon one man's ambition.

Ottokar is the first of a series of great characters – the others include Bancbanus, Hero and Rudolf II – who at their various stages of moral development possess a reality and many-sided life, a life of acute feeling and revealing action, such as in English we know only, perhaps, in Shakespeare, and which is not matched in the drama of the German language. No less subtle, though using very different techniques, is Grillparzer's next study of ambition, the depiction of Rustan in *Der Traum ein Leben*.

---

[1] On the relation of tragic characters to the emotional effect of tragedy, see W. Macneile Dixon, *Tragedy* (London, 1924), and F. L. Lucas, *Tragedy in relation to Aristotle's 'Poetics'* (London, 1927). Lessing's comments on the unsuitability of wholly blameless characters as tragic heroes (*Hamburgische Dramaturgie*, 75. Stück) are pertinent to the role of Rudolf in *König Ottokar*.

Der Traum ein Leben

On the manuscript of *Der Traum ein Leben* that Grillparzer showed to Schreyvogel in 1831, the play was designated 'Spektakelstück' (*Gespr.* 615). This term was normally applied, pejoratively, to the kind of popular drama that depended too largely on extravagant stage effects; and though in atmospheric intensity and psychological subtlety *Der Traum ein Leben* wholly transcends the limitations of the popular theatre, Grillparzer's ironic use of the term testifies to his awareness of the affinities between his dream-play and the popular *Zauberstücke* of the period. The general outline of the action of the play was drawn in the first place from a short *conte* by Voltaire, *Le blanc et le noir* (1764); but the form in which the material is treated is closely related to the popular *Besserungsstücke* of the 1820s, of which Raimund's plays are the best-known examples. In these pieces the supernatural figures and magicians traditional in the *Zauberstück* use their powers to bring the central comic character to the kind of ethical regeneration that was familiar on the popular stage as the traditional ending of more realistic satirical comedy. A typical example is *Der Berggeist, oder Die drei Wünsche*, by J. A. Gleich (1819). The central figure of this piece (a role that was played by Raimund) has the symbolical name Herr von Mißmuth. Mißmuth is cured of his discontent by the beneficent mountain spirit, who grants him three wishes and fulfils them by magic; in other plays of the same type, a character's hopes and wishes are sometimes realized in a dream or dreams induced by a spirit or a magician. Mißmuth wishes for himself attractiveness to all women, enormous wealth, and phenomenal longevity; and the fulfilment of these desires brings him only trouble and unhappiness. Realizing his folly, he repents and wishes he were as he was before; and the Berggeist restores him to his former state, and spells out the moral – the common moral of the genre – that happiness lies in the virtue of modest and unquestioning acceptance of one's given lot.

The first act of *Der Traum ein Leben*, like the first act of a *Besserungsstück*, reveals the fault from which the central character suffers and will be cured by his dream. Rustan's fault is a restless ambition, a longing to escape from the constrictions of the unadventurous pastoral life he leads. This weakness is not, however, merely stated in the black and white terms of the popular stage: the exposition brings his problematic position to life by sketching

114

in his background and his relations with other characters. Thus
what we are shown at the very start, as Mirza waits for him to return
from hunting, is the depth of her affection for him. She admits
her anxiety about him (60f.), and though she tries to pretend to
her uncle, Massud, that she has complete confidence in his valour
(158ff.) her worry shows through in her anxious questioning of
Massud (178) and her relief and reproaches when Rustan finally
returns (411ff.). Moreover, when Massud tells Rustan openly of
Mirza's love for him, Rustan lays his hand on his heart and
indicates that he returns her feelings (571f.). That his ambition
has gained the upper hand over this affection, and that the peace
of Massud's home has been disrupted, is blamed by Mirza un-
equivocally on the influence of the slave Zanga (121–37) who, as
the apostle of action (379f.), scorns the peacefulness of Rustan's
present life (262f.) and dismisses as soft-heartedness his feelings
for his relatives, which blunt his resolve to set out in pursuit of
heroic adventure (344); and indeed we see the skill with which
Zanga spurs Rustan's ambition, dwelling on the fact that the
King of Samarkand has risen to his position from lowly rustic
origins like Rustan's own (292–5), and twice suggesting that
Rustan himself is a born hero and leader (296–8, 408–10). We learn
too that Rustan has been goaded by the mockery of Osmin, who
has a position in the Samarkand court and who has derided
Rustan as a mere yokel, unfit to serve the king as a warrior and
so win the hand of his daughter (519–22); Rustan bitterly acknowledges his lack of achievement so far and resolves to prove Osmin
wrong (526–30). We are also shown that Rustan's resolve has
a depth that both makes it distinctive and lends it its dangerous
strength. His restlessness is not the negative kind of general
discontent from which a stereotyped figure such as Mißmuth
suffers. He experiences a genuine need for self-expression:

> Ich muß fort, ich muß hinaus,
> Muß die Flammen, die hier toben,
> Strömen in den freien Äther... (535–7)[1]

Like Ottokar, moreover, he sees the goal of his ambition as a
noble ideal (275) – though not, even speciously, as a selfless one.

All this expository material, which gives depth to the depiction
of Rustan's ambitions, is presented in language which itself
enriches the whole atmosphere of the setting. The trochaic metre,

[1] 'I must away, I must escape, must let the flames that rage within me
blaze into the open sky...'

which Grillparzer chose for its liveliness (*Gespr.* 1100), does not easily conform to the natural rhythms of the German language (or of English): the consequent rearrangements of word order, omissions of unstressed syllables and endings, and the use of elliptical constructions give the verse a markedly stylized quality, and this is heightened by the shortness of the octosyllabic line, which the constant stress on the first syllable emphasizes. The metre has an unfamiliar ring, which makes it suitable for conveying the exotic flavour of mysteriously distant settings. Goethe uses it frequently in *Der west-östliche Divan*; Heine uses it in oriental ballads such as 'Der Asra'; in English we know it best as the metre of *The Song of Hiawatha*. And in the exotic atmosphere established by this rhythm Grillparzer stresses the oppressive peacefulness of Rustan's pastoral life by recurrent use of the word *still* (51, 57, 467, 533). But the first act is full of contrast and conflict too; and the language enhances the changes in mood through striking variations of pace. There is, for example, a great contrast between the leisured tone of factual narrative, as when Zanga reports on Osmin's behaviour at midday (485ff.), and his breathless description of the joys and excitement of battle, which finally breaks into free verse (362ff.), or the crisp exchanges of Rustan and Massud, where stichomythia gives expression to the tension between their opposed viewpoints (550ff.). Such contrasts in pace may be enhanced by the use of rhyme. That within Zanga's description of battle most of the lines 352–406 are rhymed emphasizes – and especially in the shorter lines of the later part of the speech (381–406) – the accelerated speed of the stirring narrative of rapid action. In complete contrast to this stand the words of the dervish's song (628–35), where the regular rhyming of alternate lines serves to emphasize, as it were to beat out, the importance of the moral teaching. It is this song that lulls Rustan to sleep; and in its insistence on the vanity of worldly ambition, it presents one aspect of the moral lesson that he learns from his dream.

The actual coming of sleep is shown by the use of allegorical figures, genii representing real life and dream life. As Rustan's dream begins, the torch of the genie of real life (who is drably clad in accordance with Rustan's view of his present existence) ignites that of the brightly clad genie of dream life and is then extinguished, the scene of the dream-action becoming visible behind transparent gauze curtains. This technique of representing the transition from waking to dreaming is strongly reminiscent of the popular stage, where simple allegorical effects were common. In *motivating* the dream, however, Grillparzer has done away with the spirits or magicians of the popular stage convention; he has transformed what were traditionally the effects of magic into the effects of a credible psychological process. Although the dervish's song in a sense anticipates the outcome of his dream, the dream is a natural one, not the product of a magic spell. We are well prepared for it; not only do we know of his confrontation with Osmin, we also learn from Massud (92f.) that at night he habitually dreams of battles, and his lively imagination is revealed in his use of colourful imagery (e.g. 243ff.). So now his dreaming imagination peoples a nightmare world with figures who have the form of characters familiar to him in his everyday life: Gülnare resembles Mirza, her father the king resembles Mirza's father Massud, Kaleb resembles the dervish, the mysterious 'man on the rock' is strikingly like Osmin. Even the demonically exaggerated tempter of the dream, who when he throws off his cloak appears to Rustan to have black wings (a detail drawn from the black servant Ebène in *Le blanc et le noir*) and snakes for hair (2515–18), appears in the form of the slave Zanga because the standards he represents are associated in Rustan's mind with Zanga's tempting tales and eager encouragement. The real-life Zanga has actively goaded Rustan into rebellion and adventure; but despite his real domination of Rustan's thoughts, he has on the whole remained aware of his position as a servant (408f.) – indeed, in his humorous inquiry to the audience about the disadvantages of love (438ff.) and later in his timorousness (2554f.) he is akin to the comic servants of popular stage tradition. But the dream-Zanga develops a manner of Mephistophelean disrespect, which shows at once in the derisive tone in which he dismisses the rejoicing enthusiasm of Rustan's first dream-monologue: 'Herr, und jetzt genug geschwärmt' (653).[1] As a projection of Rustan's own unconscious mind, what he represents is Rustan's own wrongful ambition, the selfish *will* which rejects the humble background of Mirza's true love:

> RUSTAN Arme Mirza!
> ZANGA   Ja, weil arm,
>   Hindert sie ein reiches Wollen.   (724f.)[2]

---

[1] 'Now sir, that's enough enthusing!'
[2] 'Poor Mirza!' 'Yes, and since she's poor she inhibits richness of will-power.'

As the incorporation of ambition he eggs Rustan on with his Mephistophelean blend of assistance and derision. That in the last moments of the dream Rustan finally sees him as having the appearance of a devil means that Rustan has at last perceived the true evil nature of the motivating force behind his own would-be self-advancement. For the series of adventures in Rustan's dream, ending in disaster and defeat, present the potential outcome of his own submission to the ambition which he has entertained and which his slave has encouraged. In *Melusina* the hero is warned that what dreams reveal must already be contained in the mind (246–9); so too Rustan has later to be reminded by Massud that his dream is only a development of his own motives and desires (2697–2701).

This dream sequence is presented with convincing authenticity, except for the fact that twice, contrary to the usual pattern of dreams, Rustan (the dreaming character) is briefly absent from the scene (1010–19, 1165–1200). In the final scene of the first act, his ambition overriding all moral considerations, he has spoken of the dervish with complete disrespect (627) and dismissed his song as nonsense (636); he has thoughts only for adventure, and as he falls asleep, he cries out: 'König! Zanga! Waffen! Waffen!' (638),[1] his mind racing with the ideas discussed in the previous scenes. The liveliness of his expectation contributes to the reality his dream has for him; and as the dream gets under way in the second act, it reflects his excitement. Filled with the invigorating feeling of liberty (639f.), the dream-Rustan compares his position to that of a bird venturing on flight and bursting at last into rejoicing song:

> Nicht mehr in dem Qualm der Hütte,
> Eingeengt durch Wort und Sorge,
> Durch Gebote, durch Verbote;
> Frei, mein eigner Herr und König!
> Wie der Vogel aus dem Neste,
> Nun zum erstenmal versuchend
> Die noch ungeprüften Flügel.
> Schaudernd steht er ob dem Abgrund,
> Der ihn angähnt. Wagt er's? Soll er?
> Er versucht's, er schlägt die Schwingen –
> Und es trägt ihn, und es hebt ihn.
> Weich schwimmt er in lauen Lüften,
> Steigt empor, erhebt die Stimme,

---

[1] 'The King! Zanga! To arms, to arms!'

AMBITION

Hört sich selbst mit eignen Ohren
Und ist nun erst, nun geboren.
Also fühl' ich mich im Raume...   (657–72)[1]

Hardly are his reflections over and Zanga's plans for deception
agreed than the adventures begin: the falsehood of Rustan's
position is demonstrated in stage action. In a sequence that
clearly draws on the opening scene of *Die Zauberflöte* (though
perhaps also on a play by Lope de Vega, *Los donayres de Matico*),
the King of Samarkand appears, pursued by a serpent (a traditional symbol of danger on the popular stage) and crying out for
help (769f.). Confronted, after his own failure to rescue the king,
by the true victor over the serpent, the mysterious figure of the
courtier on the rock, Rustan finds himself mocked, laughed at as
an incompetent shot (780f., 1083f.), as Osmin has laughed at him
(221, 517) and shown up his real lack of achievement – humiliating
details which Rustan's subconscious mind has retained and now
develops in his dream. Already the dream is turning to nightmare;
and again the language helps to build up the effect. The fluency
and unfamiliarity of the trochaic verses are particularly suited
to the swift action and strange atmosphere of the dream-world,
and contribute to the sense of eeriness that pervades it. One
device which is partly dictated by the demands of the short line
and which is used to great effect in the dream sequence is frequent
repetition, both of exclamations at moments of climax and of
names: thus Zanga's name is often repeated (e.g. 985, 1143), and
Rustan's especially rings out, as Stefan Hock has observed, in a
whole range of urgent tones, in triumph, in warning and in threat.

But from the first the nightmare effects are directly linked to
the moral issues. Thus when Zanga first advances the tempting
argument that the whole apparition of the courtier on the rock
was imaginary (807), what he is trying to have Rustan deny is
the uncomfortable truth – which the Osmin-like courtier embodies
– that Rustan is not the supreme warrior he aspires to be. Rustan
has to learn that active achievement will always escape him: he
was born to be a countryman, not a hero; born, as Osmin has

---

[1] 'No longer in that stifling cottage, hemmed in by words and cares, by
instructions, prohibitions – free, my own master and king! Like a bird
emerging from his nest, trying out for the first time his still unproven
wings: trembling he stands above a yawning abyss – dare he? Will he?
He tries, beats his wings – and is borne up and lifted! Sweetly he soars in
the mild breezes, climbs, and sings, hears himself with his own ears – and
now for the first time is truly alive! Just like that I feel in the free air...'

pointed out (522), to wield a plough, and not a sword or a sceptre. Even at the height of his dream, when he is given credit for the victory of the king's army, he himself has played no very glorious part in the battle, as Zanga recounts:

> Da sieht Rustan jenen Khan,
> Der so überstolz getan,
> Sprengt auf ihn, – zwar, wie mich dünkt,
> Ist das just der Punkt, der hinkt –
> Rustan stürzt... (1183–7)[1]

Similarly, in his very first adventure, by yielding to Zanga's advice and the lure both of the king's evident wealth and of the prospect of Gülnare's hand, and denying the claim of the banished courtier to his reward for saving the king when he himself has failed to do so, Rustan is denying the truth about himself. The courtier, then, symbolizes the truth; he represents a part of Rustan's conscience, and his toneless voice (SD/1079) and deathly pallor (SD/1061), by suggesting a certain incorporeality, point to the monitory and symbolic function of his role. Himself banished from the court for his love of Gülnare (who represents the wrongful goal of Rustan's selfish ambition) and dressed in humdrum brown, he stands for the (unexciting) standards of right and responsibility which Rustan is repressing. In arguing with him, Rustan is arguing against the dictates of conscience, and knows that his opponent is in the right (1124). It is when Rustan finds himself powerless in the fight with the brown-cloaked courtier – a fight which is based on his real-life quarrel with Osmin (cf. 478f.) – that his dream turns wholly to nightmare (1136ff.); and when he is spurred on by Zanga ('Braucht den Dolch! / Braucht den Dolch!') to stab his adversary, what we are shown is how at this stage Rustan is led on by the temptations of ambition to suppress – to silence and to 'kill' within himself – the claims of responsibility and right. The bridge from which the courtier plunges to his death is seen by Rustan as a threshold to his fortune:

> Unmensch! Halt! Nicht von der Stelle!
> Diese Brücke wölbet sich
> Als des Glücks, der Hoheit Schwelle,
> Sei es dir, sei es für mich. (1130–3)[2]

---

[1] 'Rustan saw the Khan who has been so overweening, charged at him – yet surely this is in fact the snag: Rustan fell...'

[2] 'Monster, stop! Do not move! The arc of this bridge forms the threshold to fame and fortune, whether for you, whether for me!'

The rhyming, especially the rhyme on the word *Schwelle*, puts extra emphasis on the symbolic function of the bridge; the mortal confrontation there ('Ich oder du!', 1136) represents the fact that for a Rustan fortune *can* be attained only by overthrowing the order of truth. Just as the real-life slave, spurring his master on to try his fortune in adventure, has sought to alienate his affections from his uncle and cousin (340f.), so it is significant that in the dream-adventures the first step Zanga insists on Rustan's taking is to conceal the truth about his origins (714ff.). To this first temptation Rustan falls, and later in the same act he himself orders Zanga to throw away the knapsack which might give them both away (1022–4) – a gesture which symbolizes his determined rejection of his home background. So almost from the outset he commits himself to a deception that he never rectifies; in denying his home he is denying the truth about himself – significantly, it is with a reminder of Rustan's home and family on his lips that the courtier dies (1146–8).

The potential for good in the Rustan of real life – which lends conviction to his final repentance – is suggested by the way his dream counterpart capitulates to dishonesty only after a struggle. When the king first addresses Zanga and him, that he kneels at some distance is a sign of his indecision (842/sd). It is Zanga who first actually lies (845ff.), and Rustan tries to resist being manoeuvred into deception (859f.); the lure of the prize overcomes his scruples, but he remains conscious of the falsity of his claim (cf. 912). Later, when he is committed to his denial of the courtier's claims, he twice covers up his weakness with transparent rationalizations (1030–5, 1044–6); but when his rival confronts him again, he again acknowledges the strict demands of right before once more quietening and denying them (1124–9). Moreover, no sooner is the murder committed than Rustan regrets it (1145, 1154).

As the second act ends, however, he once more sets aside his scruples for the sake of prospective reward (1163f.), and in the third act his continued refusal to face up to the wrongful nature of his adventure – in other words, his continued silencing of the voice of truth – is given visible representation in the voiceless presence of Kaleb, the murdered man's dumb father, whose role as the voice of truth is later made explicit (1725). This old man, on whom the dreaming Rustan bestows the name of an otherwise unrelated real-life huntsman mentioned in Act I (62), corresponds to the real-life dervish in standing for the standards of right now voiceless in Rustan. It is the dervish he resembles – to the alarm of Zanga (1372) and subsequently to the horror of Rustan (2710). Kaleb only regains his voice in the last act; meanwhile his silent presence suggests that the truth is in fact nagging away at the mind of the dreaming Rustan, repressed but not conquered. This shows, too, in the way that during Acts II and III the king's questions both about Rustan's origins and about the killing of the serpent become gradually more insistent, until finally Rustan confirms that he was standing 'am Felsen' (1300). Even here his phrasing avoids the issue, for *am Felsen* is South German and Austrian for *auf dem Felsen*, and while Rustan indeed stood *am Felsen* in the standard German sense, 'beside the rock', it was the courtier who stood *am Felsen* in the sense of '*on* the rock': Rustan's words take advantage of Viennese idiom to seek refuge in ambiguity, and it is left to Zanga to make the lie explicit in the following line.

Moreover, as his luck begins to change, Rustan turns against Zanga, admitting his error in following Zanga's advice (1424ff.). At this stage, as the accusation in 1435–7 makes clear, it is still only of his falsehood, not of his whole goal of fame and glory, that he repents; he has not yet perceived the essential interconnexion of end and means. Reflecting on the events at the beginning of the dream, he again distorts them by rationalization:

> Nicht daß ich den Mann erschlug!
> Hab' ich ihm den Tod gegeben,
> War's verteidigend mein Leben,
> War's, weil jener Brücke Pfad,
> Schmal und gleitend wohl genug,
> Einen nur von beiden trug.
> War's, weil er mit gift'gem Hohn
> Lauernd seine Tat versteckte
> Und die Hand erst nach dem Lohn,
> Dem bereits gegebnen, streckte.
> War es, weil – muß ich's denn sagen –
> Er und ich zwei Häupter tragen,
> Und dies Land nur eine Kron'. (1475–87)[1]

What, however, his image of the two heads seeking one crown truly symbolizes is the irreconcilability of conscience and falsehood.

---

[1] 'Not that I murdered him! If I killed him, it was in defence of my life, it was because the path across that bridge, narrow and slippery as it was, could carry only one of us. It was because with venomous scorn he lay in wait, concealed his deed, and only reached out for the reward once it was already given. It was because – if I must say it – we were two heads seeking this country's single crown.'

And now, indeed, his dissatisfaction comes briefly to a head; he expresses his regret that he has ever allowed himself to be led on to the false and giddy path of ambitious adventuring and acknowledges that he has sacrificed his integrity for a prize that was both superficial and insubstantial; the fame he once saw in the distance now seems an illusion:

> O, hätt' ich, o hätt' ich nimmer
> Dich verlassen, heimisch Dach,
> Und den Taumelpfad betreten,
> Dem sich Sorgen winden nach;
> Hätt' ich nie des Äußern Schimmer
> Mit des Innern Wert bezahlt
> Und das Gaukelbild der Hoffnung
> Fern auf Nebelgrund gemalt!
> Wär' ich heimisch dort geblieben,
> Wo ein Richter noch das Herz,
> Wo kein Trachten ohne Lieben,
> Kein Versagen ohne Schmerz! (1497–1508)[1]

Once again, the moral reflections are made to stand out by a change of pace; the rhyming of every other line gives a more measured regularity to the verse, in keeping with the pensive regret it expresses. In a popular comic *Besserungsstück* this regret at having ever left home would be the end of the dream, and Rustan would return, reconciled, to Massud's cottage. But in *Der Traum ein Leben* Rustan's self-deception is more deeply engrained, and his 'cure' is more gradual (and hence more convincing). At this stage regret is again conquered by the unscrupulousness of greed; he dismisses conscience, as represented in his mind by the shade of the murdered courtier, as a mere delusion (1516), which must not be allowed to obscure his vision of the prize that lies within his grasp (1513f.).

When, later in this act, Rustan is confronted with a new temptation, it is again given concrete form in that it is introduced by the witch-like old woman who follows Zanga into Rustan's presence (1529/SD). This grotesque figure appears only to Rustan (1608), she is only a symbol; she enters the dream as a crystallization of his feelings in the desperate situation into which his

---

[1] 'If only I had never left my home to tread that giddy path where cares come winding after – if only I had never paid for surface glitter with my heart's integrity and had never painted a mirage of hope in the misty distance! If only I had stayed at home, where the heart is still the judge, where there are no aspirations without love and no failings without sorrow!'

ambition has led him. Among those feelings are certainly both fear and (still) unprincipled ambition: from them grows Rustan's will to commit calculated murder, which creates its own evil opportunity. This will, then, is incorporated in the old woman, who *tempts* Rustan[1] by presenting him with the means of committing his second murder, the killing of the king. He tries to withstand the temptation (1592f.); but if the old woman seems repellent to him, she also fascinates him, and in the end, after a single brief moment of horrified hesitation (1716), he allows the king to drink the poisoned wine. Rustan himself realizes the fateful nature of this temptation; and in his lines

> Sieh den Becher halb geleert,
> Ganz erfüllt schon mein Geschick　　　　(1825f.)[2]

the balanced antithesis between *geleert* and *erfüllt* brings out the essential interconnexion between the goblet and the fate he is fashioning for himself. For while the murder of the king brings him to the climax of his attainment so far, all his success is still based on evil and untruth; this, indeed, is precisely what the king has tried to make clear in his dying accusation of Rustan, which Gülnare misinterprets as a commendation (1900ff.). By the time of the episode with the old woman, the dreaming Rustan has already become aware, in his unconscious mind (which is projecting the whole dream), of the guilt of that potential self which the dream is revealing to him; this awareness shows in the old woman's criticism of his lack of moral independence (1577f.), then later the subconscious sense of guilt is given expression in the warnings and accusations of the letters (1774ff.), followed by the vision of Mirza and the dervish and the vision of the courtier; and finally the dream-Rustan is surrounded by the inescapable evidence of his evil deeds – he is shown (sᴅ/1844) attempting to hide the instrument of his second murder (the goblet) under the symbol of his first (the cloak). The increasing sense of guilt which characterizes this whole third act coincides with and develops from the discovery on the river-bank of the body of the courtier in brown – a discovery which, in symbolical terms, signals the re-emergence from its suppression of Rustan's acknowledgment

---

[1] Cf. ll. 1579–81: 'Ei, ich zwinge niemand, Sohn! / Bietend reich' ich meine Gaben,/ Wer sie nimmt, der mag sie haben.' ('Oh, I do not force anyone, my son! I hold out my gifts as offerings: he who takes them is welcome to them.')

[2] 'See the goblet now half-empty, and my fate wholly fulfilled!'

of his evil deed (the 'killing' of conscience). Finally in the fourth act Kaleb regains his voice to make explicit his accusation of Rustan as the king's murderer: the truth makes itself heard again, with a certainty that can no longer be held silent.

Still finding himself – to his desperate disappointment (SD/1939) – not king, but merely consort, Rustan has to build up his power further, and we are given a miniature type-sketch of the psychology of tyranny, as he removes his enemies from power (1949ff.) and like Ottokar (*König Ottokar* 1018f.) grows suspicious of all around him (2009ff.). Yet all the time he is only hastening his fall; and the growing sharpness of his clashes with Gülnare is enhanced by skilful use of repetition and rhyme. Thus when Karkhan is pleading with Gülnare to grant Kaleb an open trial, and Rustan demurs, she begins to insist:

GÜLNARE	Billig scheint, was sie begehren.
RUSTAN	Wär' es so, würd' ich's gewähren.
GÜLNARE	Und wenn ich's nun selber wünsche?
RUSTAN	Wünsche! Wünsche!
GÜLNARE	Und befehle.

(2053–6)[1]

After the rhymed riposte-effect, Rustan's repetition of Gülnare's 'wünsche' allows full expression of the cruel scorn in his attitude to her, showing how in his now monstrous self-seeking his pursuit of his own desires runs roughshod over the desires or wishes of all others. A more extended example of the use of rhyme to set off contrasted speeches against each other can be seen in a later exchange (2153–70) in which the same rhyme occurs nine times in eighteen lines, so that Gülnare's speech has the effect of an ironic echo of Rustan's.

As the nightmare intensifies, the moment of Rustan's waking draws near. This waking is a gradual process, and is most convincingly suggested. After the dream-Rustan has tried to explain away as nothing but a feverish fantasy (2291) the whole episode of Kaleb's accusation, there follows a moment of half-waking, an escape from the high drama of the new situation, as he hears through his sleep a clock striking in Massud's cottage (SD/2294). The clock draws him one stage further out of his now shallow sleep; and from now on actions and activities in the real world begin to impinge on the dream. First Rustan – his thoughts still

---

[1] 'What they ask seems just and fair.' 'Were it so, then I should grant it.' 'And if I wish it now myself?' 'Wish it, wish it!' 'And command it!'

centring on the real world to which he has briefly half-returned – mistakes Gülnare's servant for Mirza (2301); later the fire that the dream-Zanga ignites (2351–3) can be seen as a dream-version of the light with which Mirza is moving about in the next room in Massud's cottage (SD/2356). So also her movement seems to be reflected in the dream as the noise of pursuit (2499f.); and finally the torch of decayed wood and fungus which Rustan sees in Zanga's hand (2521–3) corresponds to the lamp carried by the real-life slave, who is moving around preparing the horses (SD/2542). And when Rustan at last awakes, it is still in confusion, his cry that he is lost ('verloren!', 2538) echoing the triumphant claim of the devilish Zanga at the end of the dream-sequence; still not fully awake, he sees in the real-life Zanga the devil of his nightmare (2544ff.), takes fright (2548) at the flashing light of Zanga's lamp, which reminds him of the flash of the sword with which the dream-Zanga has threatened him (2457f.), assumes he is being held captive in the room in which he finds himself (2562), and, when Massud and Mirza first appear, assumes they too must be their dream-equivalents (2568).

This gradualness carries much more verisimilitude than the summary magic awakenings of the *Besserungsstück* routine. Another subtle variation of the convention is the brief scene in which, as the dream-Rustan sets out on his flight from Gülnare and her forces, Mirza hears him in real life, crying out in his dream (2356), and we return briefly to Massud's cottage. This scene serves to remind the audience that the disasters overtaking the dream-Rustan *are* only a dream, and at the same time points forward to the morning and the end of the nightmare after its final episode, in which the dream-hero, exposed, pursued and surrounded, throws himself off the very bridge that was to be his threshold to fortune. The sensation of falling is a characteristic ending to nightmare; and for this reason it is important that when *Der Traum ein Leben* is produced on the stage Rustan's fall (SD/2538) should be *seen* by the audience, and not left to their imagination. But while the fall is a nightmarish effect, it is also Rustan's return – which his nightmare has impelled – to the upright standards and morality of Massud and his kind. When finally he is fully awake, he realizes that the dream has given him the self-knowledge he has hitherto lacked: his mention of dawning light ('Was verworren war, wird helle', 2636) has a figurative sense as well as describing the sunrise. He has been vouchsafed a mirror to his potential self;

like the hero of any *Besserungsstück* he is cured of his discontent; and as in a *Besserungsstück* the moral teaching of the play is spelt out, affirming quiet domestic contentment and denouncing the dangerous emptiness of 'greatness' and 'fame' (2650–6). But it is important to remember that this ethical thesis is no more than a cliché of the *Besserungsstück* genre, which was taken for granted as a standard conclusion: the interest lay not in the final, often very summary, formulation of the moral, but in its illustration in the whole theatrical action of the play. This is as true of *Der Traum ein Leben* as of its equivalents on the popular stage, and the action has all the plasticity that Grillparzer consistently valued in stage works. It is characteristic that even Rustan's moral decision to renounce his ambition is not expressed in preceptive form only, but is also symbolized visually in the freeing of Zanga.

In the mood of reconciliation in which the play ends Zanga and the dervish together play the melody of the dervish's song (2707/SD), as a recapitulation of the theme of the vanity of ambition. Massud listens intently (2720f.) to the words of the song, which now take on a special sense:

> ...Schatten Worte, Wünsche, Taten;
> Die Gedanken nur sind wahr.
> Und die Liebe, die du fühlest,
> Und das Gute, das du tust...   (630–3)[1]

Rustan's *Worte, Wünsche, Taten*, his self-conceit and his desires for glory and heroism, are set behind him; in his moral conversion (*das Gute*) through the insights vouchsafed him by his dream (*die Gedanken*), he has reaffirmed (2683ff.) his true love for Mirza (*die Liebe, die du fühlest*), of which his pursuit of Gülnare was a denial. Recognizing this, Massud unites the lovers. If this ending corresponds to that of innumerable popular comedies, it also corresponds to the ending of Grillparzer's own tragedy *Sappho*: 'Und nur das *Gleiche* fügt sich leicht und wohl!' (1742).[2] Similarly the whole moral tendency which the work shares with the *Besserungsstück* genre corresponds to a recurrent element in Grillparzer's work. As early as 1812 he planned to write a continuation to the first part of Goethe's *Faust*, in which Faust was to find happiness in 'self-limitation and peace of mind' (T 1083) – the

---

[1] 'Words, desires and deeds are shadows, thoughts alone are true – and the love you feel, and the good you do...'
[2] 'And only like and like go well together!'

very opposite, in fact, of the qualities which are generally associated with the 'Faustian' spirit. In the plays of Grillparzer's maturity, it is by self-seeking or ambition that his characters from Jason and Ottokar onwards sow the seeds of their own tragedy. By its revelations Rustan's corrective dream affords him a second chance, tragically absent in the reality of the world of Jason or of Ottokar, to realize the true happiness that lies in 'self-limitation and peace of mind' or, as Rustan formulates it, 'quiet inner peace and a heart free of guilt' (2651f.). The process of self-discovery and moral self-liberation entails the renunciation of unrealistic desires; so it does for Sappho also, and the idea is expressed again in *Libussa* in two lines which are very reminiscent of the late Goethe and which might almost serve as a motto for *Der Traum ein Leben*:

> Wer seine Schranken kennt, der ist der Freie,
> Wer frei sich wähnt, ist seines Wahnes Knecht.
>
> (*Libussa* 1185f.)[1]

Erich Hock points out, in his essay on *Der Traum ein Leben*, that a similar insight is expressed in the closing lines of the poem 'Entsagung' (G 87):

> Und in dem Abschied, vom Besitz genommen,
> Erhältst du dir das einzig deine: Dich![2]

What Rustan's dream has shown is that the power and kingship for which he has longed are properly beyond his grasp, so that he has had to jeopardize his entire *moral* self, he has had to resort to deception and wrong-doing in order to achieve them. It is in this sense that the dream-Zanga's final exclamations – 'Mir! Verloren!' (2537) – seem most like a Mephistophelean claim for Rustan's lost soul, a parallel to the 'Her zu mir!'[3] at the end of the First Part of Goethe's *Faust*. For in the course of his dream Rustan's commitment to wrong has become deeper and deeper. His capitulation to Zanga's threat of betrayal (2241–54)

---

[1] 'The free man is the man who knows his limits; he who deludes himself that he is free is the slave of his delusion.' Cf. especially Goethe's maxim 'Niemand ist mehr Sklave, als der sich für frei hält, ohne es zu sein' ('No-one is more of a slave than he who believes he is free without being free in fact': *Die Wahlverwandtschaften*, II, ch. 5). Clearly, however, the self-limitation learnt by Rustan is much less positive than, for example, the purposive self-direction learnt by Faust in Goethe's Part Two. Cf. also p. 235, below.

[2] 'And in parting from what you possess you preserve what alone is yours: yourself!'

[3] Zanga: 'To me! You are lost!' – Mephistopheles: 'Hither to me!'

has exemplified the difficulty of renouncing evil once one has committed oneself to it, and his repeated appeals to Zanga for help in the final scenes of the dream further reveal the dependence of the would-be hero on his supposed servant. In this respect the implications of the piece are akin to those of *Das Goldene Vlies* – the first work Grillparzer embarked on after abandoning *Der Traum ein Leben* as a fragment in 1817–18 – in that the evil into which the dream-Rustan's ambition lures him develops into a whole chain of wrong-doing from which he is powerless to extricate himself.

Yet despite all the similarities of subject and implication between *Der Traum ein Leben* and others of Grillparzer's works, the final moral formula expounded by Rustan should in no way be seen as an expression of a general ideal or as a statement of a commended philosophy of life:

> Eines nur ist Glück hienieden,
> Eins: des Innern stiller Frieden
> Und die schuldbefreite Brust!
> Und die Größe ist gefährlich,
> Und der Ruhm ein leeres Spiel. (2650–4)[1]

The positive argument here amounts to little more than the truism that contentment lies in contentment; and in fact, precisely because this speech is built up of platitudes, it does not come properly to grips with the moral issues inherent in the play. There are higher things than contentment, and as Grillparzer's other plays confirm he does not condemn action, adventure, or eminence in themselves in any absolute sense; nor is their opposite, the quiet happiness of passive resignation, in any sense his consistent ideal.

The reason why Rustan's would-be-heroic adventuring leads him to disaster in his dream, and why he subsequently resigns himself to the plough – to which Osmin has alluded as a symbol of humdrum domesticity and weakness (522), but which also stands, as in *König Ottokar* (1921), for the life of peace – is to be sought in his own character. His dream reveals his unsuitability for the heroic stature to which he has aspired; his will – as Zanga scornfully observes towards the end of the dream (2438f.) – has outstripped his capability. Ambition is not disastrous, on the

---

[1] 'On this earth happiness lies in one thing, one alone: quiet inner peace and a heart free of guilt! And greatness is dangerous, and fame is hollow and vain.'

other hand, in such a character as Osmin, who has gained access to the court, can boast of the impression he has made there (496ff.), and can with justice scorn Rustan as an inferior. Again, for the King of Samarkand fame and worldly greatness are neither a hollow illusion, 'ein leeres Spiel', nor dangerous, either in the sense of morally corrupting or even in the literal sense (for it is only the dream-king who is killed, a piece of wishful imagination born of Rustan's ambition); yet he has risen to eminence from origins as humble as Rustan's are, and there is no suggestion that this rise was wrongful, as Rustan's is. So too in *König Ottokars Glück und Ende*, whereas it appears wrongful for Ottokar – who like Rustan lacks the self-knowledge that would teach him his innate limitations – to aspire to the imperial throne, Rudolf I, whose skill as a warrior Ottokar himself readily concedes (438f.), has the true stature of the rightful ruler, and is able to battle successfully in defence of the order of the empire. It is only those who are not born with the capacity for great achievement who must console themselves with the conception, propounded in the dervish's song, of desires and deeds as alike insubstantial, and the resignation of all 'greatness' in the name of inner contentment, 'des Innern stiller Frieden'. Such resignation is not an ideal achievement, but rather a defence: it derives from the perception of the tragedy that can ensue when the whole personality is dominated and so misled by a single motive – in Rustan's case by ambition, in other plays by love and even by excessive loyalty.

In Grillparzer's work, as the examples of *König Ottokars Glück und Ende* and *Sappho* both illustrate, positive achievement is characteristically presented in association with the idea of a supreme duty. If his works suggest a spiritual ideal, it is that state which he saw as a prerequisite for the fulfilment of his own poetic duty and which he called '*Sammlung*'. This condition, which we shall consider again in the next chapter (see pp. 159–61), is not one of negative resignation, but of inspired, creative concentration – what in the late essay 'Zur Literargeschichte' he described as 'that inner concentration...without which either a deed or a work is impossible'. This significant passage is highly characteristic in that it defines achievement not only in literary terms ('a work') but also in practical terms ('a deed'). So too in a letter of 1850 the idea of inspiration is related not only to artistic achievement but also to the valour of the warrior (B 709); so too in *Libussa* Primislaus uses the verb 'sich sammeln' in connexion with practical ('tatenschwanger') ideas (2106–9); and so too in *Des Meeres und der Liebe Wellen*, when the priest commends 'Sammlung' to Hero, he couples with the ideal of artistic achievement the ideal of the greatness of heroic action:

> Des Helden Tat, des Sängers heilig Lied,
> Des Sehers Schaun, der Gottheit Spur und Walten,
> Die Sammlung hat's getan und hat's erkannt... (951–3)[1]

[1] 'The hero's deed, the bard's sacred song, the seer's vision, the imprint and the sway of divinity – composure has wrought it or perceived it...'

4

DUTY AND LOVE

Ein treuer Diener seines Herrn

In *Ein treuer Diener seines Herrn* Grillparzer treats not selfish ambition but its diametrical opposite, selfless duty. Such duty appears, as also in the love-tragedies *Des Meeres und der Liebe Wellen* and *Die Jüdin von Toledo*, in uncompromising colours; in all three plays, to varying degrees, it is presented as harshly demanding. It was again from the medieval field that Grillparzer drew the subject of *Ein treuer Diener seines Herrn*: he chose a more or less legendary story ('eine Sage': SB 204) from the history of twelfth-century Hungary, 'the story of the Palatine Bancbanus, whose wife is dishonoured by Otto von Meran, the brother of his queen' (T 1428).

The hero of the play, Bancbanus, is designated co-regent and charged (against his will) with the duty of government and of preservation of peace and order while the king is away leading his army in battle. His young wife Erny, subjected to the advances of the libertine Otto von Meran, stabs herself. His brother Simon leads an armed insurrection, and in the fighting the queen herself is accidentally killed, so that the king returns to find his land in civil war and himself a widower like his 'faithful servant'.

The moral centre in this action is provided by the political unit, the state, which Bancban is chosen by the king not merely to serve but, as co-regent, to represent in the king's absence; but as in *König Ottokars Glück und Ende* the motivation is developed at both the political and the personal level. Throughout the action of the play Bancban and Erny stand opposed to the queen (with whom Bancban is co-regent) and her brother both in the initial political situation and in their private life. This twofold dramatic contrast springs from fundamental differences in temperament, character, and interests. Bancban is by nature cautious and peace-loving. In the very first scene, when Otto and his men sing their mocking song, he will have no action taken, for his, he says, is a home of peace (20); so later, defending peace in the state, he

132

refuses to disrupt that peace too by taking revenge on Otto. Otto by contrast is bold, ingenious, and aggressive; even the king (who has no respect for him) admits these positive qualities when the queen lists them. But he also defines what Otto lacks: moral sense.

> GERTRUDE Sagt selbst, ist nicht mein Bruder tapfer, klug,
> Entschlossen und verschwiegen, listig, kühn,
> Kein Zaudrer?
> KÖNIG   Ja.
> GERTRUDE   Was fehlt ihm also?
> KÖNIG   Sitte!
> (277–9)[1]

With the temperamental contrast in characters, then, there goes a wider contrast in attitudes and standards. Bancban and Erny have a high moral sense of duty; the queen and Otto are essentially selfish.

Professor Wells's classification of this play under 'plays of action', which he defines as 'plays with exciting action but where the characters are uninteresting', is far from satisfactory, for the portrayal of all four principal characters is executed with no less subtlety of insight than Grillparzer had displayed in *König Ottokar*. The queen is perhaps the most straightforward of them – not in the sense of everyday normality, but in the sense of clear consistency in the play. Her conduct is governed largely by her love of her brother. She herself admits that even in youth she regretted her sex and identified herself with all Otto's activities (322–6), and that still she sees him as 'the male Gertrude' (331). The lack of normal femininity that this confession suggests is borne out in Act IV, when she puts Otto's safety above that of the infant prince, her son (1602, 1620–5).[2] On her Otto is able to rely: on her intercession with the king in the first act, on her connivance in his seduction of Erny, on her defending him after Erny's death by claiming responsibility for it herself, and on her help in ensuring his escape. She never seems conscious that she is abetting immorality; it is as though, blind to her brother's faults, she is aiding the idealized Otto she praises to the king.

---

[1] 'Tell me yourself, is not my brother brave, shrewd, resolute and discreet, cunning, bold, unwavering?' 'Yes.' 'What does he lack, then?' 'Morals!'

[2] In the first manuscript version of the text she was also to address Otto as' ...mir teurer als mein Leben,/ Als Kind und Gatte...' ('dearer to me than my life, than child or husband': variant to l. 1101). Doubtless Grillparzer felt able to cut this because the point was made more dramatically – in action as well as words – elsewhere in the play.

But that Otto can rely on her so completely is one of the reasons why he himself lacks any independence of 'moral sense'.

He is a libertine, solipsistically arrogant in his libertinism. He tells Erny that his 'badness' has been fed partly by his rank, partly by his success with women (1219–25). In January 1828 Grillparzer wrote a letter to the actress Julie Löwe (B 336), analysing the character of Otto for her brother, who was to play the role in the Burgtheater production. In this letter he describes the basis of Otto's whole character as coming from these two sources – his rank and his success with women – but sums it up as 'Übermut'. It is indeed his overweening self-confidence, which has seemingly been bolstered all his life by his sister, that drives him into his involvement with Erny. He has at first little real regard for her: 'Was kümmert mich sein Weib mit ihrem blonden Haar?' he asks (160).[1] In the same speech he gives us the clues to the answer to his question. He says, for instance, that he is only pursuing her to annoy Bancbanus, who has observed his interest with a calm that has seemed to Otto tantamount to mockery (184f.); one of his principal motives, then, is vanity. He also remembers Erny's eyes, 'so grave and stern, and yet so fiery too' (165); and he remembers how she has looked long at him and then averted 'her icy gaze' (177). He has no real feeling for her, it is true, nor has she for him; but he senses that she finds him not unattractive, and he himself is attracted to her, especially by the fiery spirit in her eyes. Yet towards him those eyes remain icy, and her attractiveness is enhanced by her inaccessibility. This is a sound piece of psychology, and one that Grillparzer had explored before: Jason too admits that his interest was spurred by Medea's resistance to the attraction she feels towards him (*Medea* 465). In Otto's case, as in Jason's, it underlines the element of vanity in the motivation. Indeed, Otto now directs to his selfish ends all the positive qualities which the queen has praised in him; unhampered (as the king recognized) by moral sense, he applies his boldness, his aggressiveness, his ingenuity, to the pursuit of Erny. His aims are purely sensual: the only excuse he can offer to her for importuning her is the 'sweet allure' of being close to her (1157). But her attraction is increased still more, as Otto himself realizes (1089), by her expression of contempt at the end of Act II (898). All his interest, indeed all his self-interest, is concentrated on the pursuit; his

[1] 'What is that fair-haired wife of his to me?'

134

self-regard is at stake; he becomes absorbed in a role not merely
of libertine, but of irresistible, conquering libertine. He is so
caught up in this role that even when in Act III he indulges
in a blatant piece of seducer's flattery, telling Erny how much
her influence and affection could improve his ways (1243ff.), he is,
as Grillparzer says in the letter, 'only half a hypocrite'. He is a
creature of sensual instinct, but the fulfilling of that sensual
instinct has taken possession of him, so that he becomes totally
involved even in his gambits. His egoistic desires replace any
objective reality, they become all that exists for him. This is
precisely what Grillparzer envisaged in a note written during his
work on the play: 'This libertine, who uses his passions as a
plaything, yet in whom they are at the same time so violent that
they themselves become real for him and in the third act make
him physically ill' (T 1428). This illusive 'reality' is challenged by
Erny's rebuff – Otto twice repeats the word *verachten* in confused,
uncomprehending disbelief (899f.) – and it is shattered when Erny
commits suicide as the only way to escape from his advances.
In Act IV he suffers from what Grillparzer called 'temporary
insanity' (B 336): a condition of breakdown and confusion, a
heightened form of the restless perplexity and emptiness that
Ottokar experiences in Act IV of Grillparzer's previous tragedy,
the end of the grand illusion of *Übermut*. For the first time Otto
is brought face to face with dimensions of real experience outside
his pursuit of libidinous pleasure; and it is finally through the
further confrontation with reality in the deteriorating circumstances of the civil war that he recovers sufficiently for Bancban
to be able to entrust the infant prince Bela to his care. The
confrontation with reality is made sharper by the death of the
queen, on whose support Otto can no longer weakly fall back:
her death removes, indeed, a fundamental obstacle to his development of mature moral independence.

The nature of Otto's role in relation to Erny is expressed
mimically in the second act, where he creeps up behind her and
touches her arms with the very tips of his fingers (SD/669). The
tactile gesture is suggestive both of the sensual nature of his
approach and, in its tentativeness, of how far Otto still is at that
stage from winning Erny over or even, indeed, making any really
effective approach to her. But that she has felt his power of
attraction is a point on which Grillparzer laid much emphasis in
his notes on the play (e.g. T 1619), and rightly so. It was of Bancban

that he later remarked that there is no virtue in preserving a loyalty that is not threatened (*Gespr.* 1182), but the point holds equally good for Erny. If she were to seem wholly cold in feeling, as Otto once suggests she is (181–3), it would detract both from her humanity and from the impressiveness of her moral decision. In fact early in the first act the way she dwells wonderingly on Otto's bold serenade reveals her to be innocently interested. And with immense care – no fewer than twenty-four variant versions exist – Grillparzer revised and rewrote the scene in which Otto reminds her of the signs by which she has betrayed to him her conscious or unconscious interest: the long look with which she has measured him (713), her having returned (even if, perhaps, involuntarily) the pressure of his hand during a dance (724f.), her having stolen a lock of his hair (731ff.). He engineers Erny into promising him a tryst. Alone, she remembers that at first she had taken Otto for a better character, 'devout and good' (774); but she cannot appease her sense of guilt, and it betrays itself immediately when Bancban returns. Instinctively she conceals from him the piece of paper, the still blank piece of paper, on which she was about to write to Otto. The paper, as Bancban says, 'can only be read by God' (803); and Erny's action brings out with superb clarity how heavily the intention (as opposed to the deed alone) can weigh in moral judgments of human behaviour – a point which is otherwise not made explicit. Moreover, though the paper was still blank, Erny's reaction on Bancban's entrance – grabbing the paper, trembling, backing away from him, throwing the paper away – is such that he cannot but suspect her guilt. In his subsequent questioning of her – another scene that Grillparzer completed only after many careful revisions – he perceives that even the horror of Otto which she now expresses reveals, by its exaggerated violence, that her conscience is not wholly clear (883): in the same way we also have suspected this earlier from the vehement cry of 'That is a lie!' ('Ihr lügt!', 722) with which she has denied Otto's charge that she returned the pressure of his hand. Having formed his suspicions, Bancban refrains from accusation or condemnation; and his reasons are very revealing:

> Was gibt ein Recht mir, also dich zu quälen?
> Weil du's versprachst? Ei, was verspricht der Mensch!...
>
> (825f.)[1]

---

[1] 'What gives me the right to torment you like that? That you made a promise? Ah, the promises man makes!...'

The characteristically sardonic tone of this passage shows that Bancban realizes the irony of his argument – the guardian of morality questioning a moral commitment. It also reveals a deeper personal embarrassment, which he does not spell out: he himself bears the burden of a solemn commitment, and the difficulties it imposes make it impossible for him to moralize on the superiority of duty over personal inclinations. He has, however, earlier dismissed as selfish Erny's plea that he should lay down his office for her sake:

ERNY   Gib sie zurück denn, dieses Amtes Bürde,
               Sei Ernys Gatte bloß, mit ihr beglückt!
BANCBANUS Was fällt dir ein? Weil du nicht gern beim Fest,
               Soll ich von Hof...?   (632–5)[1]

In his rhetorical question the emphatic antithesis of the personal pronouns, the first (*du*) introducing the idea of personal demands, the second (*ich*) that of the denial of such demands in deference to a duty of public service, embodies the essence of Bancban's standpoint. What he has rejected is a temptation generated in the first instance by Otto and corresponding to Otto's selfish standards. And now again, with persuasive gentleness, Bancban puts morally right conduct ('Rechttun', 830) first. Under his influence – mature, ironical – Erny's whole character develops. From the naivety and youth of the opening scenes she has become by Act III a changed, more mature character; and it is in this development – which shows linguistically in the way she begins to catch Bancban's habit of slightly sententious aphorism (e.g. 1155f., 1242) – that she gains the resolution and courage which make her suicide possible.

Her death is quick: we see her attempting to escape from Otto but finding herself locked in, we see Otto ordering his men to seize her and Erny fleeing back across the stage, then Otto's men approaching her, finally seizing her – all this stage action bringing out how she is truly hemmed in, physically cornered (to the last Otto's approach is a physical one), and how the dagger can seem to her the sole means of escape. For when, showing the strength of her courage, she threatens to use the dagger on her attackers, Otto drives them on, reminding them that they are in armour; and it is plain that she is facing insuperable odds. She stabs

---

[1] 'Lay down the burden of this office – be simply Erny's husband, happy with her!' 'What are you thinking of? Just because *you* do not like the ball, I am to leave the court...?'

herself: she can only gasp of her sorrow and her pain before she sinks to the ground, dead. It is a climax without rhetoric, without the pathos of dying monologues. Early in 1828 Grillparzer inveighed in his diary against the German taste for theatrical rhetoric (T 1626); this crucial scene is evidence of his rejection of that taste and his adoption of naturalness as his standard in determined emulation of Lope.

In this dramatic climax Erny's suicide in defence of honour and duty bears out in the context of the love-action Bancban's standards in the main political action of the piece; indeed it is his standards that determine her sacrifice, in that her fatal defence of the moral order is made necessary by his refusal to protect her as she asks him to in Act II (811) – or rather, as he sees it, his inability to do so because of his appointed commitment to the defence of the political order. And even now he still remains passive, opposing his brother Simon and Erny's brother Peter in their campaign of vengeance. His reasons are twofold: at the personal level, on the basis of his questioning of Erny, he has to assume that she may not have been guiltless; at the political level, though his refusal to abet the revolt fails to diminish the upheaval of the political order, his position nevertheless commits him to a policy of peace until the return of the king who alone can judge the queen's part in Erny's death. In his steadfastness he may easily appear cold-hearted. Of course, to make Bancban's feelings and attitude explicit Grillparzer might have given him a monologue or a scene with a confidant, showing him wrestling with his conscience, weighing his strict duty against the dictates of his heart – for in his heart he knows as well as Simon and Peter that the queen's self-accusation, and her concomitant accusation of Erny, must be untrue. But such a scene would be impossible, for three reasons. First, the artificiality of a monologue would be quite out of keeping with the style of the play. Secondly, Bancban could not confide his doubts to some friend or courtier because his character is not of the confiding kind. And thirdly – the most fundamental point – he can have no real doubt: he is committed to his role in the state, his decision has been taken for him. He is no more free to avenge Erny than he was earlier free to protect her. But this must not conceal the reality of his feeling, the depth of his grief. When he learns of Erny's death he speaks only a single line: 'O Erny, o mein Kind, mein gutes, frommes Kind!' (1329).[1] That

---

[1] 'Oh Erny, oh my child, my good and godly child!'

here, as in the scene of Erny's suicide, Grillparzer eschews operati-
cally grandiloquent effusions does not betoken coldness in Bancban:
rather, indeed, it presents a grief so real, so piercing, that it lies
too deep for words. For the rest of the third act, while Simon and
Peter shout for revenge, and the queen protects Otto, he remains
silently kneeling by Erny's corpse. By the final act, however, he
gives full vent to his fierce anger at Otto. Three times in his first
speech he calls him a 'bloody murderer' (1691, 1700, 1718), once
'man of blood' (1721), and once more 'murderer' (1730). In the
same speech he also addresses Otto five times as 'Duke'; while his
personal feelings towards Otto are unmistakable, he remains
conscious both of Otto's rank and of their joint responsibility
towards Bela. Maintaining to the last that rational self-control
which contrasts with Otto's habitual self-indulgence, he is still
not free to follow the dictates of personal feelings. The steadfastness
and the tragedy of Bancban's position are together what is
represented at the end of the preceding act when, amid the
battle, he settles himself on the ground beside the infant prince,
his cloak covering them both: a tableau of unfreedom and
committed service amid the manifest collapse of all his policy.

The last act, after its angry beginning, becomes elegiac – a
sharp and striking contrast with the vivid theatrical activity of
the fourth act, a final quietening and dimming of mood. In it
the surviving *personae* gather, one by one, and the framework
of the action is completed, with the king's judgment of Bancban's
execution of the task set him. And the king is not the sole judge:
his verdict is qualified by Bancban himself, who in the end stops
the king from offering him the reward of new eminence (2078ff.).
For him the task has ended in tragedy. He has conquered the
egoism condemned in *Das Goldene Vlies* and *König Ottokars Glück
und Ende*; he has maintained a calm moral humanity and nobility
of feeling which, though they hide behind his pedantic manner,
cannot be summarized in terms of anything so negative as merely
obedient dutifulness; he has shown a real heroism – what Grillparzer
later called 'the heroism of devotion to duty, which is as much
a kind of heroism as any other' (SB 204). But the task which he
has executed as best he could ('wie's eben möglich war', 1971) was
beyond him; the burden imposed upon him in the name of duty
has destroyed his life, and he has no use for the eminence that
goes with such a burden. From his own viewpoint it is a massive
understatement when he says to the king:

Der Glanz, womit du deinen Diener schmücktest,
Er hat als unheilvoll sich mir bewährt.   (2085f.)[1]

And his final withdrawal is a tacit acknowledgment that he is by
his very character and nature unfitted for such eminence. Unlike
Rustan, he has not had to learn his limitations through experience;
rather experience has tragically confirmed the verity of his own
original insight: 'Herr, ich tauge nicht dafür!' (411).[2]

In his critical introduction to Goethe, Ronald Gray comments
on how Goethe's early lyrics are full of a 'feeling of being glad
to be Goethe', and how several of his heroes seem to be presented
uncritically, as it were from their own point of view.[3] At no stage
of Grillparzer's life, by contrast, does his work express a feeling
of being glad to be Grillparzer; and his approach to his heroes is
correspondingly more critical. We have already seen how hard
critics have found it to do justice to Ottokar's own conception
of his motives, which seems outweighed by his strident, arrogant
manner; and with Bancban again, whose good will is far greater,
this and his moral feeling are concealed beneath a far from pre-
possessing manner. There is much of Grillparzer in him – and it
is precisely because this is the case that in his characterization
there is a strong satirical vein. Thus Bancban is not only shown
as being much older than Erny, but as being enfeebled by his age.
In the second act, for example, the courtiers laugh at him as an
old dupe; while they do so, Erny is dancing – and Bancban by
contrast is so exhausted by his official duties that he has to have
a chair brought for him to sit down on (551). Again, in the fourth
act, he lacks the physical power to restrain Simon and his followers:
and this bias in the presentation of his character can cast an
unjust light on his moral attitudes, in that it can make his passivity
seem related to his feebleness, when in fact it is sustained with
the strength of conscientious decision. Nor is he merely old: he is
also old-fashioned. When the curtain first goes up we see him in
his home explicitly surrounded by old-fashioned things, 'old-world,
unpretentious pieces'. In his private life he is a conservative,
'opposed to innovations' (64); and in a pedantic quibble (52–4) he
displays a rather grumpy insistence on simple frankness reminiscent
of Grillparzer's father – whom Grillparzer feared in the late 1820s

---

[1] 'The dazzling honour you bestowed upon your servant has brought calamity
upon me.'
[2] 'Sire, I am not fit for the task!'
[3] R. D. Gray, *Goethe. A Critical Introduction* (Cambridge, 1967), pp. 32 and 61.

he was himself increasingly growing to resemble (T 1655). He tends
to a certain sententiousness, which is revealed in his fondness for
proverb-like turns of phrase: homely sayings (81), expressions of
patriotic feeling (25f.), or statements of moral principles (83f.).[1]
He has too much of the mentality of a born official, the fussiness
which cares about a sharp penpoint (534) and the unswerving
loyalty to duty which enables him to resist so easily the temptation
to become 'simply Erny's husband'. Grillparzer once referred to
him as 'somewhat limited' (SB 204). His unsuitedness for his
position is manifest even in the doggedness with which he sticks
to his course despite its futility; and it is just this that is brought
out in the stage action at the beginning of the fourth act when,
rebuking and even making to arrest Simon, he cannot make
himself heard through the angry cries of Simon's followers, fresh
from Erny's funeral (SD/1440), and finally collapses in the arms
of his own servants in the very act of protesting his opposition
to Simon's men (1442/SD). 'Laßt ihn,' says Simon contemptuously,
'und überlaßt ihn seiner Schwäche!' (1443).[2] That in these various
ways the characterization of Bancban contains a sharp comic
element doubtless detracted from the effect of *Ein treuer Diener*
for an age which expected its tragedies to be thoroughgoing
tragedies, unremittingly solemn and elevated; and criticisms of
the work along such lines lingered into the present century.[3] But
the fact that Bancban is not an idealized hero but has eminently
human weaknesses not only enhances the perseverance of his
heroism – for a virtue is not vitiated by the fact that its possessor
has faults in other respects – but also adds to the characterization
a whole dimension of realistic psychological truth which was altogether lacking in, for example, Grillparzer's previous portrayal of
dutifulness in Rudolf I.

This very modern realism in the characterization is in keeping
with the realistic tendencies in the language of the play. To talk
of realism in relation to a play in verse is a contradiction in terms;
but within the pentameter lines of this piece the rhythms of the
language are unmistakably the natural rhythms of speech. When
Otto, for example, is talking of Erny's eyes and remembering her
long look, a natural quality is preserved in his short phrases,

---

[1] Cf. also a number of general observations about various questions of human
behaviour: 87f., 879f., 883, 891.
[2] 'Come away, and leave him to his feebleness!'
[3] E.g. Reich, p. 151.

parenthetic additions, interrupted thought, and in his word order, which is fashioned not for elegance but for emphasis:

> Schön ist sie wohl! – Wenn dieses blaue Auge,
> So ernst und schroff, und doch so feurig auch,
> Wenn je – Ich sage dir, ich hab's gesehn,
> Wie sie im vollen Kreis des ganzen Hofes
> Die teilnahmslosen Augen, blau und groß,
> Nach mir hin richtete, minutenlang,
> In starrer, wohlgefälliger Betrachtung. (164–70)[1]

The same tendency is still more marked in the language of Bancban. When he counsels Erny to ignore Otto's attentions, and promises her respite before long, his phrasing is utterly natural; the sentences would need no revision if they were to be written out as prose speech:

> Ertrag und übersieh ihn; kurze Frist,
> So send' ich dich hinaus auf eins der Schlösser,
> Dann bist du seiner quitt... (887–9)[2]

Yet within this natural style Grillparzer can achieve telling effects. Simon, for example, badgering Bancban to abandon what he regards as his cowardly passivity, shouts out – as though Bancban had not grasped it – that Erny is dead:

> Getötet hat man sie, hat sie ermordet. (1388)[3]

This is a pure pentameter rhythm, but even in the emphatic inversion of the first phrase it is also the rhythm of natural speech. And the inversion not only lends the line balance: it creates an antithesis between the first participle and the second, so that the line builds up to the force of the final cry of brutal murder. The lack of artifice and exaggeration in these examples is in keeping with the lack of artifice and exaggerated effusion which we have already noted in Erny's suicide and Bancban's reaction to it. *Ein treuer Diener seines Herrn* is, indeed, a play in which the words, being so little stylized, lean more than ever on the mimic element of stage action. This is especially true in the climaxes, where the words of everyday are (realistically) inadequate to the

---

[1] 'Beautiful she certainly is! If those blue eyes, so grave and stern, and yet so fiery too, if ever – I tell you, I have seen her, with the whole court around her, directing her big blue eyes at me for minutes on end, indifferently, in a fixed, complacent gaze.'

[2] 'Put up with him and take no notice: just a little while, and then I'll send you away to one of the castles, and then you'll be rid of him...'

[3] 'They have killed her, murdered her.'

drama of the extraordinary. A last example to set beside Erny's
death and Bancban's grief is the killing of the queen. Pursued, she
considers for a moment standing and fighting like the man she
would like to be, and takes up the cloak and sword left behind by
'the male Gertrude', her brother:

> Ergreif' ich dieses Schwert, den Mantel hier
> (*sie rafft beides vom Boden auf*)
> Und kämpf' als Mann um meine süße Beute?   (1642f.)[1]

Then she acknowledges that she is too weak (1644) and she
throws down again Otto's cloak and sword (1646/SD) – a mimic
enactment of her rejection of her momentary plan. She flees, and
Simon and Peter rush on stage in pursuit. Seeing the cloak, they
think and act with a fateful overhaste that is matched in the rapid
economy of the language:

> (*Sie wirft Schwert und Mantel wieder hin und eilt fliehend in den Gang.
> In demselben Augenblicke treten die Grafen Simon und Peter vom Hinter-
> grunde her auf; erst später hinter ihnen Gewaffnete mit Fackeln*)
> SIMON Der Herzog war's! Dort liegt sein Schwert und Mantel.
>   Wirf deinen Dolch!
> PETER (*wirft seinen Dolch in der Richtung des Ganges; ein gedämpfter
> Schrei wird gehört.*)   (1647f.)[2]

Only in such haste is the mistake credible: and only such unadorned
language, and reliance on stage action to make its own effect, can
capture that haste in dramatic representation.

While critical opinions have long differed widely about this
play – partly as a result of misconceptions of its political implications, which will be discussed in chapter 6 (pp. 223–7) – numerous
critics have appreciated its greatness and have dwelt especially
on the vitality of its language, on its memorable act-endings, and
on its formal balance. The last act, the act of judgment, summary
and decision, is a superb conclusion, an act of sustained drama.
There are four great climaxes, one after the other: the return of
the king, the entry of Bancban, the return of Otto with Bela, and
Simon's cross-examination of Otto. Finally the tension is resolved
in the sadness and the ironies of Bancban's closing speech, in

---

[1] 'Shall I seize this sword and this cloak (*she snatches them both up from the
ground*) and, as a man, fight for these sweet spoils?'
[2] (*She throws the sword and cloak down again and escapes quickly into the
passage. At the same moment Count Simon and Count Peter enter from the
rear; armed men with torches follow, but only later.*) 'That was the Duke!
There are his sword and cloak! Throw your dagger!' (*Peter throws his dagger
towards the passage. A muffled scream is heard.*)

which he reviews his tragedy, announces his withdrawal, wanting only like an aged Romeo to set up his everlasting rest by Erny's side:

> Bei meines Weibes Leiche still zu harren,
> Bis zwei der Leichen liegen in der Gruft (2094f.)[1]

and with sardonic clarity counts the cost of having allowed himself to be exploited by the king's dependence and of having been too unquestioningly what the king counted on him to be (382), 'ein treuer Diener seines Herrn' (2122). The idea of loyalty does not sum up his whole character, but it does sum up the whole basis of his tragedy. He is faithful both in private life and in public service, and the obligations of his public faithfulness, which to him seem paramount, tragically frustrate the obligations of his faithfulness to Erny (who by normal human standards has every bit as much right to his attention), so that at the last the private faithfulness can only be expressed in a solitary watch by her grave.

Grillparzer's interest was attracted by this subject, though not for the first time, in 1825, while he was searching for a possible subject for a piece for the coronation of Empress Karoline Auguste as Queen of Hungary. His principal source was a recent history of Hungary by I. A. Fessler, but in keeping with his customary practice he treated his historical material freely. Lessing before him had recognized that verisimilitude (*innere Wahrscheinlichkeit*) is a more important criterion in historical drama than strict factual accuracy (*die historische Wahrheit*);[2] and Schiller had insisted in *Über das Pathetische* that the aesthetic effect of characterization is based not on historical but on poetic truth. So too Grillparzer perceived that a drama does not pretend to be history: it is a play, and it stands and falls by its liveliness, not by its accuracy, which in any case cannot be gauged. In his autobiography (in the section on *König Ottokar*) he illustrates his point with reference to Shakespeare's histories and to *Wallenstein*, 'Schiller's masterpiece' which, he says, even if records were now discovered establishing Wallenstein's total guilt or total innocence, would not cease to be what it is and will continue to be, independently of historical truth, for all time; and he concludes: 'The historian

---

[1] 'Quietly to wait beside the body of my wife, until two corpses lie in the grave.'
[2] *Hamburgische Dramaturgie*, 19. Stück.

knows little, but the poet must know everything' (SB 167). The facts of the historian make up only a thin thread of data about events and consequences; the dramatist has to make of those facts the whole living world that must appear a true world: a world of imaginative truth which is built on a foundation of historical fact, but which is given its verisimilitude not by objective accuracy but by subjective selection and elaboration.

Nevertheless, several factors have led critics, including Sauer, to believe that *Ein treuer Diener seines Herrn* was written in a spirit of far more objective detachment than Grillparzer's other works of the same period: the occasional nature of Grillparzer's choice of the story of Bancban; the lack of lyrical sections or monologues such as are found in, for example, *Des Meeres und der Liebe Wellen*; and Grillparzer's own later assertion that the work satisfied 'no inner need' in him (SB 204). This reminiscence is, however, misleading. A clearer indication of his feelings about the play at the time he wrote it is contained in a diary-note of late 1827, in which he recorded Schreyvogel's first discouraging reaction to it and admitted that he now agreed with Schreyvogel's strictures, but added: 'But if the play now fails to please me, it was once otherwise: when I wrote it...' (T 1620). So, characteristically, Grillparzer's discontent with the play was stimulated by adverse criticism. Indeed, in a letter written probably shortly after the diary-note he even dismissed the play as uninspired ('[ein] Machwerk', B 332); but it is again characteristic that after the successful première his reservations were only riders to a sense of satisfaction (T 1623), and his enthusiasm for it while he was writing it strongly suggests that he felt it to be composed under the compulsion of inspiration. This inspiration was not of the kind that bore lyricism, but was rather touched with sardonic bitterness and fed by the experiences of the year 1826, his love for Marie and final full knowledge of her liaison with Daffinger. His renunciation of her, and of the delights of love, in his allegiance to art seemed both right and also a bitter self-denial; and the ambivalence of his attitude to what he saw as his own duty informs his portrayal of Bancban's self-sacrificial devotion (overriding all inner qualms) to a patriotic duty. The tragic outcome, and especially the heavy personal price that Bancban pays for his devotion to duty, correspond to and reflect Grillparzer's questioning of the worth of his own achievement in the service of his 'duty' by comparison with what he sacrificed for it. At the time when he began work on the manuscript in March 1826, his self-doubts in his relations with Marie were reflected in the striking insistence in the opening scenes on the disparity in age between Bancban and Erny: it is brought out both in Otto's serenade and then, less blatantly, in Erny's first scene with Bancban, who six times in under fifty lines (64–110) addresses her as 'child'. When Grillparzer resumed work on the manuscript in October 1826, developing the treatment of Otto's pursuit of Erny, it was very shortly after Marie had borne Daffinger's child; and though, feeling that the finished play treated his own immediate situation with all too bitter clarity, Grillparzer delayed over nine months after completing and revising his text before he finally submitted it to the Burgtheater for production, when he did so it was as Marie's marriage to Daffinger was approaching and it was with a sense of vengeful exposure of 'baseness' (G 192).

These considerations raise wide questions about the relation between personal experience and creative writing. Grillparzer himself explores this problematic and often painful relation in the cycle of poems that he entitled *Tristia ex Ponto*, the composition of which coincides in part with his work on *Ein treuer Diener seines Herrn*.

Tristia ex Ponto

The *Tristia ex Ponto* (G 84, i–xvii) are the only group of lyric poems that Grillparzer published in the form of a cycle. Whereas a large proportion of his poems are essentially occasional pieces, his work on the *Tristia* extended over a decade: it is generally recognized that they form the peak of his lyrical production, and they include some of the few poems by him which are occasionally anthologized ('Der Fischer', 'Sorgenvoll').

The cycle is a sustained treatment of his problems as a dramatic poet. The Ovidian title under which it appeared in 1835 has a metaphorical sense, signifying the poet's feeling of spiritual exile, of exclusion from the realm of poetic inspiration: his 'Pontus' is a spiritual wasteland, in which inspiration seems dead. To Grillparzer, the power of inspiration was an essential basis for creative poetic work: a poem of 1831 ('Weihgesang', G 206) describes it as a bridge to the divine and the source of every eternally enduring achievement. Throughout his years as a dramatist he longed to feel its presence, and was dispirited when this recognizable inspirational state was absent, even at times when he was producing some of his finest work: in 1829, for example, when the manuscript of *Der Traum ein Leben* was well advanced, he worried because he missed the kind of burning inspiration that should fire the whole process of conception and execution 'with the most positive compulsion' (T 1698). When, on the other hand, he knew his work to have been written in a true sense of inspiration, as was the case with *Sappho*, the presence of this power served as his self-defence against what he judged to be unimaginative – because uninspired – criticism:

Was begeistert ich schrieb, das willst du mir nüchtern bekritteln;
Ist dir, nüchterner Mann! denn die Begeisterung fremd?   (G 397, iv)[1]

When the *Tristia* were begun, on Grillparzer's return from Germany in 1826, he was planning a cycle of five poems only, expressing his despondency and sense of artistic frustration at that time. Following the long-drawn-out difficulties over the censorship of *König Ottokar*, his work on further dramatic projects (*Ein treuer Diener, Des Meeres und der Liebe Wellen, Libussa*) had been sporadic and unsatisfactory. His relations with Kathi had become tense and increasingly acrimonious, and those with Marie had been soured by her involvement with Daffinger. The poem 'Vision' had caused an uproar of misunderstanding, and the *Ludlamshöhle* club had been disbanded. Grillparzer had left for Germany in late August in understandable depression about his personal affairs and his literary future. The journey had added to his tribulations the sense of inadequacy provoked by his meetings with Goethe; and though in fact he was shortly to begin the first full manuscripts of both *Ein treuer Diener* and *Des Meeres und der Liebe Wellen*, he still felt a lack of confidence and of driving inspiration. This, then, is the mood reflected in the first *Tristia*. The poem 'Böse Stunde' begins with a lament at the absence of inspiration, and the search for it leads to an attempt to define what is missing. The answer given in the concluding stanza (which, together with the previous nine lines, was written after the rest of these early *Tristia*) is that the creative impetus must be prompted by experience. The poet resolves to plunge into the activity of 'life'; by this is meant the same as in *Sappho*, contact and emotional involvement with other people:

Drum auf ins Leben, mutbewährt!
Gestrebt, geliebt, gehaßt!

---

[1] 'Prosily you cavil at what I wrote when inspired? Prosy critic! Is inspiration unknown to you, then?'

GRILLPARZER

Ist dir der Stoff erst, der sie nährt,
Fällt Glut vom Himmel auf den Herd
Und lodert ohne Rast.[1]

When it was written, this stanza formed a provisional answer to
the mood of loneliness with which the following poems are imbued;
placed *before* them, however, it seems outweighed, negated by
them. 'Polarszene' reads, indeed, like an immediate reply, denying
any capacity for lively activity: it describes the desolate wilderness
of icy winter, and compares it to the poet's inner self, in which
inspiration is lacking and all feeling dead. Nothing stirs but
fleeting thoughts, which vanish at once:

Nur schimmernde Ideen,
Im Kalten angefacht,
Erheben sich, entstehen,
Und schwinden in die Nacht.   (13–16)[2]

And such thoughts are not the stuff of poetry, but explicitly
'cold', products of what a year later Grillparzer called his 'cold
intellectuality' (T 1615). The mood that this poem recaptures is
that of the early months of 1826, the unsatisfactory winter of
slow and sporadic progress on his various projects. But on winter
follows spring: 'Frühlings Kommen', a much gayer poem, likens
the coming of spring to the entrance of a king into his castle (an
unusual metaphor, based on the image of the lost 'house' of
inspiration in 'Böse Stunde', 6), and expresses the hope – the
hope that Grillparzer himself had felt in the spring of 1826 and
which with a sense of metaphorical springtime he now nurtured
again later in the year – that the new season will bring with it
new poetic works. But 'Der Fischer' then returns to the problem
of the artist's relation to his material. The poet describes himself
as an angler, sitting quietly watching the fish in the water of
a river or lake and reflecting that if he casts his line they will
swim away and he will return empty-handed; he might be more
successful if he were to disturb and so cloud the water, but then
he would no longer be able to watch the fish. As the angler loses
sight of the fish when he sets about trying seriously to catch them,
so the poet may confuse his vision of his subject. The solution

[1] 'Out into life, then, strong with courage! Striving, loving, hating! When
once you have the material to support it, fire will fall from heaven on your
hearth and will blaze without ceasing.'
[2] 'Only glimmering ideas, kindled in the cold air, arise, take light, and
vanish into the night.'

advanced in the final stanza of 'Böse Stunde' will in fact be no solution at all if it can be implemented only at the cost of endangering the poet's detachment.

To these *Tristia* of 1826 Grillparzer added in the following year a draft version of the poem 'Reiselust' (T 1583). In this poem his weeks in Germany are compared with his earlier journey to Italy: whereas the first journey vouchsafed an escape from deep personal unhappiness (lines 17–20), the one to Germany has left him in despondency, even the meetings with the god-like Goethe having discouraged him by bringing home to him the gulf between them. 'Reiselust' was incorporated in the *Tristia* in the autumn of 1827, together with a small group of new poems: 'Verwandlungen', 'Sorgenvoll', 'Freundeswort' and probably 'Die Porträtmalerin' (though Backmann's dating ascribes it to the year 1829); and also a poem later omitted from the cycle, 'Der Halbmond glänzet am Himmel' (G 193), in which Grillparzer accuses himself of having only half-devoted himself to the Muses, and of having as a result been vouchsafed by them only a half-reward, an inspiration now already withdrawn. The 'joys of life' which he reproaches himself with having tasted to his cost are affairs of the heart. This was the time when he had just learnt of Marie's impending marriage to Daffinger; his disillusion with her, and his decision to break off their relations, found expression in two poems composed independently of the *Tristia* and not at this stage intended for inclusion in the cycle: 'Verwünschung' and 'Trennung'. All the new *Tristia* also deal more or less directly with this crisis and its effects on Grillparzer's work. In 'Die Porträtmalerin' the idea of portraits demanding to come to life is contrasted with the painter who has infused true life into his portraits only at the cost of the soul of the original – i.e. Marie, Daffinger's future wife, whom Grillparzer saw as being now (in the words of 'Trennung', 8) 'in einer furchtbarn Hand'.[1]

'Verwandlungen' is a more difficult poem. Gabriele Petrasovics has shown that it is strongly influenced by a poem entitled 'Trauer', which is one of Tieck's 'Magelonenlieder'.[2] Tieck's poem

---

[1] 'in dreadful hands'. The use of the feminine form *Porträtmalerin* is in keeping with Grillparzer's normal practice. In 1836, for example, he chanced to meet in the King's Theatre, London, a Viennese woman who had married a printer, and his diary at once refers to her as 'die Buchdruckerin' (T 3089).

[2] *Jb.* XXVIII, 58–60. The first eight lines especially echo the thought and rhythm of Tieck's poem. Grillparzer had read Tieck intensively earlier in the 1820s (cf. T 1314).

laments the transience of life and love in general terms; Grillparzer's subject is apparently more particular, but nevertheless the poem has been interpreted very variously. It has been taken as a poem about Charlotte von Paumgartten, bewailing the irrevocable nature either of past beauty or of past happiness in love. Other critics have argued that it has nothing to do with Charlotte's death, which took place after it was already begun, and have interpreted it as a poem about the present loss of inspiration and the prospect of its return. Inasmuch as the absence of inspiration is associated with a crisis in Grillparzer's relations with women, it has been related to the separation from Marie. All these readings are essentially exegetic, for the actual wording of the poem is vague. It opens with a plaint, contrasting the barrenness of present night with the sunshine of past contentment (i.e. a past happiness in love and satisfaction in poetic work); the hope of a new sunrise, expressed in the second section, is shown in the third as being frustrated – whether temporarily or finally is not immediately clear – by a death. Critics differ again as to whose death is being referred to, the poet's own, or that of an (unnamed) beloved; but the wording does not support the latter interpretation, which has to be read into the text with Charlotte's death in mid-September in mind. Indeed, in the very first section of the poem the image of the poet looking for a house he cannot find (9–12) proclaims, by its kinship with the image in 'Böse Stunde' (6), that 'Verwandlungen' shares the common theme of the cycle. The one possible allusion to Charlotte's death is in the emphatically repeated idea of 'night' in the second section, the wish that every 'night' must end as the 'night' of the poet's artistic frustration will; and this leads by association to the contemplation of his own death, which he presents as the only final obstacle to the reappearance of inspiration. This concluding section, with its image of spring sunlight, introduces, then, a positive note, a hope of inspiration till death comes.

No such note of hope is struck in 'Sorgenvoll', which describes the poet hoarding his sorrow:

> Mein Kummer ist mein Eigentum,
> Den geb' ich nicht heraus... (1f.)[1]

---

[1] 'My sorrow is my property – I shall not yield it up.' But 'herausgeben' also suggests the sense 'to publish'. The association of this poem with Grillparzer's 'hoarding' of *Ein treuer Diener* is supported by the fact that he copied the poem into his diary immediately following the note which

The particular problem to which this is related was Grillparzer's hesitation in making public one major work of self-expression, *Ein treuer Diener seines Herrn,* which he had probably still not submitted to the Burgtheater. But in the poem the mood is expressed in general terms; its tone corresponds to that of a diary-note written in mid-September: 'From the moment when I can no longer take pleasure in voicing my laments to the public I can no longer enjoy writing for them...' (T 1617). 'Freundeswort' also relates directly to these problems. It treats the advice given to Grillparzer in August by Bauernfeld in a poem 'An Grillparzer' which had exhorted him not to let his personal troubles stop him from writing. Grillparzer gave a long formal answer in the poem 'Rechtfertigung' (G 68); in 'Freundeswort' he dwells on only one motif touched on by Bauernfeld. Bauernfeld had written:

> Die Leiden singen, heißt die Leiden mildern,
> Gemalter Schmerz macht uns des wahren los.   (ll. 43f.)[1]

'Freundeswort' begins by stating briefly the case for sublimating private anguish in creative work, then counters with the objection that conventional artistic forms are vehicles for expressing imaginary sufferings ('selbstgemachte Leiden', 10) but inadequate to express the violent feelings of real experience. The only answer is presented in the final stanza: to write with all the directness and violence of experience itself.

That 'Freundeswort' does not contain any denial of the reproach it summarizes, viz. that Grillparzer's sorrows are still being suppressed in 'mute raging', not only confirms that when it was written Grillparzer had still not made up his mind to offer *Ein treuer Diener* for performance but also suggests that he can still have had no plan for the rapid publication of his *Tristia.* It was not until the spring of 1830 that he began to attempt a fair copy of the cycle; and since the final poem, 'Schlußwort', was given the number '15' when it was first copied into his diary in the following year (T 1895), it is evident that he was beginning to envisage a considerable expansion of the cycle. In the summer of 1831 he went on his walking-tour to Gastein, escaping once more from renewed involvement with Marie Daffinger, and the

---

records the eventual submitting of the manuscript of the tragedy, and which, in its doubts about the work, also reflects the same depths of despondency as the poem does (T 1620).

[1] 'To express our sorrows in song is to lighten those sorrows; sufferings portrayed release us from the sufferings of reality.'

three new *Tristia* which this holiday produced testify to the depth that his despondency had once more reached. The first, 'Ablehnung', is a rejection of unhelpful advice. The second, 'Noch einmal in Gastein', takes his stay in Gastein as an occasion to survey the disappointments which have filled the years since his last visit in 1818 (of which the greatest recent one was obviously the reception of *Des Meeres und der Liebe Wellen*). The third, 'Naturszene', describes a scene in the countryside: each of the separate phenomena of Nature seems heedless of all the rest of Nature; the grass shows no gratitude to the stream that waters it, nor the butterfly to the flowers that feed it. And amid this scene the poet too is self-centred, lost in his sorrows and thinking nostalgically of the past loves which have engendered those present sorrows.

The more hopeful tone of 'Schlußwort' corresponds to a renewal of poetic activity in the later months of 1831, when Grillparzer resumed work on *Libussa* and the *Bruderzwist*. But still the cycle was not complete. Early in 1833 he tried to make a final arrangement of poems. Those from which his choice was made included both 'Begegnung' (G 73), which fitted in very ill, and 'An die Sammlung' (G 210), an invocation of inspiration which was tentatively placed as the introductory poem instead of 'Böse Stunde'. The final revision for publication was undertaken in 1834; and this was when 'Verwünschung' and 'Trennung' were added for the first time, together with 'Intermezzo', a poem of very different mood which dates from 1832 and treats the stirring of love in the springtime. And – a massive counterweight to this 'intermezzo' of light – Grillparzer also introduced into the cycle the autobiographical poem 'Jugenderinnerungen im Grünen', which had not only been begun (in 1824) but also completed (in 1826) before any other of the *Tristia*: it deals, then, with earlier experiences than the rest of the cycle. The inclusion of this long poem radically widened the scale of the cycle. Together with 'Trennung' it provides a solid core of autobiographical writing which as it were documents and substantiates the personal suffering which the shorter *Tristia* refer to and which underlies that persistent artistic dissatisfaction which is the starting-point of the whole cycle. This detailing of Grillparzer's experience prevents the cycle from falling into that vague, seemingly baseless late-romantic melancholy which Grillparzer criticized in the lyrical poems of Lenau (T 2085): 'Jugenderinnerungen im Grünen' provides, indeed, a chronicle of Grillparzer's increasing depression in the mid-twenties. The first four quatrains, written in 1824, end on a note of achievement and promise; but the next twenty-two, composed chiefly in the following year, conclude with the agonizing unhappiness of the Kathi section; and the whole poem, completed after a gap of another year, ends on a note of almost despairing disillusion.

The various poems which gradually accumulated in Grillparzer's *Tristia* folder centre mainly, in their various groups, on the painful years 1826–8. We have traced the gradual evolution of the cycle; now a second piece of literary detection is required to unravel the implications of the finished composition. For in fashioning these poems into a cycle treating the interplay between art and experience, Grillparzer had so to arrange them that the various groups of poems were linked together in a coherent line of argument.

He achieved this by reinstating 'Böse Stunde' as the opening poem; the rest of the cycle tests its conclusion, reveals the sufferings endured in this testing, and concludes with a final reacceptance of its solution to the initial dilemma – an affirmation of the creative role of experience (however painful), since from suffering art is born.

'Böse Stunde' begins by posing the problem, the absence of inspiration, and proposes the search for it in the experience of life. 'Polarszene' presents a defeatist answer, a resigned denial of vitality, but this is immediately balanced by the hopefulness of 'Frühlings Kommen'. 'Reiselust', then, is the first practical test of the solution proposed in 'Böse Stunde', and its conclusion is negative, for travels have had only a dispiriting effect. 'Der Fischer' adds a further discouraging note about the effects of experience, but, by introducing the idea that the poet may attempt to capture the objects of his contemplation, leads directly into the main body of the *Tristia*, which treat the poet's relations with women, the testing of the solution of 'Böse Stunde' in amatory experience. The outcome is further anguish. 'Verwünschung' records his insight into the character of Marie (who, however, remains anonymous in the cycle, an archetypal representative of the inconstancy and dangerous mystery of womankind), 'Verwandlungen' the bleakness consequent upon this insight, and the elusiveness of the regeneration to which he looks forward. 'Die Porträtmalerin' rehearses the victory of his rival, and its effects, and has obvious monitory implications for the poet himself, a summary of the dangers of exploiting experience for the unscrupulous enrichment of art. 'Trennung' finally establishes the effect of the new insight, the resolve to part, and reflects again on the mysterious contradictions in the character of the daemonic woman now possessed by dreadful baseness (a fear which is voiced in line 8 and again in line 51). The poem 'Sorgenvoll' now reveals the poet's attitude to the completed affair and its outcome: his continued grief, and his brooding suppression of his feelings – a brooding mood which also informs the rejection of advice in 'Ablehnung'. Erich Hock has pointed out the balance in the arrangement of the cycle. Adapting his analysis, we may say that so far, after the introductory poem, it has consisted of two mutually balancing groups of four poems each, followed by the general restatements in 'Sorgenvoll' and 'Ablehnung' of the poet's silent sorrow. The two sections deal respectively with the poet's hopes and experiences in the field of his art (poems 2–5) and in that of love (poems 6–9). In each case the sequence starts with a poem of bitter bleakness ('Polarszene', 'Verwünschung'), which is followed by a poem of hopefulness for the future ('Frühlings Kommen' and, more problematically, 'Verwandlungen'); then comes in each case a poem looking back on painful experience ('Reiselust', 'Die Porträtmalerin'); and finally the poet faces his present deprivation, pensively in 'Der Fischer', forthrightly in 'Trennung'.

Not only is the balance between the two fields of experience maintained in the second half of the cycle (poems 12–17): the thematic pattern of the first part – introduction, plaint, reassessment – is repeated. First comes an introductory poem preparing further development: having dismissed the help of others as being of no use, the poet turns in isolation to nature in the idyllic interlude of 'Intermezzo'. This is in a formal sense the counterpart in the later part of the cycle to 'Böse Stunde' in the first (though in mood it corresponds most closely to 'Frühlings Kommen' among the earlier poems). But memories of the past immediately darken the mood again in 'Noch einmal in Gastein' (dealing with the artistic field) and in 'Naturszene' the poet is still sadly retrospective as he reflects on past love. The element of inward-looking retrospection amid nature is now expanded in 'Jugenderinnerungen im Grünen', which treats both fields of experience, telling how the fulfilment of the poet's early hopes has in fact meant only disappointment, both in human relations of friendship and love, and also in his art. His work has been 'half truth, half dream' (120), reality enriched by poetic vision, it has been true to the poet's own feelings (127f.); and yet it has met only with petty criticism devoid of vision, so that now even Nature is no longer any solace, and the poem ends on a note of profound disillusion, in continued despondency at the poet's inability to recapture that creative fire which once he knew but has now lost:

> Wenn erst ich das Verlorne wieder hätte,
> Wie gäb' ich gern, was ich seitdem gewann.[1]

The factors underlying that crisis of creativity which was the starting-point of the cycle have now been discussed in detail; but the crisis itself is still unresolved. And now once more the sequence of poems is rounded off with two poems which take stock of the poet's sufferings not in detail but as a whole; and this time they present a positive conclusion. 'Freundeswort', moved to the penultimate position in the cycle, proposes again the only answer: the sufferings which have just been described must form the basis of the poet's artistic work. This is a reaffirmation of the solution proposed in the very first poem, but now it is not merely a speculative resolve for the future, but takes account of the past which the previous poems have recounted. And so the *Tristia* end on a positive note of hope: the poem 'Schlußwort' dismisses the sufferings in art and love (treated together in the image of the piercing of the poet's heart, line 3) as a dream, rounding off the cycle with a suggestion of the return of creative power, represented by approaching strains of music, the choice of music in this symbolic role being characteristic of Grillparzer and indeed of the artistic ambience of Vienna.

In his autobiography, in connexion with the controversial poem 'Auf die Genesung des Kronprinzen', Grillparzer observes that it was his wont 'to take refuge in lyric verse only as a means of unburdening myself', and adds the modest rider that for this reason he could 'not claim to be an authentic lyric poet' (SB 211). Yet while the *Tristia* are not technically flawless – there are some obscurities, and occasional lapses into rather jingly versification and artificial diction[2] – they have genuine poetic merit. This merit

---

[1] 'If only I could have again what I have lost, how gladly would I give up what I have since gained!'

[2] E.g.: (weak versification) 'Frühlings Kommen' 12; (artificiality) 'Reiselust' 19f., 'Sorgenvoll' 11–15, 'Intermezzo' 7f., 'Jugenderinnerungen im Grünen' 112.

lies, however, not in the evocation of feeling, but in the intense pursuance of an argument. One of the characteristics of Grillparzer's work in lyric forms is that many of his poems are reflective and retrospective; where they diverge from conventional standards of lyric verse is in their rational (rather than emotional) tone. In order to write with uninhibited emotion, Grillparzer needed dramatic figures, on whom he could project that emotion; his poems tend to be built up with analogies, images suggesting parallels to his experience rather than growing directly and expressively from it. Thus in the *Tristia* the approach to the underlying experiences seems, in general, analytical rather than lyrical. Symptomatic of this tendency is the occasional reduction of the problems being dealt with to abstract formulations, as, for example, in 'Böse Stunde':

> Wärst du das Wie und brauchst ein Was?
> Nur Was durch ein Warum? (21f.)[1]

or in 'Reiselust':

> Drängt's den Mißmut abzustreifen
> In gedankenloser Hast? (3f.)[2]

Again, 'Verwünschung' is a statement about rather than a portrait of Marie's character, the contradictory traits being not illustrated but listed. This intellectualizing tendency does not, however, betoken any lack of deep and genuine feeling: Hock, making this point in his article 'Grillparzers Eigenart als Lyriker', borrows a phrase used by Oliver Elton about Byron's lyrics, which are also informed by 'a kind of passionate thinking'. Indeed, the *Tristia* contain passages of great power. This is particularly true, perhaps, of the poems 'Verwünschung', 'Trennung' and 'Jugend-erinnerungen im Grünen', written in iambic pentameters which with their length and regularity suit the reflective mood of retro-spection: especially fine is the famous passage in 'Jugenderin-nerungen' treating Grillparzer's relations with Kathi (73–104), an account of eloquent clarity. The disillusion in his relations with Marie also receives memorable, more softly modulated expression in the closing lines of 'Die Porträtmalerin', and his whole dilemma in respect of poetical work is finely expressed in 'Der Fischer',

[1] 'You [= inspiration] are the "how", but need a "what"? – and before that a "why"?' (i.e. inspiration affords the possibility of poetic creation, but depends on material and motive).

[2] 'Is the urge there to cast off ill-humour in thoughtless haste?'

a beautifully balanced poem that is marred neither by clumsiness nor by artifice:

> Hier sitz' ich mit lässigen Händen,
> In still behaglicher Ruh',
> Und schaue den spielenden Fischlein
> Im glitzernden Wasser zu.
>
> Sie jagen und gehen und kommen;
> Doch werf' ich die Angel aus,
> Flugs sind sie von dannen geschwommen,
> Und leer kehr' ich abends nach Haus.
>
> Versucht' ich's und trübte das Wasser,
> Vielleicht geläng' es eh;
> Doch müßt' ich dann auch verzichten,
> Sie spielen zu sehen im See.[1]

Here the mood of detachment which elsewhere detracts from the emotional immediacy of Grillparzer's lyrics is intrinsic to the subject of the poem, the very premise of which is the poet's own sense of detachment. The implications for the poet in the analogy with the contemplative angler are clear. Grillparzer is reproaching himself with lacking any creative urge: the angler of the poem is sitting indolently, 'mit lässigen Händen', watching the fish but not even attempting to catch them. Underlying this is the old doubt, expressed in the early note T 45 and repeated in another note in 1826, about the power to capture in artistic form the vision of the imagination: just as casting the line frightens the fish away, so in the mere act of trying words and phrases to capture an idea the first high poetic conception becomes lost, ungraspable, because in seeking to give it shape the poet falls back too readily on his analytical reason: '...the process of giving form brings me closer than is proper to working with my intellect' (T 1554). Moreover, experience is not only elusive and difficult to recapture: it must itself endanger the poet's very powers of vision, in so far as these depend on the collected detachment of contemplation. Only by daring to gain experience will he gain the essential artistic impulse (and his material) – this was the conclusion of 'Böse Stunde' – but in gaining it he will lay himself

---

[1] 'Here I sit with idle hands in quiet and peaceful ease, and I watch the little fish playing in the sparkling water. They race about and come and go; but if I cast my line they swim away at once, and I return home in the evening empty-handed. If I tried clouding the water, I might perhaps be successful; but then I should have to do without watching them playing in the lake.'

open to the criticism later expressed in 'Der Halbmond glänzet...', the charge of self-indulgently neglecting art in favour of (pleasurable) experience of 'life'.

The central question here is whether contemplation in withdrawal is essential to the poet, or in fact inimical to his work. The idleness of the angler's hands in 'Der Fischer' points to the latter answer; in this sense the poem represents a significant step towards the final commitment in 'Freundeswort'. The decision with which Grillparzer finally resolves his dilemma is one that is at least adumbrated at one point in *Sappho*; for during her first infatuation with Phaon Sappho argues that art must be fed by life (276f.). In her case, however, this is merely an imprecise romantic dream, a piece of self-delusion, and the ending of the play amounts to a rejection of the real implications of her resolve to find the source of her art in life ('Die Kunst zu schlürfen aus der Hand des Lebens', 283). In finally reaffirming the supremacy of her poetic calling, Sappho yet accepts death, and an end to her work, rather than reaping the potential poetic advantage of her suffering in the affair with Phaon. The *Tristia* testify to a far more mature and perceptive view both of the creative process and of the poet's position; but still the expression of the new resolve lacks the certainty of complete confidence. The 'Schlußwort' is brief, a weak counterweight to the long catalogue of tribulations which has preceded it and which it nominally dismisses; and while from his experiences Grillparzer did indeed draw the material for further dramatic work, and while he did frequently acknowledge the nature of his work as a lament (*Klage*) born of his suffering,[1] nevertheless he was still prey to the doubts expressed in 'Der Fischer'. Recurrently he saw 'distraction' in all its forms as the principal enemy of inspiration, an obstacle to his own work: that 'discontented distraction of mind' of which he complained in his diary for 1829 as 'growing and becoming more dangerous with every day' (T 1720). The secret of inspiration he described as lying in the concentrated direction of the emotional and intellectual faculties: 'Die eigentliche Begeisterung ist die Hinrichtung aller Kräfte und Fähigkeiten auf *einen* Punkt, der für diesen Augenblick die ganze übrige Welt nicht sowohl verschlingen, als repräsentieren muß' (T 3406).[2] This note, which was written in

---

[1] E.g., T 1617 and G 192, both of autumn 1827.

[2] 'True inspiration is the concentration of all one's powers and capacities on a single point, which for that moment must not so much engulf the rest of the world as represent it.'

1838, goes on to discuss how the individual faculties are quickened in this concentration, so that the heightened mental or spiritual condition that is characteristic of inspiration is induced, while the object of the concentration – the subject of the work of art – is as it were lifted into independent life. The idea that the work of art must become a focal point taking the place of the whole world is also advanced in a slightly earlier note (T 3205), where Grillparzer writes of art as being based on 'exclusiveness'.

In association with the idea of complete concentration Grillparzer also uses the term *Sammlung*; one note of 1826, for example, refers to the state of *Sammlung* in a way that makes it appear a pre-condition for inspiration: '...Und doch entsteht nichts Großes ohne Ausscheidung, ohne Hinrichtung auf *einen* Punkt, ohne Sammlung' (T 1413). And he goes on there to relate this capacity for *Sammlung* to genius: 'Ich möchte das Vermögen sich zu sammeln in höchster Potenz als gleichbedeutend mit *Genie* erklären...'[1] A literal translation of *Sammlung* as 'composure' is inadequate to convey the meaning with which Grillparzer endows it. It must be understood in a special, and essentially active sense, that of the complete possession and control of all the faculties, which may then be concentrated on a single task or a single subject. It is a dedicated, solitary 'composure' which nurtures creative achievement: 'Sammlung, jene Götterbraut,/ Mutter alles Großen' (G 56).[2] In *Des Meeres und der Liebe Wellen* the nature and importance of *Sammlung* are expounded by the priest, who describes it as the motive force of all the greatness of the universe,

> ...den mächt'gen Weltenhebel,
> Der alles Große tausendfach erhöht
> Und selbst das Kleine näher rückt den Sternen.
>
> (948–50)[3]

When Grillparzer uses this image of a 'motive force' in his diary, it is to describe the significance of inspiration in his own life:

[1] '...Yet nothing great can be achieved without exclusion, without concentration on *one* point, without creative "composure". I might equate the capacity for this "composure", in the highest degree, with genius.'

[2] 'Composure, bride of the gods, mother of all that is great.' While Grillparzer's longing for (and faith in) inspiration is a fundamentally romantic feature of his outlook, clearly the ideal of *Sammlung* is also related to the classical conception of the harmonious and whole personality: see chapter 6, pp. 234f.

[3] '...the mighty motive force that exalts a thousandfold all that is great and brings even the trivial closer to the stars.'

'Inspiration is the sole motive force of my nature' (T 1413); and the priest numbers poetic creation among the achievements of *Sammlung*:

> Des Helden Tat, des Sängers heilig Lied,
> Des Sehers Schaun, der Gottheit Spur und Walten,
> Die Sammlung hat's getan und hat's erkannt,
> Und die Zerstreuung nur verkennt's und spottet.
>
> (*Des Meeres und der Liebe Wellen* 951–4)[1]

The list of ideal achievement covers all fields, the artistic and the contemplative as well as the active and heroic. But most characteristically Grillparzer thinks of achievement in artistic terms. He has the priest warn Hero against his own enemy, 'distraction'; as its opposite the priest uses the term 'Ganzheit' (983), which Grillparzer also applied to Beethoven.

It is in relation to Beethoven, his fellow-artist, that he gave perhaps his most powerful portrait of the genius of creative solitude (*Sammlung*) and utter self-dedication (*Ganzheit*). While the music Grillparzer most admired was not that of Beethoven, but that of Mozart – he found Beethoven's later work in particular too daring formally, 'over-lyrical' and too strongly emotional (T 2174) – he recognized in Beethoven a man of genius who in all his solitude had been sustained by creative concentration. In the memorable funeral oration which was spoken over Beethoven's coffin in March 1827 by the actor Heinrich Anschütz, he spoke of Beethoven as a man who was devoted to art and found in it a justification and defence against the barbs of life, who in the solitude which nurtured his art (i.e. in the avoidance of the distraction that endangers *Sammlung*) was misunderstood by the world and earned the reputation of being hostile and without feelings, but who in fact as an artist attained that supreme humanity on which his immortality would be founded. The point about self-dedication is made again in the worthy companion piece which Grillparzer wrote for the unveiling of a monument by Beethoven's grave later the same year, and which ends with a panegyric extolling Beethoven as one who had truly known the creative power of inspiration, and who had wholly devoted himself to his one task: 'Nach *einem* trachtend, um *eines* sorgend, für *eines* duldend, alles hingebend für *eines*, so ging dieser Mann

---

[1] 'The hero's deed, the bard's sacred song, the seer's vision, the imprint and the sway of divinity – "composure" has wrought it or perceived it, and only distraction knows it not and mocks.'

durch das Leben.' And in this concentrated aspiration, the distractions of life, of love, of self-indulgence, were set aside by a
man driving himself on in his inspiration: 'Nicht Gattin hat er
gekannt, noch Kind, kaum Freude, wenig Genuß. Ärgerte ihn ein
Auge, er riß es aus, und ging fort, fort, fort bis ans Ziel.' He is a
unique example of that *Sammlung* that Grillparzer defines as 'concentration on *one* point': in Beethoven's life there was no fragmentation of effort or potentiality, but that integrity of self-dedication,
that complete, undistracted inner harmony that Grillparzer here
calls *Ganzheit* ('integrity' or 'wholeness'): 'Wenn noch Sinn für
Ganzheit in uns ist in dieser zersplitterten Zeit, so laßt uns
sammeln an seinem Grab';[1] for – so the oration concludes – Beethoven provides an example for all humanity, an example of
inspiration that bears witness to the mysterious divine powers
at the heart of all life. That the *Ganzheit* or *Sammlung* conceived
by Grillparzer involved a complete solitude is clear from the
passage in *Des Meeres und der Liebe Wellen* where the Priest talks
of it; he makes it clear that for the unfragmented development
of the inner (imaginative or visionary) life, it is necessary to
withdraw completely from the pressures of life, and from its
wounds (what in the oration for Beethoven's funeral Grillparzer
called 'des Lebens Stacheln'):

> Doch wessen Streben auf das Innre führt,
> Wo Ganzheit nur, des Wirkens Fülle fördert,
> Der halte fern vom Streite seinen Sinn,
> Denn ohne Wunde kehrt man nicht zurück,
> Die noch als Narbe mahnt in trüben Tagen.   (982–6)[2]

The implications of this are irreconcilably opposed to those of the
Tristia. In the 'passionate thinking' of his lyrics Grillparzer
achieved an insight of which he never fully convinced himself, and
experience of love, however sweet, runs counter to duty in his
tragedies; its appeal may be overwhelming, but still it is shown
as a force that fatally undermines duty and clouds vision.

---

[1] 'Striving for one aim, concerned for one aim, suffering for one aim,
sacrificing everything for one aim – that is how this man went through
life. He had neither wife nor child; he scarcely knew pleasure and had little
enjoyment. If his eye offended him, he plucked it out and went on, on, on
to his goal. If we still have any feeling for integrity in this fragmented age,
let us gather by his grave!'
[2] 'But anyone whose striving is directed inwards, where only wholeness,
fullness of effort, yields achievement, must keep his mind far from the
strife – for no-one can return without wounds whose scars remain, reminders
in dark times.'

Love

In all the works by which Grillparzer first made his name he had already portrayed love as a dangerous force, destructive of human happiness, disruptive of human personality. In *Die Ahnfrau* Bertha sings in the first act of the happiness of love, but by the end of the second act she is already lamenting that her love of Jaromir has been poisonous as well as blissful; that it has brought to an end the golden days of innocent contentment; that the roses of love are thorny growths:

> Dornen, die zwar Rosen schmücken,
> Aber Dornen, Dornen doch,
> In dem glühendsten Entzücken
> Fühl' ich ihren Stachel noch.　　　　　(1555–8)[1]

In *Sappho* too, as we have seen, the equilibrium of the heroine is broken by the violent love she conceives for Phaon. Both Bertha and Sappho fail to find any solution other than suicide to the situation into which they are brought by their hapless love.

The emphasis in *Das Goldene Vlies* is laid more on the irresistibility of love. In the opening scene of *Der Gastfreund* Medea shows her scorn for a Colchian girl who has yielded to her feelings for a man, instead of asserting her willpower. Medea cannot believe that the feelings can override the will:

> Wie konnt' es denn geschehn,
> Wenn du nicht *wolltest*? Was ich tu', das will ich...　　(65f.)[2]

In *Die Argonauten* her own will is subjected to the same test. Her intention is to help her father against the Greeks: 'Der Wille kann viel,' she reflects, ' – und ich will' (247);[3] and reaffirms the decision, 'Medea *will*!' (254). After her first encounter with Jason, and his first kiss, she is confused, and already senses that the experience has cost her her control, her integrity of personality: she speaks of it as her 'destruction' (564). Twice, against her apparent interests, she saves Jason's life: each of the first two acts of *Die Argonauten* ends on that note. By the third act, she has

---

[1] 'Thorns – graced by roses, it is true, but still thorns even so – and in my most ardent rapture I still feel their pricks.'

[2] 'How could it happen, if it was not your will? Whatever I do, it is my will to do...'

[3] 'The will can do much – and this is my will.'

learnt to admit the power of love, which she describes as a mysterious and irrational force, independent of the will:

> Es gibt ein Etwas in des Menschen Wesen,
> Das, unabhängig von des Eigners Willen,
> Anzieht und abstößt mit blinder Gewalt;
> Wie vom Blitz zum Metall, vom Magnet zum Eisen,
> Besteht ein Zug, ein geheimnisvoller Zug
> Vom Menschen zum Menschen, von Brust zu Brust.
>
> (1012–17)[1]

But while recognizing that love can exercise this mysterious magnetism, she is still determined that it can be resisted, and that she will not yield to it:

> Und ich will nicht – Medea will *nicht*!   (1027)[2]

During the long wooing-scene she says very little and remains completely silent throughout Jason's attempts to extort a confession of her love for him. She remains silent – though tearful – during the subsequent confrontation of Jason and Aietes, until Jason comes to take his last farewell of her, and takes hold of her hand. Aietes challenges him – how dare he touch her? – and Jason lets her go, and unwittingly summarizes her whole attitude towards him: 'Sie will nicht' (1324). He bids her farewell for ever, and turns and goes; and then it is that Medea too turns, stretching out her hand after him and calling 'Jason!' (1327). Within ten more lines she has confessed her love: put to the crucial test, her proud will has been routed.

The love to which she falls victim is a power which strikes across all the differences that divide Colchian and Greek; it uproots Medea from her true home, and it destroys her clarity of vision as a seer, which she insists she vitally needs (*Die Argonauten* 1010; *Medea* 120). Even when she has realized the depths of Jason's selfishness, she has to admit to Kreusa that she loves him still (*Medea* 661). It was because of this unshakable love that, interpreting wishes that Jason would not put into action himself, she played her part in the death of Pelias (*Medea* 1070–94); it is because of this love that her jealousy of Kreusa develops to the length of murder. The fire which Medea describes Jason as having

---

[1] 'There is something in man's being which, independently of its owner's will, attracts and repels with blind power: as between lightning and metal, or magnet and iron, there is a mysterious pull from person to person, from breast to breast.'

[2] 'And I will not – Medea will *not*!'

lighted within her (*Medea* 619–23) takes on destructive reality in the flames of Kreon's palace.

In Grillparzer's next play, Ottokar's rejection of Bertha von Rosenberg arouses in her feelings of such violence that she loses her reason altogether; and a further treatment of the destructive effect of love on the life of its victims is contained in the earlier of Grillparzer's stories, *Das Kloster bei Sendomir*.

This is a minor work of a mere two dozen or so pages, which in style is strikingly similar to the summary that Grillparzer wrote out in his diary in 1820 of the plot of *Das Bettelweib von Locarno* (T 762). Grillparzer described Kleist's story as gruesome ('schauerlich'). The same epithet is valid for *Das Kloster bei Sendomir*, and the Kleistian economy and tenseness of style with which it is told heighten the atmospheric intensity. Grillparzer did not designate it as a *Novelle* when it was published; but the tale concentrates on the horrific action – the 'highly unusual event' ('unerhörte Begebenheit') of the traditional German *Novelle* – and does not deepen into the kind of exploration of character that was Grillparzer's *forte*; it remained no more than an 'Almanach-Novelle', a magazine-story – he used this term of it when writing to Paul Heyse in 1870 (B 1736).

It is set in seventeenth-century Poland, and records the story of the founding of a monastery, which is told there by a monk to two German travellers. They learn in the end that the monk is himself Starschensky, the central character of the story, from the proceeds of whose estate the monastery was built. His story is essentially that of his marriage. Elga is beautiful, but a different kind of character from himself: he has been solitary from youth, she is fun-loving and extravagant. His first contact with her opens a 'new world' to him (p. 10); but his love for her involves him in mortgaging his own property to help her family. Their eventual marriage is clouded by her changeability, then by his suspicions that she still loves a cousin, Oginsky, and that Oginsky is the father of her child. In retribution for her unfaithfulness, he demands that she kill the child; she is about to do so to save herself when he kills Elga instead, and sets fire to the watch-tower on which the action has centred.

The love that has bound Starschensky to Elga is a destructive passion. Until he becomes involved with her, he has had no close relations with women, partly out of shyness, partly out of a sense of self-preservation and delight in his independence (9);

he has shielded himself from the possibility of discontent or suffering: 'to him, the absence of displeasure was itself pleasure' (9). This is clearly a much more negative kind of integrity than that possessed and lost by Sappho, or by Medea; nevertheless, the love in which Starschensky is caught finally destroys all 'self-possession' of every kind just as it does for the heroines of Grillparzer's early tragedies.

In his mature love-tragedies the force of love is the same: it is presented in a more attractive light, but still it remains irresistible, dangerous and potentially destructive.

Both Grillparzer's love-tragedies were conceived in the early 1820s. The most important of his sources for *Des Meeres und der Liebe Wellen* was Marlowe's poem *Hero and Leander*; he was also influenced by Shakespeare's *Romeo and Juliet*, which he had read with enthusiasm as early as January 1817 (*Gespr.* 52). For *Die Jüdin von Toledo* he drew especially on Lope de Vega's play *Las paces de los Reyes, y Judia de Toledo* and a story by Jacques Cazotte, 'Rachel ou la belle juive' (1788), together with Cazotte's preface. He worked alternately on the material for the two plays early in 1827, during his entanglement with Marie von Smolenitz; in the summer of that year, in one of an important series of notes on *Des Meeres und der Liebe Wellen*, he wrote that Hero should have 'something of the equanimity' of Marie.[1] But while *Des Meeres und der Liebe Wellen* was completed two years later, *Die Jüdin* appears not to have been taken up again after the end of 1827 until 1839, when Grillparzer read Michael Enk's *Studien über Lope de Vega Carpio*; then he resumed work on it again in the last months of 1848. In keeping with his dominant interests in this period, the political element in the play took on greater importance; and – also in keeping with the general tendency of his later works, which were written for the drawer rather than for the stage – there is an increase in reflective passages, especially in the last two acts.

Des Meeres und der Liebe Wellen

The first of Grillparzer's love tragedies is his dramatic masterpiece. Some years after completing it, he wrote that in it he had tried to combine the classical and the romantic (T 3247); the subject is treated with romantic warmth of feeling, but the form is classically

---

[1] These notes of summer 1827 are given in *Wke.* 1/19, 232f.

simple. The action too is much simpler than in his two preceding plays. This is especially evident in the first half of Act III and the whole of Act IV, in which (in contrast to the upheaval and warfare which fill the middle acts of *König Ottokar* and *Ein treuer Diener*) little outwardly 'happens': they are scenes of waiting, in which tension is built up either in monologue (Act III) or in discussion and planning (Act IV). After the histories, the audience's expectations were perhaps cheated at the première; it was from the fourth act onwards that the play was coolly received (T 1893). But so experienced a man of the theatre as Laube also approached the last two acts with reservations when he revived the play successfully in 1851. In one of his books of theatrical memoirs, *Das Burgtheater* (1868), he recalls that he concentrated all his efforts on the production of these acts; and in his study *Franz Grillparzers Lebensgeschichte* (1883) he suggests that notwithstanding the psychological accuracy of the fourth act its opening scene should be deleted in performance, in order to reduce what he sees as an essentially undramatic retarding element. The whole emphasis in the play, however, is on 'psychology' – that is, on portrayal of character; and it achieves its dramatic power partly by the sympathetic portrayal of the heroine, who unsuspectingly brings herself to tragedy, but also by the precision and circumstantiality with which the development of the tragedy is shown. It is consequently particularly rewarding to follow the main action of this play in detail, noting the subtlety with which the characterization is built up and the action advanced. The coherence of the action and the emotional conviction that its presentation carries achieve that effect of utter inevitability which is the hallmark of great tragedy.

Whereas in *König Ottokar* the hero finally repents, and in *Ein treuer Diener* Otto comes to his senses and Simon and Peter submit to the authority of the king, the dramatic conflict in *Des Meeres und der Liebe Wellen* is built on a disparity in standards which reveals itself only gradually, but which finally proves to be absolutely irreconcilable. The source of the tragic outcome is that Hero takes upon herself the duty of a priestess of Aphrodite-Urania. In that position she must forswear all earthly love; and such renunciation proves to be completely at odds with her true nature. In the opening scene, before her ceremonial investiture, we learn that she is assuming her position as priestess by choice, taking advantage of a privilege of her family (23). But her bearing

throughout the act shows that she can have no real understanding
of the full implications of her decision: indeed, she tells the priest,
who is her uncle, that there has in effect been no decision to take
(145). Her approach to the coming ceremony is one of unreflecting
enjoyment, even of self-indulgence: this is suggested when she
compares her position in the community of the temple where she
has been brought up for the last seven years to a swimmer stretching
his legs in the comfortable luxury of a stream warmed by the
summer sun (151) – a highly inappropriate analogy for one on the
verge of forswearing sensual pleasures – and is confirmed by
the pride she displays in the rich garments she is to wear for the
ceremony (403f.). She has no conception of the kind of solitude
she is committing herself to; indeed, she queries the suggestion
that her life will be lonely at all (123f.). When the priest talks to
her of that communion with the divine which she should already
have practised, she admits that the gods have not vouchsafed
her the gift of vision (185); she does not see that this is an implicit
admission of her unsuitability for the role of priestess, but is
quite satisfied with herself as she is: 'Laß mich so wie ich bin, ich
bin es gern' (138).[1] Her lack of insight into her situation becomes
still clearer when she builds on her comparison of herself with
the swimmer to justify her willingness to remain in the temple as
priestess:

> Wer, wenn er mühsam nur das Land gewonnen,
> Sehnt sich ins Meer zurück, wo's wüst und schwindelnd?   (159f.)[2]

The irony of this image is that it corresponds exactly to the
position Leander will be in in Act IV; but the depth of feeling
which will underlie his resolve is something which at this stage
is still beyond Hero's experience and understanding. What she
sees in the temple is a refuge from the dangers of life outside:
a refuge, that is, from an outside world which she conceives of
in negative terms because she is ignorant of its positive side. The
young men in it she imagines as being coarse and selfish, like her
brother who is abroad seeking his fortune (300–10). Her view of
the temple as a refuge is confirmed when she talks of it to her
mother as a place without war or wounds (389). Her 'choice', in
fact, is a piece of escapism, irresponsible because uncomprehending:
she has still a childlike quality, which Leander's friend Naukleros

[1] 'Let me stay as I am, I like being like this.'
[2] 'Who, having just painfully reached land, yearns to be back in the swirling, desolate sea?'

perceives (628f.). When she boasts to her mother of 'the joy of quiet self-possession' ('das Glück des stillen Selbstbesitzes', 392), the words are meaningless, for her 'self-possession' is only the naive self-sufficiency of immaturity. Her true self is still unawakened. It is equally meaningless when she protests that she is becoming a priestess out of recognition that this course is right (334f.), for no valid moral judgment can be made without any sense of the moral implications of the decision involved.

The Hero of Act I is a moral innocent; and throughout the play she continues to lack moral awareness. In Act II this lack shows in her inability to see why the priest forbids her to sing the sensual song about Leda and the swan (729). In Act III it shows when she admits that the priest has been right in his warnings (1005), but means by this only that she has indeed been attracted to Leander, not that the priest's whole case is right. In Act IV, after she has given herself to Leander, it shows in the impatience with which, amid her almost comic sleepiness, she longs for evening, when he will return to her.[1] It also shows in her conversation with the priest: she first fights shy of claiming that she knows her duty and then, forced to affirm a sense of duty, proceeds to define 'duty' in utterly inadequate terms (1728–34). Her lack of any sense of guilt in this act was a basic element in Grillparzer's conception of her role. In one of the memoranda of summer 1827 he wrote that Hero must never put special emphasis on the fact that her relations with Leander are forbidden or liable to punishment, and that there must be no trace of nervousness about her: she has regained her emotional balance, but now with a new 'feeling of being a *woman*'.[2] In Act IV, the amorality of innocence has given way to a more mature amorality, that of devotion to love. And even in Act V, before Leander's dead body is discovered, Hero talks of taking a decision, as though she still had time to do so (1868–72): we see that still she has not faced either the fact that she is committed to the obligations and duties of a priestess, or the fact that she has already transgressed against the laws of that vocation. She still has no sense of moral guilt. Even after the discovery of Leander's body she does not blame her own conduct in yielding to him and encouraging him to make a second visit. Instead she turns accusingly on the priest, though she does not

---

[1] See ll. 1438, 1674, 1748; for her comic sleepiness, see ll. 1281 and 1441.
[2] 'Gefühl als *Weib*': this very phrase goes right back to Grillparzer's first draft plan of the play (T 322), but the idea is amplified in the later notes. See *Wke.* I/19, 232.

know his full responsibility. She blames herself only for having relaxed her watchfulness and fallen asleep, so allowing the lamp she set up to guide Leander to be extinguished (1954, 1990).

That in abjuring love Hero is not only committing herself too early but still more fatefully is acting against her own nature is suggested in the first act by two incidents in particular. The first concerns a male dove which intrudes into the sacred grove and which, as a symbol of sensual love, must be removed, in accordance with the strict law of the temple. This episode points forward suggestively to the later intrusion of Leander, for Hero the very embodiment of profane love, into the strict seclusion of her tower; and Hero's reaction – revealing of her natural sensuality – is to show sympathy for the dove, as opposed to the law of the temple, and to stroke its feathers (346/SD, SD/359), as later she will stroke Leander's head (1195/SD). The second suggestive incident occurs during the initiation ceremony itself. When she comes to take her solemn farewell of Hymenaeus, she forgets the words she has to repeat. The priest makes her proceed at once with the sacrifice; but obviously her renunciation of Hymen has been left incomplete, and in a way which suggests her subconscious unwillingness to make such a renunciation. Moreover, her hesitation is directly connected with her feelings, already aroused, for Leander. Naukleros later reminds Leander of Hero's confusion:

> Nach dir hin schauend stand sie zögernd da,
> Ein, zwei, drei kurze, ew'ge Augenblicke... (643f.)[1]

What utterly confuses her is the sight by Hymen's statue of a Leander who is – as Naukleros later says – 'Hymen's true likeness' (586), and it is in his kneeling posture beside the statue of Hymenaeus that Hero later remembers him (757): he remains in her mind, associated with the statue of the god she has failed properly to renounce.

When her thoughts return to Leander that evening in her tower, and she admits to herself that she has been attracted to him (1008f.), she resolves that she will avoid any emotional involvement, which would have hitherto unsuspected dangers:

> Ich weiß nunmehr, daß, was sie Neigung nennen,
> Ein Wirkliches, ein zu Vermeidendes,
> Und meiden will ich's wohl... (1010–12)[2]

[1] 'She stood there hanging back, looking at you, for one, two, three brief, timeless moments...'

[2] 'Now I know that what they call attraction is real and must be avoided, and avoid it I will...'

But love has already struck with its mysterious suddenness; it took root in the very first act, and was signalled in Hero's backward glance at the end of the act as she pretended to adjust her shoe. Her resolve *now* to avoid the snares of the affections comes two acts too late; and indeed, she quickly dismisses the subject, telling herself that after all Leander is far away and has disappeared from her life (1014–16). She takes off her cloak, her companion in all the experience of the day, and with it sheds her experience (1017–20). This action has often been commented on. It has a double force, for while what Hero means is that she is forgetting all about the encounter with Leander, in fact the cloak is the one she donned for her initiation, so that what she is in effect shedding is a symbol of her priesthood. And indeed she does not turn her thoughts at all to her new calling, but is restless (1021); her mood is the very opposite of that *Sammlung* which the priest has taught her to seek and which would be appropriate to her role as priestess, 'dedicated to pious service of the gods' (1007). She looks round the tower, itself the guardian and the symbol of her inviolable isolation; and her fancies catch, almost hopefully, at the slightest noise (1025). She moves over to the window and looks out over the Hellespont, as though subconsciously rejecting the narrow confinement of the tower; she sets her lamp beside the window, and admires the still beauty of the waters. The stillness of the atmosphere, together with Hero's restlessness, produces a growing sense of expectancy; and it is now that Hero – who in her childlike naivety talks directly to her lamp, as previously she has done to her cloak – bids the lamp shine out through the night like a star: 'Sei du ein Stern und strahle durch die Nacht' (1035). We learn later that it is precisely as a star, a star of hope, that Leander sees the light across the waters (1112); when, however, Hero remembers that it might really be seen (1036), she quickly puts the lamp down on the table. She adds that when she finally puts it out altogether the spark of feeling within herself must be extinguished with it (1038f.). But she does not put it out yet; instead, as she undoes her hair she hums to herself the words of the forbidden song of Leda and the swan, unmistakably sensuous lines about Leda stroking the soft feathers of the disguised adventuring Zeus, which are also reminiscent of the episode with the dove. Gradually her thoughts return to Leander:

> Ja denn, du schöner Jüngling, still und fromm!
> Ich denke dein in dieser späten Stunde,

DUTY AND LOVE

Und mit so glatt verbreitetem Gefühl,
Daß kein Vergehn sich birgt in seine Falten.
Ich will dir wohl, erfreut doch, daß du fern;
Und reichte meine Stimme bis zu dir,
Ich riefe grüßend: Gute Nacht!   (1054–60)[1]

And from outside her window comes the echoing 'Gut Nacht!' from Leander, who has swum the Hellespont and climbed her tower. It is a magical theatrical moment, which obviously owes much to the balcony scene in *Romeo and Juliet*; it is also a moment of irony, when Hero's illusions about Leander's distance are shattered and her pretence of mere innocent good will is suddenly to be put to the test. It comes, as Papst has pointed out, exactly half-way through the text, and it is the pivotal point of the action. For it is a climactic realization of the mood which has been building up within the unsuspecting heroine and to which in the second half of the play she will abandon herself with tragic consequences.

She, however, is first bewildered, then horrified as Leander appears in her window. The tension here is so high, and the emotion so delicate, that this scene is particularly vulnerable to being spoiled by poor performance. Hero's exclamations have to be spoken with great histrionic skill if the tension of the situation is not to be impaired by unintentional comedy: 'Ein Haupt! – Zwei Arme! – Ha, ein Mann im Fenster!' (1065).[2] But then, when she grasps the situation, she at once orders Leander back: 'Zurück! Du bist verloren, wenn ich rufe' (1067).[3] This is another vital moment, a potential turning-point, but its outcome is certain. Thrice before Hero has threatened to call for assistance. In the opening scene of the play she threatens – albeit only half-seriously – to call the priest to report Ianthe's teasing (86). In the second act she twice threatens to call for guards to evict Leander and Naukleros after they have accosted her (735f., 751ff.). In each case her threats are proved vain: indeed, on the last occasion, far from calling for guards, she allows herself to be persuaded to sit down beside the two men. So we are prepared for her failure to call for help against Leander as he clambers into her room. Papst argues that there is a tension or conflict between Hero's

---

[1] 'Oh handsome youth, gentle and good! I am thinking of you at this late hour, with feelings that lie so serenely on me that no offence can lurk below their surface. I wish you well, though glad that you are far away; and if my voice could reach you, I would call out to bid you "Good night!"'
[2] 'A head! – Two arms! – A man at the window!'
[3] 'Get back! If I call out you are lost!'

171

conscious will and the subconscious impulses of her love; but it is here above all that Grillparzer's heroine differs from Marlowe's, whose 'every part / Strove to resist the motions of her heart'. Though Grillparzer's Hero continues to protest, in fact, surely, the battle is lost before it is fought; it is lost at the moment when she threatens Leander, 'Zurück! Du bist verloren, wenn ich rufe' – and does not call.

From this point on we are shown, stage by stage, how she gradually gives ground before the irresistible onslaught of her feelings. At first she continues with her attempt at firmness, and she orders him not to move (1072); she means he must not advance further, but from his point of view 'Dort steh und reg dich nicht' is already an advance on her initial command that he get back. When she has heard his story of his heroic swim, she quickly betrays her concern as he stands shivering in wet clothes (1095), and is prepared to let him rest a while before he returns (1097f.). The next step is an apparent admission that she might have been his had he not approached her too late (1129f.). In the following speech she renews her plea that he return to Abydos, but argues from expediency rather than from principle: she appeals to him by telling him of the disgrace that faces her (1138–40). He must go – but by a less dangerous route than he came (1142–5); and no sooner has she in this way again betrayed her concern for his well-being than she hides him in her room from the patrolling temple guard (1152–5). When this danger is past, the emotional temperature is raised still further when Leander accidentally touches her shoulder in the darkness (1164). This first contact comes later than in Marlowe's poem, where it occurs in the temple; but it is a moment of equal tension. 'He touch'd her hand; in touching it she trembled', recounts Marlowe: so now Hero starts up at Leander's touch; she sends him back for the lamp and bewails her guilty position (1166). Leander begins to thank the gods for their escape, but Hero rounds on him: 'Entsetzlicher!' She wishes he had drowned or had fallen when scaling her tower; and then suddenly it is not he but the picture her words conjure up that is 'dreadful', and her tirade peters out in inarticulate horror: '...Entsetzlich Bild! – Leander, o – !' (1177). That a speech which has begun as a fierce attack on his intrusion ends with a wealth of emotion so confusing that Hero can manage only an 'O – !' of instinctive dread is itself utterly revealing of her feelings. Her concern for the danger he faces in the sea is so live and so disturbing that now she imagines the sea as wild and dangerous (1196) where previously she saw its present peaceful-ness (1026ff.); and Leander exploits her concern in order to win from her the promise of another meeting (1208–10).[1] She rapidly yields further ground. First she assigns the place (1213–15), but talks of a tryst to take place a year hence, on the day of the next festival (1220). Then immediately – more seriously – she suggests a day ten days away (1221); and then under further pressure from Leander she reduces the wait still further: 'Komm morgen denn!' (1229).[2] (Though rightly famous, this is another line that is at the mercy of clumsy performance: it must be spoken with utter naturalness if a crudely comic effect is not to intrude.) Now at last Hero can give open expression to her concern for his safety in the sea (1230ff.); and though for the third time she holds back from his embrace,[3] he once more works on that concern (1247f.), this time to win from her a kiss that finally is only a prelude to the full consummation of their love.

In Act IV, Hero's eagerness to set up her lamp to guide her lover once more across the Hellespont leads her to seize an opportunity to pretend to fetch a letter which the priest tells her has come from her parents (1749f.). This is not the first time she has practised small deceptions. At the end of the first act she pretends to look over her shoulder at her shoe, and looks back at Leander. In the second act (820) she tells her uncle that Leander is sick – as Naukleros has earlier told her (742) – and that that is why she has stopped with the two young men. And in the third act she pretends to be alone in the dark in the tower when in fact shielding Leander. All these deceptions are necessitated by, and are reminders of, the wrongfulness of her love ('wrongfulness' not in an absolute sense, but in relation to the vows to which she has committed herself). But as we have seen, she has no real sense of guilt, and least of all in the fourth act. Her uncle perceives the new maturity with which she faces him (1738). She is out of reach of that kind of creative self-possession which he teaches, but in her 'feeling of being a *woman*' she is now at last fully herself, and

---

[1] His approach is strikingly akin to that of Marlowe's Leander: '...This head was beat with many a churlish billow, / And therefore let it rest upon thy pillow.' For a full account of Grillparzer's debt to Marlowe, see the edition of the play by D. Yates (Oxford, 1947), Introduction (pp. xxxii–xxxv) and notes.

[2] 'Then come tomorrow!'

[3] l. 1234. The previous instances are in ll. 1187 and 1201.

she stands in open dramatic conflict with him, spurning the duty and the standards which he represents.

The priest is a character introduced into the legend by Grillparzer to provide a convincing dramatic link between the love of the two principals and Leander's death in the storm. In most earlier versions, including both Chapman's continuation of Marlowe's poem and Schiller's ballad 'Hero und Leander', Hero's torch, whose light guides Leander across the Hellespont, is extinguished by the winds themselves – as indeed Grillparzer's Hero assumes has happened (1955). In many versions of the well-known folksong treatment, 'Es waren zwei Königskinder', the heroine's candles are extinguished by a shadowy figure, a treacherous nun ('eine falsche Nonne'). One such version is that included in *Des Knaben Wunderhorn* (1806–8):

> Da saß ein loses Nönnechen,
> Das tat, als wenn es schlief',
> Es tat die Kerzlein ausblasen,
> Der Jüngling vertrank so tief.[1]

It is this rather sinister figure that Grillparzer has developed in the role of the priest. In another of the notes of summer 1827 he recalled that originally the priest was to have the 'role of fate' and accordingly to be 'remote' and 'cold'; but he added that that plan would have to be modified. In the finished work, the priest is not only the agent of retributive doom but also the apostle of moral duty. In this representative role, he is insistent on truthfulness (416). In fact, however, he too stoops to deception, sending Hero off to the harbour (1461f.) to fetch a letter that he already has in his possession (cf. 1349/SD): he does this to keep her occupied, so that she will be all the more surely asleep at night when he plans to bring about the downfall of the intruder. Later he attempts to conceal Hero's connexion with Leander from Ianthe (1910–13) and uses threats to ensure Naukleros' secrecy (1993); and Wells, recalling the alarmist account Hero herself gave to Leander of how her disgrace would be shared by her family (1138f.), even infers that the priest's concern is for his own safety. But all his deception hangs together with a determination to execute what he sees as his duty, and he acts in what he believes to be Hero's own interest. He resorts to intrigue only in an attempt to ward off the danger which he believes threatens

---

[1] 'A lecherous nun was sitting pretending to be asleep: she blew the candles out, and the youth drowned deep.'

her both from without (from the intruder) and from within (from
her own state of mind). He brings about Leander's death (and
hence, in the end, causes Hero's also), but this action and his
whole attitude to Hero in Act v are clearly determined by his
unrelenting hope that he may still restore her equanimity and
rescue her for her priestly office (e.g. 1999–2003). The standards
that justify his intrigues are explicitly divine, he sees himself as
an agent of the divine:

> In meinem Innern reget sich ein Gott,
> Und warnt mich, zu verhüten, eh's zu spät! (1365f.)[1]

To the last he sees Leander's death as being the work – and,
implicitly, therefore the responsibility – of the gods (1905f.), and
he tells Hero that it is the gods' way of indicating the magnitude
of her crime:

> Die Götter laut das blut'ge Zeugnis gaben,
> Wie sehr sie zürnen, und wie groß dein Fehl. (1927f.)[2]

In the face of Hero's plight such moralism can only seem callous,
and must forfeit our sympathy. Admittedly, the priest does not
at this stage realize the depth of her involvement; his tragic
limitation is that his own purity of devotion leads him consistently
to underestimate the strength of her feelings for Leander. He has,
however, seen her collapse (1903/sp), and his continued severity
shows at the very least an unattractive lack of imagination and
of sensitivity. Here and in the fourth act, where his role is that
of intrigant, there is some validity in Grillparzer's own subsequent
comment (coloured no doubt partly by the reactions of the original
audience): 'Above all the figure of the priest has come off badly'
(T 3247). In combating and defeating the force of love, the
character retains too much of the sinister quality of the treacherous
nun of folksong.

Surveying the critical literature on the play, Papst observes
that critics who see the dramatic conflict in the play not as one
within Hero but rather as one between love and an externally
imposed duty judge negatively the ethical values represented by the
priest. Such a negative judgment is not, however, necessary. It is
true that the whole idea of a lifelong renunciation of love – the
given basis of the tragedy – may seem arbitrary and unnatural;

---

[1] 'A god stirs within me and warns me to prevent it before it is too late!'
[2] 'By shedding this blood the gods have proclaimed for all to hear how deep
their wrath is, and how great your crime.'

it is true that in consequence the priest appears harsh, that in contrast to the overwhelming naturalness of Hero's love his precepts seem rigid; and it is true that the other characters in the play judge him unsympathetically, Naukleros charging him with selfish authoritarianism (860) and Ianthe with folly (2107). But while he acts ruthlessly, the demanding code of duty he represents is essentially a positive one: he is the guardian of the 'composure' and complete self-dedication ('Ganzheit') which, he believes, are necessary for vision and achievement alike. It is an ideal which makes absolute claims; and when he compares the priestess to spring-water whose power of reflection is impaired even by the first ripples on its surface (991–5), the action of the play demonstrates the validity of his point. His warning in the same speech that it is impossible to plunge into the fray of life without receiving lasting wounds (985f.) is matched in the last scene of the play by Ianthe's reaction to Hero's experience:

> ...Nun, ich will auch nimmer
> Ein' Lieb' mir wünschen, weder jetzt, noch sonst:
> Besitzen ist wohl schön, allein verlieren!   (2017–19)[1]

This resolve to avoid all involvement in love is an extreme reaction, but no answer. What Ianthe, and the audience, face is the familiar dilemma that to involve oneself in the fullness of life is to run the risk of 'wounds' or even of destruction, but to withdraw from it is to deprive oneself of the richness of experience. Ianthe views the problem from Hero's point of view, not from that of the positive inspirational values represented by the priest; and if in the end these positive values fail to outweigh the values of feeling which are made alive in the love of Hero and Leander, and if in the final analysis the priest himself remains unsympathetic, it is because in the audience, as in the heroine, the ideas he teaches are swept away by the compelling beauty and truth of the love which ripens in Act III and reveals its full violence in the final act of tragedy.

Hero finally acknowledges that Leander's death is the vengeance of the gods (2048). But this recognition of the divine will is insufficient to sustain her, inadequate to prevent her collapse and death. Her love for Leander has become for her an authority far more forceful than that of the service to which she innocently dedicated herself. Love, as Hero tells Leander, has the power to

---

[1] '...I will never wish for love, not now or ever: to possess is wonderful, but oh! to lose!'

extinguish the divine light of vision (1189), but it casts a light
of its own. Hero's whole spirit is filled with the light of Leander's
love:

> Der du einhergingst im Gewand der Nacht
> Und Licht mir strahltest in die dunkle Seele... (2060 f.)[1]

It is the light of love, made symbolically real in her lamp, that
draws him across the Hellespont. When he compares the light of
the lamp to a net spread over the sea (1112–15), this image has
its tragic irony in that the 'net' into which Leander is being led
is – as the realist Naukleros sees (1560) – a mortal snare. But Hero
and Leander are guided to tragedy by the light of love only
because they have met a day too late, so that Hero has already
committed herself and ringed herself around with strong protectors
– both the priest and also the very waves of the sea, which become
stormy and cruel in the face of her defiance of her duty, and which
symbolize both in the play and in the antithetical formulation
of its title the elemental, unrelenting quality of the eternal force
of duty.

It is because Hero's choice of priestly isolation was an unknowing choice that its finality seems unjust when the triviality
of her self-indulgent mood is replaced by the powerfully real
experience of her love for Leander. Their love is of the deepest
kind. Naukleros, who admires Hero's looks, approaches beauty
in purely physical terms (621–6), but Leander demands respect
when he talks of her (654). His love for her is something far more
than mere sensual attraction: their love finds physical fulfilment
as an expression of the real depth of emotion which joins them
and in which both find the fullness of life. The motif of 'life' is
stressed as much as in *Sappho*, but now with far wider sense: for
whereas Sappho is wrong in thinking that in experience of love
she can escape from barren isolation, for Hero and Leander, to
whom the breaking-down of enforced isolation is expressly
forbidden and in the long run impossible, their love is indeed life
itself. Its vitalizing effect on Leander is manifest in Act iv in the
dispelling of all his old melancholy and in his spirited defiance of
Naukleros' attempts to keep him in Abydos. The life-giving
quality that Hero experiences in him is conveyed when in a
voluptuous image of embrace she identifies him with the breeze
blowing across the sea from Abydos (1812–14); and at the outset

[1] 'You who came clothed in night and cast light into the darkness of my
heart...'

177

of Act v her confidence that he must still be alive is founded – so close is her identification of life itself with her love – solely on the fact that she is herself alive (1864). After she knows of his death she says he was 'everything' to her ('Er war alles', 1975); and later she takes off her garland, the symbol of the priesthood she has sacrificed, and her belt, the symbol of the virginity she has given up to him, and gives them to be laid in his grave, symbols of herself, of all she had to give:

> All was ich war, was ich besaß, du hast es,
> Nimm auch das Zeichen, da das Wesen dein. (2055f.)[1]

As surely as the priest knows that his standards are right for the priesthood, Hero knows that her love was right for her, she knows intuitively that for her, 'Ganzheit' cannot lie in priestly isolation but must lie in union with Leander. Hence the bitter certainty with which she accuses the pitiless gods who (she believes) have killed Leander (1955–64), in whom all the life of Nature was contained (1977f.), and whose death is an end of all life (1980f.) and of light (2060ff.): and hence finally the utter emptiness of heart with which she dies, a bleakness all compressed into her last despairing cries of Leander's name (2088f.).

After completing the play Grillparzer feared that the ending was 'too theatrical' (T 1709), and the première seemed to confirm that fear (T 1893). But in its directness it is all the more effective for not being rounded off by the kind of concluding moralizing that unbalances the end of *Medea*. What it achieves is, indeed, a perfect balance: the tragic victory of a representative of right over the guilty innocents, who by every standard of compassion are no less right.

Die Jüdin von Toledo

Whereas in Grillparzer's first love-tragedy the action concentrates from first to last on Hero, in the second Rahel appears only in the first three acts. Because of this, and because of the mainly political nature of the last two acts, the dominant role in the work is that of the king, Alfonso VIII of Castile. This is also the case in the play by Lope that was Grillparzer's principal source.

Lope, indeed, devotes the whole of his first act (in a play of only three acts) to Alfonso's youth: it shows him as a boy of

---

[1] 'All that I was, that I possessed, you have it: take the token too, since all it represents is yours!'

ten preparing to defend his crown against the claims of his uncle, Fernando of León, and taking the castle of a recalcitrant nobleman. When Grillparzer reread *Las paces de los Reyes* in 1850 or 1851, the one criticism he had to make of it was that as a result of Lope's organization of his material, the love-action, which was the dramatic core of the piece, was denied full scope. The first plan Grillparzer made for his own play in 1824 shows that he intended the love-affair to be central in it (T 1330); yet the finished work is open to criticism very similar to that which he levelled against *Las paces de los Reyes*. The restriction of Rahel's role to the first three acts made it possible to give fuller treatment to the political situation, in which Grillparzer became increasingly interested during the later years of his work on the text; but the result is that the work falls into two distinct halves of quite different character, the love-tragedy proper and a largely political afterpiece.

The preliminary material which Lope treats in his first act is compressed by Grillparzer into a single speech of expository narrative (101–41). In this speech the king's part in the actual struggle for power is minimized: as a mere child (138), he was a passive symbol rather than an active participant, 'Fahne mehr als Krieger noch' (134). He was, then, untainted by intrigue and bloodshed, he was morally worthy of his exalted position as king; and it is against the obligations inherent in that position that his subsequent failure is measured. He was carried to power, he recalls, as a defender of the rights of his people, 'eurer Rechte williger Beschirmer' (127); and he promises to lead the defence of his people against the threatening Moors (271). This danger is mentioned in Lope but is not central; in Grillparzer it becomes an ever-closer threat to the supreme order of the state, which is presented as having divine authority – 'Die heil'ge Ordnung, die er [*scil.* Gott] selbst gesetzt' (1238).[1] The king's duty is absolutely clear: in Garceran's words,

> Der Feind steht an den Grenzen, und der König
> Gehört zu seinem Heer...　　　　　　　　　(867f.)[2]

Alphons knows his duty (733f.), knows that he is wrong to evade it (902) – but still he dallies, demanding three days more with the beautiful Jewess, Rahel. As he acknowledges, his conduct is made

---

[1] 'The sacred order which God himself ordained.'
[2] 'The enemy is at our borders, and the king belongs with his army...'

doubly serious by the fact of his kingship: 'Was andern Laune, ist beim Fürsten Schuld' (711).[1] After Rahel's murder, he admits his errors to the queen (1375, 1422, 1490), and defines them explicitly in terms of his neglected duty as ruler of his kingdom:

> Ein König, der an sich nicht gar so schlimm,
> Hat seines Amts und seiner Pflicht vergessen.   (1438f.)[2]

The psychological basis for the king's conduct, formulated in Grillparzer's first plan and brought out clearly in the completed text, is his inexperience, especially in love. At the outset, like Hero, he has still to be awakened to love. It is true that he is married, but his marriage was his first experience of women (182f.); in Act IV he speaks of himself and his queen as having been like children at the time of their marriage (1379–81). It was, indeed, his very devotion to his political and military duties that had hitherto precluded attention to the attractions of 'life':

> Als Knabe schon den Helm auf schwachem Haupt,
> Als Jüngling mit der Lanze hoch zu Roß,
> Das Aug gekehrt auf eines Gegners Dräun,
> Blieb mir kein Blick für dieses Lebens Güter,
> Und was da reizt und lockt, lag fern und fremd.
>   (177–81)[3]

He has had little more experience since. 'Ich selbst hab' nie nach Weibern viel gesehn,' he says,[4] contrasting himself to his confidant Garceran, who is 'a connoisseur' (353f.); and he repeats the point almost verbatim shortly afterwards (396). It is because he is conscious of Garceran's superiority in this respect that he warns him against attempting to play the interloper with Rahel (379–81). In Act II, with a growing wistfulness conditioned by his thoughts of Rahel, he again talks of his inexperience with women and contrasts this with Garceran's experience and resulting confidence, which he envies (444–50); and that his fears of Garceran as a potential rival are not wholly unjustified becomes clear in Act III, when Rahel too contrasts them both and expresses her admiration for Garceran's graces in amatory matters, which the king lacks (920–7).

---

[1] 'What in others is mere caprice, is for a sovereign guilt.'
[2] 'A king, not all that evil in himself, forgot his office and his duty.'
[3] 'As a weak boy with a helmet already on my head, and as a youth sitting high on a charger with a lance in my hand and my eyes turned towards the threatening foe, I had no eyes for the good things of this life, and its attractions and temptations were distant and unknown to me.'
[4] 'I myself have never given much attention to women.'

Alphons's love for Rahel involves a loss of innocence, in two senses. First, he matures to a fuller understanding of life: 'Seit ich sie sah, empfand ich, daß ich lebte' (1688).[1] Secondly, his love is a moral downfall. Garceran tells him that the attraction Rahel has had for him is that of Eve for Adam (993–5); his loss of his purity in duty follows the pattern of the eternal fall of man. And Garceran – who finds the conduct of his supposedly adult king reminiscent of the adventures in which he himself indulged in his youth (876–8) – perceives that the emotional violence of this fall is directly attributable to Alphons's inexperience:

> O, daß doch dieser König seine Jugend,
> Der Knabenjahre hast'gen Ungestüm
> In Spiel und Tand, wie mancher sonst, verlebt!...
>
> Und nun ist auch der Widerstand besiegt,
> Den die Erfahrung leiht dem oft Getäuschten,
> Zum bittern Ernst wird ihm das lose Spiel.
>
> (851–3; 863–5)[2]

Like Hero, Alphons is defenceless in a way that only heightens the dangerous power of his emotion when it is finally aroused.

In linking Alphons's liaison to its political context Grillparzer was not merely following his source in Lope, but could also draw on a contemporary example of comparable defection from duty on the part of a ruling monarch. The scandalous affair between King Ludwig I of Bavaria and the dancer Lola Montez came to a head politically in 1847 when the king overthrew the ultramontane government of Karl von Abel, which opposed Lola Montez's naturalization. The eventual consequences of the affair included the expulsion of Lola Montez and the abdication of the king. That Grillparzer saw in this episode a parallel to the position of his own King Alphons is suggested by his description of Lola Montez in the spring of 1847 as a woman 'in whose arms a king became a man' (G 285); and his continued interest in the affair is attested by a series of epigrams composed in 1847 and subsequent years.[3] When he resumed work on the second and third acts of *Die Jüdin* in 1848 and 1849 this topical interest may not only

---

[1] 'It is only since first I saw her that I felt I was alive.'
[2] 'Oh, had this king only spent his youth, the turbulent years of impatient boyhood, in frivolous play, as so many do!...And all resistance, which experience lends to the man who has often been deceived, is in his case now overcome: the empty game is turning to bitter earnest.'
[3] G 1058, 1069, 1102, 1226, 1227.

have determined the political emphasis of the entire last two acts but may also have influenced the monitory treatment accorded to the king.

Alphons appears, in a sense, to be harshly treated by his queen and the grandees of his kingdom. That they meet in convocation in his absence, as though he were dead, serves partly to bring out dramatically the idea that he has abandoned the basic reality of his life, his duty in the state; in fact, however, he has offended against no actual law, but solely against the moral law. He is judged, in short, not by the written laws, which are inadequate to deal with this issue, but by the higher law of his duty, which the state embodies; and it is in service of the state that he abdicates in favour of his son and sets out to atone for his guilt by defending the 'sacred order' against the Moors. The abdication is clearly a demonstrative gesture, a symbolic restoration of moral purity in the leadership of the state. In practical terms, however, the efficacy of the gesture seems dubious, in that it must elevate and put at risk once more that same vulnerable innocence that was Alphons's own downfall. The ideal ruler, such as Rudolf I, is a father-figure to his people; Alphons has fallen short of this ideal precisely because in experience he has been 'no better than a grown-up child' (453). Moreover, while as an act of atonement his commitment to the battle against the Moors is clearly positive and constructive in a way that (for example) the self-immolation of Sappho is not, nonetheless dereliction of supreme duty is not easily atoned for. The historical Alfonso VIII was in fact heavily defeated by the Moors at Alarcos in 1195, and reversed this defeat only in 1212, two years before his death; and while the action of the play does not extend to this battle, and its outcome is left unstated,[1] Alarcos has been mentioned by name as a theatre of war (732), and the strength of the enemy has been stressed (e.g. 266) enough to suggest that in his dutiful and promised protection of his people he will be no more successful than he was in the protection he promised Rahel.

The character of the woman who exercises so fateful a power over him is problematic. What he encounters in her is, as Garceran puts it, 'das Weib als solches, nichts als ihr Geschlecht' (859),[2] the female of the species with all her unpredictability and coquetry:

---

[1] No more than in *König Ottokar* and the *Bruderzwist* is Grillparzer attempting to give a full and accurate historical picture: his interest is in the dramatic situation centring on the love-affair and Alphons's moral problem.

[2] 'woman as woman, nothing but her sex'.

capricious, unreflecting, sensually appealing, at once naive and calculating. The depth of her love for the king is arguable. Even in Act III she tells Garceran that she has never known the full force of love (957–9); but when the king has left her and she fears he will not return she tells her sister Esther that she has truly loved him (1136). Since this is the last line she speaks in the play, the final impression that we gain of her feelings for him is positive. But Rahel is a creature of impulse, and these words, like all her words, are true only for the moment they are spoken. Even her feelings about herself are changeable. One moment she is sobbing on Esther's shoulder in her fear of death (1104–8), the next her attention is caught by a necklace with amethysts and pearls which Esther has brought her (1109f.). To the king she remains a mystery;[1] he remembers her as having the solipsism of a child (1666f.), yet also 'all the faults on the face of the earth': folly, vanity, weakness, cunning, obstinacy, coquetry, avarice (1456–8). Garceran describes her as having been 'lecherous and wanton, full of malicious tricks' (1837); and to the king even her beauty appears in retrospect to have reflected this side of her character (1849–51). Nevertheless, he senses that – unlike the queen – Rahel was herself, was natural; this is a point he makes in Act IV (1497f.) and again in Act V:

> Sie aber war die Wahrheit, ob verzerrt,
> All, was sie tat, ging aus aus ihrem Selbst,
> Urplötzlich, unverhofft und ohne Beispiel.　　(1685–7)[2]

Grillparzer's sources had presented him with a heroine whose hold over the king was 'not without a suspicion of sorcery' (T 1330). Grillparzer underlined this point heavily in his diary; but from an early stage in his work on the play he conceived of the king as being 'bewitched' only in a figurative sense. This motif is developed in the finished work. The queen believes Rahel to have truly bewitched the king, but Alphons knows better:

> Umgeben sind wir rings von Zaubereien,
> Allein wir selber sind die Zauberer.　　(1429f.)[3]

---

[1] Grillparzer knew (and could draw on his observation of) just such a mysteriously contradictory personality in real life: cf. 'Trennung' (G 84, ix), stanzas 4–7 ('Ein Rätsel warst du mir...', l. 17). The lines about Rahel's 'Wahrheit' (1685–7) also correspond to an insight expressed in the same poem (l. 67). Cf. also T 1639.

[2] 'But she was truth itself, even though distorted: everything she did sprang from her very self, spontaneous, unexpected and unique.'

[3] 'We are surrounded all about by sorcery, but we ourselves are the sorcerers.'

He insists that the attraction Rahel has had for him is a natural attraction:

> Und wenn, statt Zauber, rätselhaft du's nennst,
> Daß jemals sie gefiel, so stimm' ich ein
> Und schämte mich, wär's nicht natürlich wieder.
> (1460–2)[1]

The miniature of her that holds his love even when he is far away from her has 'magical' powers only in that it shows her in all her entrancing beauty. Rahel is herself well aware of that beauty (604) and of her magnetic attractiveness (724).

Her spontaneity, and her consequent capriciousness, are part of her fascination for the king, as Wells points out in his analysis of the play. But the basis of her hold over him is, quite simply, her physical attractiveness. This was a central point in Grillparzer's first detailed plan, and it derives directly from Lope, though it is treated by the two dramatists in characteristically different ways. In Lope, it is the king who, having seen Raquel bathing, dispatches Garcerán to fetch her (II, 4); in Grillparzer it is Rahel who is the aggressor – who, indeed, deliberately sets out to force herself (and her attractions) on Alphons (69ff.). This change of emphasis is indicative of Rahel's role in relation to the king: that of a disturbing influence endangering his devotion to his duty, his 'Ganzheit'. It is significant that Rahel is trespassing when the king sees her in his gardens, just as Leander meets Hero 'on forbidden ground' (*Des Meeres und der Liebe Wellen* 565). In Lope, moreover, the king is so swiftly and so completely captivated by Raquel's naked beauty that his infatuation overcomes his horror when her clothes show that she is a Jewess; in Grillparzer, a sense of love grows slowly within the king, gaining its dominion over him gradually and revealing itself, as Wells shows, in his irritable jealousy of Garceran. But though Grillparzer's characterization differs from Lope's, he makes the manner of Rahel's appeal no less clear. The king succumbs to a constant current of sensual feeling, which is established, and vividly suggested, at their first confrontation. Where the queen has turned away from Rahel's appeals for protection, the king does not; Rahel throws herself at his feet, her arms holding his right foot (312/SD) – and gripping it so hard, indeed, that later he still notices the effects (387f.). Then, raising her head, she starts to take off her jewelry to offer it as a ransom: after her jewelry she takes off a costly oriental neckscarf she is

---

[1] 'And if, instead of "magic", you call it "mysterious" that she ever appealed to me, then I agree – and would be ashamed, were it not in fact so natural.'

wearing, so that her throat is bared (316/SD). She sinks back again; then in fear of being killed, she points to the jewelry (330/SD) and lays her cheek against the king's knee (331/SD). The immediacy of this physical contact is something characteristic of Grillparzer's love-actions; the powerful effect of contact and touch is also brought out strongly, for instance, in the relations between Zawisch and Kunigunde (*Ottokar* 881, 945f.). But this quality of physical immediacy in scenes such as that between Rahel and the king in the first act of *Die Jüdin* is something which can make its full effect on the audience only in performance on the stage; when F. O. Nolte cites the play as an illustration of what he holds to be Grillparzer's failure to achieve the 'thickness' of 'truly sensuous art', one cannot but wonder whether he ever saw this scene acted well. The effects build up right until the end of the act. The king entrusts Rahel to Garceran's care, and thanking him she conjures up two potent images: first, her throat (now bare) severed by the hangman, and secondly her breast as a shield for the king against the foe (375f.). Alphons exclaims that it is 'a beautiful shield' (377).

By Act II his whole mood is affected. He questions Garceran about his past philandering, imagining him singing serenades in the scented air of a moonlit night and being led to his mistress – who, he insists, must have black hair (457–77). Their conversation is followed by one with Isak, Rahel's father. Isak tells the king (whom he has not recognized) of how she has taken his portrait from the wall and pressed it to her breast (548). Alphons goes quickly to the house; not in anger, as Isak fears, but to see her (549). Rahel is talking of hanging the portrait by her bed, and looking at it when she is undressed (573–7); she sits facing the picture, addressing it, pretending that she is the queen, insisting that Rahel has attracted the king, and is comparable only to herself (598–604). 'Gesteht!' she insists. 'Gefiel sie Euch? Sagt ja!' And the answer comes from the listening king: 'Nun ja!' (604).[1] It is an equivalent to Leander's 'Gut Nacht!' in *Des Meeres und der Liebe Wellen*: in both cases the single line contains both the wish and then the answer, proclaiming the arrival of the lover; and all the magnetic, 'magical' sensual appeal of Rahel, who has pressed herself against his knee, bared her throat, and pressed his picture to her breast, is expressed in Alphons's exclamation, full of sensual clarity, 'Und wie das wogt und wallt

---

[1] 'Confess! Did she attract you? Say yes!' 'Then – yes!'

und glüht und prangt!' (641).[1] What most he remembers of her after her death is her 'voluptuous form' (1705).

Because the king's love for Rahel is fundamentally sensual, there is a temptation for the reader to dismiss it – by comparison, perhaps, with the love of Hero and Leander – as superficial. This is, indeed, a mistake the king himself makes. Such is the human capacity for self-deception that throughout the first three acts he never fully realizes the extent of Rahel's hold over him. He misleads himself into thinking of his affair as phantasmal (904), easily dismissed, a mere dalliance (910). But we cannot dismiss as superficial an emotion whose strength is sufficient to bring a king to the very brink of forfeiting his kingdom. Even after Rahel's death Alphons has still to free himself of her spell, which lives on in his mind: indeed, while he has in her presence admitted, and repeated, his liking for her (604, 610), it is only when she is dead that he fully professes his love and claims his exclusive right to it (1669–73). The elegiac tone of his praise is in a vein familiar in Grillparzer's work: the speech is a more eloquent counterpart to the grieving affection which in the final pages of *Der arme Spielmann* Barbara displays for the dead Jakob. By this time, however, the Rahel Alphons is recalling is already an idealized memory, and the illusion is shattered when he is brought back to reality by seeing her corpse. Just as Hero finds herself estranged by the sight and the coldness of Leander's dead body (*Des Meeres und der Liebe Wellen* 2028–32), so the sight of Rahel estranges the king from his image of her, and his reaction is expressed in mime: he looks down at his two hands and runs each one over the other 'as though to cleanse them'. Then he makes the same cleansing motion over the upper part of his body. Finally he raises his hands to his throat and moves them round it. In this posture he stands, staring, with his hands to his throat (SD/1813). It was her throat that Rahel bared, crying that she did not want to die (319); he promised her his protection (617), and she is dead. His failure towards her forms a parallel to his failure to his people, whom he has promised to protect (271) and whom he has neglected for the pleasures of love. He has failed by putting self before duty, with fatal results for Rahel and dangerous ones for the security of his land.

The representative of duty in the play, the anti-sensual counterweight to the sensuous Rahel, is the queen, Eleonore. She is an English Puritan; and that her (apparent) coldness is typically

---

[1] 'And how her breast surges and swells! How glowing, how radiant!'

English is made explicit – rather glibly – by the king in the first act (210–12). The contrast between her and Rahel is made mimically clear at their first confrontation. Rahel kneels before the queen, asking her protection (304–6): she reaches for the queen's hands, and the queen turns away from her. When Alphons does not turn away, Eleonore spells out the contrast between his position, 'caught' by Rahel, and her own:

KÖNIGIN   Wollt Ihr nicht gehn?
KÖNIG   Ihr seht, ich bin gefangen!
KÖNIGIN   Seid Ihr gefangen, bin ich frei. Ich gehe.   (333f.)[1]

In the second act they confront each other again. When Rahel dresses herself in a cloak and crown that she has found among costumes from the previous year's Shrovetide play and poses as the queen to address Alphons's picture, she forces an unspoken comparison between herself and the queen in whose position she has put herself – and this comparison is then enacted in fact when the queen enters in person. The real queen faces the costume queen; the standards of reality confront those of the king's fantasy, and the realist Esther quickly takes both crown and cloak away from Rahel.

Alphons is not sparing of criticism of his consort. Even before he has met Rahel he suggests that Eleonore is too perfect to be wholly lovable (184–6); and in the fourth act he criticizes her to her face for her cheerless virtue (1499–1503), and even suggests that it is in part responsible for his lapse, which he presents as a form of escape (1504). Psychologically, this makes sense, and as a piece of motivation it is not without parallel in Grillparzer's work: Ottokar too has escaped from a loveless marriage, that with Margarete, into dalliance with Berta von Rosenberg. Alphons's argument in Act IV of *Die Jüdin von Toledo* develops out of a point he has made earlier about himself – his fear that 'der Mensch, der wirklich ohne Fehler,/Auch ohne Vorzug wäre' (163f.).[2] This he now applies by implication to Eleonore: true virtue, he says, is a whole range of separate, colourful virtues,

Und nicht ein hohles Bild, das ohne Fehl,
Doch eben drum auch wieder ohne Vorzug.   (1507f.)[3]

Still later he repeats that virtue ('die Tugend') must be not only 'worthy of respect' but 'lovable too' ('liebenswürdig auch', 1910f.).

[1] Queen: 'Are you not coming?' King: 'As you see, I am caught!' 'You may be caught, but I am free. I am going.'
[2] [that] 'a person utterly without faults were also without excellence'.
[3] '...And not a hollow idol that lacks all faults but for that very reason lacks all merit too.'

Tugend and *Liebenswürdigkeit*: these are complementary qualities embodied in Eleonore and Rahel respectively. Each wholly lacks what the other represents. The queen, in short, stands for a correct, unyielding morality. The moralistic and anti-sensual elements in her nature combine in her attitude to marriage, which she describes as sacred and therefore justifying what is otherwise repulsive:

> Ist denn die Ehe nicht das Heiligste,
> Da sie zu Recht erhebt, was sonst verboten,
> Und was ein Greuel jedem Wohlgeschaffnen
> Aufnimmt ins Reich der gottgefäll'gen Pflicht?   (1202–5)[1]

Hers is an uncompromising attitude, and a narrow one; she can forgive the king, for such is the meekness of virtue, but she has so little feeling for sensuality that, as she admits, she is quite incapable of understanding his lapse (1377f.).

It falls to the queen to demand Rahel's death (1199): her reason, uncompromisingly presented to the assembled grandees, is Rahel's violation of the sacred law of marriage (1208ff.). The coquette is condemned by the voice of moral duty; and in this respect Eleonore's role is akin to that of the priest in *Des Meeres und der Liebe Wellen*. Yet despite all her Puritanical sternness, she is much more than a figure of cold retribution. In planning that it should be Eleonore who insists on Rahel's death Grillparzer noted in 1827: 'The queen shy, *seemingly* cold, an Englishwoman ...' [my italics].[2] Particularly after his experience of England in 1836, he could not be satisfied to take over the stereotyped character of Lope's 'icy angel' (*ángel tan helado*, II, 3), and if he makes the king's view of her as a typical Englishwoman seem facile, this is a subtle indication that the king does not at that stage appreciate her true character. In fact, Eleonore's coldness *is* only apparent: it is at least in part a reserve which hides both determination and real feeling. When the king begs her forgiveness and seeks reconciliation in Act IV, she agrees with immediate gladness (1363), and holds out her hands to him – a welcoming gesture which expresses warmth by its diametric contrast with her refusal to take Rahel's hands in the first act. She displays the same warmth in the final act, when Alphons returns to the stage after viewing Rahel's corpse: what she sees is not his anger but – with an immediacy that betrays otherwise unspoken depths of

---

[1] 'For is not marriage the most sacred state, in that it justifies what is otherwise forbidden and exalts into the realm of duty, pleasing to God, what is an abomination to every virtuous being?'

[2] *Wke.* I/21, 369.

jealous love – the fact that he has taken off Rahel's picture (1819f.). The light these incidents throw on her character suggests that if the king is right in comparing Eleonore and himself, as they have been hitherto, to children (1379–81), then she has already developed a broader humanity and proved herself, as he believes her, 'nicht unzugänglich...dem innern Wachstum' (1393).[1]

The play as a whole does not match the formal balance of *Des Meeres und der Liebe Wellen,* and the impulsive Rahel lacks Hero's range of tragic feeling. In one respect at least, however, *Die Jüdin* marks an advance on what Grillparzer himself saw as the shortcomings of his earlier love-tragedy: if he suspected the priest in *Des Meeres und der Liebe Wellen* of being too forbidding, in *Die Jüdin* the forces of duty – a loving queen and a loyal state – are no less right, and significantly more sympathetic.

Esther

There is one more work which has to be considered together with Grillparzer's love-tragedies. This is the fragmentary play *Esther,* the principal source for which was the biblical Book of Esther. When Grillparzer finally abandoned the work as a fragment in 1848, he had completed two acts and forty lines of the third. We learn at the outset of the king's separation from his queen, Vasthi (on grounds based on Esther i. 11–12), and of the plan of Haman (who combines the role of the biblical Haman and that of 'the king's servants' of Esther ii. 2) to find a replacement for Vasthi in the king's affections. Esther is chosen because of her beauty to be brought before the king, and Mardochai (the Mordecai of the Authorized Version) enjoins her to conceal her race. Mardochai at once appears a figure of conviction and sureness – a contrast both to the king, who feels isolated and insecure among his courtiers (227–71), and to the court itself, where favour, as Haman warns Esther early in the second act, is precarious and fleeting (541f.). Immediately after this warning, the king enters, weary of the sycophancy of the court:

> Wie widerlich! nur immer sich zu hören
> Und alle andern leerer Widerhall.   (584f.)[2]

Esther boldly urges him to reinstate Vasthi, and tries to defend her against his criticisms:

---

[1] 'not closed...to spiritual development'.
[2] 'How hateful it is always to hear only oneself, all others being but an empty echo!'

KÖNIG Wohl also denn, du kennst sie nicht, die Frau,
Für die du sprichst, du lobtest sonst sie minder.
Denn sie ist stolz.

ESTHER   Auf dich.

KÖNIG   Rachsüchtig.

ESTHER   Gib
Ihr nichts zu rächen.

KÖNIG   Eifersüchtig.

ESTHER   Herr!
Die Eifersucht der Fraun ist Liebe stets...   (662–6)[1]

Struck by Esther's directness and her refusal to flatter him, and hopeful of her affection, the king chooses her as his queen. Mardochai learns of a plot against her by Vasthi's supporters; and in the fragment of the third act his warning is brought to Esther and read by the king. The completed text, then, breaks off with the story at a point equivalent to Esther ii. 22.

In between Grillparzer's conception of the play and the main stint of work on the manuscript in 1839–40, two significant events both heightened his interest in and clarified his attitude to the story. The first was the death in December 1829 of the Archduchess Henriette, the Protestant wife of Archduke Karl: this rekindled a public controversy about religious tolerance that had first been sparked off by their marriage in 1815. The second was a rereading in 1831 of Lope de Vega's play *La hermosa Ester*, which Grillparzer had probably read twice in the 1820s, but which now more than ever captured his imagination: 'This Lope de Vega is taking a greater hold on me than is good for a modern poet,' he wrote. 'He is Nature itself...' In particular he noted Lope's depiction of the relation of Aman to Mardocheo, Aman's feeling of almost physical suffering at the thought of someone who refuses him the respect he is due. This confirmed Grillparzer's own conception of Haman's character, which had probably been influenced by earlier reading of *La hermosa Ester* and which he had jotted down in note-form in 1830: 'The fact that Mardochäus does not bow his head before him weighs him down like an illness. This contempt, while everyone else kneels before him, prevents him from eating and from resting. Vanity his chief characteristic.'[2] It is possible that Grillparzer also knew Racine's *Esther* (and may have derived

---

[1] King: 'You cannot know her, then, the woman whom you defend, or you would praise her less. For she is proud.' 'Of you.' 'Vengeful.' 'Give her nothing to avenge!' 'Jealous.' 'Sire! Women's jealousy is always love...' *Wke.* 1/1, 450.

from it his spelling of the name Zares, in contrast to the Seres of Luther's Bible); but this is only speculation.

The first 731 lines of Grillparzer's text, concluding with the king's choice of Esther to be his new queen, were published and performed in the 1860s. Grillparzer's restriction of the material published was doubtless founded partly on the sense that the first scenes made a well-rounded picture on their own, as he is reported to have told Emil Kuh (*Gespr.* 1116), but still more on the fact that – as he told Professor Robert Zimmermann in January 1866 – the final scene of the second act leads on too clearly into further material. The conversation with Zimmermann (*Gespr.* 1176) is one of two in which Grillparzer discussed how the work might have developed had he completed it. The other was with Auguste von Littrow-Bischoff in May 1868 (*Gespr.* 1212). They are to some extent mutually contradictory, particularly about the ending; but the later conversation is reported with such circumstantiality that there can be little real doubt that Grillparzer's intentions, especially with regard to the delineation of Esther's character, were in accordance with what he revealed to Auguste von Littrow-Bischoff. It is possible to piece together in outline how the action would have continued. In Act III the king would frustrate the plot against Esther by having her exchange the poisoned goblet with his own, so forcing the cupbearer Bightan – who wants not to kill the king, but to reunite him with Vasthi – to confess. Haman meanwhile would be planning to gain the king's permission for persecution of the Jews. According to Grillparzer's conversation with Zimmermann, Haman would have been won over to Vasthi's side by his wife, Zares; and according to the conversation with Frau von Littrow-Bischoff, Bightan would support his plans. The third act would close with the scene between the king and Haman, 'a major scene about the rights of the state in relation to religion, about the position of religion in the state, about freedom of conscience, political rights and ecclesiastical dogma' (*Gespr.* 1212). In Act IV, Mardochai would demand that Esther save her people from their persecution by revealing to the king that she is a Jewess. Unwilling to imperil her own happiness, she would refuse, but in another crucial scene she would be brought to submission by the authority of Mardochai's learning. And now there would follow a scene (corresponding to the fifth and sixth chapters of the Book of Esther) in which Esther would come unbidden before the king, he would come across Mardochai's name in the chronicle and resolve to reward him, and Haman would unwittingly recount the honours which Mardochai is to receive but which he thinks will be for himself. The last act would include Esther's banquet, at which Haman would beg her for mercy, and she would refuse. According to Zimmermann's account, Grillparzer planned that only Haman would be killed, and that the ending would not be strictly tragic. But he told Auguste von Littrow-Bischoff that Zares would also die – and perhaps Esther too, 'after she has become corrupt'; or she might lead 'a life of torment with the morbidly agitated king, after Haman's role of indulging the ruler's whims has fallen to her'. One of the reasons Grillparzer gave for not completing the work was the prospect of official reaction and censorship. The theme was too similar to the controversy surrounding Archduke Karl: indeed, the whole subject of religious tolerance and the relationship of religion and politics, which was to be central in the third act, would have guaranteed that the work could never have been performed or even printed. As a result, he said, all his interest in proceeding with it died (*Gespr.* 1212).

A further reason for his diminishing interest in *Esther* must undoubtedly have been its similarities with his two love-tragedies, which had also been planned in the 1820s and which were both eventually completed. The subject of a king who falls in love with a young Jewess is one common factor with *Die Jüdin von Toledo*, and another is the problem of the ruler's prime duty to his state: in the *Esther* fragment the king's advisers are concerned with his reactions to Vasthi's departure because the business of the state is suffering (101, 171f.). On the other hand, the relationship between Esther and Mardochai is strikingly similar to that between Hero and the priest in *Des Meeres und der Liebe Wellen*: Mardochai, like the priest, is the learned voice of duty (in this case Esther's duty to her race), and Esther has no more conception of her duty to her people than Hero has of hers as a priestess; indeed, she explicitly describes to Mardochai an ideal of love which is based on personal feeling, and not on wider ideals or causes (346–56). The completion of *Des Meeres und der Liebe Wellen* and then the resumption of work on *Die Jüdin von Toledo* meant that essential elements in the *Esther* fragment had been developed or were being developed elsewhere.

As for why Grillparzer chose to resume work on *Die Jüdin von Toledo* in 1848 rather than on *Esther*, there are also intrinsic factors in his plan for the latter work which must have contributed materially to his inability to continue and complete it. According to Frau von Littrow-Bischoff's account, Esther was to appear in the end as a thoroughly unworthy character (that is, a figure related to Elga in *Das Kloster bei Sendomir*). 'I had intended the heroine as a *lover*, not as a figure of *virtue*', Grillparzer observed; and he argued that 'the seeds of corruption' are present in her character from the start, in that by concealing her race and religion she gains the throne by dissembling. But while Esther is capable of denying her religion and her kin, she does so for love – in a cause, that is, which (rightly or wrongly) can be regarded as more valid in such beings as Esther than the principles she offends against: comparable examples are Hero's desertion of her duty as priestess and Juliet's of her family. She attracts the king by making, or appearing to make, no effort to attract him; how genuine her attitude is Haman cannot decide (533–5), but her genuine love for the king shows in her concern for his safety rather than her own (946f.), which is wholly in keeping with the conception of love she has outlined to Mardochai (354f.). She is a realist; she is assertive and self-possessed; in the palace she appears unsophisticated but watchful, to the king she is both shrewd and frank and maintains her self-confidence to the point of impudence.[1] She does not have Hero's charm; but nor is she a villainess, and she shields Haman from the king's anger (574–6) as generously as Hero shields Ianthe from the priest's (*Des Meeres und der Liebe Wellen* 103f.). In short, for Esther to end as a scoundrel would entail a change in her character of a kind that is insufficiently foreshadowed in the opening acts. It holds true of all great characters in literature, even if it is not always apparent in characters of real life, that the germ of what they develop into is present from the start, and must be revealed to be so; in the case of Esther, Frau von Littrow-Bischoff was justified in expressing her surprise at the fate in store for the 'sweet creature' of the first scenes. But even had he revised the published fragment and developed the motivation of Esther's character, Grillparzer would have faced a thankless task; for while it may be artistically rewarding to show that in the worst of us there is good which can prevail, it is less so (certainly according to nineteenth-century standards) to show the evil in the best of us.

[1] E.g. 331–5 (assertiveness); 378–80, 426f. (realism); 456–60 (self-possession); 477–89 (watchfulness and lack of sophistication); 526 (shrewdness); 595 (frankness); 641–52 (near-impudence).

5

COMEDY AND THE THEATRE

'Theatrical' Novellen

We have now met Grillparzer's work in three separate fields: his plays, his poems, and his two short stories. It was essentially as a dramatist that he thought of himself; he regarded as secondary not only his lyrics but also, despite the success of *Der arme Spielmann*, his prose writings. He once wrote to Heckenast, the publisher of *Der arme Spielmann*, that stories were not at all his line (B 663). This is over-modest as an assessment of his achievement in narrative form; but it certainly seems that his narrative technique in both his short stories shows his natural feeling for *dramatic* action. He once remarked that he could see his characters standing before him as he wrote (*Gespr.* 13); and clearly this vivid power of visualization applied to his narrative as well as his dramatic writing. One of the most striking features of his stories is his use of gesture rather than speech to express emotion. As a device in prose narrative, this is by no means peculiar to Grillparzer, but is in fact common in the *Novellen* of the Poetic Realist period. Towards the end of Annette von Droste-Hülshoff's story *Die Judenbuche*, for example, after Friedrich Mergel's return to his home village, he sits carving a wooden spoon, and he cuts it in two: the simple report of this accident serves to suggest his preoccupation. Effects of this kind are, however, particularly marked in Grillparzer. The opening pages of *Das Kloster bei Sendomir* contain two good examples. When the monk Starschensky is asked what man beloved of God founded the monastery, Grillparzer describes him bursting into scornful laughter, putting such intense pressure on the chair on which he is leaning that it breaks, and directing a fiery glance at the travellers before stalking out of the room (p. 8). Nothing is said – what we are given is, as it were, a stage direction, and Starschensky's actions serve to suggest the violence of his feelings. A page or so later, as he is about to start his story, he is described as sitting motionless, his head on his chest, before he rouses himself and begins: again the

194

physical posture, described with the precision of a stage direction, serves to suggest the (now changing) mood of the central figure.

Dramatic features are equally striking in the second story. Symbolic values are brought out by visual effects such as the use of Jakob's hat or the chalk line down the centre of his room. His timidity is revealed in physical trembling – both in his approaches to Barbara's home (60f.) and, in old age, when he is surprised by the approach of the narrator (49). His story is punctuated with theatrical gestures: an example is the way he points at his body with both hands to explain why Barbara would not have liked to be married to him (74). The *Novelle* is brought to a close with a tableau-effect, with Barbara having locked the violin in a drawer and the narrator looking back to see her standing with tears streaming down her cheeks (81). Also reminiscent of the technique of drama is the dialogue at climaxes, where speeches tend to be shorter and sharper, with an effect akin to stichomythia: examples are Jakob's first conversation with Barbara, about her song (58f.), his first encounter with her father (62), and the scene with Barbara in which his financial ruin is discovered (71–3).

Both stories have been dramatized. *Das Kloster bei Sendomir* was dramatized by Gerhart Hauptmann early in 1896, and *Der arme Spielmann* by the Austrian dramatist Rudolf Holzer in 1913. The problems that Hauptmann and Holzer faced are instructive about the qualities and virtues of their sources. When Grillparzer's contemporary Nestroy attempted a dramatic version of *Martin Chuzzlewit* (*Die Anverwandten*, 1848), his chief difficulty was in selecting his material: within the scenes he borrowed he could often re-use Dickens' dialogue with little alteration. This is precisely what Hauptmann and Holzer could not do: Grillparzer's stories provided the (theatrical) mimic element, action and gestures, but dialogue largely remained to be added.

Hauptmann was able to fashion the action of *Das Kloster bei Sendomir* into dramatic form by the simple expedient of turning the monk's story into a dream, dreamt by a traveller at the monastery. One result of this is a noticeable change of perspective, in that Elga, rather than Starschensky, occupies the central position in the action, and this is reflected in Hauptmann's title, *Elga*. Otherwise Hauptmann follows the main outlines of Grillparzer's story until the tragedy, where he stops short after Oginsky's death, and does not show the murder of Elga. But he necessarily expands Grillparzer's story, developing and inventing dialogue, increasing the roles of minor characters (including Oginsky) and introducing other characters; and as a result, both the language and the action seem diffuse in contrast to the tautness and economy of the original. Moreover, partly as a result of the process of expansion – which has Oginsky introduced as early as scene 3 and shows his complicity with Elga, and which throughout makes the feelings and thoughts of the characters more explicit – the character of Elga appears much less mysterious than in Grillparzer's story. One of the possible critical objections to the story is that Elga's behaviour is too mysterious, that her conduct is insufficiently motivated and hence lacks verisimilitude; but in changing the balance and clarifying the motivation, Hauptmann sacrifices much of the sense of inexplicable horror which is an essential ingredient of the sensational atmosphere of the story.

Holzer's version of *Der arme Spielmann* is entitled *Stille Musik*, and concentrates on Jakob's relations with Barbara. It is a still less successful attempt at dramatization than *Elga*. This is partly because though Holzer broadly follows the events of the *Novelle*, the story and the characters are sentimentalized. Of course, the whole tone of the original depends on the effect of the dual narrative, and it is not possible to reproduce this dramatically; but in dispensing with the narrator, Holzer's version sacrifices the distancing effect his narrative provides. Moreover, like Hauptmann, Holzer has had to expand and to make explicit, and above all to invent dialogue in place of the essential laconism of the original. Jakob particularly, because the events are not summarized in his own discreet narrative but enacted on stage, seems much more loquacious than in the original; Barbara's song, too, is actually played, instead of being merely described: rather banal words take the place of Jakob's mysterious description of its general effect – 'Steigt gleich anfangs in die Höhe, kehrt dann in sein Inwendiges zurück und hört ganz leise auf' (59)[1] – and are used as a sentimental *leitmotiv*. It is, however, significant that again and again the stage directions describing gestures and actions are based directly on Grillparzer's narrative. In the first act Barbara laughingly claps her fiancé hard on the back (from p. 61); she leans over sideways to point to the music of the song without setting aside her basin of peas and beans and she reacts to her father's *volte-face* on learning Jakob's true identity only by

[1] 'Right at the beginning it soars high, then returns into itself and comes to a close very quietly.'

stroking back her hair (from p. 62). She withdraws her arm when
Jakob wants to kiss her hand, as she does at the office in the
original (59). In the second act, Holzer retains the whole action
in which Jakob puts his arms round Barbara while she is reaching
up on tip-toe to a shelf, and she whirls round and slaps his face,
and also the long kiss he gives her through the glass pane of the
door (from p. 69). He also uses the episode in which Jakob in
confusion takes Barbara's father's hat by mistake instead of his
own – though in the play this is after the discovery of Jakob's
business venture, and he is given his own hat not laughingly as in
the original (70) but in anger. In Barbara's farewell visit she
slowly shuts Jakob's drawer, as in the original, leans against the
cupboard, bursts into tears and then sinks sobbing on a nearby
chair (from pp. 74f.); and the play ends with the same action as
the story, Barbara placing the violin in the drawer, locking the
drawer, and again bursting into tears. Clearly the modern dramatist's imagination was caught by these theatrical touches in the
prose story – touches characteristic of Grillparzer's own dramatic
imagination.

Writing comedy

The vividness of action and gesture which characterizes Grillparzer's dramatic style is based, as we saw in chapter 2, on his
conception of drama as an essentially theatrical, and hence visual
art. It must appeal to the audience, the 'jury', with real immediacy;
and it must entertain. This is the sense of his aspiration, expressed
in 1828, to prove himself 'precisely that half-way house between
Goethe and Kotzebue that our drama needs' (T 1626) – combining,
that is, the universality and poetic quality of the former with the
magnetic audience-attraction of the latter. In the 1849 essay
'Über das Hofburgtheater' he affirmed: 'Die Schaubühne ist...
da, um dem Publikum Kunstgenüsse zu verschaffen': the purpose
of the theatre is to give aesthetic pleasure, to entertain. Even
a tragedy is still first and foremost a play. This very Viennese
point is made explicitly in the autobiography, where Grillparzer
reminds the German writers of the day 'daß ein Trauerspiel, so
traurig es sein mag, doch immer auch ein Spiel bleibt' (SB 126).[1]

---

[1] 'that a tragedy, however tragic it may be, is always a *play*'. A similar
concern is expressed in a similar phrase in a letter written from Vienna
by Mozart while he was working on *Die Entführung aus dem Serail*: he
insisted 'that...the passions, whether violent or not, must never be so
expressed as to repel the listener, and the music, even in the most horrific

In view of this concern with entertainment it is perhaps surprising that his mature plays include only one full-length comedy. But he was always interested in comedy, and his *juvenilia* include several short comic pieces of various kinds. The most notable are three one-act playlets, *Die unglücklichen Liebhaber* and *Die Schreibfeder*, both in prose, and *Wer ist schuldig?*, in alexandrines. Also among his early works is a fragmentary translation of the first act of Gozzi's *Il corvo*, dating from 1814. These and other early works show his familiarity with conventional subjects and techniques of comic drama: the treatment of love, marriage and intrigue, and the use of misunderstanding as the mainspring of the comic action.

The list of his uncompleted plans and the quantity of short prose satires he composed throughout his creative life show how lasting this interest in comedy was. Moreover, to a far greater extent than the German classical dramatists whom he otherwise sought to emulate, he tended to include in his tragic works from *Ottokar* onwards scenes of episodic comedy. Examples include the opening of the second act of *Ein treuer Diener*, with Bancbanus's clumsiness, pedantic legalizing and fussing over liking a sharp pen; Hero's father wheezing through his obviously prepared speech (*Des Meeres und der Liebe Wellen* 232ff.); and Isak accepting bribes from petitioners at the beginning of the third act of *Die Jüdin*. In the thirties he also lent assistance to Bauernfeld in the construction and polishing of a series of comedies, a service for which Bauernfeld gave him generous credit in his memoirs, *Aus Alt- und Neu-Wien*. Bauernfeld draws attention particularly to the fact that the psychological point of the ninth scene of the final act of *Die Bekenntnisse* was suggested by Grillparzer. This is, in fact, a crucial scene, in which the heroine, disguised as a young lieutenant, is cured of her old love for one of the male characters by hearing him compare her unfavourably with another woman. The presentation of her reactions shows a depth of characterization that is rivalled in Bauernfeld's works only, perhaps, by the portraits of jealousy in *Helene* and of hot-tempered egoism in *Der Selbstquäler*; and it is probably not mere coincidence that these two plays are also among those in which Grillparzer is known to have taken a friendly interest.

Despite all his obvious inclinations to dabble in comedy, it was

situation, must never offend the ear, but must give pleasure – must, that is, always remain *music*' ('daß die Musick...allzeit Musick bleiben muß': to his father, 26 September 1781).

not until the mid-thirties that he embarked on his own full-length comedy, *Weh dem, der lügt!*. A decade and a half had passed since he had first read his source, an anecdote in the *Historia Francorum* of Gregory of Tours; since then he had elaborated his plans for the play only in a series of drafts and notes written in the years 1821–6. He began writing, and completed the first two acts, not long after the first performance of *Der Traum ein Leben*, an indication of the badly needed encouragement and invigoration he drew from the 'total success' of his dream-play. His faith in his art was renewed; and this optimism is reflected in the story of Leon, who indeed sees himself as something of an artist (502) and is regarded in the same light by Kattwald (619), and who serves Bishop Gregor, his master and his ideal, in a spirit of selfless devotion. He asks no reward, and retains his confidence in his allegiance even when his task of freeing Atalus seems thankless and disagreeable (1249) and even when he is denied the satisfaction of taking pleasure in his work (1572); and at the end he is rewarded with positive achievement in the fulfilment of his mission, and with personal happiness in the hand of Edrita.

It has been suggested that Grillparzer's interruption of the writing of *Weh dem, der lügt!* after the first two acts may have been a consequence of the illness and death of the Emperor Franz in the early months of 1835 and the subsequent news that conditions in Austria would not change under his successor, Emperor Ferdinand. Certainly by the summer of 1835 Grillparzer had temporarily lost interest in completing the play, and the poem 'Wenn der Vogel singen will' (G 218) – though it was probably not written until late the following year – testifies to the depressing and restricting effect on his work of prevailing conditions. He compares himself to a bird who needs a branch upon which to sing:

> Gebt mir, wo ich stehen soll,
> Weist mir das Gebiet,
> Und ich will euch wohl erfreun
> Noch mit manchem Lied.

But Germany is storm-swept, Austria plunged in darkness:

> Und so schweb' ich ew'gen Flugs
> Zwischen Erd' und Luft,
> Und kein Platz dem müden Fuß,
> Als dereinst die Gruft.[1]

---

[1] 'Give me somewhere to alight, show me that place, and I will give you pleasure with many more of my songs...And so, always on the wing, I

Conditions at home seemed, perhaps, particularly constricting in contrast to conditions abroad; for in the meantime Grillparzer had travelled to France and England. This journey was undertaken as a curative exercise: 'I had imposed the journey on myself as a kind of penance, as an attempt to accustom myself again to people and to external activity' (T 3042). But he set out without high hopes (T 2868), and was on the whole depressed by Paris: he found himself constantly confronted with irritations, 'these little *ennuis*, these recurrent vexations' (T 2930). An Englishman by the name of Brant, who befriended him there and gave him English lessons in preparation for the next stage of his journey, was a less than inspiring teacher, and was also mean, a fact which involved Grillparzer in a hated diet of poor food eaten on the cheap and other privations and annoyances, such as walking even in wet weather (T 2973), sitting in the cheapest seats in the theatre (T 2946), and on one occasion undergoing a disastrous cheap haircut which left Grillparzer with nothing but 'a small selection of alternately short and long hairs, so that I looked like a scarecrow and cursed the day I was born' (T 2979). He enjoyed his meetings with Meyerbeer, Börne and Heine; on occasions he was very impressed with French cuisine; and he was also impressed with Etienne Arnal when he saw him at the Théâtre du Vaudeville. Nevertheless, when he left Paris on 15 May, it was in low spirits: 'poor weather, poor rooms, ill humour' (T 3042).

His diary for his subsequent visit to London (T 3046–3135) was probably kept rather irregularly, and may even have been completed retrospectively after his return to Vienna; but it makes very lively reading, for despite his anticipatory fears about his inability to cope with the English language (T 2929), and despite his recurrent complaints about the English Sunday, his stay was clearly very enjoyable. He was delighted with the beauty of London and with English food, and he indulged in a great variety of activities and entertainments, including frequent visits to the theatre. By the time of his departure on 16 June, he was in altogether brighter spirits; and he not only retained this mood on his journey home as far as Munich (where news reached him of his brother Karl's insanity and self-accusation) but also, as Bauernfeld's report reveals, recovered it to some extent in Vienna.

His journey also fulfilled its curative purpose in restoring his

hover between earth and sky, and there is no place for my weary foot – except, some day, the grave' (ll. 9–12, 29–32).

creative energy. Significantly, what especially impressed him in the London theatre was the standard of English comedy, which he found 'at a high level of perfection' (T 3075). And indeed we may well be reminded of the mood of his own comedy by his later memories of the English theatre and in particular his praise of the English comic actors: '...One perceives in their lighter characters that they can also be serious when the need arises – and that is what distinguishes true humour from wit and joking' (SB 227). Just such a combination of gaiety and seriousness is characteristic of Grillparzer's Leon. Clearly we may surmise that his visit to London – together with his continued interest in Bauernfeld's work – stimulated his renewed interest in *Weh dem, der lügt!*; and when, some ten months after his return home, he resumed serious literary activity it was with an achievement of a kind he had striven for for nearly twenty years: the completion of his play in one burst of uninterrupted work.

Weh dem, der lügt!

Thematically, Grillparzer's only mature comedy is closely related to his tragedies. The story is one of duty to an ideal; the working-out of the plot depends on a complex series of deceptions and self-deceptions, both knowing and unknowing. 'Weh dem, der lügt!' Leon is warned by Bishop Gregor (385); with this principle he embarks, at the end of the first act, on his adventures, and those adventures are brought to a triumphant conclusion in the final act as, with the same words, he demands justice of God (1688).

It is Gregor who introduces the question of truth and untruth in the long speech in which he prepares his notes for a sermon (118ff.). His argument covers problems that had occupied Grillparzer's interest since his early years under the strict aegis of his father's 'wellnigh incredible rectitude' (SB 103). In particular it takes up themes discussed in two diary-notes of the twenties. The first was written in 1822: fired by a reading of Rousseau's *Rêveries du promeneur solitaire* (4e promenade), Grillparzer argued that no lie is defensible as harmless, since social life depends on mutual trust, which even the slightest untruth must undermine (T 1041). The second, written in the second half of 1827 in conjunction with the composition of *Tristia*-poems, is a powerful self-indictment – 'Liar, liar, abominable liar...' – in which he accused himself (only to deny it again at once) of feigning feelings he had not experienced (T 1584). No less scrupulous, Gregor regards truth as the basis of morality, to which all conduct is related and on which all worthy human relations are based; and he sees sin as dependent on untruth, whether conventional lying or inner untruth. He himself lives up to his standard of inner truth in, for example, his conscientious refusal to deflect the church moneys that he administers into the strictly private purpose of paying the ransom that will liberate his nephew Atalus from captivity (304–6). Indeed his attitude even seems over-rigorous when he tells Leon that the truth is more important than Atalus' life (345) and that he would return him to captivity if he discovered that his rescue had involved untruth (374–6); but here he is exaggerating his severity as a means of stressing his argument to Leon, and when Atalus is finally brought home Gregor does not receive him with such unyielding rigour.

What stands out in Gregor's attitude is that his concern for truth is essentially a *moral* concern. His office as bishop – as with Rudolf I's position as Holy Roman Emperor in *König Ottokars Glück und Ende* – has moral rather than strictly religious weight in the play. The service of God stands as a conventional symbolical representation of the service of good, of 'the eternal Law' (T 641). What Gregor sees working in Leon is 'the spirit of Good' (381), and when he goes on to link his motto with the enjoinder 'Sei dir selber treu und Gott' (384),[1] his point is the linking of truth with moral steadfastness. He sees truth as the supreme virtue;[2] but it also serves to represent all virtue. That not only truth, but wider standards of good conduct are the touchstone of his judgments is confirmed in the final act, in his attitude to Atalus and Edrita: he disapproves of Leon for having parted Edrita from her father (1751), and he warns Atalus against snobbery (1767–72).

When he is first confronted with Leon, Gregor inclines to moralize, punctuating their dialogue with leisurely sententious observations (191f., 393–6). Leon by contrast seems much more mentally nimble: he deploys his argumentative skill in reasoning that he has to account for himself as the guardian of the bishop's body, just as the bishop is the guardian of his soul (221–3). Of course an argument with the representative of morality and duty is not one that Leon can win: he begins by accusing the bishop of

---

[1] 'Be true to yourself and to God!'

[2] This is an idea that is also expressed elsewhere in Grillparzer's plays: cf. *Des Meeres und der Liebe Wellen* 414–16; *Ein Bruderzwist in Habsburg* 1919.

meanness, but then he himself has quickly to move to the defensive. Nevertheless Gregor's scrupulous moral argument about saving money and his description of his very gradual saving are put firmly in perspective by Leon's decided view that the method is too slow (304–20). His own quick impulsive planning leads him into trouble with the bishop's recurrent demand for truth:

LEON   Das muß man anders packen, lieber Herr.
             Hätt' ich zehn Bursche nur gleich mir, beim Teufel! –
             Bei Gott! Herr, wollt' ich sagen – ich befreit' ihn.
             Und so auch, ich allein. Wär' ich nur dort,
             Wo er in Haft liegt! – Herr, was gebt Ihr mir? –
             Das ist 'ne Redensart, ich fordre keinen Lohn. –
             Was gebt Ihr mir, wenn ich ihn Euch befreie?
             Wär' ich nur dort, ich lög' ihn schon heraus.
GREGOR Weh dem, der lügt!   (321–9)[1]

But at once he reaffirms – rightly – that Gregor's attitude is unhelpful in practice:

     Da bleibt nichts übrig, als: wir reden Wahrheit
     Und er bleibt, wo er ist.   (331f.)[2]

Gregor, however, knows that on one occasion already to have told the truth would have secured Atalus' release (161–4), and he sternly insists to Leon that the high standards he represents will be rewarded (379). In this way the anecdote in Grillparzer's source is developed, the whole expedition being related to truthfulness. Leon accepts his mission on Gregor's terms, 'in full seriousness' (370), but also in a spirit of adventure, as a kind of wager (377).

His willingness to take on this mission without prospect of material reward corresponds to the whole spirit in which he serves Gregor: he has already told Gregor's steward that he works not for money (39) but because he has regarded Gregor as an embodiment of greatness and nobility (48, 66), and he thinks of leaving his service only when he suspects him of falling short of this perfection (67ff.). Won round again in his confrontation with Gregor, he sets out trustfully, his words 'Ich ziehe fort mit Gott...'

[1] 'We must attack that quite differently, my Lord. If only I had ten lads like myself, by all the devils! – I mean "by Heaven", my Lord – then I would free him. And so I will, alone. If only I were where he is imprisoned! – What will you give me, sir (that's just a manner of speaking: I ask for no reward) – what will you give me if I rescue him? If I were only there, I'd get him out by lies!' 'Woe to him who lies!'
[2] 'Then there's nothing else for it: we'll speak the truth, and he'll stay where he is!'

(409)[1] echoing the equally dutiful Rudolf I; but he has not yet grasped the full spirit of Gregor's precepts, which centre on trust among mankind ('das Vertraun, das Mensch dem Menschen gönnt', 373). When he approaches his first crucial encounter with Atalus' captor, Kattwald, he is mindful of Gregor's standards of truth and steadfastness; but precisely because he is thinking of the letter of the precepts rather than their spirit, he is dubious of their efficacy:

> Leon, sei erst Leon. Und eins bedenke:
> Weh dem, der lügt! – So mindstens will's der Herr.
> (*achselzuckend*)
> Man wird ja sehn. (424–6)[2]

It is in this uncomplicated, carefree fashion that he faces Kattwald and establishes himself in his household. All his sprightly confidence now stands comically at odds with his supposed position as a slave, and there is sustained irony in the scene in which he haggles successfully over the price for which he is to be sold (527ff.) and then proceeds to bully Kattwald into agreeing his conditions of employment. Kattwald regards him as impudent (1066); so, less indulgently, does Atalus (865), towards whom Leon adopts a telling line of laconic frankness (e.g. 903). But Kattwald also accepts his frankness of manner as amusing (1109), and his daughter Edrita too praises him as being (in contrast to Atalus) cheerful and gay (822).

Frankness of manner, however, is not quite the same thing as veracity of word. In selling himself to Kattwald, Leon bends the truth at least once, when he describes himself as being well-mannered ('von den feinsten Sitten', 466). His first encounter with Edrita also begins badly: he is busy in the kitchen, she asks him what he is doing, he replies sarcastically that he is chopping wood (638) – a riposte ironically meant, but strictly offending against the letter of Gregor's instructions. At other times, when Leon tries to tell the truth, he is very much a literalist: told not to sing, he whistles instead (571). And he adopts towards Kattwald a kind of super-frankness: he openly and repeatedly threatens to abscond, and then admits that he is going to escape with Atalus.[3] While this is literally true, Leon is saying it in the hope that it will not be believed, and as Edrita later spells out to him this is in effect deception of a kind (1132ff.). Though he is observing the

---

[1] 'Now I set out, and God is with me.'
[2] 'Leon, be true to yourself. And remember one thing: woe to him who lies! – At least that's how the Bishop wants it. (*Shrugging his shoulders:*) Well, we'll see!'
[3] See ll. 532, 546, 848–50.

letter of his task, he is betraying that trust between fellow-men that Gregor has essentially commended. It is also deceitful in effect when, having been caught red-handed stealing Kattwald's key, he tells Kattwald that he now has the wrong one; for while (after Edrita's substitution of the keys) this is the truth, Kattwald understandably does not believe it because it is Leon who is saying it:

KATTWALD   ...Dort häng ihn hin.
LEON   Es ist derselbe Schlüssel nicht.
KATTWALD   Dort, sag' ich!
LEON (*zum Boden gebückt*)
    Man muß den andern suchen.
KATTWALD   Tausend Donner!
    So narrst du mich von neuem? Dort der Platz!
LEON   Doch wenn's der rechte nicht?
KATTWALD   Es ist der rechte.
    Weil du's bezweifelst, grad'.   (1088–93)[1]

Before this episode, Leon has still been sceptical about the efficacy of the bishop's prohibition, and has still been giving it a try in an adventurous spirit (1052–7); but the success of the whole escape operation finally convinces him. Moreover, there have already been signs that he has begun to shed his initial carefree naivety. This is suggested particularly by his encouragement of Atalus:

    Eur Oheim harret Euer – hört Ihr wohl?
    Leis mit den Abendwinden, deucht mich, dringt
    Zu uns her sein Gebet, das schützt, das sichert,
    Und Engel mit den breiten Schwingen werden
    Um uns sich lagern, wo wir wandelnd gehn.   (986–90)[2]

His invocation of the idea of angelic protection reveals that he has developed a sense of the loftiness of the duty on which he has embarked on Gregor's behalf. Enjoining Atalus to play his part in the escape, he adds the same pious 'mit Gott' as he last used when departing from the bishop (1014). When he finds the right key in the lock, he thanks heaven for its protection (1130f.),

---

[1] 'Hang it up there!' 'It is not the same key.' 'There, I tell you!' (*Leon, bending down over the floor:*) 'We must look for the other one!' 'Great Heavens! You're trying to make a fool of me again? Up there, I said!' 'But if it's not the right one?' 'It *is* the right one – I know because you question it.'
[2] 'Your uncle is waiting for you, and – can you hear? – I sense that with the quiet evening breezes his prayers reach us, protecting and defending us; and angels will be with us on our way and spread their wings about us.'

and in the fourth act, during their flight, he tells Atalus to put his trust in God (1261). Even Edrita is impressed by his praise of Gregor's sanctity. She has some knowledge of Christian priests:

> Sie lehren einen einz'gen Gott. Und wahrlich,
> (*seine Hand berührend*)
> An was das Herz in gläub'ger Fülle hängt,
> Ist einzig stets und eins. (1155–7)[1]

She too, then, recognizes the universal validity of the good that Gregor represents and Leon serves.

It is Edrita, however, despite her earlier criticism of Leon's subtle deceptions, who advises that they should pretend to the ferryman that they are travelling on Kattwald's behalf (1193–5), and who does in fact lie to him (1502f.), just as she has earlier lied to Galomir and so helped his capture (1435). Leon, after kneeling in prayer for a few moments (1496/SD), firmly commits himself, with the Lutheran formula of conviction, 'Ich kann nicht anders' (1525)[2] and risks telling the full truth. It pays off once more. He draws the lesson, 'Man ist nicht klug, wenn man nur klügelt' (1542),[3] and the ferryman enjoins them to thank God for his guidance (1546f.). When finally, having crossed the Rhine and reached the walls of Metz, they are caught up by their pursuers, Leon again refuses to budge from the truth. He admits openly where Edrita and Atalus are sleeping (1638); but then again he offers a prayer in need (1656ff.). A church bell rings, a token of answer (1676/SD); and as the gates of the city are about to open, he has recourse to a final urgent prayer:

> Ich bitte nicht mehr Hilfe, nein, ich fordre –
> Ich bitte immer noch, ich bitte, Herr!
> Als ich von deinem frommen Diener schied,
> Da leuchtete ein Blitz in meinem Innern;
> Von Wundern sprach's, ein Wunder soll geschehn.
> Und so begehr' ich denn, ich fordre Wunder!
> Halt mir dein heilig Wort! – Weh dem, der lügt!
> (1682–8)[4]

---

[1] 'They teach one single God. And in truth (*touching his hand*) what the heart clings to in the fullness of its faith is always One.'

[2] 'I can do no other.'

[3] 'One is not *wise* when one just tries to be *clever*.'

[4] 'No longer do I *ask* for help, I *demand* it! – O Lord, I ask it still, I ask it! When I was leaving thy pious servant, a light blazed within me; it promised miracles – a miracle must happen. And so I beg – demand – miracles! Keep thy holy word! For woe to him who lies!'

He challenges the ideal he has come to believe in to produce the just reward which its representative, Gregor, promised. And Metz is indeed in Frankish hands.

Only once during the long flight has Leon deviated from the high standards he has now set himself: after the tricking and capture of Galomir, he takes advantage of Galomir's plight with a sophistic denial of responsibility that certainly abides once again by the letter rather than the spirit of Gregor's instruction:

> Es war nicht meine Wahl, doch ist's geschehn,
> Und da es ist, benütz' ich es zur Rettung.
> Bleibt sitzen, Herr, Ihr seid in unsrer Macht. (1420–2)[1]

In relation to Edrita's escape, however, he interprets his brief according to the spirit:

> Ich habe meinem frommen Herrn versprochen:
> Nichts Unerlaubtes, Greulichs soll geschehn
> Bei diesem Schritt, den nur die Not entschuldigt...
> (1322–4)[2]

Edrita, who was genuinely unwilling to marry Galomir and has joined in the escape of her own accord, and who is disappointed in Leon's attitude towards her, accuses him of being fairer to his opponents than to his supporters (1330–5): she calls him a man of the arid letter of the law ('Mann des Rechts'), and later she again accuses him of sticking with selfish rigidity to the letter of the truth (1443–7). In fact though Leon has tried to prevent Edrita from joining him and Atalus (1321ff.) he acknowledges a moral responsibility, which is still worrying him at the beginning of the fifth act and which he faces squarely in its darkest colours. He thinks anxiously of how he must account for himself to the bishop:

> Sein letztes Wort war Mahnung gegen Trug,
> Und nun, wie bunt, was alles wir vollführt.
> Die Tochter aus dem Vaterhaus geraubt.
> Geraubt! Gestattet mindstens, daß sie folge.
> Wie werd' ich stehn vor meines Herren Blick? (1590–4)[3]

---

[1] 'It was not by my choice, but it is done; and as it's so, I'll use it for our escape. Stay seated, sir, for you are in our power.'

[2] 'I gave my promise to my godly master; nothing forbidden, no outrage shall be committed through this step, which only necessity excuses.'

[3] 'His last words were a warning against deception – and now how lurid [or 'confused'] all that we have done has been! A daughter abducted from her father's home – abducted? At the least I permitted her to follow me. How shall I stand and face my master?'

When he is finally before Gregor, he does not deny that he is at fault in having brought Edrita (1738), and Edrita has to do it for him, taking the blame on herself (1739–41). Leon, in fact, is over-scrupulous in the account he gives of himself, and admits humbly to an excessive degree of failure:

GREGOR Nu, hübsch gelogen? Brav dich was vermessen?
           Dem Feinde vorgespiegelt dies und das?
           Mit Lug und Trug verkehrt? Ei ja, ich weiß.
LEON   Nu, gar so rein ging's freilich denn nicht ab.
           Wir haben uns gehütet, wie wir konnten.
           Wahr stets und ganz war nur der Helfer: Gott! (1718–23)[1]

In showing so little faith in Leon's ability to adhere to his instructions – a scepticism that is quite justified by the spirit in which Leon began his adventure – Gregor does not speak in threatening wrath, but with a calm acceptance of human fallibility (an acceptance which, however, in no way controverts the purity of his ideal *standards*). And straightway, in trying to conceal his affection for Edrita, Leon himself gives a final demonstration of that fallibility (1783–6). The bitter prospect of losing Edrita forces the truth out of him, and there follows a highly charged exchange (1792–9):

EDRITA War ich gleich anfangs dir nicht denn geneigt?
LEON   Doch in der Folge kam's gar bitter anders.
           Du gingst mit Atalus.

(At a non-tragic level, an echo of the experience of Medea.)

EDRITA   Ei, gehen mußt' ich,
           Du aber stießest grausam mich zurück.
LEON (*auf Gregor zeigend*)
           Es war ja wegen dem. Er litt es nicht.

(The standards of duty have overridden the call of inclination – not with tragic consequences, but still to Leon's real unhappiness.)

           Sollt' ich mit Raub und Diebstahl zu ihm kehren?

(Once again, an over-scrupulous interpretation of the standards imposed by duty.)

EDRITA Du aber stahlst mein Inneres und hast's.
LEON   Und willst dich doch vermählen?

[1] 'Well, told lots of lies? Made lots of boasts? Deceived the foe with this pretence and that? Descended to falsehood and deceit? Yes, yes, I know...'
'Well, of course we haven't come out of it with completely clean hands – we looked after ourselves as best we could. God who has helped us – he alone had complete truth and integrity.'

(With neat wordplay, Edrita reproaches Leon with the responsibility he also has to her; he replies with a bitter reproach, and an unjust one, for she has already indicated that she will not marry Atalus (1775f.).)

EDRITA   Ich?
          (*mit gefalteten Händen den Bischof vertrauensvoll anblickend*)

(For her too the standard is inescapable: 'Weh dem, der lügt!' And she replies not to the letter of Leon's question, but to its spirit:)

                                    O nein![1]

In this, as the bishop sees, there is both truth and untruth, and in a famous speech he admits the confusing coexistence of truth and untruth in the real world (as opposed to the ideal order), finishing with an allusion to the parable of the sowing of seed (Matthew xiii. 24ff. – the words 'Unkraut' and 'Weizen' are those used in Luther's translation)[2] which emphasizes again the fundamentally moral bias of his concern:

> Wer deutet mir die buntverworrne Welt!
> Sie reden alle Wahrheit, sind drauf stolz,
> Und sie belügt sich selbst und ihn, er mich
> Und wieder sie; Der lügt, weil man ihm log –
> Und reden alle Wahrheit, alle. Alle.
>
> Das Unkraut, merk' ich, rottet man nicht aus.
> Glück auf, wächst nur der Weizen etwa drüber.[3]

It is from this slightly quizzical summary of the ironies of the situation that he goes on to unite Leon and Edrita, providing the

---

[1] 'Well, did I not like you from the very first?' 'But later that changed sharply. You came with Atalus.' 'I had to come with someone; and you rejected me, cruelly.' (*Leon, pointing to Gregor:*) 'On account of him; he would not have allowed it. Was I to return to him an abductor, a thief?' 'But you had stolen my inmost self, and have it still.' 'And yet you want to marry?' 'I, marry? (*With hands clasped, she looks trustingly at the Bishop*) Oh, no!'

[2] Grillparzer's library included a modernized version of Luther's translation. (See *Wke.* II/12, 97ff., 'Verzeichnis von Grillparzers Bibliothek'.) Cf. also *Nathan der Weise*, v, 5, ll. 3476–8.

[3] 'Who will interpret the muddle of this world? Each of them is speaking the truth, and they are proud of it; and she is deceiving herself and him, he is deceiving me and her; he is lying because he has been lied to – and yet they are all telling the truth. All of them. – I see we shall never root up the tares. So be it, provided the wheat will spring up over them!'

traditional happy ending of comedy. Gregor has been proved worthy of Leon's trust, a true and just ideal: the only flaw in his character, his bad education of Atalus, will be corrected (1711f.). Leon has come through his mission with as much success as it is possible to demand in the 'buntverworrne Welt': he has made errors of judgment, but he has on the whole acted with good will and in good faith, and has avoided those deceitful means which – as Rustan's dream illustrates – are symptomatic of selfish ends. Whereas Rustan's selfish ambition in defiance of his rightful destiny leads in his dream to disaster, Leon by his selflessness retains what Rustan's attempted advancement of self endangers, 'Des Innern stiller Frieden / Und die schuldbefreite Brust', and his service is crowned not only with success but also with the reward of Edrita's love.

This is a happy ending indeed. Nevertheless the reflective mood of the final scene is far from the conventional gaiety of comedy. *Weh dem, der lügt!* is a play of two moods, with sharp contrasts built into its very structure. The central acts are full of rapid action, matched by rapid dialogue full of swift exchanges; the first and last acts, on the other hand, have a serious deliberative tone, which is reflected linguistically in the generally more leisured tempo of the dialogue and in long speeches such as the bishop's reflections on his sermon and Leon's monologue outside Metz (1567–1620). The contrast is particularly marked in Leon's role. In the middle acts – as also in the opening scene of the play – the language he speaks is eager and active, in keeping with his character. Confronted, however, with the moral certainty of his ideal, as represented by Gregor, his cheeky loquacity breaks down: he admits that he hardly knows how to talk to the bishop (336) and at a moment of moral insight he simply falls to his knees (SD/380). In *König Ottokars Glück und Ende* this gesture of penitence and insight comes only in the final act; precisely because it is so long delayed, Ottokar's story is a tragic one. That Leon acknowledges his rightful duty at the very outset of *Weh dem, der lügt!* is a prerequisite for the development of the action towards the happy ending.

A further linguistic contrast is built up within the central acts between Leon and the Germanic barbarians. Leon, with an ironic understatement suggesting his superior sophistication, finds Kattwald 'somewhat incomprehensible' (456). And the very opposite extreme to his loquacity is Galomir's completely inarticulate speech: in the whole work he speaks only some two dozen words of more than one syllable, most of those being expletives or in exclamations, and nearly all in unformed sentences. The general contrast between the civilized and the barbarian, to which the language contributes in this way, has sometimes been seen as a parallel to the contrast between Greece and Colchis in the trilogy. But the contrast in *Weh dem, der lügt!* is defined in terms that belong essentially to the vocabulary of the eighteenth-century idea of *Humanität* – the contrast between the high potential of humanity and undeveloped brutishness. Schiller, for example, contrasts 'Tierheit und Menschheit, Naturzwang und Vernunft-freiheit'[1] (*Über das Pathetische*), and in another well-known passage Herder affirms:

Das *Göttliche* in unserm Geschlecht ist also *Bildung zur Humanität*... Humanität ist der Schatz und die Ausbeute aller menschlichen Bemü-hungen, gleichsam die *Kunst unsres Geschlechtes*. Die Bildung zu ihr ist ein Werk, das unablässig fortgesetzt werden muß; oder wir sinken... zur rohen Tierheit, zur *Brutalität* zurück.[2]

The very terms of such arguments are echoed by Gregor when he tells Leon that Atalus is a prisoner

> Wo noch die Roheit, die hier Schein umkleidet,
> In erster Blöße Mensch und Tier vermengt.   (290f.)[3]

Gregor's standards are essentially akin to those of Goethe's Iphigenie, who incorporates an ideal of 'pure humanity' based on truth ('O weh der Lüge!', IV, 1) and trust; and Leon's adventure is an example of human development in the spirit of this eighteenth-century humanitarian ideal: he learns to appreciate 'das Vertraun, das Mensch dem Menschen gönnt'.

Gregor's description of the Franks tallies especially with the animalistic character of Galomir. And while here he dismisses the greater polish of his own people as a mere façade, in general the contrast between the two nationalities has a sharp edge to it. It is striking evidence of Grillparzer's utterly unromantic approach

---

[1] 'brutishness and humanity, the compulsion of nature and the freedom of reason'.

[2] 'What is divine in our species, then, is a development to full humanity. "Humanity" is the harvest, the yield of all human efforts – the art of our species, as it were. The task of developing towards it is one which must be carried on without cease, or we shall sink back into raw animality, into brutishness' (*Briefe zu Beförderung der Humanität*, XXVII, 1794).

[3] 'Where the brutal rawness, that here is cloaked by outward pretence, still in its primeval nakedness links man with the brute.'

to the Germanic past; implicitly it is also pointedly relevant to
the French and German peoples of Grillparzer's own time, with
the French equated with the civilized, and the Germans with the
barbaric. It is the Franks who are the masters of the table: 'Hier
nährt man sich,' Leon tells Kattwald, 'der Franke nur kann
essen' (497).[1] In their initial confrontation, Kattwald has a single
refrain: 'Wie teuer ist der Mann?', repeated over and over again;[2]
and the selfish materialism of his people is confirmed by Edrita
when she distances herself from it and claims an aesthetic sense
otherwise alien to the east bank of the Rhine:

> Ich bin nicht, wie die Menschen oft wohl sind:
> Ei, das ist schön! das soll nur mir gehören,
> Und das ist gut, das eign' ich rasch mir zu.
> Ich kann am Guten mich und Schönen freun... (1159–62)[3]

Kattwald and Galomir are the principal comic roles among the
Germans, Leon and Atalus among the Franks. Together with
Gregor and the spirited Edrita, they make up a well-differentiated
range of characters, and the roles of Atalus and Kattwald in
particular include effective comic moments. Kattwald, as well
as being grossly gluttonous, shows a cruelty which justifies his
awesome reputation as a tyrant: he would rather have his daughter
injured than have her escape (1555–7). Yet he is cajoled by Leon
into employing him on his own terms, and is finally completely
cowed:

EDRITA (*kommt*) Was ist denn hier für Lärm?
KATTWALD   Pst, pst! Der neue Koch.
EDRITA   Für den Ihr so viel Geld – ?
KATTWALD   Ja wohl. Sei still!
Er weist uns sonst noch beide vor die Tür.   (615–17)[4]

Atalus, who Gregor has admitted had a soft upbringing (360),
gives himself airs that ill befit his position as a prisoner. Not only
does he try to impress Edrita by stressing his social superiority
over Leon (813ff.); he refuses to serve in the kitchen (801f.) and
is unwilling to lower himself to the manual work of digging (972).

---

[1] 'Here you feed – only the Franks know how to *eat*.'
[2] 'What will he cost me?' See ll. 506, 510, 515, 516.
[3] 'I am not as people often are – "How lovely! I want that for myself alone!
And that is good, I'll grab that quickly for myself!" – I can take pleasure
in the good and in the beautiful.'
[4] Edrita (*enters*): 'What's all this noise, then?' 'Hush! – The new cook.'
'For whom you paid so – ?' 'Yes, but keep quiet! Or else he'll turn us
both out.'

Both of these operations are essential to Leon's plan, and Atalus' reluctance to be rescued, together with the imminence of Galomir's proposed marriage to Edrita, adds both to Leon's difficulties and to the tension of the action. Atalus' would-be dignity comes a comic cropper towards the end of Act II, when he is smugly preparing to enjoy Kattwald's discomfiture of Leon – who has refused to carry a basket of herbs into the kitchen – only to have Kattwald turn on him instead and make him do the carrying (858–70).

When Bauernfeld first heard the text of *Weh dem, der lügt!*, he objected that Atalus' change of heart on the way home and the improvement in his bearing were inadequately motivated (*Gespr.* 683). This is a fair criticism, though the flaw might be less serious within the conventions of comedy (where consistency of character need not be as important as in tragedy) if it were compensated by richer comic effects. Bauernfeld had a still stronger and more cogent objection to the characterization of Galomir. He interpreted him as 'eine Trottelfigur' (an idiot-figure). The role was also played in this way at the première. In later years Grillparzer repeatedly expressed the view that Galomir should not be a 'Trottel', but animalistic, a Caliban, brutish rather than half-witted, 'tierisch, aber nicht blödsinnig' (T 3491). But in fact his own text leaves the way open for the misunderstanding: Edrita speaks of Galomir simply as stupid, 'der dumme Galomir' (705, 1221), Kattwald rather condescendingly allows for his not thinking much (881), and this impression is strengthened both by his awkwardness in practical action and by his inarticulate speech.

Leon too to some extent falls short as a comic figure. The reasons for this are not far to seek. In the first place, Grillparzer's bent in comedy was for irony and mordancy, as in the satires or the sardonic portrait of Bancbanus, and the outgoing zest of a figure like Leon was alien to his nature. Secondly, comedy arises from effects of incongruity, which depend on contrast and disparity; and while as we have seen there are scenes of comic contrast between Leon and other characters, notably Kattwald, Leon's role is not one with comic *inner* contrasts. This point becomes very clear if we compare him with the central figure in another comedy about untruth, *Der zerbrochene Krug*. Unlike Leon, Adam is untruthful, and his every deception reveals the truth about his own untruthfulness, which stands in drastic incongruity to his position as a judge. Leon's resolution in abiding by his mandate produces a correspondence between character and duty which, though it makes the happy ending possible, is not conducive to comic effects. A contrast between duty and inclination is for Grillparzer the stuff of tragedy; but in harmless form it would also be a more fruitful subject of comedy than Leon's obedience. That he may have sensed this problem is suggested by a diary-note of the mid-1830s in which he discusses Leon's role (though uncertainty as to the exact date of the note makes it impossible to be sure whether he is planning his characterization or discussing how Leon should be acted): 'Leon must be portrayed trying faithfully to obey the bishop's command but constantly over-stepping it through his own exuberance; hence also his self-reproaches and penitence' (T 3302). An interplay between excessive zeal and remorse could well be comic, but in fact there is relatively little of it in the play, since by the time Leon's moral sense has developed enough for him to be given to self-reproaches his initial impulsiveness has declined and his adherence to the bishop's precept is practically complete.

It is indeed in those acts in which the moral issues are foremost – that is, the first and last acts – that the play is least effective as a comedy. It begins with a piece of lively stage action, as Leon draws his kitchen-knife in mock-attack on the terrified steward. After this the first scene is essentially one of exposition, achieved through Leon's complaints. Though there is some wordplay (15f.) it is on the whole rather a slow scene, and Leon's anecdotes about having to sell back a bargain purchase of venison (25ff.) and about having seen the bishop kiss money he has saved (88–98) are not in themselves very comic. Once Leon's task is set and his standards established, the comedy lies in the ironies and un-certainties of his precarious progress along the narrow path between truth and untruth, and Grillparzer plays on various perceptions – that even when the truth is told it may not be seen as such, since in human society the truth is simply not expected, and hence not recognized; that the truth can be used to deceive (this is the sham truth of literalism); and that in this 'buntverworrne Welt' deception and self-deception are possible even with the best will. But in treating these several and overlapping grades of truth and untruth, the language of the play militates against the unrestrained gaiety of true comedy. Again a comparison with *Der zerbrochene Krug* is revealing: Kleist's language is racy, earthy, full of ingenious quibbles; Grillparzer's by contrast is much stiffer and more stylized. The over-literary quality is especially marked in the reflectiveness of the fifth act:

> LEON   Ich wünschte Flügel unserm Zauderschritt,
>   Doch wag' ich's nicht, das Schläferpaar zu wecken.
>   Sie sind ermüdet bis zum bleichen Tod... (1583–5)[1]

And indeed until the complexities of the final reckoning there is no verbal comedy at all in the whole of this last act.

Nor is the last act full of opportunities for comic acting and stage business, which in practice is where much of the comedy of the play lies. The opening incident of Act I has already been mentioned. Then the scene between Leon and Gregor can be enlivened by comic action: Leon's fear at the account Gregor gives of the destructive power of God (186) can be expressed in comic mime, and at this stage of his development it would also be legitimate to play for comedy when he falls to his knees in fear as Gregor speaks of God in stern and loud tones (379f.). Much can be made too of his horrified haste in picking up his knife and apron rather than letting the bishop do it (194) – a complete contrast to his defiant pose of protest. As soon as he sets out on his adventures, the scope for comic action is wide: examples include his miming of the act of fine appreciation of taste (486–90), his chopping at Edrita's fingers with his kitchen knife (646/SD), his attempt to cement his friendship with Edrita by embracing her (680/SD), his furtive and tentative entrance into Kattwald's room (1046/SD), and his pretence of looking for the key under Kattwald's foot (1076f.). And if he subsequently grows less boisterous, there are a whole succession of set pieces of visual comedy involving the other figures: Kattwald's gradual falling asleep (1111–13), Atalus' appearance, muddy and wet, after his digging (1201f.), the collapse of the bridge with Galomir on it (1220/SD), Kattwald's vain attempts to climb out of a window (1230/SD), Galomir's clumsy attempts to catch Edrita (1372/SD, SD/1387), the episode in which Edrita, Atalus and Leon trick him out of his weapons (1410–15). Critics consistently miss how much of this visual comedy, depending on mime and action, *Weh dem, der lügt!* contains; and yet it is characteristic of the theatrical nature of Grillparzer's dramatic style. It is, however, comedy of a superficial

---

[1] 'I would wish our hesitant pace the speed of wings – and yet I dare not wake the sleeping pair. They are utterly exhausted.' (Literally: 'wearied unto pale death'.)

kind, and a poor substitute for wit; and it goes ill with the manner of a verse play, in which verbal wit would be much more in place. Moreover, in having *Weh dem, der lügt!*, with its horseplay and moral reflections, billed as a '*Lustspiel*', which suggested a comedy of wit, Grillparzer materially contributed to the failure of the première.

The première

There were certainly other reasons for the audience's displeasure. Chief among them was the insensitivity of the production, particularly in the interpretation of the role of Galomir which – despite the advice Grillparzer himself had given to the actor, Karl Lucas – aimed at farcical caricature (*Gespr.* 1100). Presented with a fool, the audience was not to detect a Caliban. Sections of the audience doubtless disapproved of the action for showing the triumph of a lowly (and, moreover, cheeky) cook over noble adversaries. They disapproved, too, of the attitude of Edrita (supposedly a German countess) to Leon, and of the egalitarian implications of Gregor's rebuke to Atalus in Act v (1767–72). Reich overestimates this aspect of the work when he talks of the play as being 'democratic' in effect, 'a trenchant satire against the aristocracy and its privileges', for there is no direct social criticism in it, nor political radicalism: but certainly the figure cut by Atalus is conspicuously unheroic, and the picture of the German nobility as represented by Kattwald and Galomir, together with the comparisons drawn between German culture and French, gave offence.

Nonetheless, all these really very trivial irritants were of secondary importance beside the principal objection, that the whole manner of the play did not live up to what its billing as a *Lustspiel* led the audience to expect. In the heyday of Bauernfeld they expected from a Burgtheater comedy the elegant, if shallow, wit with which Bauernfeld's society pieces sparkle. Moreover, at this particular juncture they also had clearly defined expectations about the subject-matter of the play.

For the whole occasion has to be seen against the background of Bauernfeld's feud with the critic Moritz Saphir, into which Grillparzer was drawn through his friendship with Bauernfeld. It was the success of *Der Traum ein Leben* that encouraged Bauernfeld to have *Fortunat* performed; but it was refused by Deinhardstein for the Burgtheater, and by the time it was performed in the Theater in der Josefstadt Bauernfeld had already published his essay 'Kritik und Kritiker unserer Zeit', in which, without actually naming Saphir, he obviously alluded to him. Saphir responded by referring in the *Theaterzeitung* to Bauernfeld's essay as being by a 'very mediocre author', and this drew Grillparzer's riposte, 'Meine Ansicht'. After Saphir's critique of *Fortunat*, Bauernfeld was quick to gain revenge by caricaturing him as the philosophizing servant Unruh in his next play, *Bürgerlich und Romantisch*: 'Wahrheit?' asks Unruh, 'Was ist denn wahr? Man kann alles plausibel machen. Lesen Sie nur meine Theaterkritiken' (III, 7).[1]

By the following year Bauernfeld and Saphir were waging open war. *Der literarische Salon* is a polemical literary satire, directed against Saphir and Adolf Bäuerle, the popular dramatist who was also editor of the *Theaterzeitung*. It shows how the generous but gullible patron of a critical journal is duped by the self-styled geniuses who contribute to it. One of them, Morgenroth, sells him supposedly original manuscripts of a letter by Homer and of a correspondence between Shakespeare and Calderón on the Romantic spirit. The journalists have no scruples about their critical methods:

WENDEMANN	Nur hübsch geschmeichelt und gestreichelt –
MORGENROTH	Zur Not was Weniges geheuchelt?...
WENDEMANN	Dem Feinde Hohn –
MORGENROTH	Und Übermut.
WENDEMANN	Tod seinem Werk –
MORGENROTH	Sei's noch so gut. (II, 6)[2]

In his review of the piece, Saphir adopted a pose of wide-eyed innocence in face of the open attack on himself, and eloquently damned the play for its lack of action and its colourless characterization. Neither he nor Bauernfeld lost by the furore. At the beginning of 1837 Saphir became editor of *Der Humorist*; and after *Der literarische Salon* had been banned the public thronged to see *Bürgerlich und Romantisch*, which in box-office terms became the most successful of all Bauernfeld's comedies, and avidly followed further attacks and counter-attacks in the press.

This, then, was the immediate background to the première of *Weh dem, der lügt!* – and the very title of the work awoke expectations that Grillparzer might be offering a companion piece to

---

[1] 'Truth? But what is true? One can make anything plausible. Just look at the reviews I write!'
[2] 'Plenty of flattery and buttering-up – ' 'If need be just a little hypocrisy?' 'Towards all opponents, scorn – ' 'And arrogance.' 'Death to their work – ' 'However good!'

Der literarische Salon. The theatre was packed to overflowing; after a long wait, there was inevitably a sense of anti-climax, and, with Saphir's clique active, the audience was only too ready to be led into voicing open disapproval. 'They behaved...coarsely and stupidly, without any respect', Bauernfeld noted in his diary. 'One cannot serve a literary comedy to these Bœotians.' Then came the reviews. Saphir's, which appeared in the *Humorist* on 10 March, was not well-argued, but it was long and damned the comedy with mocking invective.

Grillparzer's immediate reaction to the criticisms was, characteristically, compressed into an epigram, expressing his refusal to be drawn into the mud-slinging:

> Was hängt ihr euch an mich und meinen Lauf
> Und strebt dem Höhern plumpen Dranges wider?
> Ich zieh' euch, merk' ich, nicht zu mir herauf,
> Doch ihr, weiß Gott! mich auch zu euch nicht nieder.
>
> (G 689)[1]

It was left to Bauernfeld to counter more positively. His sketch *Weh dem, der dichtet!* not only testifies to his loyalty but also illustrates his understanding of Grillparzer. It centres on a poet for whom the public still express affection but whose latest play they dislike. This play is very dear to its author: he speaks of it as part of his very life, and later he repeats that it contains a part of himself. He is encouraged by a friend, who sees the play as a problem which the public will solve in time and as one of the poet's most self-revealing works. The poet himself, however, still feels himself condemned by the public; he is still worried by the thought 'Die *Wirkung* erst vollendet das Gedicht' (sc. 5),[2] and he ends with the lament 'Weh dem, der dichtet!'

Grillparzer lacked Bauernfeld's natural resilience. Whereas Bauernfeld was able to get over the failure of *Fortunat*, to capitalize on the banning of *Der literarische Salon*, and in later years to admit the wit of Saphir's reviews, Grillparzer was unable to make light of criticism and failure. Not only was his confidence undermined as always by the naggingly deterrent force of his own self-criticism; he accused the public and the critics of lack of understanding (T 3342) and came to feel increasingly that he was

---

[1] 'Why do you cling to me and my career, and why are you so crudely intent on opposing what is above you? I perceive that I shall not raise you to my level; but by Heaven, nor will you drag me down to yours!'

[2] 'The work is only made complete by its effect' [i.e. its effect on the audience and its reception by them].

living in an age alien to inspiration and imagination, 'a prosaic age' (SB 127). His sense of being completely out of harmony with his times was strengthened further both by the literary climate of the forties and by the momentous political developments of that decade, and remained with him till the end of his life. In her memoir, Marie von Ebner-Eschenbach records that in his old age he gave the impression that he had withheld his later works from the public not by way of revenge on them but out of sheer distaste.

6

POLITICS AND CULTURE

Attitudes and standards

Politics never figured among Grillparzer's chief interests as long as his life centred wholly on his literary activity and ambitions; but the conduct of public affairs and trends in the political climate impinged on his work, in three ways particularly. First, he was denied creative freedom by being forced to spend his working days serving the government as a civil servant, with only slow advancement; when Richard Wagner met him in 1848 he summed up the incongruity of his position in his wry observation that Grillparzer was the first dramatist he had seen in official uniform (*Gespr.* 1485). Secondly, he was subject to the restrictive discipline of censorship. Thirdly, he believed that the reception of his plays by the Viennese public reflected changes in the whole climate of contemporary opinion.

While Vienna, with its artistic tradition and rich cultural life, remained his home, it is striking how completely his one story whose action is set there lacks the sentimentality with which the Viennese often regard their city; and while he always felt for Austria a patriotic affection that received its best-known expression in the long speech of Ottokar von Horneck in the third act of *König Ottokar*, the affection often tends understandably to be blended with frustration, as in a characteristic diary-note of 1822: 'There seems to be no place for me in this country, and yet I would do anything and suffer anything rather than leave it' (T 1132).

His position as a minor official made him particularly vulnerable in his relations with the censor, and though his plays eventually achieved performance, he had in the process a series of brushes with authority which made life in Austria seem impossible for an active writer (SB 180): the temporary banning of *Die Ahnfrau*, the long delay with *König Ottokar*, and the attempted withdrawal of *Ein treuer Diener*. His poems too ran into trouble either with the censor or with the royal family: first 'Campo vaccino', then 'Vision', then 'Klosterszene', then 'Auf die Genesung des Kronprinzen'. He saw the last of the scandals as blighting his whole future: 'I feel that I am ruined. By that wretched poem I have queered my pitch with the Emperor's successor too, and there will never be an end to my persecution' (T 2073). The earlier episode involving the 'Campo vaccino' poem continued to rankle in the late 1830s (T 3327), and in 1853 he included a full account of it in his autobiography (SB 155–8). Also in his early middle age continued fears of censorship contributed, as we have seen, to his eventual abandonment of *Esther* as a fragment, in the belief that its subject was too delicate for publication or performance ever to be permitted. In the will that he wrote in 1848 the slowness and half-heartedness of his progress on *Libussa* and *Ein Bruderzwist in Habsburg* are by implication attributed partly to their having been written 'at the time of the most severe intellectual oppression' (B 684). The same term, 'Geistesdruck', occurs in an epigram composed a few months earlier:

> Die Knechtschaft hat meine Jugend zerstört,
> Des Geistesdruckes Erhalter... (G 1115)[1]

Grillparzer's difficult position in relation to the system of censorship was commented on sharply by visitors from outside Austria – not only by those with whom he was in sympathy, but also by such writers as the critic Wolfgang Menzel in the early thirties and Gutzkow in the mid-forties (*Gespr.* 563/ii; 862). Grillparzer himself, feeling by the mid-twenties that he was 'at most tolerated as a writer' (B 323), formulated his frustration shortly after the difficulties with *Ein treuer Diener* in an image of the Metternich 'system' crucifying genius:

> Auszeichnung hier erwarte nie,
> Denn das System verbeut's,
> Man hängt das Kreuz nicht ans Genie,
> Nein, das Genie ans Kreuz. (G 485)[2]

His continuing sense of constriction and frustration emerges clearly from a diary-note of 1829: 'An Austrian writer should be held in higher esteem than any other. Anyone who does not completely lose heart under such conditions is truly a kind of hero' (T 1698). Even after the encouragement of the successful

---

[1] 'Servitude, which perpetuates intellectual oppression, has ruined my youth.'

[2] 'Expect no distinction here, for the system forbids it: they don't pin crosses on genius, but nail genius to the cross.'

première of *Der Traum ein Leben*, he was soon comparing his
position as a writer to that of a bird imprisoned in a narrow and
stuffy cage, and unable to embark on full flights of song:

> Man kann weder fliegen noch singen,
> Wenn der Raum nicht rein und weit;
> Ein Vogel und ein Dichter
> Im Käficht nicht gedeiht.   (G 216)[1]

Less than a year later, in Paris, he suddenly felt a longing to be
back in Vienna, but had to qualify it: 'If only that disgraceful
intellectual oppression did not obtain there...' (T 2953). The
burden of working in such an atmosphere, in face of his successive
brushes with authority, together with the burden of his official
duties, is finally summed up in the bleak reflection in his memoirs
of 1848: 'Despotism wrecked my life – at least my literary life.'

He was fiercely critical of Metternich as the architect of this
despotism. One poem of 1837, 'Des Kaisers Bildsäule' (G 92),
compares the Metternich era with that of Josef II, presenting the
present as an age of injustice, in which Josef's reforming achievements are being laid waste. Other poems of the 1830s include
a bitterly ironical attack on the oppressiveness and inefficiency
of Metternich's financial policies (G 217) and a scornful epitaph,
written prematurely in 1839 when Metternich fell seriously ill, in
which he describes him as a rogue and a fool, a deceiver of others
and finally of himself (G 743). In an essay on Metternich written
in 1839 both the chief aims of his policies and his actual achievements are described in very negative terms: 'In short, at the end
of Prince Metternich's career he must face the fact that his
conservative policy has failed in both its aims, the repression of
liberalism and the maintenance of the status quo..., and that
this is his fault – that it has failed as an inevitable consequence
of his measures.' In 1842 Grillparzer called Metternich's opinions
'antediluvian' (T 3594) and applied the same epithet in an epigram
to the whole 'system' (G 821). Earlier, his poem 'Warschau' (G 77)
recorded how, in fulfilment of the international policy fashioned
by Metternich, the European powers stood passively by while the
spirit of freedom was stamped out. In 1836 he expressed in his
diary his hope that the rising tide of political liberalism in the
rest of Europe would influence Austria, forcing it 'out of its
present infamous condition' (T 3194). A possible case of how this

---

[1] 'One can neither fly nor sing without space, pure and boundless: neither
a bird nor a poet thrives in a cage.'

would work in practice is discussed in a fragmentary essay of 1844, 'Preußische Konstitution': if Prussia were to receive a good constitution, Austria would, Grillparzer foresaw, have its own constitution in ten years. And throughout all this period, the heart of his criticism of Metternich's government was the repression of intellectual and artistic freedom – what in 1850 he summed up as '[die] Geistesanfeindung des früheren Systems' (B 709).[1] When he was in Berlin in 1826, what most he envied was the comparative intellectual freedom Prussia seemed to enjoy. 'Art and learning are free...' (T 1543).

Despite all his criticisms of the Metternich régime, however, and despite his praise in 1831 of the liberal poet Anastasias Grün as one fighting for truth and justice (G 212), Grillparzer himself never held radical opinions as extreme as, for example, those of Grün or his own friend Bauernfeld, though he mixed with several leading liberals, especially in the *Ludlamshöhle* club and later in the 'Concordia'. Those of his plays with a political content, from *König Ottokar* to *Die Jüdin von Toledo* and the *Bruderzwist*, attest his belief in an immutable order of things, whose political reflection is the hierarchical state,

> ...jene weise Fügung,
> Die Gott gesetzt und die man nennt den Staat
>
> (*Bruderzwist* 1543f.)[2]

The ruler, whether emperor or king, is the representative and guardian of this inviolable order, and though man-made laws are necessarily imperfect – this is a theme that emerges both in the *Bruderzwist* (2338–40) and in *Libussa* – the citizens of a state owe loyalty to their ruler. Grillparzer's views were far removed, however, from the notion of the absolute state expounded by Hegel (of whom he had nothing good to say). His conception of kingship, as embodied in Rudolf I in *König Ottokar*, involves an ideal of *service*, and he was aware of the dangers of absolutism. *Die Jüdin von Toledo* shows the dire results when a ruler neglects his duty to the state he serves. And *Ein treuer Diener seines Herrn* also has anti-absolutist overtones.

Yet in Grillparzer's own time *Ein treuer Diener* was largely taken as 'an apologia for slavish subservience' (SB 204), both by suspicious liberals and by their opponents. This approach was perpetuated by prominent critics up to the late nineteenth century,

---

[1] 'the hostility of the former "system" to things of the mind'.
[2] 'that wise disposition which God ordained and which we call the state'.

and while perceptive commentators soon tried to scotch it – Reich, for example, wrote of 'the democratic tendency' of the work – the play has continued to be read as having ultra-conservative political implications by recent critics including Alewyn and Sengle,[1] who have interpreted it as expressing an anti-revolutionary loyalism. These rather limiting political interpretations have adversely affected the popularity of the play: despite its dramatic power and theatrical effectiveness it has been one of the least performed of Grillparzer's works.

We have already seen, however, that the political action and the private (love) action involve the same contrast in standards. In private Bancban stands for peace (20) and for right:

> Nur eine Schmach weiß ich auf dieser Erde,
> Und die heißt: Unrecht tun!   (83f.)[2]

So too as a political figure he is a 'man of peace' (1418), standing for order and law, and opposing Simon and Peter because their demands for vengeance (*Bahrrecht*) in Act IV, their insistence on taking the law into their own hands, are a denial and an upheaval of true law. In the love action he is opposed to Otto, who disturbs the peace and deliberately seeks to anger him;[3] and the impingement of Otto's selfishness on the political action lends him within it a role similar to that of Don Cäsar in the *Bruderzwist* – that of a destructive element, endangering the established order. In Gertrude too a lack of moral standards goes together with a deficiency in political responsibility. She shows this deficiency in Act I when she presses Otto's claim to be co-regent, putting her feelings for him above her duty to the state. She later puts her feelings before her moral duty also; for though she has accepted moral responsibility for his conduct during the king's absence (303f.), in the event she becomes his accomplice in his pursuit of Erny and shields him after Erny's suicide by pretending that she herself has killed her. Her shortcomings in both spheres emerge again during the flight in Act IV, when she is concerned to ensure Otto's safety before that of her own child – an attitude which from the political viewpoint is a dereliction of her duty to the future of the state, which the young prince embodies. Bancban by contrast attempts to serve the state in as wholly selfless a

---

[1] Friedrich Sengle, *Das deutsche Geschichtsdrama. Geschichte eines literarischen Mythos* (Stuttgart, 1952), p. 104.
[2] 'I know of only one disgrace in this world, and that is to do wrong.'
[3] See ll. 137, 158, 184.

spirit as that affirmed by Rudolf I. Just as Rudolf regards himself no longer as Rudolf – that is, as an individual – but solely as the Emperor, the embodiment and servant of all Germany (*König Ottokar* 1786–90), so in the pursuance of his duty Bancban sees himself, together with the queen, as representing the absent king and, by implication, all that he stands for (539f.). In this conscientious selflessness, despite his limitations, Bancban shows up the members of the royal house itself: not only Otto and Gertrude, but also the king himself.

The king takes no part in the main action of the play. He appears only in the first and last acts, setting the action in motion and judging its outcome. Nevertheless he too is conceived with a new realism, in contrast to the idealized characterization of Rudolf I: though he presents himself as a father-figure towards his subjects (1858f.) he displays a fallibility that falls far short of the ideal of kingship. His judgment is weak, his demands unreasonable; and he allows himself to follow his inclinations and affections in the exercise of his power, in a way that Bancban does not. In Act II, for example, Bancban not only draws (for Erny) a distinction between himself as Bancbanus and himself as regent (630f.), but also acts on this distinction; the king in the previous act has drawn a similar distinction between himself as husband and as monarch (216f.) – but has *not* acted by it. For though he is well aware of Otto's lack of moral sense (279), and though the queen's attitude to her brother is plainly so indulgent that her promise to control him carries little conviction, Andreas is nevertheless willing to give way to her pleas and appoint Otto co-regent. When he is deterred by the news that Otto is absent and has been out all night, he still persists in handing power over to his queen, who has shown her own unsuitability by her championing of Otto. If she is misled by her feelings for her brother, so the king in less degree is misled by his feelings for her, adjudging her just and shrewd (413) in the teeth of the evidence; and he pays the penalty in the tragic irony of her accidental death. Moreover his judgment is at fault in the appointment of Bancban to a position for which he too, though in a different way, is unsuitable. Admittedly, among the characters of the play there are no alternative choices, and certainly Bancban is a worthier regent than Otto. But he warns the king that he lacks strength (384–6), and protests that he is not suitable (411); and clearly it is limited vision on the king's part to insist on Bancban's appointment and to fail to see

that the dispositions he is making are doomed to failure. The true
potential of the situation is brought out in stage action, when
Gertrude refuses to give Bancban her hand to kiss (sd/398). The
king actually asks, in annoyance, if disharmony is breaking out
before he has even left (401); but he fails to think this perception
through to the practical consequences. Instead, very unfairly, he
threatens Bancban with ignominy if the peace is broken (421ff.) –
when in fact it is endangered by his own appointment of Bancban
against the queen's wishes – and if he should break his word (427),
when in fact he never gave it (383). Fuerst, discussing the opening
scenes of the play, points out that they run in parallel – Bancban's
farewell from Erny, King Andreas' from Gertrude – and from the
contrast between Bancban's language (ironic, staccato, grumpy)
and the more elevated, majestic tones of the royal pair he argues
that the king alone of all the characters in the play stands above
caricature as an ideal figure, without human weaknesses. But as
we have seen, the king's actions in this very scene in yielding to
Gertrude and then insisting on Bancban's appointment – imposing
it on Bancban against his will and against his better judgment –
are by no means the actions of an ideal ruler. On the contrary,
they are arbitrary, and have disastrous consequences: for the
country they mean civil war, and for Bancban personal tragedy.
The monitory advice that Bancban gives, kneeling, to the infant
prince Bela in his final speech is clearly directed only nominally
at Bela, and is really also a reminder to the king of his duties, in
which he has fatefully failed: duties of justice (2111) and self-
discipline (2113f.).

In his autobiography, discussing the attempt made by Emperor
Franz to proscribe the work under the pretext of acquiring
exclusive rights to it in perpetuity, Grillparzer writes that the
reasons for the Emperor's displeasure were a mystery to him
since the play was, after all, 'loyal to a fault' (sb 206). It must
indeed have been galling that the play was attacked from the
left for 'servility' and at the same time from the right, presumably
for the reverse. Nonetheless Grillparzer's disclaimer of any
knowledge as to the Emperor's motives carries little conviction
when the whole action of the play is based on an example of.
misuse of power by an absolute ruler. Bancbanus's loyalty is
wilfully exploited; and while he is shown as serving the monarchic
state altruistically, his allegiance to his duty is maintained at so
great a cost that his unquestioning loyalty to the state or the

royal house seems excessive, and the authority that prescribes it seems wholly unjustifiable. All the implications of his task and its results are unfavourable to the authoritarian imperial system such as obtained under Emperor Franz and Metternich.

Though Grillparzer was to claim that one of the original attractions of the Bancban theme was that it would meet few objections from the censor (SB 203), and though the text was in fact passed without difficulties, there are several further, less fundamental features which might well have aroused the censor's suspicions and which may have contributed to the official disapproval after the success of the Burgtheater production. The relative superficiality of these points illustrates the difficulty of the potential restrictions with which a dramatist in Grillparzer's Austria was hedged about. For example, Otto describes the court as an environment which helped to condition his shortcomings (1221); and he himself openly exploits his position of privilege (156f.). It was always dangerous to portray immorality within a royal family; and of course for a figure such as Bancban to respect a figure such as Otto simply because he is the king's brother-in-law (43) does appear absurd. Again, while Grillparzer does not overemphasize the nationalist implications in his material (in early versions of his manuscript Otto and his men were explicitly required to wear German dress, but in the final version this detail was deleted), nevertheless the revolution is one led by Hungarian nobles against a German queen and her brother who have abused their power and expressed contempt of the virtuous qualities of the Hungarian people (951). And in the 1820s merely to depict a revolution was to court disfavour in the multinational Empire.

Ein treuer Diener was not conceived as a political play, but as a tragedy of loyalty set against a historical background. The basis in Grillparzer's experience for the questioning of absolute duty was apolitical. It is characteristic of all but his last works that their specifically political significance is secondary, and that the political 'message' to be derived from them is at best fragmentary. What caught his interest in the political field were single events or policies which threatened to affect his career or which offended against his ideals; and the side of his interest which was caught was not the creative, imaginative side – the interest of the poet – but that of the 'intellectual'. His reactions to the world of political affairs tended, then, to be reflective and critical reactions to single items of news. The form which lent itself best to the expression of such reactions was the epigram, and Grillparzer's epigrams form the clearest cumulative testimony to his political position.

In 1834 a striking diary-note includes the comment 'Political events alone interest me, with absurd intensity' (T 2112). Symptomatic of this growing interest was the keenness with which he attended parliamentary sessions both in Paris and in London. In the later 1830s and the 1840s, after his retirement from activity as a dramatist, his attention turned still more to the dramas of public life. His epigrams increased in frequency; and whereas he had once been subjected to censorship and even, he suspected, persecution (T 3327) by the right-wing establishment, he was now increasingly exposed to criticism from the radicals and liberals. He himself claimed, however, that he was not and had never been an extremist in either direction, but that he preserved a sensible moderation:

> Als liberal einst der Verfolgung Ziel,
> Schilt mich der Freiheitstaumel nun servil,
> Nicht hier noch dort in den Extremen zünftig,
> Ich glaube bald, ich bin vernünftig.   (G 1108)[1]

He was indeed always uncommitted to any political faction. If from the late thirties onwards his position seems more conservative than previously, this is less because of a real shift in his own opinions (that he was never illiberal in outlook is confirmed by his vote for Auersperg and Bauernfeld in April 1848) than because of a shift in the trends about him. As the liberals became more vocal and more influential, he became increasingly aware of the dangers of extreme developments of progressivism, nationalism and materialism. He saw gaining strength in public affairs ideas that he regarded as equivalent to the 'prosaic' intellectual and artistic trends which ensured his withdrawal from the theatre after the failure of *Weh dem, der lügt!*

About the art of others he was able to remain robustly clear-thinking. The so-called 'Swedish nightingale', the soprano Jenny Lind, first appeared in Vienna in 1846 and was subjected to critical attacks from Moritz Saphir; when she was due to return to perform in the next Fasching, Grillparzer leapt to her defence with an

---

[1] 'Once persecuted as a liberal, I am now denounced as "servile" by the frenzied champions of "liberty". I belong to the sect of neither extreme – I almost think I must be sensible.'

epigram that resolutely affirms the invulnerability of beauty to sniping attacks:

> Der Hund bellt an den Mond,
> Der leuchtet wie gewohnt,
> Gibt sich durch Strahlen kund
> Und bleibt der holde Mond,
> So wie der Hund – ein Hund.   (G 1038)[1]

But when his own works were under attack, he found himself only too vulnerable; with that sense of 'shame' that he had felt at performances of *Die Ahnfrau* (T 204), he felt that in his writings he was baring something essentially intimate. His poetic works contained, he felt, the real core of his life. This is the sense of his remark that his poems were his biography, which he developed by explaining that he was withholding his poems from publication in a collected edition because it might reawaken painful memories, and concluding that his nature was 'terribly susceptible' (*Gespr.* 1148/vii). The same 'susceptibility' made him keep the manuscripts of his last three tragedies locked away in his desk, out of the reach of theatres and critics: not only was he himself dissatisfied with the plays, he told Wartenegg, he also feared their failure at a time when (as he said in the same conversation) he was out of harmony with the standards of the public (*Gespr.* 1088). Similarly he consistently refused to authorize a collected edition of his plays, even after Laube had revived most of them in the Burgtheater. The climate of the age, he felt, was unfavourable:

> 'Warum gibst deine Werke du endlich nicht heraus?'
> Mein Freund, bei schlechtem Wetter hält man sich gern zu Haus. ·
>
>   (G 1594)[2]

The sense of being at odds with the cultural trends of his times was not a new one. In the early stages of his career the literary scene was dominated by the Romantic school, to which he felt opposed in every respect. His diaries of the 1820s show that he was strongly critical of the creative writers among the German Romantics, including Friedrich Schlegel, Tieck and Novalis.[3] He was wholly out of sympathy with the individualism of Romantic philosophy. In practical social terms, he regarded individualism, linked to the growing materialism of the nineteenth century, as

---

[1] 'The dog barks at the moon; the moon shines on as usual, declares itself by its rays and remains the lovely moon – just as the dog remains a dog.'

[2] 'Why don't you publish your works at last?' 'My friend, when the weather is bad one prefers to stay at home.'

[3] See T 1224, 1310, 1679, 1682.

one of the most dangerous trends of the time. A typical warning is contained in a poem of about 1817:

> Eigennutz, die gefräß'ge Hyäne,
> Eigenliebe, sich Gott und Altar,
> Selbstsucht, wetzend die gierigen Zähne,
> Lüstern schlürfend des Bruders Träne –
> Austria! *Das* deiner Feinde Schar! (G 141)[1]

A note on the explicitly political dangers of 'the predominant egoism' is contained in his diary for 1830 (T 1826). But the most heartfelt of Grillparzer's criticisms of Romanticism related to the literary sphere. He was opposed to the intellectuality of the aesthetic criticism of 'the omniscient Schlegels' (T 624). He condemned A. W. Schlegel's tendency to reduce works of art to abstract or philosophical ideas (T 200); and his grievance at the treatment of his own early works in this spirit was later forcefully expressed in the poem 'Jugenderinnerungen im Grünen' (133ff.). In his autobiography he sums up the position by saying that as early as 1817 he felt that he was the last poet in an age of prose (SB 127).

The distinction between 'poetry' and 'prose' is based on Grillparzer's constant insistence that the realm of imaginative art is separate from that of intellectual knowledge ('geistiges Wissen', T 3310). In an essay of 1834, 'Über den gegenwärtigen Zustand der dramatischen Kunst in Deutschland', he described the post-Romantic situation in which, by the admixture of emotional and imaginative elements, philosophy had become a kind of poetry, whereupon imaginative literature was all but turned into philosophy. Modern literature tended to descend into 'prose' not just in its trivial respects, but 'precisely when it aspires to imaginative art ["Poesie"]: for its highest flight is to the sphere of intellectual thought, whereas nothing is poetic but feelings' (T 2768). The imaginative quality of true art should lift it out of the realm of ratiocination – two characteristic statements of this, both dating from the late 1830s, are: 'Doch Prosa *spricht*, die Dichtung *singt*' and 'Prosa und Poesie unterscheiden sich wie Speise und Trank'.[2] There is a proper distinction between

---

[1] 'Self-interest, the voracious hyena; self-love, its own idol and altar; self-seeking, sharpening its greedy teeth, avidly drinking a brother's tears – those, Austria, are the host of your enemies!'

[2] 'But prose speaks, poetry sings' (G 665); 'Prose and poetry differ like food and drink' (G 742). The diaries of the same period contain several similar formulations: T 3412, 3492, 3493.

the realms of philosophy and art, and in Grillparzer's view it was characteristic of modern German literature that this distinction had broken down: 'They adulterate poetry with philosophy and philosophy in turn with poetry', he wrote in the late essay 'Zur Literargeschichte'. He made the same point in the late 1830s (T 3362), and reworked it as an epigram in 1840 (G 762); and the poem 'Die Schwestern' (G 90) ends with the plea:

> Kehr, deutsche Prosa, rück zur sichern Erde,
> Nimm wieder Flügel, deutsche Poesie![1]

Similar plaints about the decline of contemporary literature to 'prose' are expressed in poems of the early 1840s (G 257, 260). One form that he particularly regarded as typifying this decline in practice was the *Novelle* (T 3281), because of the tendency of the Realists to treat everyday trivialities; this is the prejudice behind his emphatic refusal of the designation 'Novelle' for *Der arme Spielmann* in 1846 (B 652). It was, on the other hand, his suspicion of the dominance of ideas, whether political or philosophical, that underlay his aversion to the literature of *das Junge Deutschland* – though he admitted that such writing had a quality of directness which was at least preferable to the obscurities of the Romantics (T 2856) – and later to Hebbel (T 4038) and Richard Wagner (G 1690). In the field of philosophy, the tendencies to individualism, abstraction and over-intellectualization seemed to be combined most completely in the speculative work of Hegel, which Grillparzer condemned as 'phantasmagoric' (T 3881) and as 'the most monstrous product of human presumption' (T 4269). It was the contrast with Hegel that increasingly heightened Grillparzer's respect for Kant (T 2010): what he saw in Kant's work, as opposed to Hegelian 'presumption', was 'objective recognition of the limitation of humanity' ('Zur Literargeschichte').

In his criticisms of German culture in the nineteenth century, Grillparzer was swimming against the tide; but he was not alone in making them, nor the first to do so. Hölderlin, for example, in the short epigrammatic odes that he wrote in the last years of the eighteenth century ('An die Deutschen', 'Die scheinheiligen Dichter') voiced criticisms of the Germans of his time as being too completely dominated by the intellect; they are condemned at the end of *Hyperion*, too, as including 'thinkers, but no human beings'. Hölderlin saw the civilization of his time as cut off by

---

[1] 'German prose, come back down to earth! Take wing again, German poetry!'

its own philosophizing reflective tendencies from that perception of and sympathy with the divine forces of nature which he regarded as essential to the development of true 'humanity'. He contrasted the limited thinking that depends on the intellect ('Verstand') with the fuller understanding that is born of inspiration and intuition ('Ahnung'). It was with a very similar sense of priorities that Grillparzer condemned Hegel's work as 'an unsuccessful attempt to solve the mystery of the world purely by the use of reason' ('Zur Literargeschichte').

It was partly in reaction against the prosaic, ratiocinative thinking and literature of his own times that from the end of the 1830s he increasingly devoted himself to reading Lope de Vega. He had appreciated the 'truth to nature' of Lope's work as early as 1824 (T 1379); a poem of 1839 ('Lope de Vega', G 308) compares Lope to the great Spanish navigators, exploring 'all the coasts of nature'; and in the copious notes that Grillparzer made on his works from that year onwards 'truth to nature' ('Naturwahrheit') is a recurrent term of praise. One play, *El duque de Viseo*, prompted the reflection: 'Lope de Vega's perceptions are drawn from the deep well of feeling, and they call on us to *think* only as much as the aspect of nature itself does...'; another play, *Vida y muerte del Rey Bamba,* moved him to praise Lope as 'the most perfect protest against the literature of ideas' and to contrast him with 'our modern world, immersed in logic-chopping and abstractions'. Lope's example doubtless helped to strengthen his unwavering resolve 'not to yield to the intellectual and tendentious literature of our day' (T 3354). But his resistance to the inhospitable temper of his age – his sense of which was inevitably sharpened by the reception of *Weh dem, der lügt!* – forced him into an increasing isolation:

> Die Zeit, sie eilt so schnell voraus,
> Und ich, ich blieb zurück...[1]

he wrote in 1839 (G 99); and as the radicals and progressives gained strength in politics and the Realists in literature, he finally felt he was living in an altogether alien age; in 1859 he wrote:

> Ich komme aus andern Zeiten
> Und hoffe in andre zu gehn. (G 1590)[2]

The increasingly alien age of his middle and later years was, in

---

[1] 'Time races ahead so fast, and I have stayed behind...'
[2] 'I come from other times, and hope to go to other times.'

the words of an epigram by Bauernfeld, 'the age of phrase-mongering' ('die Zeit der Phraseologie'); and Grillparzer recognized this earlier than Bauernfeld did. After the revolution of 1848 he criticized contemporary slavery to libertarian trends, which he saw as a denial of true freedom (G 1225), and the blinkered egalitarianism that rode roughshod over established tradition (G 130). All the slogans about progress failed to convince him that genuine progress had been made, or that things were not even moving backwards (G 1228). He was suspicious of democracy. Immediately after the July Revolution in 1830 it seemed at least preferable to the 'appalling policy of stagnation' that obtained under Metternich (T 1826), but when 1848 came he admitted in conversation (*Gespr.* 951) and in verse that he had no faith that the masses were ready to participate in government. These doubts are expressed most clearly in the poem 'Der Reichstag' of 1849 (G 130). He still believed in monarchic rule: 'Daß einer herrsche, ist des Himmels Ruf' (*Libussa* 1193).[1] His poem in honour of Radetzky in 1848 (G 128), which followed Radetzky's defeat of the Piedmontese at Santa Lucia in early May, was inspired by his view that Radetzky was the last bulwark of a monarchy in collapse – though nothing could stop the liberals from condemning his patriotism as mere servility (G 1197). He saw the revolution, in fact, as threatening to destroy the very state itself (*Gespr.* 951), and, indeed, as presenting all the signs of a declining civilization (T 4042).

In his memoirs of 1848 he mentions his 'lack of enthusiasm for liberty'. The libertarian trends, both the movement towards democracy and what he calls 'the ridiculous issue of nationalism', were threatening to disrupt the whole Austro-Hungarian Empire. The danger as Grillparzer saw it came to a head in 1848: he perceived '...that the movement of 1848 threatened to destroy my fatherland, which I love with childlike devotion'. Despite all his criticisms of the Metternich régime – criticisms that he did not relax – he now saw the beneficial side of the policies of its architect, 'who with all his faults was the only man who would have had the mind and energy to limit and control the onrush of events'. He was particularly concerned about the disruptive effects of separatist nationalism, which was especially strong in the Slav countries (where it had derived powerful stimulus from Herder), but which was also a factor at every stage of the revolution in

---

[1] 'That there should be one ruler is Heaven's decree.'

Vienna. Grillparzer's criticism of the nationalists is sharply expressed in the most famous of all his epigrams:

> Der Weg der neuern Bildung geht
> Von Humanität
> Durch Nationalität
> Zur Bestialität. (G 1182)[1]

After the Austrian defeat of 1859 he felt 'inwardly shattered by the convulsions of my homeland' (B 997), and after the defeat of 1866 he expressed his fears for the unity of the multi-national Empire: 'What is to become of our Czech and Magyar homeland now?' (B 1397). The events of 1866 not only undermined Austria's imperial position but also endangered her close relation to Germany. Grillparzer commented ironically in an epigram on her humiliation in leaving the Confederation (G 1769), and in the autumn of 1866 spoke of himself as being 'without a homeland' (*Gespr.* 1186). In the following year he emphasized his role as a *German* writer (G 1778), and he continued in his last epigrams to express his sense of cultural severance (G 1768 and 1861).

Here we are approaching the core of his political standpoint, the unity within the fragmentary corpus of his political utterances. His primary concern is not with political issues in the narrow sense, but with the whole cultural life and tradition which the government of a country reflects and should maintain. Not long after the 1848 revolution, Bauernfeld spoke of him as exhibiting an excessive 'hatred' of the Germans (*Gespr.* 970); but it is quite clear from his memoirs of 1848 and other notes and essays that what his dissatisfaction with the progressive movement in Germany, both as a political movement and in its literary expression, was based on was the conviction that it went with a wider cultural immaturity. His standards were those of the mature culture of the eighteenth century, the standards of *Humanität*. Herder defined *Humanität* as the achievement of reason and justice, and saw it as 'the aim of human nature'; the means and goal of its development lay in the perfectibility of man, which he affirmed as no mere illusion. What most saddened Grillparzer about the events of 1848 was, he wrote, that they shook any belief in human perfectibility (T 4042). Herder defined human development as a process of self-realization:

---

[1] 'The course of modern culture leads from humanity through nationalism to bestiality.'

Vollkommenheit eines *einzelnen* Menschen ist also, daß er im Continuum seiner Existenz Er selbst sei und werde. Daß er die Kräfte brauche, die die Natur ihm als Stammgut gegeben hat; daß er damit für sich und andre wuchere.[1]

It is just such a process of perception and practical acknowledgment of their natural talents and responsibilities that characterizes the development of such figures as Rustan, Leon and Alphons; and it is in this sense that we should also read Grillparzer's praise of Beethoven, in the funeral oration, as having been a 'human being in the fullest sense of the word' and the formula for just government spoken by Bancbanus to the infant Bela: 'Laß dir den Menschen Mensch sein...' (*Ein treuer Diener* 2115).[2] Sometimes the idea of the wholeness of personality is expressed rather negatively, in terms of self-defence rather than development: 'In Selbstbewahrung liegt zuletzt die Ruh' (T 2919);[3] but equally Grillparzer's ideal of *Sammlung*, the concentration of all the faculties, has (together with its inspirational overtones) a clear kinship with Goethe's conception of the highest human achievement – attained by the ancient Greeks – as depending on the harmony of the natural faculties, physical, intellectual, spiritual, 'wenn die gesunde Natur des Menschen als ein Ganzes wirkt' or 'wenn sich die sämtlichen Eigenschaften gleichmäßig in ihm vereinigen'.[4]

As early as 1810 Grillparzer was already standing by the eighteenth-century standards of reason and enlightenment in criticizing Austria, which he described as a country 'where reason is a crime and enlightenment the most dangerous enemy of the state' (T 94). His criticism of the 'system' was founded on the conviction that it sacrificed 'the noblest needs of man' (T 1826) – that is, that it repressed the intellectual, cultural and spiritual life of the nation. The same criticism is made in the poem 'Warschau' of the conservatives in international politics:

[1] 'The perfection of a single man consists, then, in his being and becoming himself in the continuum of his existence, in his using those powers that he inherited from Nature, and in his putting them to profit for himself and others' (*Briefe zu Beförderung der Humanität*, xxv). See also *Ideen zur Philosophie der Geschichte der Menschheit*, 15. Buch.

[2] 'Allow your people to be human beings!'

[3] 'Peace lies ultimately in preservation of the self' (the last line of the first complete version of the poem 'Entsagung': the revised version of this conclusion is quoted on p. 128).

[4] 'when all the healthy nature of man works as a unified whole' and 'when all his qualities are harmoniously united' (*Winckelmann und sein Jahrhundert*, 'Antikes').

Die Freiheit hassen sie, doch nicht alleine,
Nicht mehr als all, was stammt vom ew'gen Geist,
Und atmend lebt im hellen Sonnenscheine,
Was wärmt, erhebt, was denkt und unterweist.   (G 77)[1]

And it is precisely the same priorities that inform Grillparzer's later criticism of the liberal movement. The whole traditional basis of human life is endangered – 'Gelöst ist des Gewohnten altes Band' (G 125)[2] – and cultural standards are undermined: the word 'Bildung' is a key word in the poem 'Der Reichstag', and presents the key to his discontents with the claims of the egalitarianists:

'Allein die Bildung sei jetzt allgemein' –
Als wäre Bildung eine fert'ge Größe,
Die man, wie ins Gefäß den firnen Wein,
Ein Totes in ein Unlebend'ges gösse!'[3]

Again, his criticisms of the separatist movements were based on a strong sense of a priority of cultural and spiritual values over purely practical ones; he expressed this very clearly in a letter of 1861 in which he addressed a Hungarian correspondent as his compatriot, dismissing the distinction of 'nationality' and insisting: 'Das Beste, was der Mensch sein kann, ist er als Mensch' (B 1014).[4] He made the same point again in 1866, speaking to a group of students who had brought him formal congratulations on his seventy-fifth birthday: 'I too am all for liberty; but I hate humbug, and these awful conflicts about nationality should not arise in civilized countries. For me, the human spirit is higher than all else, and it recognizes no exclusively national attitudes' (*Gespr.* 1178). It is the humane standards of the eighteenth century whose undermining is defined in the regression from *Humanität* via 'nationalism' to 'bestiality', a regression back to brutishness. For Grillparzer these standards were the inviolable basis of his whole cultural outlook; and this as well as a purely artistic ideal

1 'They hate freedom, but not freedom alone – not more than all that comes from the eternal spirit and lives and breathes in the bright sunlight, all that warms and elevates, all that thinks and teaches.'
2 'The age-old bond of custom is severed.'
3 '"But culture", they say, "is universal now" – as though it were a standard measure, that one could pour lifeless into a lifeless vessel, as old wine is poured into a glass!'
4 'Man is as Man the best that Man can be.' Cf. one of Goethe's *Zahme Xenien*: '...Je mehr du fühlst, ein Mensch zu sein, / Desto ähnlicher bist du den Göttern!' ('The more you feel a human being, the more you are like the gods!')

is the sense of the epigram that he first drafted in 1844 (G 893), revised in 1846 (G 993) and wrote out again both the next year (G 1043) and again in 1853 (G 1317):

> Nur weiter geht das tolle Treiben,
> Von vorwärts!|vorwärts! erschallt das Land;
> Ich möchte, wär's möglich, stehen bleiben,
> Wo Schiller und Goethe stand. (G 993)[1]

Grillparzer's long interest in politics is reflected in his last plays, and it is because of the profundity of their treatment of broad political and cultural issues that *Libussa* and *Ein Bruderzwist in Habsburg* in particular are widely regarded as being among the most important of his works. Neither matches up in entirety to his own ideal of essentially theatrical drama, and in 1849 he explained his refusal to publish them in his own lifetime by their lack of 'that essential principle of life which perception alone vouchsafes and which can never be replaced by rational thought' (T 4025). But they both reflect his criticism of the materialist tendencies of his time, his sense of living in an age of cultural and political decline, and his concern for the humanitarian and cultural standards he saw being debased.

Ein Bruderzwist in Habsburg

Ein Bruderzwist in Habsburg is a work rich in characterization and in memorably expressed insights into the course of politics and history. It is, indeed, widely regarded – especially, perhaps, by critics more interested in the ideas expressed in the work than in its theatrical effectiveness – as being among the very greatest of Grillparzer's tragedies. Naumann adjudges it his most powerful work; Nadler describes it as the most powerful historical tragedy in German.

The action is set in the early years of the seventeenth century, and treats the developments leading up to the outbreak of the Thirty Years War. Amid the partisan plotting, the Emperor is shown as trying, wisely but in vain, to maintain a balance between the religious and political factions, and so to hold off the war. As in *König Ottokar*, Grillparzer has condensed and simplified the historical material, and has drawn together events which in fact

---

[1] 'On and on the frenzy goes: "Forward! Forward!" rings through the land. I should like, if it were possible, to stand still where Schiller and Goethe stood.'

extended over more than a decade.[1] The play concentrates on the rivalries within the House of Habsburg, exploring the characters of the principal participants. All the chief figures and motifs are introduced in a superbly organized first act which, like several of Grillparzer's expositions, begins with apparently separate scenes that build up gradually to the entry of the central character. The first scene features the Emperor's natural son, Don Cäsar; the second the Emperor's brother, Archduke Mathias, and Mathias' counsellor Bishop Klesel. Only then does Rudolf II himself appear. He dominates the second half of the act; then in the next act the focus shifts back to the ambitious Mathias.

At the end of the play the focus is again on Mathias. Towards the end of the fourth act we hear that elegiac tone that is usually the hallmark of Grillparzer's last acts as Rudolf reviews his failure: 'Ich habe viel gefehlt, ich seh' es ein...' (2296).[2] Finally he collapses, and Duke Julius laments the effective conclusion of his reign: 'Der Kaiser starb, ob auch der Mensch genese' (2436).[3] His story is complete, and the curtain falls; but the play is not over. In Grillparzer's concern to bring out the whole perspective of the action, and perhaps with the sense of linking the material of the work with that of Schiller's *Wallenstein*, a fifth act follows, like an epilogue: the political action is pursued, its consequences spelt out. For though the central figure has already left the scene, his tragedy as Emperor is not merely a personal one, but that of his whole empire. The last act shows Mathias achieving the power that has been his goal, but doing so only against a background of disaster for which he himself is responsible: the Thirty Years War is breaking out, and the cries of 'Vivat Mathias!' from the crowd outside the imperial palace in Vienna provide an ironic accompaniment to his realization of the truth. He kneels, beating his breast: 'Mea culpa, mea culpa, / Mea maxima culpa' (2917f.). He remains kneeling, covering his face with his hands, as the cries of *vivat!* continue outside. And now the final curtain falls. Because the two levels of the work, the character study and the political action, are not completely integrated, it comes in effect almost as a second ending to the play; but it is a magnificent ending nonetheless.

Mathias is the last of the long line of figures in Grillparzer's dramas whose ambition outstrips their true capacity. His tem-

---

[1] The historical background is summarized by Wells, pp. 106–8.
[2] 'I acknowledge that I have been much at fault...'
[3] 'Even if the *man* Rudolf recover, the *Emperor* is dead.'

peramental instability and lack of strength of character are brought
out with convincing circumstantiality. They are, indeed, clearly
revealed in the second scene, when after a single reverse he is
willing to give up all his aspirations, all his claims to the succession
(117–21), for what Klesel derides as the 'pastoral happiness' of
a provincial retirement (127). Encouraged by Klesel, Mathias
allows his ambition to surge up again, and is soon thinking of
building up his military power (184). And yet, when he actually
confronts the Emperor, he subsides at once into complete humility,
and, kneeling, declares himself

> Bereit, mein Herr und Kaiser,
> Die Rechte alle, die mein Eigentum,
> Und die man mir beneidet, aufzugeben,
> Mein Erbrecht auf die österreich'schen Lande,
> Die Hoffnung, einst zu folgen auf dem Thron,
> Für einen Ort, um ruhig drauf zu sterben. (208–13)[1]

Rudolf is well aware of his brother's limitations, and of the vanity
which conceals them from him:

> ...Wir beide haben
> Von unserm Vater Tatkraft nicht geerbt,
> – Allein ich weiß es, und er weiß es nicht. (446–8)[2]

Consequently he accords him what he thinks will be only a nominal
command in the field (456–61); and at the beginning of the second
act his criticisms of his ability seem justified, when Mathias' army
is demoralized and complaining of lack of leadership (531, 566).
Mathias does not lack bravery, as he proves by his rash desire to
continue the war against the odds (727). What he lacks is resolution.
Klesel spells this out accurately when (in order to allay Archduke
Max's concern at his power over Mathias) he goads his lord into
resolute disagreement by suggesting that he lacks decisiveness and
firmness of purpose (1008f.); and he talks later of his 'uncertainty
and lack of decision' (2665). Mathias is guided only by his vanity,
and for his part in the tragedy Rudolf has only scathing condemnation and finally pitying compassion:

> Nur *einen* tadl' ich, den ich hier nicht nenne;
> Den ich verachtet einst, alsdann gehaßt,

---

[1] 'Ready, my Lord and Emperor, to renounce all the rights that are mine
and for which I am envied – my hereditary right to the lands of Austria,
my hope of succeeding one day to the throne – for a place where I may
die in peace.'

[2] 'Neither of us inherited energy from our father; but I realize it, and he
does not.'

Und nun bedaure als des Jammers Erben.
Er hat nur seiner Eitelkeit gefrönt,
Und dacht' er an die Welt, so war's als Bühne,
Als Schauplatz für sein leeres Heldenspiel.   (2310–15)[1]

The play ends with his apparent political success; but he is cheated of all pleasure in the achievement of his goal by his own realization of his selfishness. He has acted with the unscrupulousness of a Jason or a Rustan; and just as for Jason at the end of the trilogy 'the dream is over...', so Mathias sees his 'dreams of future deeds' disappear (2911) as he is left facing harsh reality, the political catastrophe he has brought about.

Klesel too is motivated by self-interest, at a different level: it emerges in the last act that as well as gaining high ecclesiastical office he has consistently safeguarded his material interest (2500–8). The Emperor regards him as cunning (1403); and indeed he is a born politician, and an opportunist, as we see from the way he turns his disagreement with Mathias to advantage, manoeuvring the other archdukes into electing Mathias to enforce the peace treaty. Earlier in the second act, his horror when he fears that Mathias may be dead (665) suggests that he needs Mathias as much as Mathias needs him; but nevertheless it is, as Max suspects, Mathias who is Klesel's echo, and not the other way round (851f.). Rudolf too sees that Klesel's function is to infuse into Mathias the energetic decisiveness that he lacks (1403–5); and the full extent of Mathias' dependence on him emerges in the last act, when Ferdinand has had Klesel captured and Mathias is left alone, anxiously helpless without his guidance (2780, 2799). Both Mathias and Klesel are creatures of present opportunity; they typify the limitations of the whole alien political world around Rudolf, and inevitably act counter to his plans:

Gemartert vom Gedanken drohnder Zukunft,
Dacht' ich die Zeit von gleicher Furcht bewegt,
Im weisen Zögern sehnd die einz'ge Rettung.
Allein der Mensch lebt nur im Augenblick,
Was heut' ist, kümmert ihn, es gibt kein Morgen.   (2301–5)[2]

---

[1] 'I blame only one man, whom I shall not name here, whom I once despised, then hated, but now pity as the inheritor of disaster. He has pandered only to his vanity, and if he has thought of the world about him it was as a stage, a setting for his empty heroics.'

[2] 'Tormented by the thought of the threatening future, I thought our age must share that fear, and saw in prudent delay our only salvation. But Man lives only in the present: what happens today is what concerns him, and he sees no tomorrow.'

Rudolf's foresight is unique; it is part of his deep insight into the whole harmony of creation. But as we are also reminded in *Libussa*, practical human activity is a sphere 'where too much insight is destructive of achievement' (*Libussa* 419).

It was on Rudolf that Grillparzer's preparatory notes about the play centred, from the very first note in 1824 onwards. He felt a special sympathy for him, and it is generally acknowledged that there is much of Grillparzer's own character in Rudolf's. He is grumpy, melancholy, given to brooding. He is a student of Spanish – even, indeed, of Lope. He is indecisive, and feels unequal to his task; indeed his achievements might appropriately be summed up in one of Grillparzer's later descriptions of his own career, 'Gescheit gedacht und dumm gehandelt' (G 1688).[1] One of the reasons for Rudolf's shortcomings as a practical politician is that in his heart, in contrast to the intensity and urgency of the militants, his interests do not lie in the field of political action. In the first act the keen interest that he displays in Lope and in paintings and precious stones stands in marked contrast to his refusal either to read political dispatches or to see his nephew (and possible successor) Archduke Ferdinand (197ff.). He reads wistfully in Lope of the 'ring of forgetfulness' (206f.): the obvious implication is that he is oppressed by his obligations and – at least at times – lacks the will to face them. While he recognizes the importance of his duty, his awareness of his lack of practical energy (447f.), together with his fears about the limitations of his foresight, leave in him not only scruples but also a lack of confidence in his ability to discharge his duty. The emphasis on Rudolf's sense of inadequacy, and the detail of the characterization, achieve an effect of realism and a breadth of humanity which are much more convincing than the idealized characterization of the Emperor in *König Ottokars Glück und Ende*. Like the king in *Ein treuer Diener*, Rudolf II is fallible. Moreover, unlike Andreas, he himself knows this; and precisely this further humanizing touch adds the most fundamental source of his political weakness.

There are, nevertheless, two important characteristics that Rudolf II has in common with Rudolf I. The first is his strong sense of duty: he makes it clear that he wears his crown not from inclination, but from a consciousness of his responsibility (1488ff.). The second is his conservative political outlook. He believes in a divine order of creation (*Ordnung*, 427f., 1264), and defends

---

[1] 'Clever in thought and stupid in action.'

established social differences as being akin to the established differences of the natural world (1612ff.). The equivalent of the divine order in the secular world is the established political unit whose guardian he is. His aim is to prevent the disintegration of the old political order in the anarchy of the new:

> ...Soll nicht der Grundbau jener weisen Fügung,
> Die Gott gesetzt und die man nennt den Staat,
> Im wilden Taumel auseinandergehn. (1543–5)[1]

He compares his own conservative role to that of the binding that holds together a whole sheaf of corn:

> Ich bin das Band, das diese Garbe hält,
> Unfruchtbar selbst, doch nötig, weil es bindet. (1163f.)[2]

He takes up this image of binding again in the fourth act (2396); and though by then it is clear that he has failed in his aim, the one argument with which he has been able to build up his own resolve to act is that he must prevent civil war (1465–9): his first priority remains the preservation of 'the honour of the empire' (1663).

Rudolf's conception of the order of creation is not only expounded in his speeches but is also reflected more indirectly in his interest in astrology; he sees the stars as part of the vast chain of creation, the 'first works' of the creator (400). This interest in the stars is one of the characteristics of the historical Rudolf that Grillparzer has built on and given new significance. It also bears on another element of Rudolf's outlook. He regards the stars as a model: in the regularity of their movement, they seem free of that selfishness which he observes all about him in human, and especially political, activity. His ideal is to be, like the stars, 'gelehrig fromm, den eignen Willen meisternd' (414);[3] his moral standard is summarized in the motto of the order of 'knights of peace' that he has founded: 'Not I, but God alone' (1221).

He decorates Duke Julius with the medal of this order in the course of a long scene of discussion at the beginning of Act III. His utterances here are reflective, leisured, philosophic, as they are also in his long speech to Ferdinand in the first act (391ff.),

---

[1] '...if the whole structure of that wise disposition which God ordained and which we call the state is not to collapse in the frenzied tumult'.
[2] 'I am the binding that holds this sheaf – fruitless in itself, but necessary because it binds.'
[3] 'piously receptive, mastering individual will'.

his speechifying both to Rumpf and to the delegates in Act III (1454ff.), and his last long speeches in Act IV, rich in images, similes and metaphors. One of the unusual features of the play is the extent to which the action is retarded by passages of reflection, argument and narration. The narrative passages, a natural result of the compression of historical material, include scenes at the beginning of Act II (536ff.) and in Act IV (2027ff.) in which the progress of battle is described; and in Act III we learn of the rise of Mathias at second hand, through Prokop (1383ff.). The passages of discussion include the long scene of argument between the archdukes in Act II and the scene at the beginning of Act V in which Ferdinand and Klesel weigh up possible political developments. Scenes of argument and reflection are essential to an action which depends on political calculation; and Rudolf's speeches in particular enhance the dramatic effect in that they serve to bring out a fundamental feature both of his character and (consequently) of the situation: his tendency to reflect instead of to act. Around him is a pervasive mood of urgency and threat, which is built up in sharp reminders, recurrent images of time threatening and pressing. 'Es drängt die Zeit', says Mathias (926); so too does Ferdinand's henchman in the fifth act (2672). Ferdinand himself speaks of 'der Drang der Zeit' (2822). And Rudolf uses similar expressions:

> So dringt die Zeit, die wildverworrne, neue,
> Durch hundert Wachen bis zu uns heran.   (321f.)[1]

And again, he speaks of 'drohnde Zukunft' (2301) and says 'Das Neue drängt' (2394). The contrast between the ever-growing threat of this disruptive future and Rudolf's constant delaying is the chief source of the dramatic tension of the play. The length of his speeches is admittedly alien to Grillparzer's usual dramatic style; indeed even in a lively and imaginative production a theatre audience tends to grow restive. But despite the problems it presents for stage production the *Bruderzwist* is genuinely dramatic, an exception to Grillparzer's rule that the genuinely dramatic must be theatrical. The reflective speeches stand out in sharp and intended contrast to the urgency of the political intrigues; their very length – time ticking by – draws out the tension as events close in on Rudolf and heightens the sense of inevitable

---

[1] 'Thus the new age of wild confusion forces its way upon us past a hundred guards.'

tragedy both for himself and for the ideals that he extols in his speeches but is powerless to defend in action.

Rudolf's indecision in the most momentous political and military matters is not matched by a similar slowness to act in the more limited and particular cases where he has to dispense justice within his own court and family circles. This disparity is commented on, indeed, by Julius of Brunswick:

> O daß er doch mit gleicher Festigkeit
> Das Unrecht ausgetilgt in seinem Staat,
> Als er es austilgt nun in seinem Hause! (2193–5)[1]

Towards Don Cäsar and also towards Russworm he appears harsh; in political matters weak. Wells has argued that this apparent discrepancy is not a case of inconsistency, but arises from Rudolf's own awareness of a distinction between conscientious behaviour in private life and conscientious political behaviour. Certainly, because he is so far-seeing he understands, as the other characters do not, how impossible it is to predict developments in practical politics:

> Denn was Entschlossenheit den Männern heißt des Staats,
> Ist meistenfalls Gewissenlosigkeit,
> Hochmut und Leichtsinn, der allein nur sich
> Und nicht das Schicksal hat im Aug der andern;
> Indes der gute Mann auf hoher Stelle
> Erzittert vor den Folgen seiner Tat,
> Die als die Wirkung *eines* Federstrichs
> Glück oder Unglück forterbt späten Enkeln... (1695–1702)[2]

The condemnation of statesmen in general is phrased so sweepingly and so sharply that it suggests an undertone of anxiety in Rudolf's argument, as though he were rationalizing his temperamental aversion to political decisions; but the gist of the argument itself is clear. Decisions, once taken, will always have consequences which cannot be foreseen – partly because, as he observes much later, a decision is always liable to be perverted as it is acted on by others (2290–5) – and it is in the political field that this consideration must weigh most heavily, because of the scale of the

---

[1] 'Oh, had he only eradicated wrong-doing in his state with as much firmness as he now eradicates it within his house!'

[2] 'For what to men of politics passes for decision is mostly unscrupulousness, arrogance and irresponsibility, which considers only itself and not the fate of others – whereas a good man in high office trembles at the consequences of his action, which by one stroke of the pen bequeaths fortune or misfortune to distant descendants...'

consequences. As historical events develop, they gather momentum beyond the control of their initiator, however altruistic his motives. Rudolf, moreover, is so ultra-scrupulous that, as he admits later in the same speech, he does not even trust his own motives.

Inasmuch as his reasoning presents convincing arguments against action, his indecisiveness appears to be not merely temperamental but a matter of deliberate and well-considered policy. His guiding aim is to preserve the peace of the empire; and it is for this reason – as a calculated choice, not a mere matter of weakness – that he prefers to pursue a war against the Turks rather than risk civil war (1193f.). His long success in keeping the forces in the empire in precarious balance – the image of a balance is one he himself uses (1419f.) – is later conceded by Ferdinand, in relation particularly to the religious issues between the warring factions (2485f.). When Rudolf seems to shrink from powerful action, a strong motive is his belief in the need not to upset the balance that he is preserving:

> Zudem gibt's Lagen, wo ein Schritt voraus
> Und einer rückwärts gleicherweis verderblich.   (1175f.)[1]

Hence his faith in 'prudent delay' as a realistic policy. In this respect his position, a stable conservatism warding off every change in the balance of power, is comparable to the role that Grillparzer came to believe Metternich might have played in the late 1840s. Rudolf's policies can only be associated with Metternich to a limited extent. In the first place, Rudolf's concerns are essentially anti-Philistine. In the second place, Grillparzer's conception of Rudolf's dilemma long antedates his quickening sympathy for Metternich; it was as early as 1828 that he noted about Rudolf, 'The tragedy is...that he perceives the coming of the new era while the others do not, and that he senses that any action will only hasten its coming.'[2] The situation in the tragedy, then, was conceived as a *dramatic* situation rather than as a reflection of political actualities. Nevertheless, the change of emphasis in Grillparzer's political views in the 1840s must undoubtedly have stimulated his later work on the play, and is reflected in the text; the action and arguments of the *Bruderzwist* anticipate and warn against the revolutionary situation that came to a head a few weeks after the play was completed.

---

[1] 'There are, moreover, times when a step forward and a step back would be equally disastrous.'
[2] *Wke.* I/21, 148.

Yet while Rudolf can argue a justification for his policy, what that policy amounts to in practice is still something essentially passive, a policy of letting things happen. This passivity has its psychological roots in his self-doubts, and the action of the play largely confirms the validity of those doubts. Three times Rudolf does commit himself to decision and political action; and each time it is against his own better judgment. First, though he says unambiguously that it is unwise (452f.), he allows Mathias his command in Hungary, as a token of conciliation, and deceives himself that he is only giving him somewhere to 'play' at his 'heroics' (1287). Secondly, he signs the charter granting the Protestants freedom of worship. Thirdly, although he knows it is too late (1724), he allows Leopold to lead his army into Bohemia. Various motives underlie this last fateful error. As we know from the first act, he feels a strong affection, almost admiration, for Leopold: he realizes he is 'a spoilt coxcomb', but his wariness of his own motives seems to nurture something of an envy for a carefree character who unconcernedly follows his inclinations. He is also angered by the arrival of Klesel (1777): angered, we assume, by the humiliating prospect of negotiating peace terms with the *éminence grise* behind his brother's treachery. He acts, then, from impulse, impelled by wounded pride. As a motive for going to war this is no better than that which sways Ottokar. His action is wholly unworthy of his usual wisdom and scrupulousness; and the catastrophic consequences prove all his worst fears about the potential nature of political decisions. But even Rudolf's three decisions are in reality scarcely more active than his policy of delay: in each case, though for differing reasons, what he does is to yield to expediency. In each case his decision is one of weakness. In a sense, indeed, the only *strong* decision taken by Rudolf that impinges on the political issues in the play is his ignoble condemnation of Don Cäsar.

For the distinction that Wells draws between private and public moral action is surely only partly valid; to argue that Don Cäsar's misdeeds 'have concerned his private life' and that what Rudolf has from the start felt able to punish is 'the immorality and selfishness of the individual' is to discount the point that Don Cäsar's conduct has *for Rudolf* a political significance. That the scenes featuring Don Cäsar should be linked in this way to the main plot was an essential element in Grillparzer's plan for the play by the mid-1820s: 'In Don Cäsar he sees the reflection of his turbulent, impious, sacrilegious age. This is the bond that ties that episode in with the whole.'[1] Of course Don Cäsar is for his father a living example of the unpredictable consequences of human actions, and this no doubt partly accounts for Rudolf's determination to discipline and control him. But what he chiefly sees in Don Cäsar is a creature of the disturbed new age:

> Die Zeit, die Zeit! Denn jener junge Mann,
> Wie sehr er tobt, er ist doch nur ihr Schüler,
> Er übt nur, was die Meisterin gelehrt. (324–6)[2]

And later he restates the point, observing that the times need to be 'curbed':

> Don Cäsar! Wie mein Innres sich empört!
> Der freche Sohn der Zeit – Die Zeit ist schlimm,
> Die solche Kinder nährt, und braucht des Zügels.
> (1342–4)[3]

The principal function of Don Cäsar in the play is to represent at an intimately individual level the disruptive spirit of the age, which is otherwise seen only in political and military terms. The conception of him as a mere creature of his times, not responsible for his lack of standards but reflecting a whole new trend in history, would make the rigidity of his punishment impossibly callous if it were only Don Cäsar's private life that Rudolf were punishing. But in fact his condemnation of Don Cäsar is intended as a gesture of condemnation of 'the new age of wild confusion', and it is just this that is suggested by his careful choice of words:

> Er ist gerichtet,
> Von mir, von seinem Kaiser, seinem –
> (*mit zitternder, von Weinen erstickter Stimme*)
> Herrn! (2188f.)

Wells rightly points out that Rudolf avoids the word 'Vater' and substitutes 'Herrn' as a deliberately impersonal term, 'following his ethic of impersonal devotion to principle'; and surely the considered wording suggests the impersonality of the condemnation, so that the choice of the words 'Kaiser' and 'Herr' to describe his own position suggests that Rudolf's judgment is fashioned on an imperial scale.

---

[1] *Wke.* I/21, 109.
[2] 'The times, the times! – For that young man, however much he raves, is but their pupil: he only practises what they teach.'
[3] 'Don Cäsar – how my inmost heart revolts! – Brazen son of this age! These times are bad which nurture such offspring, and need to be curbed.'

He shows equal impersonality in his condemnation of Russworm
in the first act, confirming his decision with a bald 'He is to die!'
('Er stirbt!', 270). The first scene of the play has shown Russworm
to have an old-fashioned dignity that is the very opposite of
Don Cäsar's bearing; and Rudolf's inflexibility makes a distinctly
arbitrary impression. We suspect that he is, as Don Cäsar says
(266), in an ill temper, and that he remains inflexible because
Don Cäsar pleads for Russworm. The impression given is, in fact,
that even here it is Don Cäsar that he wants to punish rather than
the unfortunate Russworm; and this impression is confirmed when
it is on Don Cäsar, and not on Russworm, that his subsequent
reflections centre (324ff.), and when he explicitly talks of punishing
Don Cäsar: 'Deshalb nun tadl' ich jenen Jüngling, straf' ihn...'
(338).[1] His harshness, then, is founded on his anxiety about
Don Cäsar and all he represents; and this explains too why (as
we learn later) he arranges a gruesome public (that is, exemplary)
execution of Russworm, in Don Cäsar's presence (1974–6).

The representative role of Don Cäsar is one of the features of
the play in which aspects of Grillparzer's critical view of his own
age are most clearly reflected. One of the principal elements that
he rejected in the cultural life of the nineteenth century was, as
we have seen, the exhaustive intellectuality of its critical and
philosophical literature. It was an age not of imagination but of
rational and scientific certainties, an age of 'Wissenschaft'. His
mistrust of this tendency is reflected in *Libussa* when the heroine
traces what she sees as the culturally retrograde development
of mankind back to man's eating of the fruit of the tree of
knowledge (*Libussa* 2325), and in the *Bruderzwist* in the characterization of Don Cäsar. What draws him to Lukrezia to the last
is, as he stresses, a hunger for knowledge: 'Als einz'ge Leidenschaft
der Wunsch: zu wissen' (1916).[2] He repeats: 'Mir ist's, sagt' ich,
um Wahrheit nur zu tun' (1984).[3] For Lukrezia remains a mystery
to him to the end (indeed, her part is too brief and her alleged
guilty liaison with Belgiojoso is insufficiently motivated for her
to be more than a mystery to us, despite several echoes of other,
earlier treatments of Grillparzer's experience with Marie von
Smolenitz). It is in keeping with the nature of Don Cäsar's role
that his search for knowledge is directed at woman – 'Was ist es

[1] 'And that is why I blame that youth, and punish him...'
[2] 'My single passion: the wish to *know*.'
[3] 'My sole concern, I said, is with the truth.'

auch: ein Weib?' (1902).[1] For his pursuit of Lukrezia also corresponds at a sensual level to the selfishness of the age as a whole. If the Emperor condemns him, as Julius says, to die like a mere animal (2185), this accords with Rudolf's view of the immoral selfishness, the denial of true humanity, that he discerns in the rapacious mob: 'Im Haufen steht die Tierwelt gar zu nah' (1480).[2]

The Protestants, whose demands are the immediate cause of Rudolf's fears, profess themselves selfless and claim to be prosecuting a cause higher than themselves:

> Freiheit der Meinung und der Glaubensübung,
> Was jedem Menschen teurer als sein Selbst. (1528f.)[3]

Rudolf, however, sees them as motivated by selfishness (336), as seeking power (1231). To Julius, he describes the political consequences of the Reformation as lying not only in the danger of religious wars (1449f.) but also in a breaking-up of the whole political and social order, with material standards increasingly dominant (1236ff.):

> Der Reichsfürst will sich lösen von dem Reich,
> Dann kommt der Adel und bekämpft die Fürsten;
> Den gibt die Not, die Tochter der Verschwendung
> Drauf in des Bürgers Hand, des Krämers, Mäklers,
> Der allen Wert abwägt nach Goldgewicht.

And so moral and spiritual values will fall into disrepute:

> Der dehnt sich breit und hört mit Spotteslächeln
> Von Toren reden, die man Helden nennt,
> Von Weisen, die nicht klug für eignen Säckel,
> Von allem, was nicht nützt und Zinsen trägt.

And the vision leads into nightmare, an egalitarian democracy founded on a chorus of demands for 'rights,' and amounting to no better than mob rule:

> Bis endlich aus der untersten der Tiefen
> Ein Scheusal aufsteigt, gräßlich anzusehn,
> Mit breiten Schultern, weitgespaltnem Mund,
> Nach allem lüstern und durch nichts zu füllen.
> Das ist die Hefe, die den Tag gewinnt,
> Nur um den Tag am Abend zu verlieren,

[1] 'For what *is* woman?'
[2] 'In a crowd, the world of the brute is much too near.'
[3] 'Freedom of thought and of worship, which is dearer to any man than his very self.'

Angrenzend an das Geist- und Willenlose.
Der ruft: Auch mir mein Teil, vielmehr das Ganze!
Sind wir die Mehrzahl doch, die Stärkern doch,
Sind Menschen so wie ihr, uns unser Recht![1]

In this scene (which was completed in 1845) Grillparzer is very clearly writing about the nineteenth century, particularly about the so-called spectre of socialism; and the cry 'Uns unser Recht!' echoes in *Libussa* also. In the *Bruderzwist*, Rudolf's fears are reiterated one after the other, either by himself or by Duke Julius: that the new age is one of base self-interest (1473f.), that the masses (the 'Volk') are a mere mob, without responsible individual judgment (1534f.), that from the legalization of Protestantism will follow mob rule (1578), and that what will pass for 'right' will be nothing more than the majority having its own way (2131).

It is to escape this uncongenially threatening political reality that Rudolf pursues his scholarly and occult interests (besides astrology, he is also interested in magic and alchemy) in solitude. He goes to extremes to preserve this solitude – we learn that when people have addressed him he has even threatened them with his dagger (1417f.) – because he feels that the true life of his mind, his perceptiveness, depends on such solitude, away from the present world (1160f.). The present age is one in which he sees not only political disruption, but the threat of a wider decline in standards. Talking of the times that have nurtured Don Cäsar, he asks:

Schaut rings um Euch in aller Herren Land,
Wo ist noch Achtung für der Väter Sitte,
Für edles Wissen und für hohe Kunst? (327–9)[2]

Once again, the terms he uses have a clear relevance to the 1840s. On 6 March 1849 Stifter wrote to Heckenast lamenting the events

[1] 'The princes want to break off from the empire, then the nobles come and fight the princes; and want, the child of extravagance, delivers them in turn into the hand of the burgher, the tradesman, the broker, who sets all values by the weight of gold. *He* puffs himself up, and he sneers on hearing talk of fools acclaimed as heroes, of wise men who are not wise about their purses, of anything that does not bring gain or interest – until at last from the deepest depths there emerges a monster, ghastly to behold, with broad shoulders and gaping jaws, greedy for all things but sated by none. That is the scum that wins the day, only to lose the day again at evening because lacking mind and will. They cry: "I want my share, or better still the whole! We are the majority, we are the stronger, we are men as you are: give us our rights!"'

[2] 'Look all about you throughout the world: where has respect survived for the morality of our fathers, for noble learning and great art?'

of the previous year: '...ein Leben, wo Sitte, Heiligkeit, Kunst, Göttliches nichts mehr ist und jeder Schlamm und jede Tierheit, weil jetzt Freiheit ist, ein Recht zu haben wähnt, hervorzubrechen; ja nicht bloß hervorzubrechen, sondern zu tyrannisieren.'[1] Stifter's concern is with the disruption of morality, art and religion; so too Grillparzer has Rudolf describe his times as 'wildverworren' because their standards of morality, their achievements in learning and in art are in decline. Later Rudolf expresses his conviction that the fragmentation of the church will involve a fragmentation of human perception of the truth (1359f.), and later again he gives a clear warning that to undermine the continuity of the traditional faith exposes the whole order of human society to the danger of collapse (1645f.). The seventeenth-century claims for religious freedom serve, in the context of the play, to represent the dangers inherent in the claims of the socialists and political nationalists of the nineteenth century. But the concerns expressed in Rudolf's role are broader than the specific issues either of the post-Reformation period or of the nineteenth century. Like those expressed in *Libussa* also, they are directed at the whole cultural and spiritual condition of mankind. The climax of Rudolf's nightmare vision of the future as he expounds it to Duke Julius is that the developments he foresees will involve a breaking down of all the standards and ideals of human achievement in a new barbarism, in which the slogans of equality will be misused to complete a levelling-down, a degradation of the human condition:

> Aus eignem Schoß ringt los sich der Barbar,
> Der, wenn erst ohne Zügel, alles Große,
> Die Kunst, die Wissenschaft, den Staat, die Kirche
> Herabstürzt von der Höhe, die sie schützt,
> Zur Oberfläche eigener Gemeinheit,
> Bis alles gleich, ei ja, weil alles niedrig.   (1269–74)[2]

[1] '...a life in which morality, holiness, art, the divine no longer matter and – because we have liberty now – everything slimy and brutish thinks it has the right to break forth – indeed not only to break forth, but to tyrannize.'

[2] 'From the womb of our own times the barbarian will spring forth, who when once uncurbed will bring down all that is great from its protective heights: art, learning, the state, the church – down to the level of its own baseness, till all are equal – yes, because all are low.'

Libussa

The plot of *Libussa* leads up to the legendary founding of the city of Prague in the eighth century, and the play culminates in the long prophecy made by the heroine at the foundation ceremony. This prophecy has a valedictory quality which may justify our considering *Libussa* last among Grillparzer's works, though it was not the last to be completed. The historical or legendary material was derived by Grillparzer mainly from W. Hájek's *Bohemian Chronicle* (which he read in the early 1820s when he was working on the background of *König Ottokar*) and the eighteenth-century version of the Libussa story in Musäus's *Volksmärchen der Deutschen*. The action of the play centres on Libussa's love for Primislaus and her union with him; their relation is both personal and political.

From the idyllic opening scene in which Libussa and Primislaus first meet, the manner and atmosphere of the piece are those of legend rather than of the conventional history play. It is stressed, for example, that Libussa and her sisters are partly of supernatural origin (202, 2211) and have supernatural powers; and while the two principal characters are drawn in depth, the subsidiary figures are presented not as individuals but rather in a symbolic spirit. Libussa's two sisters always appear together, not separately; so too do the three noblemen who aspire to Libussa's hand. These three noblemen, whose names and characteristics are borrowed direct from Hájek, are types, who between them represent the qualities which in Libussa's view should be combined in the ideal ruler she will marry:

> Nun, weiser Lapak denn und starker Biwoy
> Und mächt'ger Domaslav, die ihr euch teilt
> In das, was ich im Mann vereint mir denke,
> Hört denn ein Rätsel... (664–7)[1]

That Libussa sets her riddle, that Primislaus poses her another, and that their union is settled only when the riddles are solved, is another of the elements that give the play its atmosphere of legend or fairy-tale.

These fairy-tale elements combine oddly with the political element and the urgent political seriousness of the prophetic ending. *Libussa* is, indeed, an uneven work, and its very language

---

[1] 'Now then, wise Lapak, strong Biwoy and mighty Domaslav – who each have something of what I look to find united in a man – listen to a riddle...'

betrays this unevenness. It takes on, for example, an essentially lyrical quality when Primislaus speaks of female beauty, and implicitly of Libussa (1640ff.). But there is also dry and involved wordplay, as when Kascha plays on *stören* ('...störend / Und selbst gestört, zerstörte sie den Kreis', 1163f.),[1] or Primislaus on *sprechen* and *Sprache*:

> Weil ohne Worte du versprichst und sprechend
> Der Sprache deiner Anmut *wider*sprichst.   (1879f.)[2]

Or again, there are several passages of extended argument and reflection: indeed, Franz von Dingelstedt, who as director of the Burgtheater was responsible for the first performance of the play in 1874, adjudged the whole last act to be weak in dramatic effectiveness and even went so far as to suggest that, to avoid political controversy, Libussa's prophecy could simply be omitted.[3] The prophecy is in fact a climactic development of the most profound themes of the play, and is not dispensable; but the reflective (and also the lyrical) elements in the text are undeniably undramatic, in that they slow down the action, without adding tension as the arguments and reflective passages in the *Bruderzwist* do: indeed they substitute discursive speech for action.

Moreover, the framework on which the political ideas are imposed is an incongruously light one. It includes such trivial features as the riddles or as the use of wild coincidence to advance the action, in the meeting of Primislaus and the three nobles in the second act. It includes a whole intrigue of comic misunderstandings. Thus while Primislaus speaks his praise of Libussa, she is, as he knows, listening to him; this makes for a situation of dramatic irony which then broadens out into a moment of farce when she has him let down through a trapdoor. No doubt one of the functions of the comic elements is to place the characters in a recognizably down-to-earth setting, and so to avoid the danger of over-abstraction; but although the personal and political conflicts in the play are linked by a common contrast in standards between the chief characters, the comic element is so dominant in the love-action that the reversion to the serious political theme

---

[1] 'Disturbing, and herself disturbed, she has destroyed our circle.'
[2] 'Because you promise without words, and, speaking, contradict the language of your innate grace.'
[3] Dingelstedt's reports on all three of Grillparzer's last completed plays are quoted by Karl Kaderschafka, '*Ein Bruderzwist in Habsburg* auf der Bühne' in *Grillparzer-Studien*, hrsg. von Oskar Katann (Vienna, 1924), pp. 229–31.

and the development of a tragic atmosphere in the final act gives the effect of a formal break. Grillparzer was very aware of this unevenness; and his avowed dissatisfaction with the rather prosaic development of the middle acts, by contrast with the poetic and visionary level of the first act (*Gespr.* 14), and with the riddle-motif in particular as being too rationally contrived (T 1930), slowed down his work on the text in the early 1830s. Similar dissatisfaction influenced his decision not to publish the work when it was finished: he told Emil Kuh that the 'intrigue' in the middle acts took the work out of the tragic sphere, and that even the last act fell short of the quality of the first (*Gespr.* 1148/iv).

It is perhaps the supernatural element, however, that modern readers find hardest to accept. Libussa's sisters are – as Libussa has hitherto been – recluses, who devote their lives to contemplation and the occult, and who are cut off from the realities of the practical world. They are magicians, and are versed in astrology (1312); their interests, as Libussa summarizes them, are the moon and stars, herbs, and ciphers (400). Kascha's power is over the whole natural world (209f.), and includes the gift of healing (166); Tetka's realm is that of the spirit: she speaks of it as a realm of light, and she will not sully its purity with the standards and tasks of government:

> Nutzen und Vorteil zählen,
> Aus Wahrheit und Lüge wählen,
> Recht erdenken, das kein Recht,
> Dafür sucht einen Sündenknecht.
> Mein sonnig Reich strahlt hellres Licht... (220–4)[1]

Kascha confirms that the spiritual light they both enjoy is dependent on their solitude (242f.), and develops this point again in the third act:

> Wer gehen will auf höhrer Mächte Spuren,
> Muß einig sein in sich, der Geist ist eins.
> Wem's nicht gelungen, all die bunten Kräfte
> Im Mittelpunkt zu sammeln seines Wesens,
> So daß der Leib zum Geist wird, und der Geist
> Ein Leib erscheint, sich gliedernd in Gestalt,
> Wem ird'sche Sorgen, Wünsche und das Schlimmste
> Von allem, was da stört – Erinnerung,

'To count profit and advantage, to choose between truth and lies, to invent a law of rights that is not the law of Right – for that you must look for a sinful mortal. My sunny realm radiates a purer light.'

Das weitverbreitete Gemüt zerstreun,
Für den gibt's fürder keine Einsamkeit,
In der der Mensch allein ist mit sich selbst.   (1144–54)[1]

The ideal she describes here – the concentration of the entire mind on the single object, and the exclusion of every kind of external distraction – corresponds closely to the conception of *Sammlung* extolled by the priest in *Des Meeres und der Liebe Wellen*. Kascha and Tetka, then, and previously Libussa too, enjoy the kind of creative contemplation that engenders inspired achievement; in fact Libussa uses the verb 'sich sammeln' later when she prepares herself for her final inspired prophecy: 'Und soll ich sammeln mich wie sonst im Geist...' (2238).[2]

Kascha and Tetka – representing an ideal of inspired perception – appear three times in the play, commenting on Libussa's career at crucial stages. They appear after her first meeting with Primislaus, when their father has died and Libussa inherits his crown. They appear again after the failure of Libussa's first attempt to govern by herself; and their rejection of her wish to return to her life with them leads to her union with Primislaus. They appear again at the end, after she has yielded to Primislaus's wishes and delivered her last prophecy. The effect of these appearances is to present Libussa's career in a framework of comment: her progress is held up and judged against the standards of inspiration.

Her situation has obvious similarities with that of the poetess Sappho. Just as there is a disparity in rank and in gifts between Sappho and Phaon, so Libussa is to Primislaus 'Du Hohe' (21, 268), while his work appears to her as something lowly, 'irdisch niedres Tun' (418). She is forbidden to marry, because of her rank and, so she tells him, for other reasons as well (42–4); but though she is at first reluctant to accept her late father's crown, she is attracted by the promise of involvement in human life. There are echoes of Sappho's criticism of the barrenness of the laurel and of Melusina's rejection of her sisters' 'dreaming content-

---

[1] 'He who seeks to follow the path of higher powers must be united within himself: the spirit is one and indivisible. He who has not succeeded in *collecting* all his sundry powers in the centre of his being, so that the body becomes mind and the mind appears a body, joined in a single form, he whose scattered thoughts are distracted by earthly cares, by desires and (the worst of all the forces that disturb) by memory – thenceforth he will never know that solitude in which man is alone with himself.'
[2] 'And if I am as formerly to collect myself in spirit...'

255

ment' (*Melusina* 128) in Libussa's description of her sisters' occult occupations as 'monotonous' and 'bare' (401). Her contact with ordinary mortal humanity has been signalled visually at the start by her appearance in peasant costume (18f.), and this very costume now fills her with a longing for sympathetic contact with the realities of warm-blooded life:

> Dies Kleid, es reibt die Haut mit dichtern Fäden
> Und weckt die Wärme bis zur tiefsten Brust.
> Mit Menschen Mensch sein, dünkt von heut mir Lust,
> Des Mitgefühles Pulse fühl' ich schlagen... (402–5)[1]

She accepts the crown and commits herself to a life of involvement and responsibility; and with this development goes another, also endangering her *Sammlung* – what Kascha, using the same term as Hero in *Des Meeres und der Liebe Wellen*, calls '*Neigung*':

> ...Wozu noch kommt, daß in der letzten Zeit
> Die Neigung, scheint's, die Neigung zu dem Mann,
> In ihrem edlen Innern Platz gegriffen... (1157–9)[2]

And the result of Libussa's involvement both practically and emotionally with ordinary humanity is that like Sappho she estranges herself from her true ambience:

> Du hast vermengt dich mit dem Irdischen,
> Bist ausgetreten aus dem Kreis der Deinen. (2269f.)[3]

This is a close echo of the lesson Sappho learns, the danger of stepping 'aus der Seinen stillem Kreise'. And though Libussa is not betraying a duty, she too is sacrificing standards of achievement. By her involvement with 'life' she loses her earlier command over her magical powers (2142): her visionary gift is weakened, and she realizes that to exercise it at the foundation of Prague will require her to force herself to a fatally taxing effort (2161f.). The motif is further widened by the introduction of political implications: Libussa's vision is out of accord with the 'new age' – 'Kann ich nicht wirken in der Zeit, die neu...'[4] (2275) – and this new age is described in terms which, as with the seventeenth

---

[1] 'This garment rubs the skin with its coarse threads, and rouses warmth deep in the breast. To be a human being among human beings now seems to me a happy lot: I sense the pulse of fellow-feeling beat within me.'

[2] 'It has, moreover, seemed of late that affection, a fondness for a man, has seized a place within her noble heart.'

[3] 'You have mingled with the earthly: you have withdrawn from the circle of your own kind.'

[4] 'If I cannot function in this new age...'

century in the *Bruderzwist*, correspond to and express Grillparzer's view of the nineteenth century.

The representative of the new age is Primislaus. In contrast to the learned sisters, he is a mere countryman, an illiterate (1425); in contrast to the first speeches of Kascha and Tetka, which are full of the names of constellations, his discussions of society, rank and the achievements of government make use of imagery drawn from the garden (1720–3) or from agriculture (2125–9). He has the practicality of the countryman. But his language also betrays something else: he lacks the simplicity of the countryman. As Škreb has pointed out, Primislaus does not speak the same kind of language as Libussa; his language is more stilted. The contrast is marked even in the first scene:

PRIMISLAUS   Du Hohe, Herrliche!
           Wie zierst du diese ländlich niedre Tracht!
           Das Bild der Schwester, die mir kaum entschwand,
           Es tritt in dir neu atmend mir entgegen,
           Dasselbe Bild, doch lieblicher, gewiß.
LIBUSSA   Auch für die Kleider Dank! du mein Erretter!
           Wenn Rettung ja, wo die Gefahr nicht groß.
           Ich half mir selbst, glaub nur! erschienst du nicht.
           Doch nun erfülle ganz dein schönes Wort
           Und bring mich zu den Meinen, wie du wolltest.
PRIMISLAUS   Dein edler Leib, bedarf er nicht der Ruh'?
LIBUSSA   Ich hab' geruht, nun ruft mich ein Geschäft.   (20–31)[1]

Everything Libussa says here is straightforward, a direct expression of natural feelings, simply and naturally phrased. Primislaus, by contrast, is flattering and temporizing: his tone is both more full of pathos and at the same time more calculating, in every phrase his language is more artificial, more complex, more stiffly literary. In his combination of practicality of interests and unnaturalness of expression, he embodies attitudes not unlike those Grillparzer mistrusted in the literature of the nineteenth century in Germany. When Grillparzer began work again on his manuscript at the beginning of 1845, he summarized the essential outline of the

---

[1] 'Noble, illustrious lady! How you exalt this lowly rustic garb! The image of my sister, who is but newly lost to me, confronts me again in you, breathing anew – the self-same image, but certainly more lovely.' 'My thanks also for the clothes, my rescuer! – If it is "rescue" when the danger is not great. Believe me, I should have managed had you not appeared. But now make good your kind promise and take me to my home, as you wanted to.' 'Your noble body has no need of rest?' 'I have rested: now a task calls me.'

story in the note 'Feeling / Intellect / Return to Feeling'.[1] In his wooing of Libussa, as in his political attitudes, Primislaus is the voice of the calculating intellect.

His whole contact with Libussa seems at first unreal to him, it is like a dream (62). There is a total contrast between his attitudes and standards and those of Libussa's sisters. He sees their contemplative existence as merely 'unfruitful reflection' (2178) – he judges in terms of practical 'fruits' – while by their standards, as Wlasta rehearses them, Libussa's marriage to him and her involvement in his practical work are restrictive and nugatory, 'enges Treiben um ein Nichts' (2213). The dramatic picture of their relations that Grillparzer gives is far richer than a mere interplay between 'feeling' and 'intellect';[2] but in these personal relations, as in politics, Libussa places her trust in intuitive feeling, Primislaus is the realist, more practical, more matter-of-fact. At the height of their misunderstandings what he insists on is his 'rights' (1744). As a political legislator too he stands for the rights of the law which he is indeed called on by Libussa to establish (977, 1000).

The system that Libussa establishes in her attempt at lone rule is one based on fraternal, 'childlike' trust (444ff.); her formula 'das kindliche Vertraun' corresponds to the 'reines kindliches Vertrauen' of Goethe's Iphigenie (v, 6). Money is done away with (535); a mercenary father, trying to prevent his daughter from marrying a poor suitor (530), is rebuked by Libussa (643f.). Later she praises the traditional conservative virtue of contented 'moderation', 'Genügsamkeit' (2057) – the watchword of the *Biedermeier* era. Her idyllic society is based on 'feeling'; it is untainted by the materialism and the progressive spirit that Primislaus comes to display. It is also an unrealistic conception, which takes little account of human nature. The matriarchal character of her rule provokes the dissatisfaction of her subjects: this emerges gradually at first,[3] then is given open expression by Biwoy (571–80). Domaslaw's theme is the problem of establishing 'rights', which he voices first to the other nobles (566), then to Libussa (921); and the cry for 'rights' builds up towards the end of the second act into an insistent chant, a crystallizing of opposition: 'Ich will mein Recht' insists a disputant (896), and

---

[1] *Wke.* I/20, 388.
[2] Significantly there are close echoes (1587, 1680f.) of the section in 'Jugenderinnerungen im Grünen' (G 84, xv) dealing with Grillparzer's own relations with Kathi Fröhlich (ll. 76, 88).
[3] See ll. 513, 560, 567.

again: 'Mein Recht! / Ich will mein Recht' (957f.) – a plea that goes on 'O wäre hier ein Mann, / Der ernst entschiede, wo es geht um Ernstes',[1] and precipitates Libussa's capitulation.

She stresses that she is opposed to insistence on 'rights' (897ff.): she condemns the idea as being against the divine order. Individual rights militate against the true communal sense she has tried to build (903), and against fraternal love (905f.). The codifying of rights in formal law can amount to no better than formalized injustice:

> Und Recht ist nur der ausgeschmückte Name
> Für alles Unrecht, das die Erde hegt. (907f.)[2]

In *Esther* too the problematic nature of 'right' is brought into discussion, when it is seen as standing in contrast to the idea of advantage:

> Man sprach hier viel von Nutzen und von Vorteil.
> Nur eines ward noch nicht erwähnt: das Recht. (208f.)[3]

The quibbling speech in which Haman answers (212ff.) shows how easily the idea can be abused in practice. Libussa too takes her stand against 'Nutzen' (928), and for that very reason against the idea of 'rights'. Nevertheless, she cedes to her subjects' demand for a man to rule them, and sends for Primislaus to be her consort. It is a union which her maidservant Wlasta comes to regard as in contradiction of her inmost being (2205); and Wlasta puts this objection in extreme terms to Primislaus himself:

> Mein Jammer ist, daß ich die Hohe, Hehre
> Muß unterwürfig sehn dem Sohn des Staubs. (1950f.)[4]

But Libussa gives her answer in her final dialogue with her sisters:

> KASCHA   Wir warnten dich.
>   Warum hast du an Menschen dich geknüpft?
> LIBUSSA   Ich liebe sie, und all mein Sein und Wesen
>   Ist nur in ihrer Nähe was es ist.
> TETKA   Sie aber töten dich.
> LIBUSSA   Vielleicht. – Und doch:
>   Der Mensch ist gut. (2453–8)[5]

[1] 'Oh, if we only had a man to take serious decisions where serious things are at stake!'

[2] 'And law is but the decorative name for all the injustice that the world harbours.'

[3] 'There has been much talk of profit and advantage; only one thing has not been mentioned – what is *right*.'

[4] 'My grief is that I must see my august, exalted mistress subservient to a creature of the dust.'

[5] 'We warned you! Why have you linked yourself to mankind?' 'I love them,

This affirmation of humanity is expressed with that absolute simplicity which is the hallmark of Libussa's utterances. It emphatically underlines her belief that even if humanity 'kills' her (that is, uses her up) in the process, she is only fulfilled in contact with humanity; the spirit of inspiration has its true fulfilment through the innate nobility of man.

Primislaus, by contrast, is a man of the letter rather than the spirit. His appointed function is to organize the legislative and financial administration of Libussa's society; this is a practical mission which, as Libussa recognizes (1324–8), must work in practical terms and by practical standards, rather than by her intuitive ideals of wisdom and goodness. His priorities, then, are those of practicality (1990), he has to judge not in absolute ideal terms but according to what he sees as the advantage of the community as a whole:

> LIBUSSA Das Edle selbst, das wohltut höherm Sinn,
> Weist er zurück und duldet das Gemeine,
> Wenn allgemein der Nutzen und die Frucht.
> (1968–70)[1]

His standards are material ones; the worst enemy of man is, in his eyes, famine (1263). He ushers in a 'new age' (1978). This involves breaking down traditional ways and privileges, which are symbolized in the age-old forest surrounding the castle of Libussa's sisters. This forest has to be cut down (1979–81), the solitude of the sisters is shattered; Primislaus, after all, reckoning by practical and material terms, regards that solitude as fruitless. If he values Libussa's gifts, it is not because of their intrinsic

and all my being is what it is only with them.' 'But they are killing you.' 'Perhaps – and yet: Man is good.' While this line (2458) is another direct echo of the Kathi-section of 'Jugenderinnerungen im Grünen' (l. 83, 'Der Mensch ist gut, ich weiß es, denn sie lebet'), the idea of faith in humanity is of course linked more broadly with Grillparzer's eighteenth-century standards. Libussa's opposition to the idea of 'rights' and self-interest is also expressed in terms familiar from the eighteenth century. Thus Goethe's Tasso criticizes an age in which '...jeder glaubt, / Es sei auch schicklich, was ihm nützlich ist' ('...everyone believes that what is useful to himself is also proper': II, 1); Schiller's Wallenstein is reminded that the world is ruled by considerations of 'advantage' ('Denn nur vom Nutzen wird die Welt regiert': *Wallensteins Tod*, I, 6); and Schiller wrote elsewhere of 'der Nutzen', in the sense of 'practical utility', as 'the great idol of the age' (*Über die ästhetische Erziehung des Menschen*, 2. Brief). Cf. *Libussa* 220, 928, 1970, 2335, 2373, 2484.
'He rejects even what is noble and pleasing to high minds and tolerates baseness if it brings general fruit and profit.'

quality but because he sees an opportunity to exploit them for practical political ends, as propaganda for his new city:

> Ich wünsche dieses Werk als Götterwille,
> Als einen Wink von oben angesehn.   (2133f.)[1]

And although he is willing to call off the ceremony when she does not want to attempt a formal prophecy, he has no sympathy for her refusal and no understanding of her reasons (2169). In short, he has no understanding of Libussa, of the spirit of poetry in his age of prose. His ascendancy is underlined by two formal features of the play observed by Joachim Kaiser. Whereas the principal roles in the first act are those of the magically gifted sisters, by the fourth act it is Primislaus who is central, and his physical presence throughout almost all the act brings out the dominance of his personality and his policies. As the whole balance of the play changes in this way, the character of the verse changes also in that the proportion of rhymed lines steadily diminishes from act to act. Rhyme is perhaps the most obviously 'poetic' device in Grillparzer's verse; its gradual disappearance corresponds to and subtly suggests the weakening of the spirit of poetry in Primislaus's age.

Primislaus's foundation of Prague is described in terms which clearly point forward from the Arcadian setting of the play to the prosaic liberalism of Grillparzer's time. He sees the city as establishing a new social order, a rationally organized community (2016–19); to the nobles, however, it is suspect as undermining their position in the traditional order (2289 f.). Libussa fears that this organized society will entail a loss of human individuality, that is, of true freedom of spirit (2033); Primislaus's defence lies in the principle of progress (2027) and the slogans of liberty, the progressive clichés of the nineteenth century:

> Wir wollen weiter, weiter in der Bahn,
> Ich und mein Volk, als Bürger und als Menschen.   (2191f.)[2]

This 'weiter, weiter' corresponds exactly to the attitude attacked both in the *Bruderzwist* and in Grillparzer's epigrams (G 993; see p. 237, above).

The fullest judgment of all that Primislaus stands for is given

---

[1] 'I wish what we are doing [the foundation of the city] to be seen as the will of the gods, as a direction from above.'

[2] 'We want to go onwards, onwards in our course, I and my people, as citizens and as men.'

in Libussa's prophecy, which looks forward to the future in which the trends that characterize Primislaus's policies are realized and developed. She presents the development as a Fall (2325), and repeats the charge that Primislaus's city acts by practical and material standards rather than by moral absolutes:

> Der Staat, der jedes einzelne in sich verschlingt,
> Statt Gut und Böse, Nutzen wägt und Vorteil
> Und euern Wert abschätzt nach seinem Preis.   (2334–6)[1]

She also repeats her charge that in this kind of society the freedom of individuality will be undermined (2344ff.); and she accuses its trading interests of being rapacious (2342) and of exploiting resources, abroad as well as inland, for selfish ends (2379f.). She sees the old order breaking up, the 'age-old bonds' of life severed (2351); she sees self-interest paramount (2373f.), and all nobility of spirit forced out by evils masquerading under the slogans of liberty and equality:

> Das Edle schwindet von der weiten Erde,
> Das Hohe sieht vom Niedern sich verdrängt.
> Und Freiheit wird sich nennen die Gemeinheit,
> Als Gleichheit brüsten sich der dunkle Neid.   (2384–7)[2]

As the age of Libussa ('das Hohe') is superseded utterly by the age of Primislaus ('das Niedere'), so both the trust in which Libussa put her political faith and the inspiration that she and her sisters embody will be lost (2391). She foretells that the city will flourish (2400), that its people will be thorough ('tüchtig') and worthy ('bieder', 2402) – the virtues of the nineteenth-century middle class – but without any understanding of the wider sense of life (2463). The picture Grillparzer gives here of narrowly unseeing diligence closely matches the criticism of the Germans made by Hölderlin nearly fifty years earlier both in *Hyperion* ('Wenn selbst die Raupe sich beflügelt und die Biene schwärmt, so bleibt der Deutsche doch in seinem Fach') and in the hymn 'Der Archipelagus' ('Ans eigene Treiben / Sind sie geschmiedet allein...').[3]

---

[1] '...The state, which swallows up all individual parts, which weighs not good and evil but profit and advantage, and calculates your worth by its own values.'

[2] 'All that is noble will vanish from the world, all that is exalted will see itself supplanted by what is low. And baseness will call itself "liberty", and black envy set itself up as "equality".'

[3] 'Even when the caterpillar grows its wings and the bees swarm, the German never looks up from his work' (*Hyperion*); 'To their own labour alone they are riveted' (*Der Archipelagus*).

Finally, Libussa asserts again her belief in the goodness of man (2461ff.) and foresees that the time will eventually come when man will sense his spiritual emptiness (2474), and when a new age of vision will dawn:

> Dann kommt die Zeit, die jetzt vorübergeht,
> Die Zeit der Seher wieder und Begabten. (2482f.)[1]

It will be a time of divine regeneration:

> Die Götter wohnen wieder in der Brust... (2488)

The next line underwent many reformulations, attempts to capture in a single word the supreme quality of this restored divinity. Grillparzer tried several words which correspond to the eighteenth-century humanitarian ideal: 'menschlich fühlen', 'Menschheit', 'Menschlichkeit', 'Menschenwert', 'menschlich sein'. He tried words which correspond to the moral of *Der Traum ein Leben* and his *Faust* plan: 'Seelenfriede', 'Selbstbeschränkung'. He tried the opposite of cold reason, 'Ahnung' (intuition). But finally he settled for the human quality which is most categorically opposite to the self-seeking and presumption of his own age:

> ...Und *Demut* heißt ihr Oberer und Einer.[2]

In looking forward to the age of regeneration, Libussa's prophecy itself traces a development which corresponds to the formula 'Feeling/Intellect/Return to Feeling'. Even here, however, Grillparzer's writing falls well short of political optimism. By comparison, for example, with the immediacy of the hope expressed in Hölderlin's chiliastic hymns such as 'Germanien' and 'Friedensfeier', the concluding promise of a new Golden Age seems distant, so that it far from outweighs the bleakness of the main part of Libussa's prophecy. The emphasis even at the end is on the fact that the time of vision is an 'age that is now passing'; and the profound cultural pessimism of Libussa's vision is given dramatic substance in her death. Tetka's warning that the humanity to which Libussa has given herself will kill her is proved right; and as the curtain falls both her sisters throw down their belts, the insignia of their visionary solitude, and follow Libussa. Primislaus's age is left bereft of visionaries, and of vision.

Grillparzer's formula suggesting a cyclical progress from an age

---

[1] 'Then the age which is now passing will come again, the age of seers and of the gifted.'

[2] 'The gods will dwell once more in the human breast, and supreme among them will be Humility.'

of 'feeling', through its dimming, and on to a new age of 'feeling' refers in the first place to Libussa's own development, her initial state of natural inspiration, her contamination by the prosaic world of everyday, and her prophecy, for which she summons up once more all her powers. Gisela Stein, concentrating on Libussa's tragedy, tends to dismiss the political overtones of the work: 'Wherever political ideas enter into the work,' she says, 'they are basically reflections of Grillparzer's own surroundings and of importance only in so far as they serve to highlight the tragedy of inspiration in an uninspired age.' But to dismiss the political element as only environmental is to overlook some important points: that politics is about environment, that Grillparzer's political position was inevitably related to the world around him, and that a critique of that world forms the nub of the political prophecy which comes at the very climax of the play. It is a prophecy – or rather, as Fuerst calls it, a 'necrologue on the history of Europe' – that deserves to be taken seriously. Its standards, like Grillparzer's own, are essentially humane: indeed, in delivering it Libussa makes her sacrifice in a spirit of altruistic humanitarian service:

> Um meinetwillen soll kein Reifbedachtes
> Und vielen Nützliches zugrunde gehn. (2246f.)[1]

If the prophecy is pessimistic, it is not unrealistic: much of what it contains is absolutely justified by the history of Europe both in the nineteenth century and since. The cultural conservatism that informs both this play and the *Bruderzwist* is constantly relevant whenever valuable cultural traditions and spiritual standards are threatened, whether by commercial or by bureaucratic forces, whether in the name of the majority, of efficiency, or even of humanity: whenever the humanitarian ideals that have impelled real progress shrink into mere slogans, bandied rather than understood. To defeat repressive reactionary politics such as Grillparzer condemned as a form of 'Geistesanfeindung' in Metternich's police state is progress indeed; but progress too can have destructive effects. In every generation – this is the lesson of Grillparzer's last plays – mankind has to be resolute in preserving its humane ideals and breadth of vision, and in guarding against the danger that 'all that is noble will vanish from the world'.

---

[1] 'Nothing that is maturely pondered and useful to many shall come to nought for my sake.'

SELECT BIBLIOGRAPHY

There are a large number of editions of Grillparzer's works, and a vast amount of secondary literature on his work and his times. The following list is confined to the standard texts and to secondary works that can be recommended as both substantial and stimulating.

The sections relating to individual works follow the same order as the treatment of the works in chapters 2–6. References without full titles (e.g. Reich, pp. 117–40) are to the monographs listed in the section of General Critical Studies, p. 266.

EDITIONS

Sämtliche Werke, hist.-krit. Gesamtausgabe, hrsg. von August Sauer und Reinhold Backmann (43 vols., Vienna, 1909–48). The standard edition, with full critical apparatus; referred to below as *Wke*.

Sämtliche Werke, Ausgewählte Briefe, Gespräche, Berichte, hrsg. von Peter Frank und Karl Pörnbacher (4 vols., Munich (Hanser), 1960–5). The text is based on the Sauer/Backmann edition, with revisions; in two verse plays, *Des Meeres und der Liebe Wellen* (from l. 1452) and *Ein Bruderzwist in Habsburg* (from l. 1223), there are slight divergencies in the line numbering. The notes are confined to explanatory material.

CONVERSATIONS AND MEMOIRS

Grillparzers Gespräche und die Charakteristiken seiner Persönlichkeit durch die Zeitgenossen, hrsg. von August Sauer (7 vols., Vienna, 1904–41). Vols. 1–6 (1904–16) = *Schriften des Literarischen Vereins in Wien*, I, III, VI, XII, XV, XX. Vol. 7 = *Jb*. (Neue Folge) I (1941).

Among the separate sources from which the material of the collected edition is drawn, the most important are:

'Aus Bauernfelds Tagebüchern', hrsg. von Karl Glossy, *Jb*. V, 1–217, and VI, 85–223.

Costenoble, Carl Ludwig, *Aus dem Burgtheater 1818–1837. Tagebuchblätter*, hrsg. von Karl Glossy und Jakob Zeidler (2 vols., Vienna, 1889). Numerous corrections of the text are contained in the final volume of the *Gespräche*.

Foglar, Adolf, *Grillparzer's Ansichten über Litteratur, Bühne und Leben* (2. Aufl., Stuttgart, 1891).

Littrow-Bischoff, Auguste von, *Aus dem persönlichen Verkehre mit Franz Grillparzer* (Vienna, 1873).

GRILLPARZER

A handy collection of Grillparzer's notes and comments on his works has been published in the series *Dichter über ihre Dichtungen*: *Franz Grillparzer*, hrsg. von Karl Pörnbacher (Munich (Heimeran), 1970).

HISTORICAL AND CULTURAL BACKGROUND

Barea, Ilsa, *Vienna. Legend and Reality* (London, 1966). Survey of the cultural history of the city.

Lothar, Rudolph, *Das Wiener Burgtheater* (Leipzig, Berlin, Vienna, 1899). Illustrated history of the theatre for which Grillparzer wrote.

Macartney, C. A., *The Habsburg Empire 1790–1918* (London, 1968). Standard political history.

Rommel, Otto, *Die Alt-Wiener Volkskomödie. Ihre Geschichte vom barocken Welt-Theater bis zum Tode Nestroys* (Vienna, 1952). Authoritative history of the influential drama of the popular theatres in Vienna.

Sauer, August, *Probleme und Gestalten*, hrsg. von Otto Pouzar (Stuttgart, 1933), pp. 141–94: 'Bauernfeld und Saphir. Ein Kapitel aus der Geschichte der Wiener Theaterkritik'.

Taylor, A. J. P., *The Habsburg Monarchy 1809–1918* (London, 1948).

GENERAL CRITICAL STUDIES

Backmann, Reinhold, 'Grillparzer und die heutige Biedermeier-Psychose', *Jb.* XXXIII, 1–32.

Bauer, Roger, *La réalité royaume de Dieu. Etudes sur l'originalité du théâtre viennois dans la première moitié du XIXe siècle* (Munich, 1965), pp. 393–475. Considers the plays in relation to their sources.

Fuerst, Norbert, *Grillparzer auf der Bühne. Eine fragmentarishe Geschichte* (Vienna, Munich, 1958). History of the interpretation and reception of Grillparzer's plays in the theatre.

Hofmannsthal, Hugo von, 'Rede auf Grillparzer' (1922), reprinted in Hofmannsthal, *Prosa* IV (Frankfurt a.M., 1955), 112–31.

Kaiser, Joachim, *Grillparzers dramatischer Stil* (Munich, 1961). Stimulating study of Grillparzer's style and technique.

Nadler, Josef, *Franz Grillparzer* (Vaduz, 1948, reprinted Vienna, 1952). The only full-length intellectual biography.

Naumann, Walter, *Grillparzer. Das dichterische Werk* (Stuttgart, n.d. [1956]).

Nolte, Fred O., *Grillparzer, Lessing and Goethe in the Perspective of European Literature* (Lancaster, Pa., 1938), pp. 29–96.

Reich, Emil, *Franz Grillparzers Dramen* (3. Aufl., Dresden, 1909).

Wells, George A., *The Plays of Grillparzer* (London, Oxford, 1969). Expounds elements of the dramatic technique in the completed full-length plays.

Yates, Douglas, *Franz Grillparzer. A Critical Biography*, vol. 1 (Oxford, 1946). Study of genesis of works up to *c.* 1830.

SELECT BIBLIOGRAPHY

GRILLPARZER'S POLITICAL WORKS (GENERAL)

Alewyn, Richard, 'Grillparzer und die Restauration', *Publications of the English Goethe Society* (New Series) XII (1937), 1–18.

Backmann, Reinhold, 'Grillparzer als Revolutionär', *Euphorion* XXXII (1931), 476–525. Detailed corrective to traditional misconceptions of Grillparzer's 'conservatism'.

Bietak, Wilhelm, 'Grillparzer – Stifter – Feuchtersleben. Die Unzeitgemäßen des Jahres 1848', *Deutsche Vierteljahrsschrift für Literaturwissenschaft und Geistesgeschichte* XXIV (1950), 243–68.

Enzinger, Moriz, *Franz Grillparzer und Therese Utsch* (Vienna, 1963).

Hock, Erich, *Franz Grillparzer. Besinnung auf Humanität* (Hamburg, 1949).

Hofmannsthal, Hugo von, 'Grillparzers politisches Vermächtnis' (1915), reprinted in Hofmannsthal, *Prosa* III (Frankfurt a.M., 1952), 252–9.

Kuranda, Peter, 'Grillparzer und die Politik des Vormärzes', *Jb.* XXVIII (1926), 1–21.

'DIE AHNFRAU'

Komorzynski, Egon, '*Die Ahnfrau* und die Wiener Volksdramatik', *Euphorion* IX (1902), 350–60.

Krispyn, Egbert, 'Grillparzer and his *Ahnfrau*', *Germanic Review* XXXVIII (1963), 209–25.

Minor, Jakob, 'Zur Geschichte der deutschen Schicksalstragödie und zu Grillparzers *Ahnfrau*', *Jb.* IX (1899), 1–85.

Morris, I. V., 'The *Ahnfrau* Controversy', *Modern Language Review* LXII (1967), 284–91.

Noch, Curt, *Grillparzers 'Ahnfrau' und die Wiener Volksdramatik* (Leipzig, 1911).

Sauer, August, 'Einleitung' in *Wke.* I/1, xli–lxxix.

'SAPPHO'

Klarmann, Adolf D., 'Psychological Motivation in Grillparzer's *Sappho*', *Monatshefte* XL (1948), 271–8.

Müller, Joachim, *Grillparzers Menschenauffassung* (Weimar, 1934), pp. 19–26.

Vordtriede, Werner, 'Grillparzers Beitrag zum poetischen Nihilismus', *Trivium* IX (1951), 103–20.

See also Reich, pp. 54–76; D. Yates, pp. 31–58.

'DER ARME SPIELMANN'

Politzer, Heinz, *Franz Grillparzers 'Der arme Spielmann'* (Stuttgart, 1967). Excellent short appreciation.

Silz, Walter, *Realism and Reality. Studies in the German Novelle of Poetic Realism* (Chapel Hill, 1954), pp. 67–78.

GRILLPARZER

Stern, J. P., *Re-interpretations* (London, 1964), pp. 42–77: 'Beyond the common indication: Grillparzer'.

Swales, M. W., 'The Narrative Perspective in Grillparzer's *Der arme Spielmann*', *German Life and Letters* (New Series) xx (1966–7), 107–16.

See also Naumann, pp. 20–32.

'DAS GÖLDENE VLIES'

Dunham, T. C., 'Symbolism in Grillparzer's *Das Goldene Vlieβ*,' *Publications of the Modern Language Association of America* LXXV (1960), 75–82.

Lesch, H. H., 'Der tragische Gehalt in Grillparzers Drama: *Das goldene Vlieβ*', *Jb.* XXIV (1913), 1–54.

Münch, Ilse, *Die Tragik in Drama und Persönlichkeit Franz Grillparzers* (Berlin, 1931), pp. 33–43.

Stiefel, Rudolf, *Grillparzers 'Goldenes Vlieβ'. Ein dichterisches Bekenntnis* (Basler Studien zur deutschen Sprache und Literatur, XXI, Bern, 1959).

'KÖNIG OTTOKARS GLÜCK UND ENDE'

Naumann, Walter, 'Grillparzer: *König Ottokars Glück und Ende*' in *Das deutsche Drama vom Barock bis zur Gegenwart. Interpretationen*, hrsg. von Benno von Wiese, Bd. I (Düsseldorf, 1958), pp. 405–21.

Silz, Walter, 'Grillparzer's Ottokar', *Germanic Review* XXXIX (1964), 243–61.

Staiger, Emil, *Meisterwerke deutscher Sprache aus dem neunzehnten Jahrhundert* (4. Aufl., Zürich, 1961), pp. 163–85: 'Grillparzer: *König Ottokars Glück und Ende*'.

See also Fuerst, pp. 91–100; Reich, pp. 117–40; Wells, pp. 83–105.

'DER TRAUM EIN LEBEN'

Hock, Erich, 'Grillparzers Drama *Der Traum ein Leben*', *Zeitschrift für Deutschkunde* LIV (1940), 49–65.

Hock, Stefan, '*Der Traum, ein Leben*'. *Eine literarhistorische Untersuchung* (Stuttgart, Berlin, 1904).

See also Reich, pp. 186–98.

'EIN TREUER DIENER SEINES HERRN'

Baumann, Gerhart, *Zu Franz Grillparzer. Versuche zur Erkenntnis* (Heidelberg, 1969), pp. 30–44.

Politzer, Heinz, 'Verwirrung des Gefühls: Franz Grillparzers *Ein treuer Diener seines Herrn*', *Deutsche Vierteljahrsschrift für Literaturwissenschaft und Geistesgeschichte* XXXIX (1965), 58–86.

Sauer, August, '*Ein treuer Diener seines Herrn*', *Jb.* III (1893), 1–40.

Schaum, Konrad, 'Grillparzers Drama *Ein treuer Diener seines Herrn*', *Jb.* (3. Folge) III (1960), 72–93.

See also Fuerst, pp. 121–42; Reich, pp. 141–63; D. Yates, pp. 121–35.

SELECT BIBLIOGRAPHY

'TRISTIA EX PONTO'

Backmann, Reinhold, 'Grillparzers *Tristia ex Ponto*', *Jb.* XXXI, 7–47. Traces the genesis and development of the cycle.

'Anmerkungen' in *Wke.* 1/10, 305–14. Notes include interpretative commentaries on all the poems except 'Jugenderinnerungen im Grünen'.

'Jugenderinnerungen im Grünen', *Jb.* XXXII, 10–42.

Hock, Erich, *Das Schmerzerlebnis und sein Ausdruck in Grillparzers Lyrik* (Germanische Studien, 187, Berlin, 1937, reprinted Nendeln/ Liechtenstein, 1967). Includes interpretations of most of the poems and a discussion of the construction of the cycle.

'Grillparzers Eigenart als Lyriker und der Gedichtzyklus *Tristia ex Ponto*', *Archiv für das Studium der neueren Sprachen* CLXXVI (1939), 1–11. Deals with style and construction.

See also D. Yates, pp. 91–120 and 144–50.

'DES MEERES UND DER LIEBE WELLEN'

Atkinson, Margaret E., 'Grillparzer's Use of Symbol and Image in *Des Meeres und der Liebe Wellen*', *German Life and Letters* (New Series) IV (1950–1), 261–77.

Papst, E. E., *Grillparzer: 'Des Meeres und der Liebe Wellen'* (London, 1967).

Politzer, Heinz, 'Der Schein von Heros Lampe', *Modern Language Notes* LXXII (1957), 432–7.

Yates, Douglas, 'Grillparzer's Hero and Shakespeare's Juliet', *Modern Language Review* XXI (1926), 419–25.

'DIE JÜDIN VON TOLEDO'

Blackall, Eric A., '*Die Jüdin von Toledo*' in *German Studies presented to Walter Horace Bruford* (London, 1962), pp. 193–206.

Krispyn, Egbert, 'Grillparzer's Tragedy *Die Jüdin von Toledo*', *Modern Language Review* LX (1965), 405–15.

Politzer, Heinz, 'Franz Grillparzers Spiel vom Fall: *Die Jüdin von Toledo*', *Zeitschrift für deutsche Philologie* LXXXVI (1967), 509–33.

See also Nadler, pp. 411–16; Reich, pp. 238–61.

'WEH DEM, DER LÜGT!'

Angress, R. K., '*Weh dem, der lügt*: Grillparzer and the Avoidance of Tragedy', *Modern Language Review* LXVI (1971), 355–64.

Bandet, Jean-Louis, 'Grillparzers *Weh dem, der lügt!*' in *Das deutsche Lustspiel* I, hrsg. von Hans Steffen (Göttingen, 1968), 144–65.

Hock, Erich, 'Grillparzers Lustspiel', *Wirkendes Wort* IV (1953–4), 12–23.

Martini, Fritz, '*Weh dem, der lügt!* oder Von der Sprache im Drama' in *Die Wissenschaft von deutscher Sprache und Dichtung. Methoden – Probleme – Aufgaben* (Festschrift für Friedrich Maurer) (Stuttgart, 1963), pp. 438–57.

Minor, Jakob, 'Grillparzer als Lustspieldichter und *Weh' dem, der lügt!*', *Jb.* III (1893), 41–60.
Seidler, Herbert, 'Grillparzers Lustspiel *Weh dem, der lügt!*', *Jb.* (3. Folge) IV (1965), 7–29.
See also Reich, pp. 199–216.

'EIN BRUDERZWIST IN HABSBURG'

Baumann, Gerhart, 'Grillparzer: *Ein Bruderzwist in Habsburg*' in *Das deutsche Drama vom Barock bis zur Gegenwart*... I, 422–50.
Sternberger, Dolf, 'Politische Figuren und Maximen Grillparzers', *Merkur* XVII (1963), 1142–53.
Wells, G. A., 'The Problem of Right Conduct in Grillparzer's *Ein Bruderzwist in Habsburg*', *German Life and Letters* (New Series) XI (1957–8), 161–72.
See also Naumann, pp. 33–57; Reich, pp. 262–81; Wells, pp. 106–25.

'LIBUSSA'

Hock, Erich, 'Grillparzer: *Libussa*' in *Das deutsche Drama vom Barock bis zur Gegenwart*... I, 451–74.
Škreb, Zdenko, 'Franz Grillparzers *Libussa*. Versuch einer Deutung', *Jb.* (3. Folge) VI (1967), 75–93.
Stein, Gisela, *The Inspiration Motif in the Works of Franz Grillparzer, with special consideration of 'Libussa'* (The Hague, 1955), pp. 155–200.
Wolf-Cirian, Francis, *Grillparzers Frauengestalten* (Stuttgart, Berlin, 1908), pp. 243–70.

TRANSLATIONS

Nearly all Grillparzer's major works have been translated into English, some more than once.

Burkhard, Arthur, *Franz Grillparzer in England and America* (Vienna, 1961) lists translations and quotes sample passages for comparison.
Grillparzer im Ausland (Cambridge, Mass., and Munich, 1969) lists translations into languages other than English.

INDEX

INDEX